the art of
RESPONSIVE DRAWING

the art of RESPONSIVE DRAWING

SECOND EDITION

NATHAN GOLDSTEIN

Prentice-Hall, Inc., Englewood Cliffs, New Jersey 07632

Library of Congress Cataloging in Publication Data

GOLDSTEIN, NATHAN.
   The art of responsive drawing.

   Bibliography: p. 348
   Includes index.
   1. Drawing—Instruction.   2. Composition (Art)
I. Title.
NC740.G6   1977   741   76-25001
ISBN 0-13-048629-9

10 9 8 7 6 5

Printed in the United States of America

Prentice-Hall International, Inc., *London*
Prentice-Hall of Australia Pty. Limited, *Sydney*
Prentice-Hall of Canada, Ltd., *Toronto*
Prentice-Hall of India Private Limited, *New Delhi*
Prentice-Hall of Japan, Inc., *Tokyo*
Prentice-Hall of Southeast Asia Pte. Ltd., *Singapore*
Whitehall Books Limited, *Wellington, New Zealand*

Frontispiece:
PIET MONDRIAN *Chrysanthemum*
Smith College Museum of Art

for Renee and Sarah

Art hath an enemy called Ignorance.

BEN JONSON

*O young artist, you search for a subject —
everything is a subject. Your subject is yourself,
your impressions, your emotions in the presence of nature.*

EUGÈNE DELACROIX

CONTENTS

CHAPTER SEVEN
MEDIA AND MATERIALS

the tools of drawing

CHAPTER EIGHT
VISUAL ISSUES

the forming of order

CHAPTER NINE
EXPRESSIVE ISSUES

the forming of meaning

CHAPTER TEN
ENVISIONED IMAGES

improvisations of form

CHAPTER ELEVEN
PATHOLOGIES OF DRAWING

some symptoms and defects

CHAPTER TWELVE
CONCLUSIONS

some general observations

PREFACE

The broad acceptance by the public of *The Art of Responsive Drawing* has been gratifying and inspiring. This second edition was reshaped after several years of experience with the text, and incorporates improvements in organization, visual material, and scope. As before, this book is intended for the art student, the interested amateur, the art teacher, and the practicing artist who wants to broaden his or her understanding of the processes and potentialities of drawing.

All drawings motivated by a wish to inquire and to experience—whether they are interpretations of observed or envisioned subjects—are *responsive*. They are all founded on our intellectual and intuitive judgments about a subject *and* its organized expression on the page. But the primary concern of beginning students (and most amateur and professional artists) is to expand their ability to experience and to state their world in visual terms, and to understand better the options and obstacles that confront them when drawing from nature. For this important reason, and because there is no way to fully test the aptness of responses to

imaginary stimuli, this book emphasizes drawing as a responsive encounter with our physical world. However, a new chapter (Chapter Ten) explores avenues of approach to envisioned images that benefit strongly from the skills and insights gained in drawing from nature.

Here *responsive* refers to our perceptual, aesthetic, and empathic interpretations of a subject's properties that hold potential for creative drawing. In responsive drawing, comprehending a subject's actualities precedes and affects the quality of our responses. Such drawings do more than recall what our outer or inner world *looks* like. They tell us what our intuitive knowledge informs us it *is*.

This is not a how-to-do-it book; rather, it is a kind of how-to-see-it book. The exercises in the first ten chapters are designed to help the reader experience the concepts and processes dealt with in each, and not to suggest techniques or ready-made solutions. The book explores the disguises of shapes and forms in nature; it examines the visual elements and the structural, relational, and emotive forces that constitute the language of graphic expression. I have omitted references to color and to drawings made on surfaces other than flat, bounded ones, because these aspects are incidental to the fundamentals of responsive drawing. With the exception of the drawings in Chapter Ten, most of the works shown here were made in the presence of the subject depicted. Those few that were not are included because they clearly illustrate points in the text.

The book begins by examining the factors that enable us to respond to a subject's measurable, structural actualities, its relational possibilities, and emotive character. It then proceeds to explore the concepts, forces, and "pathologies," or common (but seldom discussed) failings of perception, organization, and expression in drawing. The examination of these pathologies (Chapter Eleven) is, I believe, the first attempt to catalog the various misconceptions, inconsistencies, and errors faced by everyone who draws responsively. The pathologies discussed should enable the reader to apply a much wider range of criteria in evaluating his or her drawings.

I have not attempted the impossible task of defining all the characteristics of great responsive drawings. I have, however, pointed out those factors which, if left unregarded, make the creating of such drawings impossible.

I wish to express my deep appreciation to the many students, artists, and friends whose experiences, advice, and interest have helped to test, shape, and sustain the forming of this new edition. I wish also to thank the many museums and individuals for granting permission to reproduce the drawings in their collections.

I wish especially to thank Jonathan Goell and David Yawnick, whose excellent photographs make an important contribution to the book's clarity; Walter R. Welch and William Gibson; of Prentice-Hall, Inc., for the many considerate and generous ways in which they helped along the way; and Hilda Tauber, the production editor, Lorraine Mullaney, the designer, and Marvin Warshaw, the art director, for their skill, patience, and care in helping to give the book its present form.

My greatest debt of gratitude I owe my wife, who handled the voluminous and often intricate correspondence with museums, artists, and collectors on three continents, provided invaluable advice at every stage, and helped create the working atmosphere I needed so much. Finally, I want to express both thanks and apologies to my daughter, Sarah, now a seasoned endurer, for once again allowing for a part-time and generally distracted father.

NATHAN GOLDSTEIN

CHAPTER ONE

GESTURAL EXPRESSION

deduction through feeling

A DEFINITION

Confronted by any subject, whether a model, landscape, or still-life arrangement, most beginning students ask, "How shall I start?" The complexity of a subject's forms, values, textures, scale relationships, and position in space seem overwhelming. There appears to be no logical point of entry, no clue on how to proceed. If the subject is a figure many students—knowing no other way—begin by drawing the head, *followed* by the neck, *followed* by the torso, and so on. But such a sequential approach inevitably results in a stilted assembly of independent parts that have little affinity for each other as segments of the whole figure. Regardless of subject, this process of collecting isolated parts which should when completed add up to a figure, tree, blanket, barn, or whatever is *bound to fail—always*.

It will fail in the same way that the construction of a house would fail if we began with the roof or windows, or, realizing this as impossible, if we finished and furnished one room at a time. Such a structure must collapse because no supportive framework holds the independently built rooms together. Without an overall structural design none of the requirements common to various rooms, such as heating or wiring systems, can be installed (without tearing apart each room), because no appropriate steps of construction for the *entire* building occur. Without such a design or plan, none of the final relationships of size, shape, placement, etc., can be fully anticipated.

Every building process must begin with a *general* design framework, its development advanced by progressive stages until the *specifics* of various nonstructural detail are added to complete the project.

But before construction can start there is always the design—the blueprint. Even before the measurements and layout of the building "hardened" into the blueprint, there was the architect's idea: a *felt* attitude about certain forms, their scale, placement, texture and material as capable of an expressive order. An architectural structure really begins as a state of excitation about certain form relationships.

Similarly, the drawing of any subject should begin with a sense of excitation about its form relationships, actual and potential. Seeing these possibilities in the raw material of a subject, the responsive artist establishes a basis for interpretation. Among the first considerations in this interpretation must be the subject's overall behavior in space—how its major forms relate and act. Seeing the harmonies and contrasts of large masses, the total visual character of their directions in space, and their shape, structure, value, and scale, gives the artist important clues to the subject's essential visual and emotive nature— what we call its *gestural expression.**

To draw a subject's gestural expression is to draw the intrinsic nature of the action of its components rather than their specific physical characteristics. As in a building's construction, a drawing is also begun by conveying the gestural essentials of the *entire* subject *before* its final form is developed. And, like a building without a cohesive system of structural design to hold it together, a drawing begun without the search for a cohesive gestural pattern "collapses." Similarly, to introduce the gestural expression *after* a drawing is underway would require undoing and reworking nearly all of it.

Gestural expression must not be understood as simply the action or rhythms of a subject, although these important qualities are always part of a subject's gestural nature. It is not to be found in any one of the subject's visual properties of shape, value, or direction, nor in its type or class, arrangement of parts, or even its "mood," but rather in the sum of all these qualities. The emotive energy of gesture cannot be seen until it is experienced—it must be *felt*.

In other words, empathy—the ability to *feel with* a person or object—is required to give expressive meaning to a subject's configuration in space. The gestural character of a swimmer's body knifing into the water is fairly evident, but that of an old shoe de-

*See Kimon Nicolaides, *The Natural Way to Draw* (Boston: Houghton Mifflin Company, 1941), pp. 14–28.

mands a more penetrating search. The term *character*, as used here, should be understood as the collective temperament of a subject in a particular configuration. We attribute human attitudes and feelings to a subject's emotive state in verbal expressions such as "an angry sea" or "a cheerful fire." In the same way an artist responding to a subject's gestural expression feels a drape as "limp," a cave as "yawning," and a tree as "stately" or "gnarled." The response to a subject's gestural expression, then, is the apprehension of the nature of its total behavior in space.

In Figure 1.1, Rembrandt uses gestural means to convey the tired, resting figure of his wife, Saskia. Rembrandt *feels* (and consequently we do, too) the essence of her pose as an expression of limp weight. What Saskia is doing and feeling is as important to Rembrandt as the delineation of specific forms and textures. His felt perception of her relaxed body pressing into the pliant bedding is intensified by the forceful speed of the lines in the pillow. Their radiating action reveals the tension in strong folds produced by the pressure of weight against soft materials. Those lines *enact* as well as describe the action.

Similarly, Degas' drawing of a young woman (Figure 1.2) concentrates on the figure's overall visual behavior. In his determination to distill the figure's representational *and* abstract nature, Degas "draws through" to locate forms actually hidden from view. Notice that the artist sees the subject as tapering and lessening in action upward, and that gestural lines underlie the more developed, upper part of the drawing.

In the same way, Corot's attack, in his drawing *The Bath* (Figure 1.3) penetrates his subject's surface-state to extract its essential actions and character. Here the search for essential movements and forms applies to figures and trees alike. Note that in all three drawings relatively little emphasis is placed on contours—the beginner's trusted device for drawing. While edges are an important consideration of any subject's form, much more is revealed by discovering the essential structure and action of its masses, as we shall see in Chapter Six.

As mentioned above, gestural expression comes from the physical and emotive proper-

Figure 1.1
REMBRANDT VAN RIJN (1606–1669)
Saskia Asleep
Pen, brush and ink. 13 x 17.1 cm.
The Pierpont Morgan Library, New York

ties of a subject, and, as such, results from its *total* behavior. Drawing the gestural expression of a single figure and its immediate environment, as Rembrandt and Degas do, is fully responsive if this alone is the subject. To do so when two or more independent forms constitute the subject, as in Corot's drawing, falls short of the perceptual scope necessary to see the relational nature of the entire subject's gestural expression.

Exercise 1A suggests a means by which we can extract a subject's gestural expression. Because the search for gesture engages our feelings as well as our ability to see, and be-

cause its pervasive but intangible qualities are difficult to discern at first, many drawings will have to be made, in the manner described, before a sense for felt actions and character can be experienced and made manifest in drawing.

exercise 1A

The "rules" suggested here should be regarded as temporary aides to help you extract a subject's gestural expression. They are not intended as a "how to draw" scheme. There is only one way to draw—yours. Learning to respond to a subject's expressive character is essential to developing your way.

Use a black or sanguine conté crayon or compressed charcoal stick, and draw on an 18″ × 24″ pad of newsprint paper. Do not use an eraser (there won't be time or the need). If possible, use the human figure, draped or nude, as your subject. If no model is available use plants, house pets, simple still-life arrangements, toys, clothing, or some of the more visually interesting or fanciful furniture forms. Even your own arm can be placed in a variety of active poses and used as subject. For the present, do not use photographs; they generally inject a stiff and artificial note to a drawing. Also, the camera's monocular image lacks the sense of depth perception our binocular vision supplies, thus reducing our understanding of the subject's forms in space. If possible, draw in a standing position at an easel or any suitable support.

You will make a total of twenty drawings. The first five will be two-minute poses. The next ten will be one-minute poses and the last five will again be two-minute poses.

During the first half-minute of every drawing, *do not draw*. Instead, search for the most inclusive action of the subject by relying as much on

Figure 1.2
EDGAR DEGAS (1834–1917)
A Young Woman Singing
Lead pencil on beige paper. 48.9 x 31.2 cm.
The Louvre Museum

Figure 1.3
CAMILLE COROT (1796–1875)
The Bath
Charcoal and paper stump on brown paper. 48.1 x 20.6 cm.
The Louvre Museum

your feelings about the subject's behavior and character as your visual analysis of its proportions and other measurable matters. You may not be able to describe it verbally, but you should get an impression of the nature of its overall action, and of its major segments: fast or slow, limp or rigid, supporting or supported, straining or relaxed.

Only when you sense you are responding to both the pattern and mood of the action, when the subject is understood as "doing," as well as "being," should you begin to draw.

Use a small fragment of your drawing tool (about three-quarters to one inch long), holding it loosely by your fingertips. Do not hold it in the manner used for writing. The hard lines such a pinched grasp produces is too restricting for gestural drawing. Let your hand and arm swing freely as you draw. Be daring to the point of recklessness in stating the essence of what you see; but don't make arbitrary lines, lines not triggered by perceptions but by willful caprice. If you see a movement that runs through the entire subject, draw it as one continuous action. Try to match the energetic force, lazy ease, etc. of a movement by the way you draw it, as in Figure 1.4. Avoid lifting your drawing instrument often. When you stop to make new observations or associations of parts, simply leave your chalk touching the page where your previous mark ended and, when ready to begin again, start it moving. This is not always possible, for a new observation may take you to another area of the page. But, when it can be done, it reduces the amount of short, broken segments of line or tone which imply a faltering in the search for gesture and, indeed, promote a more hesitant and cautious attitude. And here, it is the boldest summary of the expressive action you want, so avoid the enticements of interesting, smaller considerations. If you leave the mainstream of gesture when the drawing has just begun in order to develop smaller parts, you lose the rest of the gestural qualities of the subject and depart from the *general to the specific procedure*, a step that few seasoned artists will risk or advise.

A gesture drawing is not a contour drawing. As you draw, you will almost certainly find that you cannot stay away from the edges of forms. It will require a concentrated effort and discipline to leave the "safety" of the contours and make your drawing describe the path of an arm, branch, or chair-leg in space. Occasionally using the side of the small fragment of chalk will help to check the tendency to draw the contour because the broad, foggy tone thus produced is more suited to describing the core or direction of a form, rather than its edges. Using your chalk this way also helps to keep you from being distracted by details—such a tone line is too broad for small particulars. Try to experience the forms moving back and forth in a field of space, because whatever the subject, it exists in space. Imagine your hand actually reaching in and out of the "container" of space that holds your subject as you describe the action of the forms.

Figure 1.4

Figure 1.5

In the two-minute poses you will actually draw only about one and one half minutes. This may seem brief, and it would be if you intended to make a fairly realized graphic statement. But all you want to do in these exercises is boldly grasp the subject's expressive action. In fact, the gestural essentials should be stated within the first minute. Use the remaining half-minute to check between your subject and your drawing and make further, perhaps smaller, extractions of gestural qualities.

In the one-minute poses only half of your time will be spent drawing. This will make it necessary to see, summarize, and state the gesture more aggressively. Now there will be only enough time to perceive the strongest actions and form characteristics. These drawings should be more general in purpose, more direct in handling, as in Figure 1.5. Often, one-minute drawings capture gestural characteristics more successfully than gesture drawings of two minutes or more. You become more aware of the limited drawing time and more intensely see parts massed into greater generalities of action and form. For example, a side view of a figure, legs straight, leaning over and touching his toes, might be stated as an inverted teardrop form.

Imagine you are an artist–correspondent making a visual record of a subject. If you do not use the thirty seconds to grasp the essence of *all* that you see for further development afterward, you will be unable to complete your visual report.

Your experience in speeding up the pace and broadening the scope of your summaries during the one-minute drawings will help you use the expanded time better in your last five drawings. Now, a two-minute drawing time feels more comfortable and allows you to see some of the smaller affinities, contrasts, and characteristics that evoke gesture.

Although a gesture drawing is neither a contour nor a stick-figure drawing, it is mainly through the general look and feel of mass and direction that a subject's gesture reveals itself. Therefore, in all these quick drawings, remember to concentrate on the subject's essentials, not its embellishments (Figure 1.6).

Twenty different poses of a subject present no problem when a model is used, or when you are drawing your own arm or a house pet. With still-life arrangements you may find it easier to move around the subject, rearranging some of it occasionally. Whatever the subject, the poses

Figure 1.6
ANNIBALE CARRACCI (1560–1609)
Studies for a Portrait
Pen and ink. 13.1 x 13.9 cm.
Albertina Museum, Vienna

needn't drastically change each time. Even the subtlest of changes creates new form relationships and thus, new gestures.

THE DIVIDENDS
OF GESTURAL EXPRESSION

Drawing from the general to the specific leads us from the gestural to the factual. Once a subject's general state has been established, further analysis inevitably leads to smaller, more specific contributors to it. If you continue with a gesture drawing for five minutes or more, your responses will begin to shift from the analytical depths of general states of character and movement up toward the surfaces of the forms. Like the swimmer who dives to the bottom, we *do* come up to the surface. But the perception of factual details *evolves from* our comprehension of gestural expression and cannot, as we have seen, precede it.

The search for gesture at the outset of a drawing is visually logical for two reasons: it is the necessary basis for all that follows and it cannot enter a drawing already underway. But this search for a subject's essential dynamics does more than infuse a drawing with a sense of masses related by movement. Having done Exercise 1A, you may have recognized that seeing the general character of the forms in action provides other kinds of information about the subject.

There are no less than ten important ways in which extracting gesture serves to inform and assist us in drawing. It helps us establish: (1) the proportions or *scale relationships* between segments of a subject; (2) the placement or *location* of segments; (3) the particular "tilt" or *position in space* of segments; (4) the general tonal or *value* differences between the segments; (5) the boundaries or *shape-states* of the segments; (6) the unique nature or *visual character* of the forms; (7) the *economical* and *authoritative* graphic statement; (8) the first general analysis of the volumetric or *structural* state of the forms; (9) the first general considerations of mass, space, shape, line, value, and texture as abstract elements of the organizational design or *composition* of the drawing; and (10) the drawing's emotive spirit — its *essential expressive nature*.

Many of these insights are natural byproducts of seeing *all* the subject within a minute or two. In a figure drawing begun gesturally, we may see the torso just a few seconds after we have seen, say, the right arm, the head a second or so later, the left leg a few seconds later, etc. We visually (and empathically) grasp the entire figure almost at once. The likelihood of seeing the relative scale, location, position, and so on is much improved over a piecemeal approach, since we are everywhere in seconds and draw by hovering over the entire image, advancing it on a broad front.

In gestural drawing the search for shape, position, scale, value, etc. is at first always a rough, general inquiry, because the first questions are not, "Where is it, how big, and what are its values?" but "What is it doing?" Only when we have responded to the overall behavior of the forms do we concentrate on more fully understanding their structural and surface character. Nevertheless, a reasonable approximation of where the subject's components are, and their scale and value relationships *can* be established through drawing the expressive action. It then becomes much easier to advance the drawing by studying these rough judgments and making the adjustments needed for them to convey both the physical and expressive states as you see them (objectively), or as you intend to state them (subjectively).

The severe restriction in drawing time serves to greatly increase our awareness of the relativeness of parts. No one intentionally misjudges the scale, location, or value differences of a subject's components. These errors in judgment result from failure to see relationships — associations. And these failures are most commonly the result of a sequential system of drawing wherein each part is dealt with independently and "finished" with little or no reference to other parts. In such an isolated, piecemeal approach it is mere luck when segments are in accord.

No one intentionally makes errors in perception, but many artists do alter their drawings, to varying extents, away from the subject's actual state. But these changes are based (or should be) on a knowledge of what the subject's actual conditions are. In respon-

Figure 1.7
HENRI DE TOULOUSE-LAUTREC (1864–1901)
Study for Painting "La Comtesse Noire"
Black grease crayon. 16 x 25.7 cm.
Courtesy of The Art Institute of Chicago

sive drawing seeing the state of things as they are is prerequisite to change.

Since a gestural drawing proceeds from the general to the specific, any line, value, or texture which "works," that is, which serves to declare the artist's intent early in the drawing's development, can be allowed to remain as a completed graphic remark. Because of the fluid and inclusive nature of gestural drawing, not many such lines and tones are likely to survive. Some do, and their simple, direct quality serves to influence the artist in establishing other equally economical graphic inventions. The spontaneous quality of gestural drawing and the subsequent drawing influenced by it tend to convey a sense of courageous directness. These qualities of resolute authority and economy, and the spontaneity they promote are essential to good drawing, of whatever stylistic or aesthetic persuasion.

In Figure 1.7, the gestural expression of the scene tells us much more than "horses–carriage–people"; it evokes the clatter of the carriage, the nervous energy of the animals and their speed. In this sketchbook drawing by Toulouse-Lautrec the economy of means, the authoritative handling, and the quality of spontaneity they create—the energetic *presence* of the subject were born in the artist's initial grasp of the subject's gesture.

Because we wish to see the expressive action of forms *in space*, gestural drawing requires us to move back and forth in a spatial field denoting not only the tilt, shape, scale, and (where necessary to structure or expression), value of the forms, but also some general suggestions of their volumetric nature. In Rembrandt's rugged drawing *Portrait of a Man* (Figure 1.8), the gestural drawing of the figure also conveys some broad suggestions

Figure 1.8
REMBRANDT VAN RIJN (1606–1669)
Portrait of a Man
Brown ink and wash on white paper. 7 5/16 x 6 1/8 in.
Fogg Art Museum, Harvard University
A. S. Coburn and Alpheus Hyatt Funds

about the volume of his cloak—we even sense the mass of his right arm beneath it, as well as the volume of the hat, head, torso, and right hand. Although several areas of the figure are not fully clarified as masses, there is an overall sense of his substance and weight. In John's drawing *Portrait of Woman in Hat* (Figure 1.9), the searching gestural lines are clearly in evidence throughout the drawing. We again sense the emergence of volume, even in the most sweeping gestural responses to the character of the action. Note that the influence of the graceful, curvilinear lines still echo in the more developed passages of the drawing. These two drawings, so different in temperament and intent, are alike in their manner of evolving from an initial concern with the subject's general qualities to a controlled and concise expression of its more specific properties. The desirable graphic quality of authoritative economy often guides the artist to those summaries of volume which the gestural approach frequently uncovers.

The compositional state of a subject in a bounded, flat area (dealt with in Chapter Eight) is likewise easier to evaluate by gesture's requirement to be "everywhere at once." We can thus see, within the first minutes of a drawing, the placement of the subject on the page, the general divisions of the page resulting from its placement, and the general state of any other matters relating to the drawing's order. The earlier we establish the general state of the *formal* relationships—the system of abstract harmonies and contrast that constitute a drawing's particular organizational system—the more integrated the completed drawing will be. And, for the responsive artist, a drawing's abstract

Figure 1.9
AUGUSTUS JOHN (1878–1961)
Portrait of Woman in Hat
Pencil. 9 1/8 x 12 1/4 in.
Boston Public Library

life—the nature of its plastic and emotive energies, that is, its *dynamics*—is as important as its representational state.

In *Two Barristers* by Daumier (Figure 1.10), the general state of a compositional idea is seen in the lines near each figure, which begin to search out the essential action of two more figures. Here, Daumier lets us see his very first gestural and compositional probes. Similar gestural lines underlie the more developed figures of the barristers. Note the character of the action of the two barristers. It is expressed by the action the figures convey *and* by the animated nature of the lines that denote them.

In Exercise 1A the search for the subject's gestural expression was the exclusive goal of your efforts. Whatever dividends of this approach emerged as you drew came un-

bidden. In the next exercise you will consciously look for the ten kinds of information and influence the gestural approach provides.

exercise 1B

Use the same materials and subjects as suggested in Exercise 1A. Again, draw in a standing position. Try to *feel* the subject's action and emotive state as you begin to freely search for the expressive behavior of the forms.

One purpose of this exercise is to build upon the ten "assists" provided by the gestural approach, to allow its direct and assertive nature to help you state strong and simple masses and moving actions, and an ordered pattern of visual forces on the page. Another purpose is to experience the shift from drawing the expressive action to drawing the factual state of your subject *and* its immediate environment.

Figure 1.10
HONORÉ DAUMIER (1808–1879)
Two Barristers
Pen and ink. 20.5 x 29.5 cm.
Victoria and Albert Museum, London

Figure 1.11

Because compositional design requires an enclosed area, draw a border just inside the limits of your page, as in Figure 1.11. The page itself *is* a bounded, flat field, but you will become more aware of the limits of the drawing area by using this inner border. Drawing such borders is a temporary but helpful device. If some segment of your subject warrants inclusion, let your drawing go beyond the inner border and off the page. Should you do this, disregard (or erase) the rest of the borders and use the entire page for your drawing. But the presence of the border will greatly increase the likelihood of getting all the subject on the page.

You will make three ten-minute drawings and one half-hour drawing. Again, do not draw for the first half-minute or so, but use the time to familiarize yourself with the subject's essential form-character, its moving actions, and its general design. This time, also observe the subject's overall shape, or, if it is comprised of a number of major, separate units, its several large shapes. Decide where you will place the configuration within the page and what its scale will be. Avoid drawing the subject so small that it appears as a "tiny actor" on a large "stage." Instead, use a scale that will make the subject fill a large portion of the page.

Now look around your subject to see what foreground or background material you wish to include. If the background is a blank wall, plan to place your subject on the page so that the surrounding blank areas are divided up into interesting shapes. Should there be some other objects, values, or textures around the subject you wish to

include in your drawing, consider how their scale, shape, and gestural character may relate with the subject's gestural expression. Plan to omit anything that you feel will conflict with, crowd, or confuse the drawing of your subject.

Those things you choose to include in the drawing are now regarded as an extension of your original subject. For example, if your original subject is a figure and you plan to include a chair, rug, and darkened corner of a room, your subject is now the figure and *all* these.

Begin all four drawings as if they were two-minute gesture drawings. In all four, after the half-minute or so of study, use the first two or three minutes to state the subject's gestural character (which now includes its immediate surroundings). After two or three minutes, keep searching for further, smaller gestural actions until you feel that the gestural behavior of all the major and secondary forms have been realized, as in Figures 1.12 and 1.13. In the Dufy drawing, note the engaging impartiality with which he regards the components of his subject. Note, too, the animated character of the chairs and the drawings on the wall, Dufy's economical and authoritative handling, the suggestions of volume, and the drawing's balanced and unified character. In the Carpeaux drawing we have an excellent example of the gestural approach. The economy of means and authoritative quality are impressive, for so much has been said by so few lines and tones.

In the last three or four minutes of the ten-minute drawings, revisit every part of the drawing, this time estimating the scale relationships of the forms, their position in space, and the major tonal relationships among them. In making these changes and additions to your earlier gestural perceptions, you will find that you are beginning to draw the contours of forms—you are establishing the shapes of forms (dealt with fully in Chapter Two). We saw in Exercise 1A that continuing a gesture drawing eventually brings us to the edges of forms. There it marked the end of the exercise, now it is the beginning of a shift from the concern for what the subject is doing to a search for what it looks like.

Continue to draw the contours of the forms, slowing down somewhat to follow the major changes in the directions of the forms' edges and of inner edges created by abutments between the larger facets, or *planes*, of a form's surface (the important role of planes is explored in Chapter Six). Erase any earlier gestural marks that seem to confuse or obscure the forms. Most of the gestural lines and tones *do* become integrated into the values and textures of the later stages of a drawing. It is surprising how little of the original gesture

Figure 1.12
RAOUL DUFY (1887–1953)

The Artist's Studio (c. 1942)
Brush and ink. 19 5/8 x 26 in.
The Museum of Modern Art, New York
Gift of Mr. and Mrs. Peter A. Rübel

Figure 1.13
JEAN-BAPTISTE CARPEAUX (1827–1875)

General in Court Dress
Black chalk. 14.4 x 0.94 cm.
The Louvre Museum

13

Figure 1.14
SALVATOR ROSA (1615–1673)
Study of a Soldier
Pen, brush and ink. 13.3 x 16.5 cm.
Victoria and Albert Museum, London

drawing is visible at the completion of even a ten-minute drawing. Avoid overemphasizing the edges. Contours that are heavy or hard tend to stiffen the drawing and weaken the gestural quality.

Use those values you feel are necessary to convey the general sense of the subject's masses. Avoid the "coloring book syndrome" of adding values after the drawing is developed through line. If you mean to use values, do this early in the drawing, as in Figures 1.14 and 1.15.

In these drawings, as in those of Exercise 1A, it is important to advance the entire drawing together. Again, check the tendency to settle on a particular area, developing it ahead of the rest.

As you draw, be mindful of the ten ways in which gestural drawing assists perceptions and broadens the range of your responses. It may be helpful to list them in a corner of your drawing board or sketchbook for easy reference. With so much to be aware of—and *do*—ten minutes is not much time. This restriction is intended to keep your attention focused on the subject's major dynamic and structural cues. Kokoschka's drawing, *Portrait of Mrs. Lanyi* (Figure 1.15) provides an ex-

ample of a drawing emerging from a search for gestural expression to form more substantial abstract and representational conditions. Again, in Lillie's drawing *Standing Figure* (Figure 1.16), subtler relational and structural observations overlay the gestural drawing.

Regard the ten-minute drawings as warm-ups for the thirty-minute one. At the end of ten minutes you should have developed this drawing as far as the earlier three. At this point, stop drawing for a minute or so. Look at your drawing from a few feet away. You will more easily see errors in scale, location, and direction. Additionally, you will more easily see the drawing's gestural and compositional state. Continue drawing for the remaining time, stressing the structural character of the forms. This search for volume should be a natural development of the perceptions you made during the first ten minutes of the drawing, when you felt and evoked the subject's gestural character. Many of these perceptions carried strong clues about the structure of the subject's forms. Now you are building upon the gestural expression, rather than strengthening it further. The shift from com-

14

Figure 1.15

OSKAR KOKOSCHKA (1886–   )

Portrait of Mrs. Lanyi
Crayon. 25 x 17 13/16 in.
Worcester Art Museum, Mass. The Dial Collection

Figure 1.16
LLOYD LILLIE (1932–   )
Standing Figure
Pencil. 14 x 17 in.
Courtesy of the artist.

prehending what the subject *does*, to what it *looks like* (or what you want it to look like), depends on the guidance and influence of the drawing's initial gestural qualities.

If, toward the end of the thirty minutes, you cannot see any further changes or additions to help state the dynamic and structural character of the subject—stop. In the weeks and months to come, you may find thirty minutes to be as brief a span

of time as ten minutes seem now. As you continue your study of drawing you will find more relationships in a subject and demand a more probing encounter and a more responsive result.

In the ten-minute drawings there was about as much time for stating the gestural character of your subject as for its overall structural and surface character. But in a thirty-minute drawing the gestural expression often becomes somewhat muted. While personal attitudes will determine whether gestural considerations continue to play a major or minor role, here we use gesture mainly to support the development of the subject's masses, for which there is now more time (as for example, Katzman does in Figure 1.17).

There is a danger here. If you lose too much of the gestural expression, if you sacrifice too much economy of means, if the felt and analytical quality of the drawing is too muffled by a meticulous rendering of surfaces, too much of the life and excitement of the drawing will be lost.

The shift from the expressive action to the visual, measurable actualities does not mean that you must stop your gestural responses. You may see some strong moving actions late in the drawing. Nor does it mean that some facts about the subject's measurements are not stated early. There is no such clean break in responding to a subject. Rather, it is a gradual change in emphasis.

Do several of the ten-minute drawings daily and at least one thirty-minute drawing. Do some of these in your sketchbook. Regard your sketchbook as personal and "off limits" to browsers. Be selective about who is allowed to see it, for in the early stages of the study of drawing, the wrong compliments are as harmful as the wrong criticism.

This chapter has not attempted to provide *the* way to draw, but only a way of seeing, feeling, and thinking about the forms around us. And this way leads us to an early confrontation with the factors of order, empathy, and structure that challenge all serious exponents of responsive drawing. But if the search for gestural expression is no more the key to drawing than any other of the several basic concepts necessary to an understanding of drawing, its mastery is essential and must come early in the study of drawing. Whatever graphic goals and ideals we wish to pursue, the *process* will be that of advancing our drawings from the general to the specific and not through a system of piecemeal assembly. Responsive drawings do not accumulate— they grow.

CHAPTER TWO

SHAPE

an irony

A DEFINITION

Like gestural expression, shape is a given visual quality. Perceiving a subject's gesture tells us what the subject does; seeing its shapes tells us important things about what it looks like.

The first shape drawn on a blank and bounded surface, or *picture-plane*, by its presence creates a second shape—the remainder of the picture-plane. This first drawn shape, understood as an area of active "thingness," is called a *figure*, or *positive shape*; the remaining, passive, "empty" area is called a *ground*, or *negative shape*. In this relationship positive shapes are not seen as hovering in a spatial field of depth, nor do negative shapes represent a spatial field of depth. They all should be understood as existing *on the same level*. Together, they *are* the picture-plane. Having no volume, and intending no spatial depth, shapes are *two-dimensional* (Figure 2.1).

All volumes when viewed from a fixed point offer an absolute shape delineation. Perceiving this "flat" state of a form is essential to understanding its placement, scale, and structure. What its shape *is* will largely determine what its volume and position in space *will be*.

Some of the guises of shape are difficult to uncover. When we look around us we see volumes of differing colors and textures. The several vital roles of shape in producing the impression of volume and space are not readily apparent. Seeing through the camouflage of subject's surface to shape's visual and expressive potentialities is basic to responsive drawing.

Put simply, *a shape is any flat area bounded by line or value or both*. Shapes are classified in two general families: *geometric* and *organic* (sometimes called biomorphic or amoebic). A geometric shape, as the term implies, may be for example a circle, triangle, etc., or any combination of the angular or curved boundaries associated with pure geometric shapes. An organic shape is any irregular, "undulating" shape in which extensive use of straight or evenly curved edges is minor or absent. Organic shapes tend to echo

A   B

Figure 2.1

the contours in nature. They are less severe and often more animated than geometric shapes (Figure 2.2).

As discussed above, shapes may have a positive or negative function. They may be hard-edged or vague. They may be active and gestural, or passive and stable. Shapes may be large or small, totally or only partially enclosed. They may have simple or complex boundaries, and be consistent or varied in their properties.

Because we are conditioned to see *things* rather than the spaces that separate them, learning to see negative interspaces as providing important visual information requires concentration. Notice that the shape of any object you concentrate on, in covering part of its background, creates shapes in the background. If we squint at the object and its environment there is an obscuring of detail that helps to reduce our sense of depth perception. This loss of clarity, in tending to flatten both volume and space, helps us see a sphere as a disk, a foreshortened disk as an ellipse, and a road running back to the horizon as a wedge. It likewise helps us see the contour actualities

of negative spaces. Inner divisions (shapes) can be seen in the same way. Any shape surrounding a segment can become the "subject" of *its* surrounding or adjacent shapes (including those of the segment). Inner shapes are those "offered" by the visually insistent divisions within the subject's boundaries that occur by overlap, value, or clearly abutting (and usually large) planes, as in Figure 2.3.

An important dividend of a patient study of the shapes adjacent to a form results from the common tendency to see concavities in a form's edges (especially on its shaded side) as deeper and more pronounced than they really are. Too often the forms in beginners' drawings look sort of withered because their shape boundaries undulate too much. For some reason, perhaps because we are conditioned to think of convexities as containing something, and concavities nothing, the line we draw to represent a convexity on an edge is more likely to accurately reflect the scale and degree of the observed convex passage than a line that notes a concave one. Hence, by drawing the convexities of shapes that abut a form we are simultaneously *and more accurately* establishing the form's concavities.

Exercise 2A presents a drawing problem that makes it necessary to see these "empty" shapes with all the conscious attention generally given to positive ones. Perceiving their actual configurations is necessary to understanding a subject's shape-state—an important factor in responsive drawing. As you do Exercise 2A, you should begin to *experience* the interchangeability of positive and negative shapes, and realize that the one cannot be fully comprehended without the other. In all

Figure 2.2

Figure 2.3

drawings shapes either enhance or hurt expressive order—none "ride free." Disregarding so basic a concept as a subject's shape-state blinds the student to much of its structural and dynamic condition.

exercise 2A

In doing the two drawings of this exercise, you may erase whenever necessary. In general, too much erasing gives an unpleasant fussiness, but here you can make as many changes and adjustments as you need to complete your drawings.

drawing 1.
    Using a moderately soft pencil (2B or 3B) and a sheet of tracing paper (or any paper thin enough to see through), draw a square approximately five inches by five inches. Use a ruler if you wish. Inside the square draw, in a continuous line, a simple organic shape (Figure 2.4A). Draw it large enough to allow some of its projections to touch the borders of the square, causing the remainder of the square to be seen as four or five isolated shape-segments. Leave the organic shape the white of the paper and apply a gray tone to all of the remaining shapes. The completed drawing should look somewhat like a jigsaw puzzle-piece touching each of the square's borders at least once. Avoid making the shape complex and contorted—the simpler, the better.
    The resulting ground-shapes seem to suggest a spatial field. But to *see* the shapes that comprise this spatial "cavity," disregard its impression of spatial depth and treat *all* the shapes within the square as two-dimensional divisions of the picture-plane.
    Now take a second sheet of paper and draw another five-inch square. Inside this second square, draw the organic shape again as accurately as you can, using your first drawing as your model. This time you will find that letting your hand flow across the paper will not reproduce the original shape. Your second drawing may be fairly close to the original, but it should reproduce it *exactly*. To do this, you will have to study the original with great care. You will want to see the tilt, or *axis*, of each projection and indent of the original, as well as their relative scale. As you draw, ask yourself, "What is the axis and shape of this projection? . . . of this indent? Which is the narrowest projection? . . . which the largest?" Examining the several negative shapes bordering on the organic one and ending at the limits of the square, you will see differences from your original drawing. In

Figure 2.4

adjusting these in your second drawing, you will be adjusting the organic shape as well. Soon you may find that you no longer regard the organic shape as more important than the shapes around it. You may sense that until *each* shape matches its original, the organic shape will not have been accurately drawn. As you draw, try reversing the figure-ground relationship. That is, imagine the white "puzzle-piece" to be missing from a gray puzzle. Now the white shape is a negative one. Seeing your drawing this way, continue to adjust the remaining "puzzle-pieces." To more accurately estimate the angle of a particular projection or indent, imagine a clock-face surrounding the part, as in Figure 2.4B. Try to locate the long axis of a segment by finding its position on the clock. For example, a segment that is vertical would be twelve o'clock (or six o'clock); if tilted slightly to the right, it might appear at one o'clock; and so on.
    When you cannot find any further differences between the two drawings, place one over the

other and hold them up to the light. You may be surprised at the several differences still remaining. Continue to make further adjustments based on these differences until the two drawings match.

drawing 2

When you drew the several shapes which formed the square, the camouflage of the "square-ness" that each participated in may have kept you from considering them as much as the organic shape. In this drawing combine any three shapes that form an irregular outline. Do not enclose them in a square. These shapes can have some geometric properties, as in Figure 2.4C. Again, make as accurate a duplication of this group as you can. Now the shape-state of each will be very evident. They do not contribute to a common shape strong enough to obscure an awareness of each. Instead, these shapes more evenly interact. It is important to be able to objectively regard any of a subject's shapes, no matter how actively engaged they are with others. The three shapes you have selected are, of course, collectively producing a fourth. As you draw this group, divide your attention between seeing each of the three shapes separately and seeing the greater shape they make. Recalling the advantages of working from the general to the specific, begin this drawing by roughly searching out the overall gesture and shape of the configuration first. When completed, again match the two drawings and make any necessary changes.

These exercises, or any variation of them that promotes a search for the actual state of shapes, should be practiced daily until the process becomes familiar. Seeing shapes in this objective and analytical way is one of the most necessary and powerful resources of responsive drawing—not for purposes of imitation, but for invention based on perceptual acuity.

THE SHAPE OF VOLUME

Being two-dimensional, a single shape generally cannot convey the impression of volume convincingly. Only when two or more shapes join or interact do they communicate the idea of structure and mass.

Figure 2.5

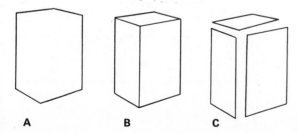

A   B   C

When shapes unite to form a volume they are seen as straight or curved facets of the volume's surface and are called *planes*. The various ways these planes abut and blend into each other determine and convey the volume's particular "topographical" state (Figure 2.3).

To interpret a subject's shape and structure we must begin by avoiding *exclusive* attention to its existence as mass in space. Instead, "read" its planes as positive shapes on the same level as the negative shapes around it. A simultaneous perception of the subject as both two- and three-dimensional then occurs. Figure 2.5 visualizes the dual role of a plane: as a discernible facet of a volume's surface, and as a shape upon the picture-plane. Figure 2.5A tells us nothing about mass or structure. We cannot tell whether it is a solid or whether the outline describes an empty interior. In Figure 2.5B, the outline of the shape remains identical: only the interior lines have been added, subdividing the original shape into three smaller ones. Seeing these shapes as planes creates an impression of volume. This volume appears solid because we cannot see any of the boundary lines that would be visible if the structure were made of glass or wire. We now understand the form to be turned to an oblique angle to the right. Further, the three visible planes strongly imply the three unseen planes necessary to our understanding of the volume as a box-form. In Figure 2.5C, separating the planes creates three shapes that suggest no more about mass and structure than Figure 2.5A does. Taken as a group, they form a Y-shaped negative area. While not wholly enclosed by boundaries, this is still "readable" as a shape. These "open" shapes occur when encompassing positive shapes provide segments of enclosure greater than segments of separation. The partially enclosed area is seen as a shape since we tend to "complete" shapes that provide strong clues to their simplest totality.*

Considering the single-shape limitations of the silhouette, some artists of the eighteenth and nineteenth centuries did quite well

*Rudolf Arnheim, *Art and Visual Perception* (Berkeley and Los Angeles: University of California Press, 1954), pp. 54–55.

Figure 2.6
NATHANIEL WEST (19th Century)
Silhouette
Cut black paper.
Courtesy, Museum of Fine Arts, Boston

mey, by stressing his subject's shape-state, provides us with an engagingly ordered division of the picture-plane in which the abstract character of the shapes expresses the same delicacy conveyed by the depiction. When an observed form is rich in textural, tonal, or decorative properties, the unwary beginner is more likely to be diverted from a recognition of its shape-character. Likewise, when shapes combine to form a volume, their individual shape-characteristics and their collective shape-state might be missed. Goodman, in his drawing *Eileen* (Figure 2.8), avoids both of these pitfalls. The strong overall shape of the hair is not visually "overruled" by its imposing dark values and rich texture, nor are the planes that "carve"

Figure 2.7
ROBERT GWATHMEY (1903–   )
Bouquet (1969)
Pencil. 29 1/2 x 23 in.
Collection of Mrs. Hillary Cranswick

in suggesting, to a degree, a sense of volume (Figure 2.6). But their efforts tend to support rather than contest the view that a single shape is understood primarily as a flat configuration and only secondarily suggests some clues about volume.

Shapes, then, tend to "offer" their edges. The simpler their interiors, the more emphasis on boundaries, as in Figure 2.7. Gwath-

Figure 2.8
SIDNEY GOODMAN (1936–   )
Eileen (1969)
Charcoal. 30 1/2 x 42 in.
Courtesy, Terry Dintenfass, Inc., New York

the head and blouse weakened by the demands of modelling the form. In fact, by showing how these planes interjoin, Goodman not only enhances the figure's structural clarity, he also provides a vigorous design of wedge-like shapes that activate the picture-plane.

This is not to suggest that edge, contour, or outline must necessarily be a dominant graphic factor. Many artists avoid emphasizing edges (see Seurat, *Sleeping Man*, Figure 4.4). But learning to search for a volume's shape-state helps us to locate those edges of

planes forming the volume's boundaries, and thus to better comprehend its inner structure.

This "flattening" of volume is especially helpful in understanding the visual state of foreshortened forms. A common error in perception is to draw such forms in a way that suggests they were seen from above or a side view. Many beginners find it almost impossible to turn a volume such as an arm or leg on end and show it as receding into a spatial field. Seeing that a form *is* foreshortened, their exclusive attention turns to the problem of explaining the mass of a form that is "telescoped," *before* they have observed its shape-actuality. In bypassing the crucial observation of the form's shape they miss an important structural truth. Like the search for gesture, the analysis of a volume's shape components must be an early perception in the act of drawing. To proceed without considering either of these acts of inquiry is to draw preconceived notions of a subject's *class*, and is not responsive to a particular subject as seen from a particular view. The seasoned artist recognizes that a subject's shape-state will change as he changes his position in relation to it. He knows that perceiving the outline of a particular form "traps" both the information that shape provides about structure *and* the form's position in space; for its position creates its shape—its "field of play."

Further discussion of the means available to understanding foreshortening volumes will be found in Chapters Five and Six. The following exercise should help you see a volume's shape-state.

exercise 2B

Place any cylindrical form (rolled sheet of paper, mailing tube, juice can, etc.) on a flat surface about twelve to fifteen inches away, and about two or three inches below the level of your eyes, so as to see a side view only. The form should be no less than eight and no more than fifteen inches in length. Correctly placed and centered, neither end plane of the cylindrical object should be visible. Using a pencil, begin your drawing in the middle of the page. Draw the shape *you see*. Draw it approximately actual size. Try to estimate the proportion between the shape's height and width carefully. Now imagine you are going to draw a foreshortened view of a wheel containing eight or ten spokes. Move the cylindrical object to the next position (where you plan to place the next spoke) and, observing two shapes now—that of the shaft of the object and one end plane—try to see them as if they were on the same plane in space. You will notice that the shape of the shaft is no longer rectangular, but appears to narrow at the farther end. Note, too, that until you have placed the object in a totally foreshortened position, the end plane will not approach the shape of a true circle. Continue to draw these spokes, moving your model each time, until you have completed the drawing. Each position will provide a new two-shape combination.

Placed just below your eye-level, even a quite long cylinder, when foreshortened, will show a smaller shaft than end shape.

This exercise warrants frequent practice. Use other simple forms such as books, bottles, or blocks. Point a finger in the general direction of your eye and draw it. Place objects before a mirror and draw them and their reflection.

Though they are composed of joined planes, simple subjects such as the cylinder, cube, apple, or pebble can be seen as a single shape. Even complicated subjects can be seen in this way. Other objects appear as a group of volumes, some of which partially block our view of others—as in a view of a still-life arrangement, a sofa, or a human figure. When studying such a complex of forms it is generally necessary to divide the subject into several shape groupings in a more or less arbitrary way—more or less because the subject itself will suggest groupings according to size, value, placement, direction, or texture. Included in these considerations should be any negative shapes present. Whether the subject is reduced to a single shape or several shape subdivisions, this simplification increases our understanding of the general shape-state of the subject, thus helping us locate the smaller shapes within. When a complex subject's general shape-state is comprehended, all subsequent departures from observed "facts" become intended, subjective choices and not the inevitable results of poor perception.

VALUE SHAPES

If a volume requires two or more shapes, what about the sphere? It would seem to have only one: the circle. But recall that shapes may be hard-edged or *vague*. The sphere, cone, cup, or any other mass formed exclusively or mainly of curved planes offer a preponderance of subtly graduated value changes. Here, the ordering of values into some manageable system becomes a necessity.

To establish shapes made of values it is necessary to group the subject's varying tonalities according to their lightness and darkness, and regard these regions as shapes. These differences in value result from the di-

Figure 2.9

rection of the light source in relation to the subject's surfaces and tend to change as the planes turn toward and away from the source of illumination. The more abrupt the change between the direction of planes, the more abrupt the changes in value will be.

To simplify the grouping of the subject's many values it is useful to establish a few general value divisions. Considering white as zero degrees and black as one hundred degrees, and calibrating a scale in degrees of ten, we have a value scale that is helpful in establishing some order out of the many and seemingly elusive value changes of a subject. Using this scale we can group the perceived values into several general divisions more easily. A four-division grouping might be: white or the tone of the paper, a light gray (30%), a dark gray (70%), and black. There will, of course, be many more than these four values in most subjects. Each of these values should be drawn as belonging to the value division closest to it in degree.

Some artists, by inclination, and when a medium allows for it, find it useful to use a value-grouping system. Then, after completing this stage of the drawing, they make whatever adjustments in value they deem necessary. Other artists will do this sorting in their mind's eye. The mental sorting will have

influenced their use of value and the completed work will reflect the tonal order of a value-grouping system.

Whether or not such divisions of tone appear at some stage in the drawing is less important than their having been consciously searched for. As the observed values are assigned to their appropriate group, larger value affinities spring up between parts of a subject, creating new shapes. These shapes may be composed of parts of several independent volumes—as would occur if we were to shine a flashlight into a darkened room. A "shape" of light could then include all or parts of several pieces of furniture, part of the floor, wall, etc. In Figure 2.9 the value-shapes in B frequently exist independently of the shapes of the volumes seen in A. Note that B shows a four-value grouping of the still life A. The early perception of these value-shapes also serves to establish scale and directional relationships among them, and helps the artist to sense their abstract behavior. Value-shapes within a form, like the overall shape that describes the boundaries of a volume, should be seen first as flat areas, and not only as existing in space upon advancing and receding terrain. Ipousteguy, in his drawing *Anatomy Study: Breasts* (Figure 2.10), utilizes the value-shapes resulting from a harsh light-source to

Figure 2.10
JEAN IPOUSTEGUY (1920–   )
Anatomy Study: Breasts (1969)
Conté crayon. 18 x 24 in.
Courtesy, Allan Frumkin Gallery, New York

Figure 2.11
KÄTHE KOLLWITZ (1867–1945)
The Mothers
Brush drawing, India ink and Chinese white.
18 x 23 1/8 in.
Courtesy Museum of Fine Arts, Boston, Frederick Brown Fund

create an image in which the pattern of values not only defines the forms, but establishes an engaging two-dimensional design. The artist, by intentionally providing as many clues to shape as to volume, creates in the image a provoking visual pulsation between its flat and structural properties.

The following exercise will necessitate a confrontation with a subject's values. It should help you to see shapes as an intrinsic part of a subject's visual condition, as well as to experience their dynamic nature.

exercise 2C

Upon a simply draped cloth of one value (towel, pillow case, or the like), arrange a simple still life consisting of nonreflecting surfaces such as un-

glazed pottery, wood and paper products, or foodstuffs in any combination of three or four objects you find interesting.

This exercise requires three drawings. Each will cause you to make a different value grouping, resulting in different value-shapes. They will provide progressively greater freedom and control in the use of value. You will also find the carving of the general masses achieved through the organization of tones progressively more convincing.

drawing 1

Group all the observed values into two divisions—white and black. Select any point near to the middle of the value scale and leave any observed value lighter than that point (nearer to the white end of the scale) as the white of the paper; any value darker than that point (nearer to the black end of the scale) should be drawn as black. Use a strong light source and arrange the forms in a way that permits the light to "explain" the volumetric nature of the objects.

Selecting a point nearer to the white end of the scale will produce a drawing with fewer white shapes and much larger black ones. Conversely, placing the point of value separation nearer to the black end of the scale will result in fewer black shapes and larger areas of white. By changing the point at which the values will be separated you can create different value-shapes which will convey new structural clues about a subject's volume, as well as different light intensity and expressive mood.

Figure 2.11 is a good example of the structural strength that this limited value system can yield. Kollwitz designs the black and white shapes both as a figure-ground arrangement on the picture-plane and as a system of volume-producing planes in space. Your drawing, too, should have the look of a bold brush drawing or a woodcut.

Using compressed charcoal or black conté crayon and a large sheet of charcoal or pastel paper, draw the still-life arrangement approximately actual size. Begin by searching for the gesture, keeping your drawing fluid and all-inclusive by reaching to all parts within the first two minutes, as described in Exercise 1A (Chapter One). At this stage you can use light lines and tones liberally; the subsequent black shapes will absorb most of them and the remainder can be removed at any later stage in the drawing's development. Begin to search for the shapes of volumes *and* value-shapes while the drawing is still in a fluid state. The values are as much a part of the subject as any other visual aspect, and the shapes they make should be an early perception.

Being limited to two values you will be unable to "shade" or "blend." But the black and white planes may, by their shape, scale, and placement, appear to "turn" or model the forms. This is a helpful restriction. It serves to keep smaller observations and interests regarding minor surface effects at bay and helps you to model the form by the larger and more important planes.

Continue to draw until your drawing suggests at least a general impression of volume. Many students are surprised to find that the sense of volume persists despite the severe tonal restriction. Though many values disappear into the black or white groupings, and many smaller planes are absorbed into them, still, the big planes that these value-shapes create convey a sense of structure.

Now study the drawing to see how the shapes relate on the picture-plane. Notice that they have certain scale, shape, and directional similarities and contrasts that produce a pattern. But does this pattern seem balanced on the page? Rework the shapes to provide a more unified and balanced state among them. But in doing so, try to strengthen the sense of solid mass further, not weaken it.

drawing 2

Draw the same subject from the same view, but use *three* values: the white of the paper to represent the lightest third of the values in the still-life arrangement; a middle tone of approximately a 50% gray to represent the middle, darker tones; for the very dark values (70% or darker) use black. This may still seem to be a severe restriction, but notice how effectively Degas used it (Figure 2.12) to create a handsome format for his visual and expressive interests. Here, the three values are used to show value-shapes both as pattern on the page and as clearly defined planes that carve the forms with great authority. Notice how, in the figure's back, the artist changes values to indicate changes in the direction of the surface terrain. Note, too, that Degas takes care to balance the three areas of dark tone.

These are things to try for in your drawing. As it develops, look for ways in which you can get the greatest "yield" of volume and dynamic spirit through these three values. As Degas' drawing demonstrates, this three-value restriction can produce a great sense of volume. Working within its limits, continue your drawing until you cannot improve the sense of structural mass and shape-order without using more than three values.

drawing 3

This will again be the same view of the still life but now use the four-value divisions mentioned on page 26. Depending on the nature of your subject's values, the lighting, and your own inclination toward lighter or darker drawings, you may wish to adjust the values. The following variation would result in a darker image: (1) white or the tone of the paper; (2) a 25% gray; (3) a 60% gray; and (4) black. Whichever four-division grouping you choose, you may be surprised by how many of the observed values can now be stated as they actually appear in the subject. Not nearly so many will have to be altered in tone (and most of these only slightly) to join one of the four divisions.

Many artists change the tonal scheme when their subject and medium change. Another drawing by Kollwitz (Figure 2.13) shows a four-value division. Notice that the artist subtly interworks these values to subdue their shape impact, but is careful not to lessen their structural function.

Figure 2.12
EDGAR DEGAS (1834–1917)
After the Bath
Charcoal with red, green and brown pastel
chalks on white paper. 17 1/8 x 13 1/8 in.
Fogg Art Museum, Harvard University
Bequest of Meta and Paul J. Sachs

Figure 2.13
KÄTHE KOLLWITZ (1867–1945)
Self-Portrait
Lithograph. 12 1/8 x 11 3/8 in.
Fogg Art Museum, Harvard University
Gray Collection

Your third drawing can be carried further, since a four-value grouping can distinguish more differences between value-shapes and can suggest subtler shape interactions. Try to use this expanded tonal range to establish some of the smaller planes. After the drawing has been carried to a firmer, more volumetric stage, you might wish to abandon the restrictions on values to get at some useful nuances and transitions of tone that will develop the forms further. However, avoid going so far as to lose the sense of shapeness and planar structure.

These three exercises are in no way intended as "how to draw" systems (though, as we have

seen, a number of notable artists have used the several formats discussed here). They are offered as one more means of organizing your observations. Their primary purpose here is to sensitize you to the value-shape as a unit of volume-building *and* pattern-making. Also, these exercises may help you feel more comfortable with the powerful but less familiar (and thus, more feared) element of value. And finally, they will enable you to see the shapes that planes and values offer the discerning artist.

Continue to use these limited value systems in drawings of a few minutes duration to extended works of an hour or longer. Apply them to different kinds of subject matter, and practice altering the lightness or darkness of a drawing by setting the range of values in different ways.

THE INTERDEPENDENCE OF SHAPE AND VOLUME

When volumes emerge from shapes, their third-dimensional quality can affect our degree of awareness to the two-dimensional life of the shapes in a drawing. It is important to recognize the power we have to increase or diminish the viewer's attention to "edgeness." To subdue and thus deny shape most of its dynamic potential deprives the viewer of picture-plane events of much aesthetic worth. For without shapes' surface tensions, their directional play, their value or texture contrasts, and their gestural and structural behavior, an important source of graphic invention is lost. The absence of a sense of shape activity, then, diminishes the means by which expressive and organizational meanings can be established. Such denial is a loss that generally leads to a fussy rendering of surfaces as an end in itself.

This seeming modification of shape considerations by those of volume has been seen by some as creating a dilemma. If emphasis on the third dimension reduces attention to the second dimension, and vice versa, how can one maintain a satisfying activity of both? A rich union of both can occur and is attested to by the drawings of Rembrandt, Degas, Cézanne, Matisse, and many others. This issue is largely absent in the works of those artists who intentionally eliminate structured, volumetric content, thereby clearing the way for the expression of concepts not otherwise possible. Paul Klee, in his drawing *The Angler* (Figure 2.14), could not have probed the visual and expressive issues necessary to him if the sense of volume continued to be a major factor in the pictorial organization of this drawing.

Nor could Rubens, in his *Study of a Male Figure, Seen from Behind* (Figure 2.15), have created his powerfully sculptured images if he had insisted on strong shape confrontations as the *primary* visual message. But unlike artists who exclude the impression of structured forms in space as a goal (although two-dimensional drawings often impart a sense of spa-

Figure 2.14
PAUL KLEE (1879–1940)
The Angler (1921)
Watercolor, pen and ink. 18 7/8 x 12 3/8 in.
The Museum of Modern Art, New York
John S. Newberry Collection

tial depth), no artist who requires a convincing impression of solid masses as part of his language of graphic expression is free of the responsibilities of the two-dimensional activities of his drawing. He must be sensitive to the ways in which the second and third dimensions can assist and spur each other on. These considerations are explored in Chapter Eight.

Actually, the dilemma disintegrates in the presence of a need to fully experience an encounter with a subject. The need to express this experience (within the framework of a personal aesthetic persuasion), not the exploration of both dimensions (or either) as an end in itself, is at the heart of responsive

Figure 2.15
PETER PAUL RUBENS (1577–1640)
Study of a Male Figure, Seen from Behind
Charcoal heightened with white. 37.5 x 28.5 cm.
Fitzwilliam Museum, Cambridge

drawing. The richest visual and expressive responses result from the richest complemental
activity between the dimensions—between
the dynamic and depictive forces. In art, one
person's dilemma can be another's motive.

SHAPE AS AN AGENT OF
DIRECTION AND ENERGY

So far shape has been considered mainly for
its role in the structural organization of volume and for its capacity to stress its two-dimensional configuration and its boundaries.
As we shall see in later chapters, shape has
other functions. In this section we want to
recognize that shape is an important agent of
direction. The familiar arrow on signs directing us to exits, shelters, etc., aims the viewer
toward a particular goal, and the shape itself
inherently suggests movement. We not only
understand it as symbolizing an arrow in
flight, but its shape-character urges us on in
the direction it points to with considerable
energy. In the first chapter we saw the compelling force of shapes when activated to convey a subject's gestural behavior. Our sense of
the arrow's "movement" is a response to that
energy. But the role of shape as an agent of
direction goes beyond gesture. If gestural expression is understood as the emotive character of movement, then directions provide the
"itinerary," the formal pattern of movement.

Shapes, whether as flat configurations
only or as stressed edges of volume, do much
to guide us in or out of the spatial field or in
any direction on the picture-plane. All shapes,
except those whose radii are roughly equal,
such as circular or square ones, suggest movement in the direction of their long axis (Figure 2.16).

Generally, the more geometrically simple
a shape the faster and more forcefully it appears to move. Compared to others in a drawing, longer shapes and those with simpler,
more sharply defined boundaries appear to
have swifter directed movement. When several shapes are arranged in a similar direction
they intensify each other's moving energy.
Conversely, the more complex the shape, the
more convoluted and/or diffuse the boundary,
the more its directional force is impeded by

A   B

Figure 2.16

shapes moving in contrasting directions, and
the less active and directional it will appear to
be. For example, in Figure 2.17, the curved
and obliquely oriented shapes of the figure
and chair, by their common direction, seem to
reinforce each other's movement-energy,
while the dark shape of the skirt, moving
counter to these shapes, is "overruled" by
them.

Exercise 2D will enable you to explore
the possibilities for control over the speed of
the forms in drawing. The last part of the exercise is useful as a preliminary drawing
probe before making an extended work, to
help determine what directional cues the
shapes of a subject offer.

exercise 2D

Using any medium, fill a sketchbook page with
three pairs of squares of the same size, making six
squares in all. We will call the first pair A1 and A2,
the second pair B1 and B2, etc.

In A1, place at any angle, a straight or simply
curved *geometric* shape that appears to move fast.
Do not let its boundaries touch any edge of the
picture-plane. Fill the rest of the picture-plane with
shapes that seem to augment its speed, as in Figure 2.18A.

In A2, redraw the original shape in A1 (a
good opportunity to practice Exercise 2A), and try
to slow down its inherent speed by filling the rest
of the picture-plane with shapes that counteract its
movement. These can appear to move faster or
slower than the original shape and can cut across
or under a small part of it to cancel its speed by
moving in an opposing direction, as in Figure
2.18B. You may use both organic and geometric
shapes for this purpose.

In B1 and B2, repeat the exercise, using an
organic shape for your original. First, try to speed it

up by adding other shapes, then slow it down. Again, both geometric and organic shapes can be used to influence the speed of the original.

In 3A and 3B, repeat the exercise, using simple geometric and organic volumes, as in Figure 2.19. In 3A, arrange forms to create an impression of vigorous movement as in Figure 2.19A; in 3B, try to slow down each form by contrasting movements in neighboring forms, as in Figure 2.19B.

There are other factors that affect the speed of a shape's direction: the differences of value between shapes, their scale and textural differences, even the haste or deliberateness with which a shape is drawn affects its directional energy. Re-examine some of your earlier drawings to see how

Figure 2.17
NATHAN GOLDSTEIN (1927–   )
Gabrielle I (1975)
Sepia ink, pen and brush. 12 x 16 in.
Collection of the author

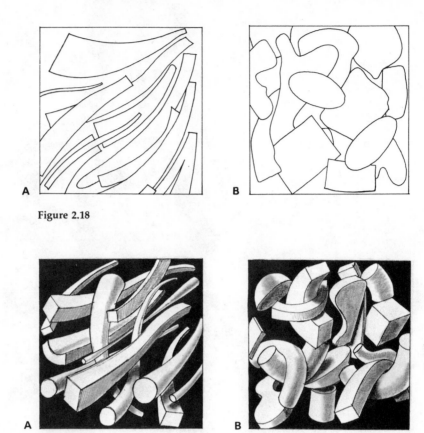

Figure 2.18

Figure 2.19

THE CHARACTER OF SHAPE

Shape can be a picture-plane "occupant," volume participant, and agent of direction. In addition to these functions shape has a quality which does not immediately serve other graphic activities, but declares the shapes in a drawing as having certain common "interests." One of these is a "familial" resemblance. Another is an interest in support of expressive as well as formal matters of visual order for more imaginative results. These characteristics among shapes, their "personality" as being clearly defined or unfocused, curvilinear or angular, boldly or delicately stated,

changing the directional energy of the forms can improve their relational order and life. Responding to the directional cues of shapes in nature and governing their movement-character are important perceptual and graphic skills.

etc., and their behavior as agents of expression, must be recognized as another given factor of drawing. Since drawing without shapes is impossible, the need to establish their collective unity—their "oneness"—*and* their suitability to the artist's expressive intent are inescapable.

In the drawing by Degas (Figure 2.12), the feeling of weighty mass, the avoidance of intricate specificities of edge, and the forceful energy of these undulating shapes establish their unity of character and expressive mood. How these differ from the character of the shapes in a similar subject is shown in a drawing by Renoir (Figure 2.20). Here, the shapes flow in an agile, rhythmic manner, more elegant than those more "plebian" ones in the Degas figure. And the shapes influence our reading of these figures. Renoir's subjects move swiftly and effortlessly; in Degas' drawing we sense strain as well as strength.

Figure 2.20
AUGUSTE RENOIR (1841–1919)
The Bathers
Red chalk. 48 1/4 x 55 1/8 in.
Fogg Art Museum, Harvard University
Maurice Wertheim Bequest

In Villon's drawing *L'Athlète de Duchamp* (Figure 2.21), the shapes are angular; their various tilts create an agitation that plays across the surface of the entire group. Most of these shapes contain value-shape subdivisions within them of a wedge-like and hence aggressively energetic character. A large measure of our impression of the figure's strength and action is due to the character and energy of these shapes. In Cézanne's drawing *View of*

Gordanne (Figure 2.22), the interlacing of geometric and organic shapes creates a handsome weave of straight and curved edges. Shapes seem to strive for a simpler, purer state. Their edges, many of them drawn and re-drawn, appear to vibrate, as if to avoid a final corraling into clearly delineated shapes. Often, Cézanne leaves open the boundary line between shapes, creating larger ones, while not losing the identify of the smaller ones. Compare Cé-

Figure 2.21
JACQUES VILLON (1875–1963)
L'Athlète de Duchamp
Blue chalk. 10 3/8 x 8 1/8 in.
Courtesy Museum of Fine Arts, Boston
George P. Gardner Fund

Figure 2.22
PAUL CÉZANNE (1839–1906)
View of Gardanne (1885–86)
Pencil. 8 1/8 x 12 1/4 in.
The Museum of Modern Art, New York
Lillie P. Bliss Collection

zanne's use of "quiet" shapes with those of Rubens (Figures 2.15, 2.23). Here, shapes twist, interlock, and strain against each other in a stormy turbulence of gestural activity.

These artists used shape's expressive power to convey meanings that mere description cannot. In doing so, they gained the unifying benefits of shapes that share a family resemblance. Neglecting or censoring the expressive power of shape-character invites a randomness of shape attitudes and thus, a muffling of intent.

Responsive drawing involves a complex of perceptions, feelings, and insights about a subject *and* an emerging drawing in which a sensitivity to the several roles of shape is only one consideration, though a crucial and often overlooked one. How shape considerations fare in the medley of responses to a subject is determined by the artist's creative intent. But if they are to play any active part in drawing, the duality of their nature must first be understood.

Recognizing the "double life" of shape in drawing makes one appreciate the ironies of (1) finding a shape's boundaries by seeing the boundaries of the shapes that surround it, (2) finding a volume's planar structure by seeing the shapes which comprise it, (3) finding a volume's direction and position in space by seeing its shape, and (4) finding a shape's expressive characteristics by feeling its emotive force. The functions of shape, only *potential* in the raw material of the physical world, if perceived by the student become some of the more important insights in his perceptual development. Left unregarded, shapes form unintended unions or stay isolated from the rest of the drawing. Such drawings are generally an assemblage of unrelated details, superficialities that do not refer to the subject's objective and dynamic essentials. They offer the viewer a visual "frosting" with no "cake" inside. And this, it seems, is the ultimate irony: that those for whom a realistic image is an important goal will not reach it until they turn from it to learn the visual and expressive abstractions that constitute the language of drawing. The contributions of shape to the language of drawing are indispensable.

Figure 2.23 (left)
PETER PAUL RUBENS (1577–1640)
Study for "Daniel in the Lion's Den"
Black chalk, heightened with white
50.3 x 30 cm.
The Pierpont Morgan Library, New York

CHAPTER THREE

LINE

the indispensable abstraction

A DEFINITION

The use of line as the primary means of drawing is universal. For most people drawing consists of using lines to represent a subject's physical limits and to mark off major subdivisions within it. Line is a visually concise and familiar device for communicating many kinds of visual information. Maps, blueprints, and diagrams utilize line's ability to symbolize organic and man-made forms. Charts and graphs use line to show concepts of weight, cost, and time. Line produces language symbols as well as visual ones—we even doodle with lines.

Our unquestioned acceptance of line as the chief means of producing graphic statements tends to blind us to the fact that line does not exist in the physical world of matter. Virtually everything we regard as a line in nature is, in fact, a thin, solid volume such as a wire, branch, or convex fold, or else a thin depression such as a wrinkle, fissure, interspace, or concave fold. In drawing, then, line should be understood as a wholly abstract device for

conceptualizing a symbol that stands for the thing seen or envisioned. With line, the measurable dimensions of a form can be stated, as can the limits of a color, texture, or value. Abutments of planes can be shown, the direction and position of forms explained as located before, behind, or alongside others in space, and movement can be suggested.

In Chapter One we found that contours emerged from gestural drawing, and we observed the way edges expressed the subject's action and basic structure. In Chapter Two we focused on the importance of edge, as indicated by line, in bearing useful information about volume. In this chapter, line as contour will be a major though not exclusive consideration. As we shall see, line in drawing is by no means limited to the delineation of contours.

A drawn line has certain given properties. It always has direction, interrupts or divides the picture-plane, has along its course one or more values, is consistent or varied in width (i.e. *weight*), and has a certain length. Sometimes a line's length is determined by

40

various calligraphic or textural requirements, and often by the artist's need to establish dimension. Line is an efficient means for noting a form's length, width, depth, and long axis. Too often the beginner restricts such observations to the measurements of a subject's outlines. But line as used to measure the distances between observed points on a form or between forms and to establish the form's specific angle in space is a fundamental consideration of objective visual inquiry, as we shall see in Chapter Six.

Lines also reveal a "personality" or *attitudinal character* mainly derived from the artist's aesthetic and intuitive attitude to line in general, and his visual and expressive responses to a subject in particular. The medium and surface used also influence a line's attitudinal character. The artist using pen and ink will produce a very different type of line than when using compressed charcoal. Not only does the medium limit the character of a line, it deflects the artist's lines onto certain tracks of usage which influence his perceptions of the subject. The medium thus influences the artist's selections. He will tend to respond mainly to those qualities in a subject that his medium and paper are compatible with and avoid those which would create technical problems or are beyond the medium's range of usage.

In responsive drawing the lines that *denote*—that describe what forms look like—also *evoke;* that is, they convey the artist's emotional responses to the forms and to their relational behavior. Consequently, all lines are partly descriptive, partly emotive. Usually, we describe the character of a line by the nature of its dominant attitude, but we should bear in mind that all lines function in both ways. Lines primarily engaged in measurements of length, width, and depth, and in direction, shape, and structural generalities are often called *diagrammatic* lines. Lines which more fully explore and emphasize a volume's planar construction and the interjoining of the form-units that comprise a complex volume are called *structural* lines. Both kinds of line, being primarily engaged with stating the artist's intellectual analysis of a form's structure and spatial condition, are not much concerned with surfaces as seen, but with their essential

constructional system—their architectural condition. Such lines, then, scan volumes searching out their relative dimensions, locations, and directions in space, and the planar arrangements that constitute their structure, rather than the textural and light effects upon them. Both of these closely related types of line are denotative, but both convey emotive qualities, if only the excitement of the artist's structural discoveries.

Lines of a strongly curvasive and rhythmic quality, often more the result of dynamic rather than structural stimuli, are called *calligraphic* lines. And some lines seem so charged with emotive energy that we regard their dominant role to be *expressive*. All lines, of course, are expressive, but some appear to issue more from an artist's intuition, empathy, and temperament than from either structural or organizational motives.

All four kinds of line may be present in some drawings, and it is possible for a single line to function in several or even in *all four ways at once* (see Rembrandt, Figure 1.1). Although in practice these qualities always overlap in various combinations, here we will briefly examine them separately, to better grasp the nature of each.

THE DIAGRAMMATIC LINE

The experience and clarification of spatial depth, dimension, shape, direction, and structure are conveyed in Giacometti's *Portrait in an Interior* (Figure 3.1). Here lines measure distance, estimate scale, and weave through space, as well as forms, to explain the environment in which the forms are located. Diagrammatic lines are investigatory and analytical. They reveal the *general* scale, shape, location, and structural nature of forms in space. As such, they are essentially spatial judgments—abstractions for the location and structural condition of parts. Giacometti's need to understand the subject's structural and spatial relationships causes him to send lines through forms, making masses appear transparent, connecting one form with another. His intense need to experience the three-dimensional *actions* of forms and planes in space—the *plastic*, as well as the structural

Figure 3.1
ALBERTO GIACOMETTI (1901–1966)
Portrait in an Interior (1955)
Pencil. 19 3/4 x 12 7/8 in.
The Museum of Modern Art, New York
Gift of Lester Avnet

nature of his subjects—and the desire to fuse form and space into a system of rhythms and tensions energize the lines and generate their darting, inquiring activity.

In Toulouse-Lautrec's drawing *Le Père Cotelle* (Figure 3.2), there is again an inquiring, diagrammatic use of line. Again, lines measure and explore the general architectural nature of forms *and* their spatial "container" by moving freely upon, through, and between forms.

All drawn lines immediately and dependably record the artist's perceptual comprehension, intent, feelings, and even his neuromuscular control at the instant they are produced upon the page. In these drawings Giacometti and Toulouse-Lautrec are deeply absorbed with visual inquiry and experience—with exploring and manipulating volume and space—and their lines tell us this. The artists, and consequently the lines they devise, are responsive to the stimuli of visual cues

Figure 3.2
HENRI DE TOULOUSE-LAUTREC (1864–1901)
Le Père Cotelle
Charcoal with colored crayon. 20 x 13 5/8 in.
Courtesy of The Art Institute of Chicago

about space, shape, dimension, and volume. And, because these are the issues that excite their interest, the lines, although primarily diagrammatic in function, also manifest an expressive quality. In these two drawings, then, perceptions preceded the artist's feelings. As both show, analytical and emotive attitudes to line are not mutually exclusive.

THE STRUCTURAL LINE

Although possessing some diagrammatic qualities, structural lines have some distinctive characteristics. They stem from the same necessity to explore and explain space,

shape, dimension, and especially volume, differing most because of their emphasis on volume building. Structural lines, in establishing the various planes of a form, are capable of modelling it with sculptural clarity. Often groups of lines are used together to create optical values that explain a subject's terrain in planar terms, and even to suggest the presence of light (see Chapter Four). Leonardo da Vinci's and Michelangelo's pen and ink drawings (Figures 3.3 and 3.4) demonstrate lines used in just this way.

A structural use of line tends to reduce attention to contours and emphasizes instead the substantiality of a form's mass. Often, as in the Michelangelo drawing, the artist using

Figure 3.3
LEONARDO DA VINCI (1452–1519)
Five Grotesque Heads
Pen and ink. 26 x 21.5 cm.
Royal Collection, Windsor Castle

Figure 3.5
PAUL CÉZANNE (1839–1906)
The Card Player
Pencil and watercolor. 20 1/4 x 14 9/16 in.
Museum of Art, Rhode Island School of Design, Providence, R.I.

Figure 3.4
MICHELANGELO BUONARROTI (1475–1564)
Standing Nude, Seen from the Back
Pen and ink. 39 x 19.5 cm.
Albertina Museum, Vienna

structural lines limits his presentation to the subject's forms with little or no attempt to develop its immediate environment. Not surprisingly, many sculptors, like Michelangelo, draw almost exclusively in structural lines. Because structural line, like diagrammatic line, is exploratory, artists often combine these two attitudinal approaches to line.

In Cézanne's drawing of a card player (Figure 3.5), the structural lines in the hat, hand, and sleeves merge with the probing diagrammatic lines that establish the shape-state of those forms. The lines in the drawing's lower half are almost exclusively diagrammatic, suggesting that Cézanne first used lines to explore forms and space throughout the drawing, developing the upper part of the figure on the information so gained. That diagrammatic line can carry gestural information is evident in some of the drawing of the card

player's legs, cloak, sleeves, and hat, as well as in the areas around the hat and head. Again, in Papo's drawing *Seated Nude Figure* (Figure 3.6), diagrammatic inquiries underlie structural statements. Notice how economical and effective the patches of massed lines are in establishing convincing masses. Note, too, that in the preceding five examples of diagrammatic and structural line drawing each is enlivened by felt and forceful responses of an engaging sort. Many students (and some teachers) feel uneasy about stressing a search for dimension and structure, fearing such an analytical approach may lead to tight or dull results. But a strong emphasis on understanding a subject's proportions and structure is not only no danger to creative interpretation and handling (unless it excludes all other considerations), it can uncover a rich source of dynamic invention, as we shall see in Chapter Six.

Figure 3.6
ISO PAPO (1925–)
Seated Nude Figure
Pencil. 14 x 16 in.
Courtesy of the artist

Figure 3.7
OSKAR KOKOSCHKA (1886–   )
Study of the Artist's Mother
Black chalk. 40.2 x 28 cm.
Albertina Museum, Vienna

THE CALLIGRAPHIC LINE

Because of their rhythmic, tactile nature, calligraphic lines usually have strong gestural qualities.* Kokoschka's chalk drawing (Figure 3.7) contains several kinds of calligraphic line, from the foggy tone-lines of the hair to the forceful lines of the clothing. Kokoschka's lines offer numerous variations of thick-thin, short-long, flowing-angular, fast-slow, and light-dark line ideas. These all function repre-

*See Roger Fry, "On Some Modern Drawings," in *Transformations* (London; Chatto and Windus Ltd., 1926).

sentationally—they denote the woman—but also reveal an independent play of line variations as a simultaneous plastic, abstract theme. And these abstract actions reinforce depictive meanings; that is, they evoke qualities in the subject that elude mere description. For example, the nature and the relational behavior of these lines help us to *feel* the firmness of the supporting arm, the differing weights of the woman's clothing, the texture of the hair, and the limpness of the reposing figure. Although, as noted earlier, all lines evoke, the pronounced activities of those lines we call

47

calligraphic seem to disclose more relational purpose, more expressive potency.

Some of the lines in Kokoschka's drawing, such as those of the chair, or the faint lines on and around the head, are as much concerned with diagrammatic searching as with calligraphic exposition. They serve as quiet, inquiring foils for the bolder declarative lines. If the drawing had an unchanging sameness of line-character, much of its *type* of calligraphic play would be lost, for one of the drawing's strengths is in its line variety.

Yet, an unvarying line, when that is the artist's graphic theme, provides another kind of calligraphic quality. Matisse's pen and ink drawing *Odalisque with a Moorish Chair* (Figure 3.8), has a consistency of line that helps create a two-dimensionally active design. Unlike Figure 3.7, where a rich variety of line assists the location of planes and edges

Figure 3.8
HENRI MATISSE (1869–1954)
Odalisque with a Moorish Chair (1928)
Pen and ink. 25 3/4 x 19 7/8 in.
The Museum of Modern Art, New York
Acquired through the Lillie P. Bliss Bequest

Figure 3.9
ALFONSO CANO (1601–1667)
Study for the Figure of a Franciscan Monk
Pen and ink. 17.6 x 7.5 cm.
Prado Museum, Madrid

and establishes solid forms, Matisse's more uniform line tends to flatten the forms somewhat by stressing the cut-out character of the edges. This occurs because contours represent the most distant surfaces of a rounded form. Emphasizing contours brings forward the receding, foreshortened planes they are meant to represent. Matisse further accents the sec-

ond dimension by creating strong, attention-getting shapes.

The lines in Cano's stormy drawing (Figure 3.9) contrast sharply with the dart and flutter of the lines in Tiepolo's page of sketches (Figure 3.10), and both these uses of line differ from the rhythmic vigor of the lines in Pineda's study (Figure 3.11), yet all

Figure 3.10
GIOVANNI BATTISTA TIEPOLO (1696–1770)
Figure of Falsehood
Pen and brown ink. 6 3/8 x 6 1/4 in.
The Art Museum, Princeton

Figure 3.11
MARIANNA PINEDA (19 –   )
Reclining Figure
Green crayon. 17 x 21 in.
Courtesy Alpha Gallery, Boston

are strongly calligraphic expressions. In each of the five preceding works the artist utilizes line's capacity for visual and expressive excitation and not its ability for description alone.

THE EXPRESSIVE LINE

As observed earlier, all lines convey *some* expressive properties. After all, they represent an artist's intellectual *and* emotional encounter with a subject, resolved through his aesthetic *and* temperamental attitudes to line, and these qualities leave *their* mark, too. Kokoschka's

drawing is sympathetic and somber in mood, the Pineda, animated and elegant—and the character of the lines tell us this. But we can regard lines as chiefly expressive when we sense in a drawing that the artist's needs to experience and share feelings *supersedes* any other motive for line's use.

Unlike the artist for whom line's expressive power is triggered mainly by visual stimuli, other artists, such as Goya (Figure 3.12), come to the blank page with an established expressive intent of another kind. For these artists the expressive character of line, though it may result in part from visual challenges and insights that occur while drawing,

Figure 3.12
FRANCISCO DE GOYA (1746–1828)
Sad Presentiments of What Must Come to Pass
(from *"The Disasters of War"*)
Etching, 4th state. 10.5 x 18.7 cm.
Print Department, Boston Public Library

receives its initial impetus and emotive potency from a need to experience and share feelings *through* and not merely *about* the representational content of the drawing. In Goya's etching, the first in a series called *The Disasters of War*, it is not the representational matter alone that expresses his ominous warning of impending doom. The character of the lines reveal this through their slashing, cross-hatched clash and the brooding tones they form. That these lines carry the grim message intrinsically can be seen by covering any portion of the etching. Even small segments cannot be seen as cheerful, gentle, or serene. Lines of such expressive force do not

come from a calm, contented attitude, but from a deeply felt anguish.

Goya's interest in visual phenomena—in structure, design, or plastic activities—exists only insofar as they strengthen his expressive message. This is not to suggest that these matters were of little importance to him, rather that they were not important as ends in themselves. They were a necessary means to the clarity of his expressive ends. His lines, then, are not the results of an aesthetic or even a temperamental "policy," but of a deeply felt and largely intuitive strategy.

Pascin's drawing *Girl in an Armchair* (Figure 3.13), shows a use of line to express a

Figure 3.13
JULES PASCIN (1885–1930)
Girl in an Armchair
Charcoal, some yellow chalk.
55.9 x 43.1 cm.
The Newark Museum

sensual, even erotic, interest in the female fig-ure. There is honest fascination evident in the slow search of the forms. These lines, *by their nature*, express the pliancy and weight of the body. Pascin delights in experiencing every fold and swell of the figure and of the yield-ing, receiving character of the sofa. Every-thing in this drawing is felt as supple and

pliant—terms that describe the character of the lines themselves. Again, covering a sec-tion of the drawing would show remaining portions capable of communicating Pascin's sensual message.

A very different kind of expression is conveyed by the rugged and resolute chalk lines in Schiele's drawing (Figure 3.14). These

Figure 3.14
EGON SCHIELE (1890–1918)
Arthur Roessler Standing with
Arms Akimbo
Black chalk.
Albertina Museum, Vienna

Figure 3.15
PABLO PICASSO (1881–1974)
Mother and Child and Four Studies of Hands
Black crayon. 13 1/2 x 10 1/2 in.
Fogg Art Museum, Harvard University
Bequest of Meta and Paul J. Sachs

lines are in complete accord with the figure's assertive stance; they evoke as well as depict.

Artists may support the emotive meanings of representational content through line's expressive powers for many reasons. Historical, religious, political, and social issues have been catalysts for such drawings.* But many other motives can and have stimulated artists to use line for expressive purposes beyond those triggered by visual issues. The lines that reveal Picasso's understanding of a mother's feelings for her child (Figure 3.15) are themselves gentle caresses.

* For an interesting exploration of such motives, see Ralph E. Shikes, *The Indignant Eye* (Boston: Beacon Press, 1969).

ON USING LINE

This discussion of the several basic attitudes to line may leave the impression that the artist makes a conscious choice among them. This is virtually never the case, although the more experience the artist has in exploring various line characteristics, the greater his control of line's "vocabulary." Still, because of certain factors, no one has complete freedom in the selection of line.

First, our choice is influenced physiologically, in the same way that we are not altogether free to choose our individual handwriting. Neuromuscular coordination and control imprints certain pathways of line-making and blocks others. These personal idiosyncracies are not easily overcome. Nor should we struggle to overcome them, for these traits form part of our unique way of drawing (or writing). And one personal style of using line is just as capable of stating our intent as any other. Second, we are influenced psychologically. Our intuitive and intellectual interests—how we like to use and see line—insist on a particular "recipe" based on the options available. This creative imperative may vary with the choice of subject or medium, and as our moods and interests fluctuate within a certain aesthetic point of view. For example, compare Toulouse-Lautrec's use of line in Figure 1.7 with that in Figure 3.2, or in his sketch of a music hall figure (Figure 3.16). Although these drawings differ from each other as much as they do from other Toulouse-Lautrec drawings in this book, all of them exhibit variations of line usage that fall within a range determined by his idiosyncratic and creative instincts. All bear the stamp of the artist's temperament and handling.

There *are* drawings which convey little line attitude. Such drawings tell us that their authors were unaware or not especially interested in line's analytical, structural, or empathic uses. They show that no benefits were gained from lines as dynamic events in their own right, or as supportive of figural content. Such line-inhibited drawings generally reveal an exclusive concern with superficial effects and appearances. But the use of line to symbolize a subject places the drawing well away from the "real."

Figure 3.16
HENRI DE TOULOUSE-LAUTREC (1864–1901)
Sketch for "Aux Ambassadeurs"
Pencil. 26.2 x 20 cm.
Albertina Museum, Vienna

To convey the experience of our visual and emotional encounter with a subject through line is possible only by utilizing line's ability to explore, act, and express.

In responsive drawing, line always functions at three levels: it *describes*, it *acts*, and it *interacts* with other lines, producing various dynamic phenomena. If description alone is the only motive for using line, we lose all of line's dynamic potential—its ability to add meanings and activities that support the depiction. Denotation alone skirts all the responsive possibilities of line and is always expressively dull. As we have seen in the previous two chapters, an exclusive concern with a subject's surface appearance blinds us to a subject's gestures and shapes. Here, it blinds us to the many possibilities for creative activity and meaning of the very means being used to make the drawing—line.

The following exercise explores the several line qualities discussed.

exercise 3A

This exercise consists of five drawings. Each should start as a two-minute gestural drawing. In each, your model will be the same: your own hand, holding a tool, letter, utensil, flower, or anything else that is not much larger than the hand, is comfortable to hold, and has some interest for you as a visual and/or expressive object.

The five drawings and the time allotted for each are:

1. calligraphic emphasis—fifteen minutes
2. diagrammatic emphasis—fifteen minutes
3. structural emphasis—thirty minutes
4. expressive emphasis—fifteen minutes
5. unrestricted line drawing—thirty minutes

For Drawings 1 and 4, use India or any black ink and a flexible pen such as a steel crow-quill or artist's sketching pen. For Drawings 2 and 3, use a stiffer pen-point. For Drawing 5, use either type of pen or both, as needed. Draw on a stiff paper, such as a bristol or vellum stock, or on any good grade of paper that has a moderately even surface. The drawings should all be about the same size, approximately 10″ × 14″. In each, try to work about actual size, but do not hesitate to work larger if your drawing requires it.

Beginning a pen-and-ink drawing may create some anxious moments for you. The earlier gestural drawings in pencil or chalk seemed "safer." Passages of light tone could be darkened and erasure was possible. It was like walking a tightrope with a net below. Here, there is no net. The foggy tone-lines, so useful in grasping a subject's broad actions and masses, and in avoiding a lapse into outlining, are not possible in this medium. Obviously we must alter our tactics.

Many artists will first make a gestural drawing in pencil *on another sheet of paper*. Tracing the original drawing in ink usually destroys its spontaneity. In any case, there is no satisfactory way to transpose the soft, light lines so natural to chalks and pencils, into pen-and-ink. Such a preliminary pencil drawing helps us to become familiar with a subject's essential action and structure, and allows for a more informing and economical use of line in the pen-and-ink gesture drawing. And using the fewest lines possible is now necessary, for almost every mark will be visible in the completed drawing.

Figure 3.17
HENRI GAUDIER-BRZESKA (1891–1915)
Standing Woman (1913)
Pen and ink. 16 1/2 x 10 7/8 in.
Collection, The Museum of Modern Art, New York

This being the case, more effort and time must be given to an analysis and summary of the forms *before* you begin to draw. Where chalks could make broad sweeps in tone, a few short lines, or even dots, must suffice to show the basic action and form-character. However, do not hesitate to use continuous lines if you wish. That such a pen-and-ink gesture drawing can convey as much about the action is evident in Gaudier-Brzeska's spirited drawing (Figure 3.17). Although intended as a final statement, it is an impressive example of how much gestural action can be grasped with a few felt, selective lines, resolutely stated.

Figure 3.18

Think of these lines and dots as clues—a kind of gestural shorthand—about the expressive action. These clues should also refer to major directions, shapes, and masses. Remember to develop all parts of the gesture drawing together (Figure 3.18).

drawing 1

Calligraphic (15 minutes). After the two-minute gestural phase, try to complete the drawing by lifting the pen from the paper as little as possible. Holding your pen upon the paper at the completion of a line, while you look up to make further observations, often leads to discoveries of nearby edges or tangential forms that allow the line to continue. This continuity gives to lines a sense of animation and promotes an economical handling, as in Figure 3.17. Although a shorter, vigorous line like Dufy's (see Figure 1.12) also suggests an energetic calligraphy, as does the rich variety of Kokoschka's lines (Figure 3.7), continuous lines more clearly reveal line's capacity for dynamic activity, and demand that you make more conclusive, simpler line judgments. However, do not hesitate to use line ideas such as those in the Dufy and Kokoschka drawings where you feel they are necessary to your drawing. But for your first attempt at a calligraphic approach to line, favoring fewer, longer ones will make you seek variations of direction, weight, rhythm, speed, and plastic play among them. By using fewer lines you will more likely become aware of their dynamic possibilities, and of just how much a single line can do. Sensitivity to line's powerfully efficient descriptive and abstract life is a prerequisite to those responses that "call forth" the calligraphic quality.

There is no one way to draw calligraphically. Your continuing study of the drawings by artists who emphasize calligraphy will reveal the endless possibilities for such linear actions. Calligraphic lines are not "free-born"—to wander where they will—but *can*, simultaneous with their representational role, offer linear configurations that are aesthetically satisfying.

In still another Toulouse-Lautrec drawing (Figure 3.19), gestural and calligraphic qualities occur throughout. We sense that Toulouse-Lautrec enjoyed the "confrontation" of contrasting types of lines, and the knowledgeable flourishes of his "handwriting" are graphic activities in their own right. The lines denote a confident mounted trooper, but simultaneously assert their own exciting existence.

With fifteen minutes to make your drawing, you need not feel hurried. Indeed, a slower-moving line permits you to make more explicit and subtler judgments. It also acts as a brake on the desire for fast flourishes which, because of their speed, may not be the result of sound observations, but of a wish to impart a calligraphic "look" to the drawing. But in responsive drawing, lines not stimulated by felt perceptions are either personal drawing cliches or aimless whimsy. The calligraphic line is always an *informing* line with a plastic life of its own.

Your goal in this first drawing is to interpret the subject as a system of forms which offer interesting linear ideas—ideas you feel extract the sub-

Figure 3.19
HENRI DE TOULOUSE-LAUTREC (1864–1901)
Horse Guard, London
Pen and ink. 26 x 26.9 cm.
Toulouse-Lautrec Museum, Albi

ject's essential character and allow for a satisfying use of line, much as you use line when writing. The lines in the completed drawing should show not only your understanding of the subject's actualities, but line interactions, affinities, and contrasts that exist as visual activities in their own right.

For the responsive artist these several functions of calligraphic (or any other) line to describe, act, and interact are ultimately inseparable. Such artists want to make permanent their impressions of, and experiences with, something they see, and they need to do so in a particularly satisfying way that *communicates*. The responsive artist does so by harnessing those dynamic forces that, to him, abstractly support the depiction. The comprehension of a subject's figural factors *and* the visual and expressive ideas used to state them, create the give-and-take between a drawing's "what" and "how" that determines the drawing's *content*, its total depictive and dynamic character. It is the artist's particular insights and innovations that make the work an invention rather than a report. And it is the quality of the negotiations between these simultaneous and mutually stimulating considerations that creates the union called art, in which the whole is greater than the sum of its parts.

drawing 2

Diagrammatic (15 minutes). After the gestural phase, explore the planes that comprise the major masses of your hand and object, and the distance separating these volumes from one another. Notice the various tilts of the volumes, their scale relationships, and the shape, scale, location, and direction of any "empty" or negative areas. Do so by a liberal use of light lines.

Your goal in this drawing is to explore and explain the subject's measurable shape, scale, spatial, directional, and structural essentials. This theme must be so insistent that responses to surface effects of texture or light are disregarded to avoid weakening the analytical search.

The calligraphic line is, to some extent, a tactile, sensual line. The sensation of touching forms to feel their terrain helps suggest ideas for line activity. Here, the goal is not to caress a form, but to tell us about its constructional and spatial condition. The diagrammatic line is primarily intellectually informing. Its expressive properties come from the artist's excitation about the visual inquiries he makes regarding the subject's important actualities, and the relational ideas they suggest to him. When a diagrammatic line defines an edge or "rides" upon a form's surface, it tells about, rather than feels that edge or surface just as the longitude and latitude lines of the globe describe divisions of that form without responding to the undulations of the earth's surface.

Like the lines upon a globe, *cross-section* lines, sometimes called *cage* or *cross-contour* lines, help to explain the *general* nature of a form's surface. Plan to use such lines wherever you feel the need to further explore a form's volumetric character, as in Tovish's drawing (Figure 3.20), where

Figure 3.20
HAROLD TOVISH (1921–   )
Contour Drawing (1972)
Pencil. 19 x 25 in.
Courtesy, Terry Dintenfass, Inc., New York

Figure 3.21
GIOVANNI BATTISTA PIRANESI (1720–1778)
Architectural Fantasy
Pen, brush and ink. 36.5 x 50.5 cm.
Ashmolean Museum, Oxford

their use evokes a powerfully sculptural image. This is more frequently useful when forms are not comprised of flat planes, but are more organic in character.

Although a line can function in more than one way at once, in this drawing try to use lines only to explore the general "architecture" of the forms and the spaces between them. These spaces, like the solid forms, should be measured and their "masses" of air explored by lines (Figure 3.1). Becoming aware of such "forms" of space is an important aid in understanding solid ones. It is helpful to imagine such a space as filled with some kind of solid but transparent material such as ice. What would its mass be? Helpful, too, is drawing through a solid form to "see" its total structure, as occurs, for example, if we draw a cube of ice. In this way we can better understand its mass, its location to other forms, and something of the spaces that separate them.

In the drawing by Piranesi (Figure 3.21), the liberal use of line helps explain the forms. Piranesi reinforces our understanding of a plane as being flat or curved, a volume's position in relation to others, and the spaces that separate and surround the volumes by using groups of lines which explore surfaces, placement, and space more fully than a single line can.

Like the Giacometti and Toulouse-Lautrec drawings (Figures 3.1 and 3.2), Piranesi's conveys a sense of excitement about the creation of a three-dimensional environment. In your drawing, regard every perception of scale, direction, etc., as an important discovery. Allow—or encourage—a sense of satisfaction about each new "find." Once you have established one or two areas in the drawing that convey a sound grasp of the masses and their spatial relationships, other, less clearly resolved, passages will call for clarification. Continue to probe these less realized passages so that the drawing, at

59

the end of fifteen minutes, will show an even standard of clarity throughout. As in Figures 3.1, 3.2, and 3.21, let your drawings "grow" to include the immediate environment of your subject, thereby including new spatial relationships.

In drawing, any kind of line can perform a diagrammatic function. When an artist uses a line to tell us something of a volume's dimensions or position, the space in which it exists, or its physical relationship to other volumes, that line, whether additionally functioning in a calligraphic or any other way, is performing a diagrammatic function.

Again, it is important to recognize that lines generally function in several ways simultaneously. When we add to these functions considerations such as line's contribution to composition and their abstract, plastic activity, we begin to see the challenges and possibilities that exist beyond the merely reportorial aspects of drawing.

drawing 3

Structural (30 minutes). This time, modify the gestural beginning somewhat in favor of a more diagrammatic search of your subject, as Cézanne does in Figure 3.5. There we saw how the diagrammatic "armature" helped to guide the structural drawing. Concentrate, then, on drawing (in a general and simplified way) the essential architecture of the major masses. But do not sacrifice the search for the gestural expression altogether, or the resulting drawing will appear stiff and lifeless.

In this drawing you will often use groups of lines, as in Figure 3.6. It may be helpful to fill a practice page with such line-groups, called *hatchings*, or, when groups of lines overlay each other, *cross-hatchings* (Figure 3.22). The few moments taken to do this exercise within an exercise will give you better control for making the various line patterns you will use in this drawing.

Now your goal is to explain the structural role of the flat and curved planes of the volumes. Also, try to convey the volumes' sense of weight. If your hand is holding a flower, show through the vigor or delicacy of your lines, and by their width and group density, the lightness of the flower, and the relative heaviness of the hand.

Instead of drawing the outline of each plane, use hatchings as in Figures 3.3, 3.4, and 3.6. Such massed lines produce optical tones which help clarify the planar modelling.

Place your hand with the object in a position that allows a single, diffused light to fall upon them. Avoid strong sunlight or a location too close to a harsh, artificial light source. These conditions create extreme and often abrupt value changes and strong cast shadows. A cast shadow occurs when a form blocks the path of light rays, leaving the area

Figure 3.22

Figure 3.23

behind the form in darkness (see Chapter Four). In your drawing, avoid cast shadows except for those small, form-revealing ones you feel will strengthen the structure. Daylight, preferably a north light (which changes least during daylight hours), will best reveal the tonal differences of the planes, and permit you to see between the forms and into their darker recesses.

Often, a plane's direction can be selected by the artist. In Figure 3.23A the same planes are drawn to carry the eye in different directions. The cubes are equally solid but we "read" them differently. When a form's structure can be stated equally well in any one of several ways, the choice of the direction of the hatching should be one that supports other issues such as compositional or expressive ones. In Figure 3.23, the lines of cylinder 1 direct our eyes along the length of the body, while those of cylinder 2 move around it, implying the existence of the cylinder's unseen back. The first cylinder is seen as moving more forcefully in a direction than the second one but tells us a little less about its volume. Usually, hatched lines drawn as moving around a form or as riding upon its surface undulations (as in Figure 3.23B), tell us more about a volume's terrain than lines that go in other directions on it.

Lines can also deny a volume's surface-state by being drawn in some direction structurally illogical to it, as in Figure 3.23C.

In Corot's drawing *Young Woman Seated, with Her Arms Crossed* (Figure 3.24), the direction of the line-groups clarifies the structure of the forms. Changing the direction of these lines would only diminish our understanding of the subject's structural nature. Therefore, indicating the direction of planes through masses of lines that ride upon them in form-revealing ways is an important method by which to convey structural conditions.

It should be stressed here that using such hatchings and cross-hatchings should not be understood as a particular *style* of drawing, but as a general and universal *process*. Many artists of very different aesthetic persuasions have for centuries applied this process of structural modelling to convey volume. Developed in the Renaissance (Figures 3.3 and 3.4), it continues to provide artists with an effective means for the manifestation of volumetric facts in original ways, as in Picasso's *Sketch of a Nude and Classical Heads* (Figure 3.25) and Goodman's *Study for Woman Holding Sheet* (Figure 3.26).

Another way to convey the impression of volume uses line-groups to show the effects of light upon surfaces. Light waves do not bend; the differing values of a form's planes represent their turnings toward and away from the source of light. When planes abut at pronounced angles the value change is abrupt, as in Figure 3.27A; but is gradual when a curved plane turns toward or away from the light source, as in Figure 3.27B. Hatching, then, in addition to establishing the directions of planes, can show the sudden or gradual changes in the surface they collectively produce.

In your drawing, use both of these form-revealing concepts to carve the forms. In de Gheyn's drawing *Woman on Her Death Bed* (Figure 3.28), both means have been used effectively. Groups of lines, *by their direction*, explain the angles of planes throughout the drawing. Notice especially how clearly the artist establishes the directions of the planes of the hands, bodice, and collar.

De Gheyn leaves as white those planes facing the light source, here falling from the figure's right side. Planes which parallel the direction of a light source receive a raking, weaker light, often called a *halftone*. These de Gheyn states as light values of several shades. The variations of these halftones are determined by the planes' slight turns toward or away from a true parallel with the direction of the light rays. Those turned well away from the light he draws as darker line-groups. Thus, by allowing the light-source to determine the *value* of the hatching, de Gheyn conveys his subject's essential structural nature by lines that explain both the direction of the planes *and* the light falling on them.

Note how well the few cast shadows are integrated among the other values, how they contribute to the pattern—the design—of the other values, and how they help explain the terrain upon which they fall. Despite the liberal use of line in this drawing, nowhere do lines deny the form. They all "earn their keep" through volume-producing tasks.

In thirty minutes of drawing *from the general to the specific*, you should have enough time to es-

Figure 3.24
CAMILLE COROT (1796–1875)
Young Woman Seated, with Her Arms Crossed
Graphite pencil. 10 7/8 x 8 in.
The Louvre Museum

Figure 3.25
PABLO PICASSO (1881–1974)
Sketch of a Nude and Classical Heads
Pen and ink. 12 3/4 x 10 in.
Courtesy, Museum of Fine Arts, Boston
Arthur Mason Knapp Fund

Figure 3.26
SIDNEY GOODMAN (1936–   )
Study for Woman Holding Sheet
Pen and ink. 8 1/2 x 11 3/4 in.
Courtesy, Terry Dintenfass, Inc., New York

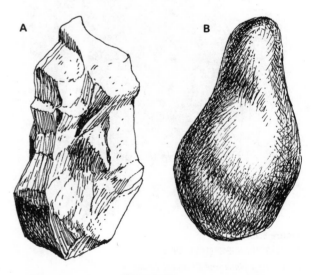

Figure 3.27

tablish many of the smaller planes that make up the volumes. Divide the planes into several value-groups as de Gheyn does, or as suggested in Exercise 2C in Chapter Two. This will help you control the many values of your subject more easily. Look for the direction a plane seems to suggest. If flat, which direction should the lines take to better explain that plane's union with adjoining ones? If curved, should the plane's hatchings move in the direction of the form's long axis or wrap around its body? The choice will often depend on the terrain adjoining the plane. Sometimes, as in reflections of highly polished surfaces, driftwood, wrinkled folds of cloth or skin, or in many highly textured objects,

the answer is revealed by these surface conditions. Look for such clues, however subtle; they can help make your drawings more structurally lucid.

Your drawing should look more carved than illuminated. Because you have emphasized planes more than the effects of light, your drawing may seem somewhat rough-hewn or blocky. With practice and experience, such characteristics can be modified or strengthened depending on your intent.

If, at the end of this thirty-minute drawing, you have established an impression of structured masses, you will have experienced a sophisticated set of visual perceptions. This is one of the more

Figure 3.28
JACQUES DE GHEYN (1565–1629)
Woman on Her Death Bed
Pen and ink. 14.6 x 19.4 cm.
Rijksmuseum, Amsterdam

demanding and instructive ways of using line. It requires your constant analysis of shape, scale, direction, and value.

The ability to control line in this sculptural way is essential to our understanding of line and to our ability to analyze and communicate the structural nature of any form. After all, we cannot draw what we cannot fully understand, and we cannot state our perceptions without a process for communicating them.

drawing 4

Expressive (15 minutes). As mentioned earlier, the attitudinal character of *any* line may be primarily expressive. In this drawing, try to advance a felt theme such as strength, delicacy, danger, anger, mystery, or joy. It will now be necessary to look at your hand and the object in it in a new way. If you have been doing these drawings in sequence, you are, by now, quite familiar with the visual issues of your subject. Now respond to its *meaning* for you. You may not be able to express your feelings in words. They may be diffuse or too interlaced with visual responses for language. That is, you may be emotionally stimulated by *visual* as well as psychological responses. But try to draw whatever your emotional response *feels* like. Let anger, joy, etc., affect the choice you make from the raw materials before you—what you will and will not use—as well as affect your "handwriting." Here, the object you selected will surely exert an influence. If you are holding a flower or a sea shell, you are not likely to respond to your subject's mood or character in the way you would if you are holding a pistol or a shrunken head. The quality of the light upon your subject may influence your feelings, as may the time of day or your emotional disposition at the time you approach the subject.

Your "handwriting" will reveal your feelings but these feelings should not supplant sound visual perception. Rather, they should act as a brake on mere copying and serve as a *basis* for selecting those cues that express your theme.

You may wish to clarify and emphasize your theme by exaggerating the bigness or littleness of some or all of the forms. You may want to alter your subject's contours, values, or the placement of its parts. Make such adjustments only when the expressive character of the lines cannot themselves intensify the feelings you mean to convey. Or, if the intended theme is conceived in a way that must include such changes, include them from the start of the gestural stage. However, resorting to distortions before expressive lines have had a chance to indicate your intent, or carrying such changes too far from the observed actualities, can create more problems than they solve. Such changes carry with them the greater risk of *unintentional* discrepancies in scale, shape, and structural clarity. Sometimes the drawing drifts so far from the subject's actualities that further references to it become useless. At least in this first attempt at expressive drawing, the prudent course would be to make only modest adjustments of the original, allowing the main responsibility for the expressive intent to be carried by the *nature* of the lines.

The tight limit of fifteen minutes for this drawing is designed to prompt your first, felt responses to be expressed. Often, in drawings without a time limit, these reactions are "censored" by second thoughts. Here, it is your feelings, advised but not dictated to by your perceptions that must be revealed through line's character. Modifying your first, intuitive responses for other, less spontaneous ones can weaken or obscure your meanings.

The expressive force of Van Gogh's *Grove of Cypresses* (Figure 3.29) is declared mainly by the swirling lines of the trees, clouds, and nearby undergrowth. Had Van Gogh drawn these trees "correctly," that is, had he held his feelings in check and only reported upon their proportions, textures, placement, etc., we would have a drawing that testified to the physical characteristics of some cypress trees in southern France, but without the compelling dynamic force of his graphic invention. Here, Van Gogh shares with us his feelings about movement and growth—the trees' animated swirl. He tells us the entire countryside and sky can be experienced as trembling with flamelike energy.

Compare this drawing with Bresdin's *Bank of a Pond* (Figure 3.30). Like Van Gogh, Bresdin tells us about the growing, animated quality of a spring landscape. But Bresdin's line is more lyrical, less driven. The scene is active but in a temperate, gentle way. He sees the foliage, clouds, and even the rocks as windblown. The breezy spring day is evoked by the graceful, rolling nature of the line. In a different mood, Daumier's *Two Barristers* (see Figure 1.10) is also animated by expressive lines that do more than describe physical facts. Their own nervous vibrations reveal the subject's movement and mood.

Segonzac's etching *Portrait of Colette* (Figure 3.31) is more than a likeness. The artist's bold, authoritative line carries some of the strength and energy of the brilliant French novelist. In your drawing also, tell us, through the nature of the lines, what your subject says to you.

Again, line can be put to any expressive undertaking—from the grim and moving message of Goya's lines in his *Sad Presentiments* (Figure 3.12)

Figure 3.29

VINCENT VAN GOGH (1853–1890)

Grove of Cypresses
Pencil and ink with reed pen. 62.5 x 46.5 cm.
Courtesy of the Art Institute of Chicago

Figure 3.30
RODOLPHE BRESDIN (1822–1885)
Bank of a Pond
Pen and ink. 16.2 x 17 cm.
Courtesy of the Art Institute of Chicago

Figure 3.31
ANDRÉ DUNOYER DE SEGONZAC (1884–1955)
Portrait of Colette (1935)
Etching. 9 1/8 x 8 1/4 in.
Collection, The Museum of Modern Art, New York
Gift of Peter H. Deitsch

Figure 3.32
AUGUSTE RODIN (1840–1917)
Two Female Nudes
Graphite pencil and brown watercolor washes
on grey paper. 30.5 x 19.5 cm.
Albertina Museum, Vienna

to the playful and provocative lines of Rodin's
sportive *Two Female Nudes* (Figure 3.32). Line im-
bued with the artist's feelings about his subject
can summon a dimension of meaning not otherwise possible.

drawing 5

Unrestricted (30 minutes). Using either or
both types of drawing instrument, begin this
drawing as you did the other four, but develop it
through any combination of line uses you wish.

Just as any line that measures space or mass
is, whatever its primary attitudinal character may
be, functioning diagrammatically, so can lines of

calligraphic, expressive, and structural qualities simultaneously undertake each other's functions.
Here, you should allow lines to convey several of
these attitudes at the same time.

We have isolated and examined these attitudes to better understand their nature and function. But avoid thinking of line as being neatly
sorted into four fixed categories. In all the drawings used here to demonstrate one or another of
these line qualities, there are lines that function in
other ways. There are diagrammatic functions in
Kokoschka's essentially calligraphic drawing, structural properties in the lines of the Goya etching,
calligraphic qualities in the Van Gogh drawing.

Additionally, we have seen that *every* line is expressive of some motive—is energized by some visual and expressive idea—either depictive, dynamic, or both. Further, bear in mind that lines can change character along their course. A line begun as a gentle inquiry may end as a furious declaration. Remember, too, that the medium and the surface used affect the "look" and even the usage of line.

In this drawing you are on your own. Do not dwell on line attitudes; instead concentrate on your visual and expressive responses that are now under none of the influences and restrictions of the previous four drawings. Having worked with each attitude has helped you understand their various qualities better. You made some judgments about their capabilities and their "feel." Much more drawing experience is needed to fully grasp their worth. But let your experiences of the previous four drawings influence your use of line in this drawing. Your attention should shift from line's uses to what it is you want to explore and convey. But your expanded repertoire of line uses should help you communicate your intent in more effective and satisfying ways.

This drawing may lack the control and clarity of meanings you had hoped for. Even though your primary attention is upon comprehension and response, it will take patience, commitment, and the experience of many encounters with subjects drawn in line before these concepts and procedures, adapted to your interests, become necessary, natural, and satisfying. As William Hazlitt observed, "We never do anything well till we cease to think about the manner of doing it."

DELINEATING CONTOUR

To delineate should be understood here as establishing the physical limits of a form or plane with any of the four line concepts already discussed. That any kind of line can be used to convey the "edgeness"—the *contours* of forms—is clearly seen in the drawings that illustrate this chapter. Whether by Cezanne, Segonzac, or any other artist, the character of their delineating lines is largely consistent with the type of line quality used throughout the drawing. Delineation then, is a task that *any* type of line can perform. But, unlike the untrained, for whom delineation is only outlining, a marking off of boundaries determined by shape, color, value, or texture, the responsive artist regards delineation to be a

volume-producing process. For him, the line that creates an edge, regardless of its calligraphic or other properties, is understood as denoting planes seen in full foreshortening, as when a calling card is held in such a way as to reduce it to a line.

And this is true whether the drawing consists mainly of contour, as in Figures 3.16 and 3.17, or is densely filled with lines, as are Figures 3.3 and 3.4. Only in drawings that avoid or subdue a sense of edge, as do Figures 3.25 and 3.30, is the issue of form-revealing delineation absent. And even then, despite the negation of a continuous contour, edge as *turning form* is implied.

The tradition of drawings which rely mainly on form-revealing contour dates back to the prehistoric cave artists of France and Spain. In Eastern Art the contour line has always prevailed. In Europe the emphasis on contour by using sharply "focused" line of a continuous nature was a dominant graphic device until the late Renaissance. Contour drawing remains a universally popular means of graphic expression because of its ability to economically state volumetric impressions of a form at its edges and even suggest conditions of the form's terrain well within its edges.

Still, contour drawing is not another attitudinal category of line but, as mentioned earlier, is an "adopted" function of any of the line qualities already discussed. As such, its function tends to set it apart. For example, in Michelangelo's drawing (Figure 3.4) the contours are essentially structural in character, but by their running at a right angle to much of the hatched lines that model the form, and by their continuity, we recognize their somewhat independent nature. That such an independence of contour can be modified is evident in the structural lines of Cézanne's *Card Player* (Figure 3.5).

For the beginner, drawings restricted to volume-revealing contours help him see the often complex state of a subject's edges with heightened objectivity. Such drawings encourage conscientiousness in the perceptual efforts required to "track" the condition of edges, similar to the kind of searching explored in Exercise 2A in Chapter Two. However, here the lines are understood to represent planes in space as seen in total

Figure 3.33
DOMINIQUE INGRES (1780–1867)
Portrait of a Lady Seated
Pencil. 11 1/2 x 8 1/2 in.
The Metropolitan Museum of Art
Bequest of Grace Rainey Rogers

foreshortening and not just the limits of a shape.

Whether or not delineation becomes an unselective tracing of edges—a kind of fussy scrutiny—depends on the artist's ability to recognize what is essential to the impression of volume and what is irrelevant or detrimental to it. Ingres' drawing (Figure 3.33) is a quite faithful denoting of his subject, but not slavish imitation. His choices and changes make each delineating line reveal volume. Also, Ingres is sensitive to the rhythmic flow that organic forms possess, and his line includes that graceful relatedness of the parts. Ingres' drawings have a knowing ease that looks deceptively simple. Far from mere copying, Ingres, despite his close adherence to the subject's actualities, developed a style of delineation so distinct that his drawings are easily recognizable.

Exercise 3B provides some suggestions for delineating contours that will help you experience line as edge *and* volume-maker.

exercise 3B

This exercise will take thirty minutes. Use any kind of pen or pencil and a sheet of good quality bond paper, approximately 18″ × 25″.

For your subject, select one or more mechanical devices that offer an interesting collection of gears, wheels, cylinders, pipes; for example, a hand-run lawn mower, an eggbeater, or a bicycle. Parts of discarded engines and even carved furniture can be used. The more unfamiliar these things are to you, the better. All too often, forms we possess some knowledge of cause us to unknowingly slip into remembered clichés about their structure. This drawing requires your sharpest perceptual acuity—not for purposes of imitation, but to ana-

Figure 3.34

lyze and understand the volumes you will be delineating. This being the case, try to favor a structural attitude to line. As such drawing becomes more familiar to you, it will reveal your own calligraphic idiosyncracies about contour. Ingres' drawing shows his "recipe" of structural-calligraphic qualities. Diagrammatic themes being often too schematic, and expressive themes too little concerned with objective analysis, most contour drawings show a blend of structural and calligraphic interests.

Arrange your subject so that parts overlap. This time, do not make a gesture drawing but begin by sighting on some edge of your subject and, drawing in a large scale (where possible, close to

actual size), *slowly* follow the edge with a single, continuous line. Lift your drawing tool as seldom as possible. Do not feel pressured to complete the drawing within the time allowed. At all times regard your line as recording the edges of planes. Do so whether the planes are flat or curved, facing you, turned away, or fully foreshortened. Because your line indicates a form's direction in space, try to feel the line moving in and out of space as it follows an edge. By increasing and decreasing pressure on your drawing instrument you can vary the value and weight of lines to help suggest a form's near and far parts. Additionally, such variations help suggest whether an edge is rounded or not. Thinner, lighter, and/or less sharply incisive lines suggest the edges of rounded forms; heavier, darker, and/or more sharply "focused" lines indicate the edges of flat planes.

Ideally, you should not lift your drawing tool more than seven or eight times during the entire thirty minutes. However, do not hesitate to do so more often if you find this restriction too limiting; or less often, if you can. While most artists do not restrict their contour line in this way, here it will help to increase your awareness of delineation as a distinct graphic activity with its own dynamic potential. A line can be kept going by continuing to find "routes" for it to take. Often, a line, having reached a dead-end, can be made to continue by backtracking. Just draw your line (as slowly and as well observed) along the same edge it came up, until you find some way out (Figure 3.34A).

As you draw, you will notice that some lines begun at a form's edge have moved into its interior, as may happen with an object such as a spiral-shaped chair leg. Follow such edges with an awareness of their coming toward and moving away from you. Each time a spiralling edge turns away and out of view, continue your line on the new edge that blocked your view. But recognize that doing this means leaving a form at one level in space to "hop" to another one located nearer to you. Sometimes an edge turns inward—"dies out." When this occurs you can either reverse your line to get back to the outer edge of the form or "legitimately" begin a new line (Figure 3.34B).

Do not use lines to suggest value. Here, you want to test your ability to perceive and lines' ability to convey volume, as edges may reveal it, without other aids.

In contour drawing you will find that the angle of interception of one line by another—the impression of space and volume resulting from perspective principles (see Chapter Five)—is as important as are particular changes along a form's edge. Perspective is a factor in all volumetric drawing, but drawings that rely on contour lines to communicate several kinds of information require the artist to be especially sensitive to the direction of edges in space. Part of the impact of such lines is in being "right" the first time. If several lines are needed to adjust the original one, there is some loss of the clean, economical control that you want to command in this drawing.

The slower the line, the more you will see. Avoid the natural tendency to speed up the line. This usually results in drawing uncertain generalities to represent intricate or subtle passages in the subject. Here, your attitude should be "the more difficult or subtle the passage, the more committed my perceptual skills will be to changes and over-lappings of edges." An extreme example of this attitude would be to draw every strand of spaghetti in a dish, just as you see them, avoiding none of their coiled, interlaced complexities. One of the frequent pitfalls of the beginner is to relax his perceptual powers when confronting a complex or unusual subject. Just at that critical moment, where continued or even intensified efforts to analyze would cause the breakthrough to the understanding necessary for the control of a demanding passage, there is a retreat to vague generality. Known as "lazy vision," this turning away from visual challenges must always be guarded against.

In this drawing, do not worry about proportions which may be awry or about poor organization. You are extracting one idea only: "Here is what I found about the volumetric properties of my subject that were capable of being stated in a few continuous lines."

Other concepts and uses of line are dealt with in Chapters Eight and Nine. While our interest has been focused here on the properties and responsive possibilities of line, we should remember that its unseen presence abounds in everything we see. In Chapter One we sensed, in the search for gestural expression, some of the linear forces that forms generate by their direction and rhythms. This sense of directional energy—of "pathways"—moving through a subject, should be permitted to influence all uses of line. We are always aware of directional force, a kind of "invisible" line, even when it runs through several forms, as when we speak of furniture "lined up" or an arm "aligned" with a leg, or when several linear directions form a discernible pattern such as the lifting upward and outward of tree branches from their origin in the trunk. Adding such "felt" lines to the line considerations already discussed, we recognize lines' powerful role in the acts of perceiving *and* drawing. We must also recognize that it is inquiry, empathy, and invention, not the desire to imitate nature that is at the heart of a knowing use of line.

You will treat line in drawing as your physiological, psychological, and aesthetic dispositions allow. Within these limits the ability to state your visual and expressive meanings through an understanding of lines' many uses is basic and calls for a dedicated, searching study.

CHAPTER FOUR

VALUE

light, local-tone, modelling, and mood

A DEFINITION

A children's riddle asks what the subject of a black sheet of paper is. The answer: a coal miner with no headlamp, in a mine at midnight. Why not? A black surface *can be* imagined to be anything—in itself, it *is* nothing. A coal miner *with* a headlamp—and there is no riddle. Forms in nature, as even the children who ask the riddle know, are revealed by light. In drawing, the impression of light is conveyed by values.

Value can be produced in just two ways: (a) by variously hatched lines creating optical grays, that is, impressions of value resulting from the collective tone of massed lines, their value resulting from the density of the hatching; and (b) by deposits of actual gray tone by chalk, pencil, or diluted washes of ink or paint.

For the student the use of massed lines to model forms provides important experiences in perceiving and explaining the direction of planes in space and is, therefore, highly instructive of the structural aspects of

volume (see Chapter Six). But the application of actual gray tones has its own versatile uses and characteristics, as we shall see.

Value, whether the result of optical or actual tones or both, is the necessary and (except for color) the only tool for modelling form with light. It gives the artist the means of showing subtle changes in a form's surface-state, and it helps clarify the relative distance between forms. Value also conveys the inherent lightness or darkness of a form—its *local-tone*. This is a given quality of all forms. It is affected by, but separate from, the light and dark areas that result from light falling on forms. The local-tone is the intrinsic value of a thing—excluding any effects of light. The local-tone of a common pearl is very nearly white; that of a lump of coal, nearly black. If we use the value scale described in Chapter Two, the pearl's local-tone is about a ten percent value, the lump of coal's, about ninety percent. Light falling on both would make them lighter and darker in places, but under most lighting conditions the darkest value on the pearl will not be as dark as the lightest value on the coal. Light is incidental to local-tone. Values, then, enable us to state a subject's intrinsic *and* incidental tonalities.

Value can also suggest a broad range of expressive meanings. How we contrast, shape, and distribute values, and the amount and manner of tonal transition among them are potent factors in a drawing's psychological mood. In the powerful seventeenth-century drawing of a triumphant general (Figure 4.1), the amount and manner of application and the bold contrast of values between the configuration and the page suggest strength and grandeur. The forward part of the horse and rider "burst" through the splashy field of tone, asserting aggressive energy. The shapes

of the tones, their spontaneous application, only loosely confined by the lines, further signify powerful force.

Like line and shape, value is a versatile compositional tool. Value can command attention to a form's direction, weight, or importance; it creates visual diversity and serves as a strong unifying agent.

Unfortunately, most beginners seldom use values. Partly due to a universal tendency to regard drawing as a process limited to line, and partly because of its relative unfamiliarity, they restrict their responsive options by an avoidance of value. When introduced to value, many beginners are uneasy about drawing large or dark tones. They are afraid

Figure 4.1
Italian, 17th Century, Venetian School
Triumphant General Crowned by a Flying Figure
Brush, pen and ink. 10 3/4 x 7 3/4 in.
Fogg Art Museum, Harvard University
Bequest of Meta and Paul J. Sachs

that such areas will be hard to manage—or re-move—that they will surely "mess up" the drawing. These are understandable concerns. But when value's functions are explained and some approaches to its use are suggested, it is often quickly adopted and controlled. How soon and how well it serves the student depends on how soon he confronts his fear and how well he understands the functions of, and approaches to, value. Drawing with line alone—freely selected as a mode of graphic expression—is excellent; but when drawings are restricted to line because of innocence or fear, it is a regrettable limitation. Value provides the only means to convey a broad range of responses which must otherwise remain stifled.

THE DISGUISES OF VALUE

Our world is a collection of colored forms in space. A lake is seen as blue, not as a value of fifty or sixty degrees; grass is green—its value not usually a conscious consideration. The beginner, if he is painting a lemon and a plum, is generally more aware of their color than their inherent local-tone. He may paint the lemon yellow and the plum purple, but his color choices may be lighter or darker in value than those of the fruits. If he is making a tonal drawing with ink, charcoal, or pencil, he will, of course, disregard the subject's colors. But often he will also disregard the values inherent in the colors, neglecting to extract their local-tone. Instead, he may draw the differing values or *value-variations* resulting from light striking the subject, as if the lemon and plum were actually white. If he does try to show their local-tone, it will often be at the cost of the value-variations. Establishing a subject's value-variations in the context of its local-tones is not likely before the student sees the difference between these two aspects of the subject's value-state. For him, color disguises local-tone. Or, seeing it, color adds to his confusion in attempting to sort out inherent values and those produced by light.

The basic skill of tonal drawing is the transposing of colored forms and the light upon them into values. However, unlike the camera, which extracts the values of illumi-nated, colored forms, the student can and must make selections from, and changes in, the observed values, for light can *distort* as well as explain both local-tone and value-variations.

Texture can also disguise both given and light-induced values. What we mean here by texture is the character of depicted surfaces and of the media used to draw them. When a surface has a pronounced, allover tactile quality like a tree trunk or silk, when it has qualities inherent in its physical composition like a calm or stormy sea, or when a surface results from the proximity of many small forms, like leaves or the threads of a lace collar—the visual activity thus generated should be regarded as texture.

Texture also defines value and color changes of either a patterned or random nature in a form's surface. A plaid shirt, a tiger's stripes, and the markings of a marble slab are examples of nontactile textures. The term also includes groups of forms when they activate a large area such as a table top or a field. A display of dishes, a herd of cattle, a crowd at a rally as in Goya's drawing, *Crowd in a Park*, (Figure 4.2)—all these can be seen as textures.

Additionally, all drawings show the texture inherent in the medium used and in the way it is used. For example, the given texture of chalk markings is grainy and rough; but the stippling, hatching, or smudging uses of chalk, while never losing their grainy character, can suggest many other textures. In Millet's drawing *November* (Figure 4.3), the rough grain of the chalk does not intrude on the delicate texture of the hatching in the sky, and seems most suited to the depictive textures of birds, branches, and furrows. Even the grain or *tooth* of the surface drawn on reveals its texture by the way a medium acts upon it. As an example, compare the texture of the chalk's behavior on the smooth paper used for Figure 2.10 with the texture of the chalk in Figure 4.3, or in Seurat's *Sleeping Man* (Figure 4.4).

The texture of some subjects, like a tree with a deeply rutted trunk, or a shrub with its countless leaves catching the light from many angles, produces such an array of values that it is difficult to judge either the subject's local-tone or the behavior of the light striking

Figure 4.2
FRANCISCO DE GOYA (1746–1828)
Crowd in a Park
Brush and brown wash. 8 1/8 x 5 5/8 in.
The Metropolitan Museum of Art
Harris Brisbane Dick Fund

Figure 4.3
JEAN-FRANCOIS MILLET (1814–1875)
November
Black chalk. 13.2 x 20.5 cm.
The Louvre Museum

Figure 4.4
GEORGES SEURAT (1859–1891)
Sleeping Man
Black chalk. 24 x 30.8 cm.
The Louvre Museum

it. Other subjects are so boldly textured that they cannot be reduced to a single local-tone. A chessboard, a zebra, a boldly patterned wallpaper or flag—or anything else that has striking and frequent contrasts in color or texture—inherently possesses two or more local-tones.

But if an intense light illuminates part of such a surface, leaving the remainder in a pronounced shadow, the surface's tonal differences are made subordinate to the strong contrast of light and shadow upon it. In Figure 4.5A a strong light strikes half a chessboard,

unifying the alternating light and dark squares of the illuminated part into a pair of values lighter in contrast to the light and dark values of the unlit part. Here, the intense light unifies the two local-tones of the board by showing their differences to be less great than the contrast between the lit and unlit halves of the board. But this is achieved at the cost of seeing the chessboard as split into two halves. In Figure 4.5B, the contrast occurs less abruptly than in 4.5A, resulting in a more unified image, without losing the impression of a strongly lighted board.

Figure 4.5

When textures can be seen as contrasts to a constant base or background, such as cattle in a field, markings on a marble slab, or polka dots on a scarf, the local-tone of such backgrounds can be better determined by disregarding the smaller "interruptions" of the base. Then too, once this tone is established, the values of the smaller units can be better gauged in relation to it.

Before such perceptually demanding differentiations can be made, we must experience the controlling of values as they relate to each other in some ordered scale. Being able to see and to govern such value relationships as discussed above is fundamental to responsive drawing. Exercise 4A suggests how this skill may be practiced and developed.

exercise 4A

You will need a good grade of bond paper, a ruler, and three pencils: a 2H, which makes a fine, light gray tone; a 2B, which makes a moderately soft, deeper tone, and a 6B, which makes deep, velvet-like gray-black tones. Using the 2H pencil, rule a horizontal rectangle one inch high and eight inches wide. Divide the rectangle into eight squares by drawing lines at one inch intervals.

Make eight values progress in even "jumps" from white to black (or as near to black as the 6B pencil permits). The first square on the left will be the white of the paper. Fill the second square with an *even*, light tone. Use the 2H pencil for the first few squares, darkening them as needed with the

2B pencil. For the next few squares, the 2B pencil, used with increasing pressure, will be needed. If necessary, combine it with the 6B pencil to establish darker tones where needed. The last squares may require the softest pencil only, but use all three in any way that helps you control the visual "meter" of the value changes.

In choosing the first light tone to put beside the white square on the far left, remember that you need to make five more value jumps before you reach the black square on the right. All eight squares must show *the same degree of difference between values*. If you make the first tone too light, the small difference in tone between it and the white square to its left sets the degree of value difference between all the values to come. Because the goal here is to have the eight values progress evenly on the value scale—where white is zero and black is one hundred—starting at the left, each square must be just over twelve degrees darker than the one on its left. In Figure 4.6 there are intentional errors in the eight values shown. These cause some squares to be too greatly separated in value from neighboring squares, while others are too close in value. Avoid such blending as occurs between squares three and four, and such splits as occur between squares four and five. Draw each tone evenly, permitting no value changes within a square. By placing lines close together in one direction, or by cross-hatching and varying the pressure on your pencil, a uniform value of any degree can be produced. The control necessary to make line-groups produce a desired even value is a helpful by-product of this exercise. Therefore, do not smudge or rub tones to get an even value. Although the smudging of tones is a valid graphic

Figure 4.6

tactic, it is too often overused by the beginner, causing overworked, fussy results that destroy a drawing's freshness and spontaneity.

When completed, this chart should be studied from a distance of nine or ten feet away. Are there any sudden breaks in the value changes? Are any values so similar they seem to blend at this distance? Do the values on the left side seem grouped together and split off from the values on the right? Are the values from left to right so light that they seem to drop off to black too suddenly? Check to see if any of the tones, including white and black, break the even progression of the values. In making any adjustments in these tones, you may find that changing one often requires changing one or more of the others.

In deciding whether or not your exercise is successful, you will be making judgments about its tonal organization, its *tonal order.* Evaluating the tonal order here—perceiving and weighing the differences between degrees of value—is similar to the way values in an observed subject are assessed. Then, too, we want to see the range and relationships of the values. If our goal is reproducing the tonal order of a subject, we must study our drawing to search for false notes—for faulty tonal judgments.

Try some variations of this chart. Here are a few suggestions:

1. Draw a ten-square value chart. Here, the value changes will be subtler, their differences more critical.

2. Draw a ten-square chart using pen and ink. The true black now possible makes it somewhat easier to show ten different values, but the inability to lighten any tone makes establishing an even pace of tones more difficult. Producing unvaried squares of tone in pen and ink is likewise more difficult than in pencil, especially in the lighter values, where dots will have to replace lines.

3. Make another 1" × 8" rectangle, but do not divide it into squares. Using your three pencils, make a *gradual and unbroken* progression from white to black. Here, the tone continually grows darker as it moves to the right. On the rectangle's far left, some white paper should remain to establish the scale's zero. Placed at a ten-foot distance, the values should flow evenly from white to black.

4. Mix eight to ten gray tones using any opaque, water-based paint, then reproduce these tones in pencil. The painted tones need not be lined up in any progression but can be used to create a small, two-dimensional painting of clearly defined shapes. In this way, along with the challenge of perceiving the values of another medium, you can, in your pencil version, practice seeing shape-actualities.

5. Cut out of magazines, construction paper, etc., ten or twelve evenly colored one-inch squares. Paste them down in a row according to their *value,* with the darkest color on the far right. Seeing the difference between a light blue and a bright orange is a demanding test of your ability to disregard a color's hue and extract its value. When this chart is completed, draw another row of one-inch squares directly below it and, using pencils, match the value of each color in the square below it.

In Chapter Two we saw that sorting a subject's values into two-, three-, or four-value divisions enables us to see the general distribution of a drawing's values in its early stages. Establishing these major value groupings *before* we draw the smaller, specific ones that constitute them will reduce the possibility of destroying the tonal character of an area—whether that character is mainly the result of local-tones or light diversity. For example, in a drawing of a sunlit interior, a white cat lying in a shadowed, far corner of the room, seen in its value *context,* would be understood to be—not white—but gray. The darker the corner of the room, the darker the value of the cat. It is easier to see the white cat as actually gray if we first search for the major value divisions created by both local-tone and light source.

Drawing values sequentially, and with no regard to the tonal order they contribute to, increases the likelihood that prior knowledge (the cat is white) may replace visual comprehension. To draw the cat in that tonal environment as actually white, forces it to "pop out" of the darkened corner's tonal condition. Or, seeing the cat as gray, it may be lost among its surrounding tones if they are stated as lighter than the existing tonal order of the corner.

Color, texture, sequential drawing, and displacing perceptions by prior knowledge all camouflage value. In order to extract a subject's tonal actualities from the visual factors obscuring them and avoid attitudes that intrude on such perceptions we must be able to distinguish between a subject's given and incidental values and to recognize the importance of an objective analysis of the relational state of these values.

THE EFFECTS OF LIGHT ON VOLUME

Just as color and texture can obscure value, so value — as light is distributed upon a form — can obscure our reading of a form's structure. Light can in fact explain, distort, divide, or unite forms. The way light's indifferent behavior is understood determines whether its effects are merely copied or controlled for responsive purposes. A drawing which tries to duplicate the values in the subject will reveal no more than the light does about volume and space. But if light's behavior is understood, the values can be "edited" — selected and altered to more fully disclose the subject's structure and spatial environment. Where the light's behavior explains a form's structure, it can be used; where light confuses or denies structure, it can be changed. In responsive drawing the artist, and not the accidental effects of light, determines what the clarity of the volume will be.

Forms appear fragmented, are seen as divided into tonal shapes when an intense light casts harsh, dark shadows across their bodies, as we saw in Figure 4.5A. Such shadows can sometimes give us a distorted idea of a form's structure or obscure important structural passages. But a moderate, well-placed light can help the artist reveal and unify complex subject matter. A tree need not be drawn leaf by leaf. Grapes, pebbles, hair, a stadium crowd, or any other subject comprised of small forms can be expressed in a unified way by values that explain the overall volume these small forms contribute to.

Until the Renaissance the manner usually employed for representing small forms was an additive one. Each leaf, grape, or pebble was delineated with roughly equal attention. A clump of leaves, a bunch of grapes, *resulted from* this patient and deliberate accumulation of virtually every member, as in the anonymous Lombard drawing (Figure 4.7),

Figure 4.7
Anonymous Medieval Drawing
Page from a Lombard Sketchbook
Pen, brush and ink. 23.9 x 17.1 cm.
The Pierpont Morgan Library, New York

where each leaf has been carefully drawn in each tree. Here the artist has drawn his conception, rather than his perception, of a tree. As drawing moved toward more objective analysis of the thing observed, the additive process declined. As ways of perceiving expanded, sensitivity to the ways volume could be summarized and conveyed also grew. The drawing by Cesare da Sesto (Figure 4.8) goes far beyond the collecting of particulars in suggesting complex masses, and does so by more than line, as in Figure 4.7. Da Sesto, although still giving much individual attention to particulars, subordinates his attention — espe-

Figure 4.8
CESARE DA SESTO (1480–1521)
Study for a Tree
Pen and ink. 15 x 10 1/8 in.
Royal Collection, Windsor Castle

sands, comprise, and does so by employing a strong light-source. Note that, in these last four drawings, the impression of light and atmosphere increases as values "take over" from line.

Treating whole trees as particulars of a general panorama—a forest—Rothbein (Figure 4.11) orchestrates light to unify the forest's "small" forms, its textures, and even the larger forms of the hills and valleys. She creates a pulsating light that seems to move across the landscape "pulling together" many small forms and explaining the greater masses they are part of. Here, light is more than the means by which the subject is explained—its pulsations and its mood are as much a part of the subject as the mountain forest it defines.

Figure 4.9
NICOLAS POUSSIN (1594–1665)
Trees in a Meadow
Pen and brown ink, brown wash, over black chalk.
24 x 18.1 cm.
The Louvre Museum

cially on the drawing's right side—to individual leaves to show the masses they collectively form. This is achieved by making use of values to suggest light falling on the tree from above and to its right side. The shading of the left side of each branch and of the trunk unify and lend substance to these parts.

Nicolas Poussin's response to trees (Figure 4.9) utilizes the impression of light to stress their gesture and mass. Here, individual leaves are only broadly suggested, the emphasis being on their collective texture and mass. In an even broader, more painterly manner, Lorrain's *Landscape with Tree and Figures* (Figure 4.10) uses values to carve the broad planes that the leaves, in their thou-

82

Figure 4.10
CLAUDE LORRAIN (1600–1682)

Landscape with Tree and Figures
Pen and bistre wash. 28.5 x 21 cm.
Albertina Museum, Vienna

Figure 4.11
RENEE ROTHBEIN (19 –)
Mountain Landscape
Pen and ink. 18 x 27 1/2 in.
Courtesy of the artist

Also responding to light as both means and subject, Dickinson, in his drawing *Cottage Window* (Figure 4.12), creates a silent and enigmatic scene in which the shadows of part of a house and porch are projected on the wall and window of a cottage, making these "ghosts" of structures that are "off stage" part of the drawing. Likewise, some trees across a broad meadow are not seen directly, but as reflections in the windowpanes. The light casts shadows that ride upon the wall, shutters, window frame, and panes, explaining their volume. In doing this, they create unusual tonal shapes that call attention to the drawing's two-dimensional design. Again, in

Seurat's drawing (Figure 4.4) light itself is both tool and theme. Here, light bathes human forms with majestic simplicity. Seurat's use of tone makes the white of the paper appear to glow—like the sun's own blinding light.

As the preceding several drawings intimate, works in which light is the dominant graphic idea imply a view of our world as existing in darkness—darkness is the norm and light the transitory, revealing exception.

Light, then, can not only be made to explain and unify forms, it can provide important visual and expressive meanings. Rembrandt's *Cottage before a Storm* (Figure 4.13)

Figure 4.12
EDWIN DICKINSON (1891–   )
Cottage Window
Charcoal. 10 7/8 x 12 7/8 in.
Atlanta University, Gift of Mr. and Mrs.
Chauncey Waddell

Figure 4.13
REMBRANDT VAN RIJN (1606–1669)
Cottage before a Storm
Pen, brush and ink.
Albertina Museum, Vienna

is a striking example of the power that the impression of light can impart. What might otherwise have been a pleasant, if ordinary, rural scene is transformed by an extraordinary control of light into a dramatic and spiritual event. And note how volume informing are the tones that create this transcendental light.

THE ELEMENTS OF LIGHT

In drawings where values represent light, the value contrasts can denote the forms, the spaces surrounding them, and the shadows they cast. These contrasts conform to six discernible divisions, regarded here as the *elements of light*. As seen in Figure 4.14, they are:

1. The lightest value on a form, or *highlight*.

2. The next lightest value, the *light-tone*, or *quarter-tone*.

3. The third lightest value, often found on surfaces that parallel the direction of the light rays, or *half-tone*.

4. The darkest value, or *base-tone*.

5. The usually weak light cast upon the side of a form turned away from the light source, *reflected light* results from deflected light rays.

6. The dark tones resulting from the blocking of light rays by solid bodies, or *cast shadows*.

In Figure 4.14, we see that the cast shadow is the one element that does not exist on the sphere. Because of its special project-

Figure 4.15

ing nature, a cast shadow behaves uniquely. Often troublesome, the cast shadow *can* effectively reveal the distance between forms, and explain the terrain of the form upon which it is cast. It can suggest the location of the light source, the time of day, and can perform compositional and expressive functions.

Cast shadows help explain spatial relationships. In Figure 4.15A, the sphere hovers above the lower of the two boxes. In Figure 4.15B, it seems to be located further back in space, resting on the higher box. In both illustrations the placement and size of the cast shadow suggest the position of the sphere in its relation to the other two forms. The two drawings are identical, but changing the cast shadow's location and size in each changes the spatial relationship of all three objects.

Cast shadows (as we shall see in Chapter Five) are projected in accordance with the laws of perspective. Their value, scale, and shape tell us the direction and height of the light source, how close it is to the objects casting the shadows, and the nature of the terrain upon which they are cast.

In Figure 4.16, the card in A and B is the same short distance from the wall. But, because the light source is farther from the card in 4.16A, its cast shadow is smaller and darker than the cast shadow in 4.16B. In each illustration we see that the radiating light rays not stopped by the card continue to diverge, leaving unlit shapes on the wall. The cast shadow in 4.16B is larger because the closer the light source is to the object receiving the light, the greater is the degree of divergence of the light rays.

Maintaining the same distance between the light source and the card but placing the card farther from the wall also increases the size of its cast shadow, in relation to the ever-

Figure 4.14

A   B   C   D

Figure 4.16

widening cone of light, as in 4.16C. Here, too, we can see that the greater distance separating the card from the wall allows more deflected light to illuminate the area of the cast shadow, lightening its value and softening its edges. Tilting the card forward, as in 4.16D causes the cast shadow to tilt backward. There are two reasons for this. First, cast shadows increase in scale as the distance between an illuminated object and the surface receiving such shadows increases, and second, the degree of divergence of the light rays increases as an object (here, the upper part of the card) approaches the light source.

As these illustrations show, cast shadows always retreat in the opposite direction from that of the light source. If we see a form's cast shadow below it, as in 4.16A, B, and D, we know the light falls from above. When the cast shadow falls above the form, we understand the light to come from below. Additionally, should a form's shadow be cast upon an uneven surface, it will "ride" and thus explain that surface's topography (Figure 4.17).

Courbet uses cast shadows (Figure 4.18) to help explain the structure of the head, by projecting shadows from one part, such as the nose, upon other parts. Notice how the shadow of the hat reveals the terrain of the right side of the head, and shadows cast by parts of the clothing explain other parts of it.

We see in the strongly contrasted values of Courbet's drawing, in the areas of subtle value-variations, and in the sense of the subject as existing in an atmosphere of light and space, a presentation of the elements of light used in a manner sometimes called *chiaroscuro* (an Italian term meaning clear and obscure, and used in the sense of light and shade). In Leonardo da Vinci's study of drapery (Figure 4.19), the strong but softly graded value contrasts demonstrate chiaroscuro's volume-revealing possibilities. Notice da Vinci's looser, broader manner, used in the earlier stages of the drawing and visible in the upper part of the figure. The drawing is a closely observed and fully realized study of light's behavior on forms. But at the beginning, da Vinci's search for the general masses of the drapery, and some preliminary line drawing, indicate that

Figure 4.17

Figure 4.18
GUSTAVE COURBET (1819–1877)
Self-Portrait
Charcoal. 27.7 x 20.3 cm.
Courtesy, Wadsworth Atheneum, Hartford

his first responses were to the subject's gestural and structural essentials. Also observe that this brush drawing, heightened with white, consists mainly of hatchings that effectively produce subtly graduated value changes. These changes, like those in the Courbet drawing, demonstrate a use of all the elements of light.

When an object such as glass or metal reflects light, or has a polished or otherwise reflective surface, as when an object is wet, the highlights upon it produce a mirror image of the light source. Highlights on objects with a matte surface denote the small areas where the greatest concentration of light rays strike a form directly. A subject's surface may vary in reflectivity, thus offering both kinds of highlights. This makes it difficult to be sure when a highlight is a reflection of a light source and

when it is an intense concentration of nonreflecting light. In the first instance—if volume through value is a goal—it can be omitted, for it is not relevant to volume, but rather to surface effects. Indeed, drawing a subject's surface effects instead of its volume cues usually obscures the latter. When a highlight is nonreflective, it should be understood as part of the form's terrain and not as an isolated, bright speck of light. Seeing it as a self-contained, little shape often makes the student treat it as something separate from the form's surface, with the result that it appears to occupy a position in space *in front of* the form's surface.

The texture of the human figure often contains both kinds of highlights. When drawing human forms, the experienced artist often subdues or even omits both reflecting

Figure 4.19
LEONARDO DA VINCI (1452–1519)
Study of Drapery for a Kneeling Figure
Brush and lampblack, heightened with white,
on bluish paper. 21.3 x 15.9 cm.
Royal Collection, Windsor Castle

and direct highlights. The intrusive nature of reflecting highlights usually warrants their exclusion. And direct highlights are relatively unimportant because they describe only a small area of a form, contributing little. If a volume has been sensitively analyzed, their inclusion is not necessary. We understand a subject's volume mainly through its major structural character. If the essential structural facts are not clear, highlights cannot contribute enough to make us understand the subject's volume.

We can distinguish whether a highlight is reflected or direct by deciding if it seems to promote a form's surface texture or its structure. To take an extreme example, imagine drawing a large, shining, steel ball bearing. Its mirroring of the light source (actual images of windows, light bulbs, etc.) and the sudden, drastic changes of value inherent in any curved and polished surface, "blinds" us to visual cues about its volume. But coat the ball bearing with a matte paint, and the value-variations that reveal its volume become visible. If both the volume and surface character of such a form are desired, placing the emphasis on volume first and surface effects second communicates far more of the form's total character than the reverse. In three-dimensional drawing the clarity of a form's volume should precede any facts about its surface characteristics.

Reducing the intensity and clarity of any highlight improves its informational function. This makes it appear to belong to the form's surface instead of floating above the drawing like a bit of confetti. In general, the attitude to highlights should be: the fewer the better, and the subtler the better.

On rounded forms, the light-tone, half-tone, base-tone, and reflected light will fuse into each other gradually. On forms composed of flat planes, they may each occupy one or more of the form's planes, as in Figure 4.20. The light-tones are usually found on all planes in positions facing the path of the light rays. Those placed at a right angle to the light's direction will be most intensely illuminated; those turned slightly away, somewhat less so. Light-tone involves the *several* light values of planes located anywhere from a right angle to the light's position just short of one running

Figure 4.20

parallel to the light ray's path. Light-tone, then, is a term that denotes a small range of values seen as having a general lightness in relation to the half-tone, base-tone, and reflected light. These terms also denote, not a single value, but a small range of values that set them apart as a discernible tonal unit in relation to other tonal units.

The several darker values that constitute the half-tone are, as mentioned earlier, generally found on planes roughly parallel to the direction of the light rays. Half-tones may sometimes be seen in areas where weak cast shadows reach the lightness of the halftone range, or in reflected light areas, as in areas A, B, and C of Figure 4.21.

A form's darkest values are located on those planes turned farthest from the path of

Figure 4.21

the light rays or wherever shadows cast by other forms block the light. On a form constructed of flat planes the darkest values are on planes facing in, or closest to the direction opposite the source of light, as in Figure 4.20. On rounded forms the values of the base-tone are not always found at the edge farthest from the light source, but are often located well inside a form's limits (Figure 4.22). This results when light rays, striking nearby surfaces, reflect back to illuminate areas of a form turned away from the direction of the light, or when weak, secondary light sources illuminate those surfaces turned away from the primary light source. The tone of an area illuminated by reflected light is determined by the intensity of the light source, the local-tone of the nearby, reflecting surfaces, and the local-tone and texture of the form itself; but is almost always darker than the light-tones and usually darker than the half-tones. The weak reflectivity of most surfaces greatly reduces the original light ray's intensity. Often, the reflected light is barely perceptible. A form on a black drape will produce a far weaker reflected light than the same form upon a white drape, and weaker still if the form itself is a dark one; if it has a matte rather than a shiny surface; or if the surrounding forms reflecting the light are located some distance away.

Reflected lights, like highlights, are generally more convincingly shown when only subtly suggested. Overstating reflected lights sometimes produces gaudy effects. At its most extreme, reflected light (or a second, opposing light source) is heightened to the value of the

light-tones, leaving a band of base-tone to run along a form's long axis or along any pronounced ridge formed by planes abutting at strong angles.

Often, a form's base-tone is not quite as dark as a shadow cast upon it by some nearby form. This difference in tone is due to the reflecting light rays being more easily able to strike those surfaces of a form turned away from the light than the more sheltered area of the cast shadow.

These six elements of light, understood as general phenomena of light on volume, can support, but not supplant, visual comprehension of a subject's structure. Analysis and intent, not an automatic dependence on a fixed system, should determine how these elements are used.

The nature of transitions between values in a drawing offers useful information about changes in a subject's surface-state that helps us understand its structure. As we saw in Figure 4.20, abrupt changes in value suggest angular terrain; gradual changes, rounded terrain. But the form of some subjects permits us to interpret their structure as reducible to either flat or curved planar units. In Figure 4.23A, the modelling of the woman's head relies mainly on curved planes, in Figure 4.23B, on flat ones. The gradual fusing of tones in Figure 4.23A enhances the sense of volume more than do the abrupt value changes in Figure 4.23B for two reasons. First, we are conditioned to expect gradual tonal changes on rounded forms. Second, because we are less conscious of the shape-state of gradual tones, we tend to be less aware of their picture-plane existence—of their two-dimensional life. But in Figure 4.23B we are at least obliquely aware of the shape-state of the black and white divisions.

Where intentional emphasis on the shapes of tones is desired, avoiding gradual transitions of tone helps to convey both two- and three-dimensional impressions. In the vigorous drawing by Matisse (Figure 4.24), this strategy helps to manifest both a woman and a powerful dynamic event—these interdependent states together are the subject. Matisse, through furious hatchings, also uses value as an agent of composition and to ex-

Figure 4.22

A

B

Figure 4.23

press his emotional responses to the subject. We will return to his drawing when we examine these additional functions of value.

"LOST AND FOUND"

In some drawings, such as Figures 4.12 and 4.18, some forms are intentionally left vague or largely hidden in shadow or dark tones that swallow up details. These devices are used in Seurat's drawing *Seated Woman* (Figure 4.25) to create a stately and timeless image. Forms emerge from and dissolve into values, their essential masses never altogether hidden by the drawing's "foggy" tonalities. Seurat shows little of the traditional chiaroscuro devices within a volume. His interest is in forming, through gradual changes in value, an image bathed in a vaporous atmosphere. A gentle haze envelops the figure, unifying it. Forms lose themselves in each other in the same way as the figure begins to dissolve into its surroundings. Yet the figure appears to be almost monumental. Had Seurat clearly focused the figure's edges it would have looked silhouetted and flat. As he drew it, it exists in

space, has volume and weight, and even seems to be illuminated. But note the sharply focused edge of the woman's back and the pronounced value contrast between it and the background. The visual "relief" provided by these departures from the drawing's "softer" handling provides strength and stability, keeping the drawing from seeming merely weak and unfocused. The impression of the torso rising like a pillar is made stronger *because* other edges and value contrasts are less forceful. This visual "crescendo"—the figure's grandeur and strength—depends on the state of edges and values *throughout* the drawing. It is like the crescendos of sound in symphonies, which are created partly by the quieter passages that surround them.

Watteau (Figure 4.26) loses and finds edges that help him emphasize the graceful sweep that envelops his subject. He diminishes the tonal contrast between the head and the background and darkens the tones of the figure *and* the wall below the arm to call attention to the flow of the woman's arm. He prevents cutting the torso by the drape and the head by the uplifted arm, by losing the edges of these forms and by avoiding value

Figure 4.24

HENRI MATISSE (1869–1954)

Figure Study (c. 1907)
Pen and ink. 10 3/8 x 8 in.
Collection, The Museum of Modern Art, New York
Gift of Edward Steichen

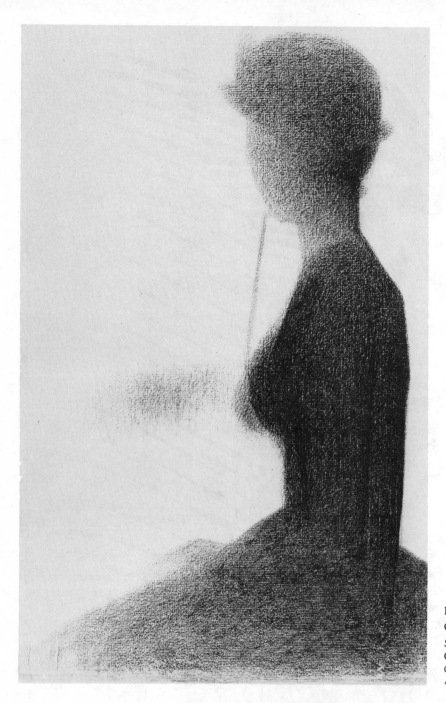

Figure 4.25
GEORGES SEURAT (1859–1891)
Seated Woman (1884–85)
Conté crayon. 18 7/8 x 12 3/8 in.
Collection, The Museum of Modern Art, New York
Abby Aldrich Rockefeller Bequest

contrasts in these places. This helps to strengthen the graceful letter S rhythm that starts in the lowered arm as a gentle movement ·and, gaining momentum, courses through the figure to end boldly in the woman's right hand, turned down to start the movement again. And the values and edges throughout the drawing support this enveloping sweep.

We feel the locomotive's power in Hopper's drawing (Figure 4.27), through his bold use of large dark tones that hide some of the particular mechanical appurtenances that a more factual drawing might provide. By losing these details in dark shapes of tone that

stress the engine's major volumes, Hopper makes us feel its heavy bulk and its immense energy.

If Hopper tells us little about the engine's "anatomy," he tells us—mainly through value—a great deal about its character and power. He even uses value to tell us that it is a bright day. The strong cast shadows, the gleaming metal (note that Hopper does not allow the highlights to "jump" off the forms) and the value-contrast between the wall and the tunnel all suggest strong sunlight.

Katzman, in his *Portrait of John Bageris* (Figure 4.28), loses edges and form-clarity in the figure's lower portion in order to amplify

Figure 4.26
ANTOINE WATTEAU (1684–1721)
Nude Half-Figure with Arm Raised
Red and black chalk. 28.3 x 23.3 cm.
The Louvre Museum

Figure 4.27
EDWARD HOPPER (1882–1967)
The Locomotive
Charcoal. 8 x 10 1/4 in.
Philadelphia Museum of Art

the dramatic potency of the figure's stance, and the assertive character of the head. Note how engagingly Katzman simplifies these forms. He finds strong shapes of tone that interwork at the dynamic level with the same vitality that he intends for the figure. As the drawing's thrust moves upward and structural clues emerge from the shapes, the form complexities of the hands, the left arm, and the upper body are engagingly simplified into a few, telling planes. Note especially the three values and the several planes that constitute the figure's right hand. In the head, the greater emphasis on smaller form-units never overrules the broader planar construction.

The use of values to suggest forms modelled by light and the tactic of losing and finding edges and forms provide versatile graphic devices. The following exercise suggests some general modes of approach to these uses of value.

exercise 4B

This exercise consists of three drawings. Because it is important to go as far as you can in developing the impression of illuminated volumes, none of these drawings have a time limit. For all three use soft, medium, and hard vine-charcoal sticks or charcoal pencils, and a charcoal or pastel paper of good quality. As you draw, use the soft charcoal for the deeper tones and the other two for the lighter ones. You may erase, but avoid erasing as an immediate solution to every misjudgment. Instead, see if such areas can be incorporated into the developing drawing. Ideally, all the tones in the first drawing should be made of line-groups. Where a particular tone or texture cannot be produced this way, some moderate adjusting of these hatchings by a kneaded eraser or a paper blending stump, called a tortillon, may be used. But blend and erase only as a last resort. Both tend to weaken a drawing's freshness and promote a concern with unimportant details. In the second and third drawings erasing and blending will be necessary at times to produce the impression of light. Then, they will be given a useful graphic role.

Figure 4.28
HERBERT KATZMAN (1923–   )
Portrait of John Bageris (1974)
Sepia chalk. 96 x 42 in.
University Gallery, University of Minnesota

Your subject should be a simple still-life arrangement, illuminated by a single light source, preferably a north light. Use no more than four or five objects on a table top. Avoid large, complicated objects or those made of highly reflective materials. Select simple, bulky objects. A drinking straw or coat hanger, being linear in character, would be a poor choice. Unglazed pottery and objects made of wood or paper, such as salad bowls or books, are usable. Shoes, mittens, hats, and handbags make interesting subjects — even the boxes they are stored in are usable (unless their surfaces are decoratively "busy," or covered with lettering or illustrations). Fruits and vegetables provide a variety of simple forms useful for the first drawing.

Draw as close to actual size as your still-life selections will permit. It is not necessary here to include all parts of each of the objects or the surface they are on. They can be allowed to run off the paper on all four sides.

drawing 1

Concentrate on the single experience of modelling the form by the value-variations upon it, and by values you select when the light does not adequately explain the terrain. Here, disregard all local-tones — assume everything in the still life to be *white*. With this in mind, begin with a lightly drawn search for gesture, shape, scale, direction, and location. Once you have established a rough drawing (much of it may be linear, but avoid stressing edges), place the several values of the light-tone in every part of the drawing where planes face the direction of the light source. Less than five minutes should elapse between the first line drawn and your search for the areas of light-tone. Avoid the "coloring book syndrome" — do not make an outline drawing of each part of the subject to fill in with tones. Line's temporary appearance at the outset (almost all the line will be absorbed into the drawing's various tones) quickly and economically establishes some basic structural relationships that assist the realization of volume as it is revealed by light. It should not be relied on to do more than help you get the drawing underway.

As you draw in the light-tone, also place it in *all* other areas of the drawing where your observations of the still life show darker tones to be (Figure 4.29). Except for any small areas intended to represent highlights, this will mean covering the entire drawing with light-tone. Because the light-tone represents a narrow range of values, use the darkest one (about a twenty-degree tone on the value scale) to place in all the areas darker than the actual light-tone areas.

Figure 4.29

Continue by placing the half-tones in *their* observed locations. Again, using the darkest of the half-tone range, place *it* in all areas judged to be darker than the actual half-tone areas. Next, place the base-tones in *their* observed locations only. Now place any darker values as might occur in some cast shadows or in small crevices between forms. Because you have been drawing tones on all but the highlight areas (if any), the reflected light areas (if any) are now toned. Adjust any reflected lights to their correct relationship with the other values of the drawing.

Remember that the entire subject is being regarded as white in local-tone, so a half-tone of say, an egg, will have the same value as say, a black shoe. This absence of local-tones will require you to make tonal judgments based on the position of planes in relation to the direction of the light. Do not merely follow the subject's value actualities. Here, the information that light provides is of more structural, than tonal interest.

When the entire still life has been established as more or less flat value-shapes, begin to carve at the borders between values where transitional tones are needed to "turn" the forms. Stress the nature of the gradual or sudden turning that occurs between the planes these shapes represent, by modelling with groups of structural lines that sculpt the forms at these planar junctions.

As you model the form, the sense of value-shapes will recede and the impression of planes forming volumes in space will emerge. Try to feel the weight and mass of each form you draw.

Make any changes in value that help explain a form's volume when the light fails to reveal the planar activity you know is there. Sometimes the light strikes a surface from an angle that does not distinguish its planar differences. Such changes in the terrain may actually be difficult to see because of the sameness of the light. Coming nearer to the subject or seeing it from another angle will help you see the planar state of poorly illuminated parts. To clarify the topography of such passages you will need to expand the tonal range. The value

Figure 4.30

differences needed to show the terrain in these "blank" areas must then be strong enough to perform their modelling function and subtle enough to stay within the value range of the passage in question. If, for example, you wish to explain the planar construction in an area of say, half-tone light, imagine a weak, secondary light raking across the planes in the blank area. Direct this second light from whichever angle would best reveal the various tilts and turnings of the planes.

As the drawing develops, check to see that the value range of one object has not grown lighter or darker than that of another. Should any cast shadows appear, remember that they are striking surfaces assumed to be white.

The background can be handled more independently. Its main function here is to provide value contrasts for the objects in the still life. In places it can freely but subtly change value to be lighter than a form against its dark side and darker than the form on its light side, as in Figure 4.30.

Because you have been using light *and* structural analysis to explain volume, the completed drawing should convey the impression of light revealing convincingly constructed masses.

drawing 2
Begin by using the same still-life objects in some rearranged order. As in the first drawing, just a few minutes should elapse between starting to draw and introducing the first tones. But now these tones should record each object's local-tone. Where an object cannot be reduced to a single local-tone, draw the two or more necessary to establish its inherent tonal character.

Draw the local-tones as flat areas whose limits determine the various shapes of your subject. These local-tones are not volume-producing val-

ues—they merely state the object's particular lightness or darkness independent of the light conditions. They can be drawn in any broad, simple way. Here, blending or working with the kneaded eraser may help produce just the degree of value you want. Except for the few, brief notations in line to get your drawing underway, line, in the sense of contour or calligraphic handling, is not needed in this drawing. But structural line-groups functioning as values will be extensively used to model the forms. The boundaries of volumes should be conveyed by the values that form the volumes. Surrounding tonally expressed forms with an outline is visually redundent—it suggests a mistrust of value's ability to establish form or edges.

Keep relating the local-tone of the *entire* drawing. As you draw one local-tone, judge its value in relation to others far from it in the still life, as well as those nearby. If your still life contains similar objects, for example, two apples, see if any value differences exist between their local-tones. Such differences, however slight, should be stated. It is often helpful to establish the subject's lightest and darkest local-tones early in the drawing. They serve as tonal "brackets"—all other local-tones are then more easily judged against these two extremes.

Be sure what you draw *is* the local-tone of an object, and not the effects of light and shade upon it. If an object possessing a light local-tone is observed in deep shadow, its local-tone should be drawn, not its darkened state—not yet. Once you have drawn all the subject's local-tones in relation to each other you can turn your attention to the modifications of the local-tones that light striking volume produces.

Two kinds of tonal change should now occur: those which convey the impression of light coming from a specific direction to strike (or miss) volumes, and those which convey volumetric information about parts of an object when the light fails to do so. Both types of change may require you to lighten as well as darken parts (or all) of every local-tone. Making charcoal lines or tones lighter is best accomplished with a kneaded eraser, which can be shaped to make fine points that enable you to make a kind of "negative" hatching—white or gray lines in areas of dark tone.

The first of these changes, those where light rays explain volume, may require that some local-tones be darkened entirely. If a light-toned form is located entirely inside an area of diminished light that results from a cast shadow, all its surfaces will obviously be much darker than its local-tone. But to have drawn this darker tone earlier would have complicated the search for local-tones by including responses to the effects of light on form. Here, you want to experience value's several roles in a more isolated way. However, many artists do in fact omit the study of the local-tones of objects, drawing the observed tonalities of the objects *and* the areas around them instead. That is, they respond to the tonal order of their subject at the outset.

With the local-tones established, you should adjust the values of your drawing to set up their tonal order. As you do, another advantage of developing the local-tones first becomes evident. It is much easier to see that a local-tone is too light or too dark by a particular degree for its counterpart in the subject, and adjust it, than it is to state exactly the right tone upon the white of the page from the start.

At this stage begin, as in the previous drawing, to search for the six elements of light. Again, draw these value-divisions with a view to their shape before you begin to model the forms with transitional values.

The major difference between this drawing and the previous one is that each form is now modelled in its own value range—the result of its local-tone *and* its position in relation to the light source. Here, an egg *is* light; a black glove, dark. Here, a half-tone in one part of the still life may differ greatly from a half-tone in another. Several dark objects grouped together, or in shadow, may merge their edges. Indeed, you should try to "lose" some edges and forms, and have others stand out in dramatic contrast. You may be surprised at the continuing readability of forms whose clarity you have subdued, and at the sense of atmosphere such tactics promote. Now, too, the shift from tonal shapes to volume should coincide with a shift in your attention from light's behavior on each form to the structural clarity of those forms not lost in dark tone. Again, some parts of the still life may not be explained by the light, or may be distorted by cast shadows. The subtle changes in value that you will make to explain the surface-state of such passages must now agree with the local-tone of each object and the tonal order of the area in which it is located.

The completed drawing should suggest a light source revealing the volume of several objects of various values. Here, the lightest value of a black glove will be darker than the darkest value of an egg if the light upon them is roughly the same.

drawing 3
Coat your paper with a layer of soft or medium vine charcoal. The value of this tone is not critical, but should not be lighter than a thirty de-

gree, or darker than a sixty degree tone. Extend the tone to the edges of your paper.

Begin this drawing as you did the other two, working from yet another arrangement of the still life. Again, begin using values within the first minutes. Now, values can be "subtracted" as well as added. With the kneaded eraser, values can be easily removed from the toned surface to give the impression of light striking planes. This removal of tone, of revealing volume the same way light does—by illuminating most those planes turned nearest to the path of the light rays—was not possible in the first drawing, and it had only limited use in the second one. Here, you actually draw the light, as well as the absence of it.

Drawing on a toned and erasable base encourages a fuller involvement with value and often results in more convincing volumes and richer tonal activity. Often, the impression of light striking forms is stronger. Generally, tonal drawings are begun on a white sheet of paper with the move toward tonality always down the value scale. Some students, in this downward progression, never reach the "lower register" of the value scale. They feel the lighter range of values to be "safer" or more manageable. This hesitancy to use darker values is abetted by the intimidating nature of the page's whiteness. As you start a tonal drawing, any tone, no matter how light, *does* seem to intrude on the purity of the white page. When this feeling restrains the student's advance upon a subject's darker tones, the result is usually similar to a photograph removed too soon from the developing tray—a weak and incomplete suggestion of illuminated volume.

In this drawing, you begin with an overall tone somewhere near the middle of the value scale, with the extremes of black and white roughly equidistant from it. For once, white is not a given condition of the drawing but must be produced by removing tone. When this is the case you are more likely to recognize that white in most subjects is present in small amounts, if at all.

Beginning with a toned surface also helps to establish a subject's local-tones, and the elements of light that model the form. If you begin with an allover tone that is close to many of the tones in the subject, it is easier to match these by making the minor adjustments required than to reproduce the precise value on the white page.

Once the search for the value-shapes has begun, the tone of the page can be altered depending upon the still life's local-tones, tonal order, and later, the behavior of the light that falls on the forms. Advance the entire drawing together. As you study the way the forms affect, and are affected by, the light rays, notice that you can better grasp the behavior of both by viewing your subject both ways. When you concentrate on a form's volumetric character, the light rays can be seen to be interrupted by it; when you fix on the light's path, it can be seen as illuminating planes according to their position in space. In the first instance you identify with the form; in the second, with the light. Doing both gives you a fuller understanding of the nature of the light *and* the volume. Each helps explain the other.

When completed, this drawing may look rather like the second one—the goals in both were the same. But here, you began with an erasable tone, and it may have resulted in a darker overall character, a wider value range, occasional lost edges, and more convincing volumes. Because the common tendency to draw tones too lightly was here circumvented by the tone of the page, your drawing may more nearly approximate the still life's actual tonal order.

Drawings in which light reveals volume should be done at frequent intervals. One or two extended tonal drawings each week is hardly too many. The demands they make on your perceptual skills increase your ability to see shape, value, scale, direction, and texture, and develop your general sensitivity to structural considerations. Even the ability to make volume-informing "pure" line drawings is improved through tonal drawing. When values are made to carve forms into being, the deeper understanding gained of the ways edges and planes contribute to the impression of volume, increases the empathy, economy, and eloquence of lines that delineate.

The drawings in this exercise may suggest other variations of tonal drawing. These three approaches are not intended as "how to" systems. Rather, their selection here provides three general modes of approach to the challenge of drawings that suggest light. How well they serve depends on your perceptual sensitivity and intent, and not on any inherent worth in the processes themselves. They are intended to promote and assist, not replace, understanding. The following variations on the study of value are helpful, and may, in turn, suggest others.

Variation 1. Using a sheet of gray pastel paper, draw in black and white conté crayons or chalks. Here, forms emerge from the page's *fixed* tone. By varying the pressure on your chalks you can produce a wide range of tones, the results of optical mixtures with the fixed gray tone. The only "rule" is never to mix the black and white chalks to produce grays. Every value from black to white

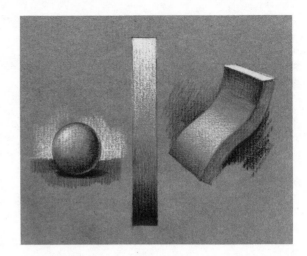

Figure 4.31

can be made without doing this. Black and white, or any tone they *separately* produce, may appear side by side in the drawing. But all grays should result from black or white being "mixed" with the gray of the page (preferably by hatchings)—not with each other. When a gray identical with the page's tone is required, let the page provide the value, as in Figure 4.31.

Variation 2. Start a tonal drawing on a stiff, white support, such as illustration board, using black and white goauche, casien, or acrylic paint. Use the paint thinly to establish the local-tones, and continue to develop the forms using black and white conté crayon or chalks. Here, the black and white paint may be mixed together to produce various grays, but the chalks should be used separately, their tones "mixing" with the underpainting to make all the value-variations that volume building requires.

Variation 3. Using India-ink washes of varying tints to develop the local-tones, continue to establish the illuminated volume with pen and black and white ink. The black and white inks may interweave in various hatchings to produce the required grays and textures.

VALUE AS AN EXPRESSIVE FORCE

Values can do more than establish local-tones, build forms, and suggest light. They can help the artist convey his emotional interests and reactions to his subject. The nature of his conscious and intuitive feelings about the subject are revealed by *what* the artist selects, omits, and emphasizes, and by *how* he organizes and draws—gives expression to—the image. Value plays a potent role in drawings that excite, calm, amuse, sadden, or otherwise affect the viewer.

Returning to Matisse's *Figure Study* (Figure 4.24), we find the values of the background and figure express powerful moving vibrations. Although we see most of these values as composed of thick lines, and even react to their furious action, the *dominant* impression of their collective behavior is more one of value than line. These values not only convey form and to some extent, light, they pulsate with vigorous rhythms, reinforcing the figure's action. The fury with which Matisse attacks the page is necessary to his expressive idea—the figure's strong forms and bold stance, and the background's envelopment of its forms. Matisse formulates value-shapes that animate and clash with great force. In the lower part of the drawing the

values seem to "invade" the figure; above, the stark white of the torso and arms "break free" of the background to give the upper body dramatic strength. In this drawing, Matisse's values are expressively descriptive *and* plastic—they inform and they evoke.

Whether Matisse's disposition to such energetic drawing had found a "cause" in the subject's potentialities, or was triggered by them, energy and idea are fused here in an image of explosive force.

In contrast with the Matisse drawing, Kuo Hsi, an eleventh-century Chinese artist (Figure 4.32), uses values to express a majestic serenity in this section of a handscroll. Tonalities range from nearly invisible nuances that describe distant peaks to emphatic contrasts in the mountainside on the right. The values suggest space, atmosphere, texture, and volume, and do so with a delicacy that expresses a stately silence. Kuo Hsi's rhythmic design, the undulations of shapes, tones, and direc-

Figure 4.32
Attributed to KUO HSI (11th Century)
Clearing Autumn Skies over Mountains and Valleys (detail)
Ink and tint on silk. 81 1/8 x 10 1/4 in.
Freer Gallery of Art, Washington, D. C.

tions, and the gentle character of his handling—the sensitive care in making the lines and tones themselves—is as delicate as the mood they convey.

Fish Skeletons by Hyman Bloom (Figure 4.33) offers an approach to value that reverses the usual role of white or light paper and black or dark drawing materials. Here, Bloom draws in white ink on a maroon surface. Depending on the subject and the expressive intent, this can be both figuratively and dynamically logical. In this instance, the reversal of light tones upon a dark surface helps convey the feeling of underwater depths—its mystery and darkness. The spikey fish skeletons are

drawn light in value—which they are. Note the flowing quality of the forms, and how the artist causes them to "flash" into bright light and then fade into the deeper background.

In his drawing *Reclining Figure* (Figure 4.34), Lebrun draws the figure's head obscured by the shadow of the hoodlike drape, as contrasting with the lines and light tones of the rest of the drawing. The shaded head becomes the visual and expressive center of emphasis—the focal point of the drawing's representational *and* abstract theme. Note that Lebrun "loses" other parts of the figure, making the tonal "crescendo" at the head even more expressively powerful.

Figure 4.33

HYMAN BLOOM (1913–   )

Fish Skeletons
White ink on maroon paper. 16 3/4 x 22 3/4 in.
Collection, Mr. and Mrs. Ralph Werman

Figure 4.34
RICO LEBRUN (1900–1964)
Reclining Figure
Pencil, ink and chalk. 19 x 25 in.
Fogg Art Museum, Harvard University
Gift of Arthur Sachs, Esq.

As the preceding drawings show, the way values are employed and the manner used to state them are determined by the responsive artist's felt perceptions of his subject, which modify and edit the observed actualities. To him, the drawing's emotive character and plastic activity—its dynamic condition—is necessary to his *total* realization of his subject. For only when a felt pattern is found for the subject's measurable but random facts, does a drawing transcend mere description and become a system of expressive order that is alive with meanings important to the sensitive viewer.

For many artists, such as Watteau, Hopper, and Katzman, the expressive intent of a particular drawing is largely triggered by their subject. Although such artists *do* bring attitudes, feelings, and ideas—their unique pyschological and temperamental tone—to a confrontation with a subject, their expressive responses are mainly stimulated by their perceptions. Thus, their use of value (and all other visual elements) is heavily dependent on what expressive potentialities they find in the subject.

Other artists, such as Rothbein, Dickinson, and Bloom, experience a deeply felt

Figure 4.35
NATHAN GOLDSTEIN (1927–   )
Ellie
Pen, brush and ink. 18 x 22 in.
Collection of Martin Robbins, Boston

"presence"; more than an idea, less that a vision, they seek forms that will make their meanings clear. They can be said to intend *before* they see. Neither kind of artist functions as he does exclusive of the other's means of approach. The perceptually stimulated artist brings certain concepts and emotions to the encounter with a subject; the conceptually stimulated artist responds to the measurable and dynamic provocations of the subject. Both require value to do more than describe.

VALUE AS AN AGENT OF COMPOSITION

Value's uses in pictorial issues such as direction, balance, emphasis, diversity, and unity will be examined in Chapter Eight. Here, it is necessary to mention, in general terms, the various ways in which value can participate in these design considerations.

Like line, value is capable of a vigorous abstract existence that can animate as well as define. For example, in Figure 4.35, the dark tones of the dress and the light ones of the background serve to intensify the sense of forceful vertical movement that enliven the figure's inactive stance.

Value can relate dissimilar shapes, forms, textures, and spatial areas. In drawings where these visual phenomena appear isolated, confused, or in conflict, value can enforce visual affinities that cause groupings, emphasis, and directions to emerge, as in Figure 4.36, where three differently working arrangements occur by changing the values of the same design of shapes. Note that while 4.36A seems balanced

and unified, 4.36B appears to be too heavy on the right side. Additionally, the vertical alignment of the black shapes is somewhat overpowering. In 4.36C, the division of the light and dark values "breaks" the design into isolated halves and weights the image too much on the left.

Charles Sheeler's *Interior with Stove* (Figure 4.37) directs our attention to the play of vertical and horizontal movements in a room's interior. Throughout the drawing values merge and contrast in a tonal pattern that activates, balances, and unites the scene into units which emphasize the strong directional force of the shapes and forms. Note how the dark tone of the stove, seen against the surrounding light tones, fixes our attention upon the stove's powerful verticality, as well as its "mystery." Through value, Sheeler makes us aware of both shape and volume, guiding us to both the two- and three-dimensional design of the image. Here, values simultaneously serve descriptive, expressive, and organizational matters.

As observed in Chapter Two, shape is a basic, given quality. It is important to recall that value always has shape. Whether as clearly defined as the shapes in Sheeler's drawing or as diffuse as a puff of smoke, the termination of a value within the boundaries of a drawing establishes its shape. Although the value-shapes in Seurat's drawings (Figures 4.4 and 4.25) are vaguely defined, he balances them with all the care that Sheeler gives to his more focused ones. Thus, in tonal drawings of whatever style or degree of subjective interpretation, the artist must visually weigh the effects of value on shape and vice

Figure 4.36

A   B   C

Figure 4.37
CHARLES SHEELER (1883–1965)
Interior with Stove (1932)
Conté crayon. 28 5/8 x 20 3/4 in.
Collection of Joanna T. Steichen, New York
Photo courtesy of The Museum of Modern Art

Figure 4.38

versa. As Figure 4.36 demonstrates, value differences can greatly reduce the visual bond between like shapes, as well as increase the rapport between unlike shapes.

Value can help locate the position in space of similar volumes when other graphic clues, such as linear perspective, fail to do so. Because of the weak value contrast, we read the hill on the right, in Figure 4.38, as farther off than the similar one on the left. Likewise, the spheres and cubes occupy different positions in space because of their value differences, despite their sameness in shape and scale. In this illustration the impression of distance given through value is assisted by our recognition of the phenomenon of aerial perspective (see Chapter Five) which causes distant objects to appear lighter in value. The position of forms in a shallow spatial field such as a still life can also be clarified by value. Then, the value of the forms relative to the value of the background determines their position in space. An object possessing a light overall tone, seen against a similarly toned background, will appear farther back than a similar, but dark-toned object located alongside it.

Value can also exist free of mass. As mentioned earlier, light can envelop several forms or segment them. In Figure 4.39, a

Figure 4.39

Figure 4.40
REMBRANDT VAN RIJN (1606–1669)
Woman Looking through Window
Pen, brush and ink. 29.3 x 16.4 cm.
The Louvre Museum

shape of light envelops a wall, dancer, and floor. When objects stand in the path of a light source, cast shadow can, as here, take on important compositional meaning. Sometimes, as in Figure 4.12, although the objects in the path of the light are "off stage," their participation in the design can be considerable.

107

We have seen that value is a potent graphic force. Its uses in drawing are limited only by our perceptual understanding and inventive wit. Its relevence to responsive painting, which, like responsive drawing attempts to shape a subject's actual and potential qualities into some system of expressive order is clear, though sometimes overlooked by the student. Many responsive painting problems are often really drawing problems, and those involving a subject's tonalities are among the most vexing to the young artist. These are more easily recognized and solved in tonal drawing than in painting, where value, like hue and intensity, is a property of color and harder to isolate for consideration.

It is no coincidence that Rembrandt was not only a great painter but also a prolific and brilliant draughtsman from his earliest days as a young aspiring artist until the end of his life. Rembrandt's mastery of value (Figure 4.40) enabled him to more inventively convey profound visual and expressive meanings through light and volume with an economy, power, and eloquence rarely equalled. His penetrating grasp of the dynamic potentials of value is amply evident in his paintings (Figure 4.41).

The development of graphic freedom—the ability to pursue your drawing interests in *any* direction for *any* purpose—depends on the comprehension and control of value's several roles in drawing. Whatever uses value will hold for you later on, its study now is essential to your development as a responsive artist.

Figure 4.41
REMBRANDT VAN RIJN (1606–1669)
Lady with a Pink
Oil on canvas. 36 1/4 x 29 3/8 in.
The Metropolitan Museum of Art
Bequest of Benjamin Altman

CHAPTER FIVE

PERSPECTIVE

the foreshortened view

.

A DEFINITION

For the responsive artist, the term *"perspective"* embraces virtually every visual clue to the disposition of volumes in space. It is an implicit condition of any form's scale, location, and direction in a spatial field. Using this broader meaning of perspective, we discover its presence in all drawings that convey a convincing impression of masses arranged in some logical spatial order. Even primitive works show some rudimentary (though possibly subconscious) employment of perspective, as in Figure 5.1, where the smaller figures on the left appear to be located farther back in the spatial field.

The broader interpretation of the term perspective, namely as clues to the appearances of forms in space, may reassure the student who feels confronted with a complex and rather dry system. Actually, for most artists the exact (and exacting) complexities that stem from the basics of perspective hold little interest. Moreover, a preoccupation with perspective generally restricts inventive freedom.

Because perspective deals with appearances, the student knows more about the subject than he realizes. In fact, he has been using many of the basic principles, and probably sensing others. What he needs to do is to clarify and expand his understanding of these principles to benefit from the specific information and control they provide.

A knowledge of perspective is helpful in three ways. First, it serves as a "checklist" for uncovering unintended distortions of the subject's actualities. Second, it encourages the drawing of more complex and/or interesting subjects, which the student might otherwise avoid. Third, it enables us to regard space and volume clues that we might otherwise not consider.

A number of perspective systems have been devised in the past. Ancient Egyptian, Persian, and Oriental artists developed visually lucid and aesthetically pleasing systems. There have been others. The system normally used in the Western world is called *linear perspective*. Like all other systems, it is not completely successful in projecting real volumes

Figure 5.1
Bushman Rock Painting of a Dance
South African Museum, Capetown

in real space onto a flat surface, without some distortion. It differs from all other systems in being based upon what forms in space look like when observed from a fixed position with one eye closed. Naturally enough, artists when drawing do move about. Indeed, many artists find the act of drawing demands a considerable amount of movement. The artist must look up and down, left and right, and frequently step back or otherwise change his original position relative to his subject. Thus, with their very first requirement often disregarded, the principles of linear perspective are best applied in a supportive rather than a methodological role.

Allied to linear perspective are some observable phenomena (the results of atmospheric conditions and particles of matter suspended in the air) called *aerial perspective*. These affect the clarity, texture, and values of subjects seen at a distance.

Together, these concepts have helped Western artists convey much observed visual fact with little intrusive distortion. But the best exponents of drawing wisely regarded perspective as a tool, and one with definite limits.

It must be remembered that in responsive drawing, results emerge from the interactions—the negotiations—between perception, intuition, and intent. The information provided by linear and aerial perspective, like all other visual information, is subject to this interpretive process. Perspective, then, is useful as a means, but has restraining tendencies as an end. When overused, perspective begins to change the purpose of drawing from inquiry and invention to imitation—which are mutually exclusive attitudes. In relinquishing inventive choice and change, we lose the means to order, expound upon, and dynamically activate the subject's random properties. And responses that amplify a drawing's visual and expressive meanings are more important than following perspective or any other convention. Any convention that unquestioningly restricts is destructive of the freedom necessary to creativity. But when used with a liberal tolerance for its accommodation to other factors in responsive drawing, perspective becomes a valuable aid.

This is especially true in the case of foreshortening. The foreshortening of forms in space is inherent in three-dimensional drawing. In fact, much of linear perspective concerns the visual nature of things moving toward or away from us at various angles. Look around you and notice how seldom you see an object centered vertically and horizontally on your line of sight. Most of what you see is of course positioned at random angles, "aiming" in different directions. Even if you confront a row of books or trees, except for the ones directly in front of you, all are being seen in some degree of foreshortening. This being so, we seldom see a form from a view that offers only one plane. Indeed, it's rare to see only one plane of even so geometrically severe a form as a cube. The seasoned artist usually avoids such totally foreshortened views of objects because they hide too much of the object's mass. A line drawing of a circle, representing an end plane of a cylinder, tells us nothing of the cylinder's length. Unless we are told the circle represents one end of a cylinder, we would have no way of deducing this from the circle itself. It could represent the base of a cone or half a sphere, or any other form that resolves itself to a circular plane at its base.

An understanding of linear perspective helps to clarify and control the impression of foreshortening in unobtrusive ways, as in Vermeer's drawing *View of Town with Tower and Windmill* (Figure 5.2). This complex arrangement of forms in space is not overbearingly aligned and rigid, but presented with the subtlety and ease that a sound grasp of perspective in the service of an interpretive intent makes possible. In fact, Vermeer has not unselectively followed the dictates of perspective. We will return later to note how he has "broken" a rule of perspective in order to strengthen a dynamic theme.

Perspective's more technical complexities tend to pull us away from the needs and purposes of free response. Most of these complexities can be inferred from the principles to be examined. Here we will concentrate on the basic principles to establish their function as general guides to perception and to show how they assist foreshortening in particular. To paraphrase Eugène Delacroix's observation on the study of anatomy, perspective should be learned—and forgotten. The residue—a sensitivity to perspective—helps perception, varying with each individual and determined by his responsive needs.

Figure 5.2

JAN VERMEER DE DELFT (1632–1675)
View of Town with Tower and Windmill
Pen, ink and washes of tone. 16 x 20 in.
Albertina Museum, Vienna

THE PRINCIPLES OF LINEAR AND AERIAL PERSPECTIVE

Linear perspective is based on six principles. Each of these provides space and volume-revealing clues, some of which have already been touched on in earlier chapters.

1. relative scale. When forms known to be the same or a similar size differ in their scale, they indicate differences in their position in a spatial field. Thus, the decreasing scale of a row of trees or fence posts suggests near and far forms in space.

2. overlapping or blocking. When a form's position interrupts the contours of one or more other forms, partly hiding them, we perceive the overlapping form to be nearer than the overlapped one. Thus, seeing less than the entire form of an object suggests its position is farther back in the spatial field.

3. relative distance and position. When forms, not overlapping, and known to be the same or a similar distance apart show a decreasing distance between them, we perceive them to be receding in space. Thus, the decreasing distance between fence posts or railroad ties suggests forms in space. Except when such forms are seen high above our eye-level, the higher a form is in our field of vision, the farther back in space it appears.

4. convergence. When lines (or edges) known to be parallel appear to aim toward each other, or converge, they give the impression of going back in space. Thus corridors, houses, railroad tracks, or anything possessing parallel boundaries in any direction, appear to recede in space if these boundaries are seen as inclined toward each other.

5. cross-section or cage lines. When forms naturally possess or are, in a drawing, given a linear-textured surface, as in the use of structural hatchings, the relative distance and changes of direction between such lines suggest volume in space. Thus, objects as different as sea shells, driftwood, cornfields, or barber poles, by their textured surface-state, suggest forms in space.

6. light and shade. When a form's value-variations result from the play of light upon it and not from local-tones, volume is suggested. Thus a cylinder whose values gradually darken as they approach its boundaries is more easily seen as a volume in space. When one form casts a shadow on another, its length, location, shape, and especially its scale and value suggest the distance separating the two forms, the shape of the form casting the shadow, and the planar surface-state of the form in the area receiving the shadow.

The common denominator in these six principles is the diminution of scale and, in light and shade, of the value contrasts of forms as they recede in space. If all or most of these principles are invoked, forms—when uninterrupted by other forms—will appear to diminish in scale and finally disappear.

Aerial perspective is based on three principles. These apply mainly to forms in deeper space, such as distant houses and hills, but are sometimes employed in drawings of forms in shallow space.

1. clarity. When forms appear less distinct in edge, detail, and general focus, we assume they are farther away than more incisively focused forms. Thus, a mountain seen at a distance appears vague and formless when compared to a nearby boulder.

2. value range. When the value contrasts between forms diminish, often becoming lighter, but always more closely related, we assume these forms to be in deep space.

3. relative texture. When forms diminish in textural clarity relative to other forms known to be the same or similar in physical characteristics, we perceive the less texturally active ones to be farther away. Thus, nearby grassy areas are seen as texturally active, those in the distance, far less so.

The common denominator in these three principles is that as distance increases, definition (clarity of focus, value contrasts, textural differences) decreases. Used together with linear perspective, if uninterrupted in space by other forms, aerial perspective will help cause forms to disappear.

These nine principles provide useful assists in the locating and structuring of masses

Figure 5.3
ALBERT ALCALAY (1917–   )
Times Square (1959)
Pen, ink and wash. 16 x 20 in.
DeCordova Museum, Lincoln, Mass.

in space. But, unless they serve *in support of some visual and expressive theme*, they may assume an unintended importance in a drawing, overruling other important responsive considerations. Seeing gesture, shape, scale, and value; responding to spirit and substance before detail and surface; permitting the interplay between facts and intent—these are first considerations to a full experiencing of volumes in space. A knowledge of perspective can serve but not replace them.

Perspective can also help the artist *subdue* volume and space. Knowing what clues convey these impressions he has greater control over involving the beholder with a drawing's picture-plane activity. Alcalay, in his drawing *Times Square* (Figure 5.3), achieves an interesting fusion of two- and three-dimensional space by stressing some perspective conditions and subduing others. Despite the severe convergence of the lines of the streets and houses, the overall configuration provides an engaging two-dimensional design.

THE HORIZON LINE

A fundamental concept in linear perspective is the horizon line. This is determined by, *and is equivalent to,* the observer's eye-level.

Whether visible or not, the horizon line is imagined as describing a horizontal line at the observer's eye-level, parallel with the ground-plane and 360 degrees around him. Being equivalent to the observer's eye-level, the horizon line is as high or low as his position is above or on the ground. To someone standing on a mountain peak, the horizon line is very high in his field of vision; for someone lying on the ground, very low (Figure 5.4).

Normally, obstacles such as hills, houses, walls, or foliage block our view of actual horizon lines. But visible or not, linear perspective requires that the horizon (eye-level) line be established in the artist's mind. This can be actually drawn or simply understood as located on a particular horizontal level on the page. Knowing its location helps determine quickly the general position of forms in relation to the artist. He sees anything above the horizon line as above his eye-level, anything below it as below eye-level. He looks at the undersides of forms located above the horizon line, and down on the tops of forms beneath it.

To better understand the horizon line as equivalent to eye-level, take the example of a room with three transparent walls, through which we seen the horizon of a lake (Figure

113

Figure 5.4

5.5A). Our eye-level is centered between floor and ceiling, equidistant from both side walls. Through an opening in the middle wall, the horizon of the lake can be seen *directly*. If we now assume the walls are not transparent but opaque and solid, the only part of the horizon visible is the small segment seen through the window-like opening. The rest of the line that formerly represented the horizon can now be seen as a painted line on each of the three walls, exactly at eye-level. Were such lines drawn on each wall near the floor, they would not form a straight line, but would incline upwards toward the horizon line on the two side walls. If they were drawn close to the ceiling on each of the three walls, the lines on the side walls would incline downwards toward the horizon line. The horizon, or eye-level line, is that horizontal level where lines that we know to change direction appear to flatten into a straight line. In Figure 5.5B, the same room is shown with several lines on the three walls. Note that extending any pair (one from each of the side walls) causes them to meet at a point on the horizon line. That point on the horizon line (your eye-level) where converging lines meet is called the *vanishing point*.

Recalling the principle of convergence, we know that lines appear to recede in space when they incline toward each other. When such lines are horizontal, that is, parallel to the ground-plane, they will always meet at a vanishing point on the horizon line. This can be seen by extending the lines on the side walls in Figure 5.5B.

In Figure 5.5C, the same room is viewed with the observer's eye-level near the floor. Now, the next-to-the-lowest lines on the three walls are the horizon line and appear as a straight line. This being the case, we no longer see the lake through the window in the center wall. Looking at 5.5B and 5.5C, we sense the difference in the level at which we view the two rooms. Through perspective the artist can not only set the stage, he can control the level and, as we shall see, the angle from which we view it.

The horizon line need not appear within the limits of the drawing. Sometimes, as in Mantegna's *Man Lying on a Stone Slab* (Figure 5.6), the horizon line is assumed to lie above the page, because the degree of inclination of the lines representing the slab's left and right sides would make it impossible for them to meet until they had traversed several inches

Figure 5.5

Figure 5.6
ANDREA MANTEGNA (1431–1506)
Man Lying on a Stone Slab
Pen and ink. 16.3 x 11.4 cm.
The British Museum, London

beyond the upper boundary of the drawing. Less frequently, the horizon line may be known to lie below the page (Figure 5.7). Assuming a minimum of movement, the artist can view his subject in one of three ways. He can center himself before its horizontal limits, as Mantegna did before the stone slab in his drawing (one-point perspective); he can stand to one side of his subject, as Mantegna did before the figure of the man (two-point perspective); or he can view his subject from a point very much above or below it (three-point perspective). Any other view is, of

course, some combination of these basic options. In Figure 5.7 it is clear that the artist's position is near the base and to the left of the buildings. Whatever the view, an artist gains helpful information by regarding the general behavior of the parallel lines (in discussing perspective, the term *line* often replaces *edge*, for purposes of clarity).

When the artist is centered and parallel to his subject, those lines he sees as *actually* horizontal or vertical do not meet at any vanishing point, for there is no convergence. Such lines, then, will appear as verticals and

Figure 5.7
CHARLES SHEELER (1883–1965)
Delmonico Building
Lithograph. 10 1/2 x 8 1/2 in.
Fogg Art Museum, Harvard University
Gift of Paul J. Sachs

horizontals in his drawing. Only those lines he sees as *diagonals*, as moving away from him, incline toward each other and meet at a vanishing point on the horizon line, as in Mantegna's drawing. Note that the lines of the slab *parallel* to the page do not converge.

Drawings in which the artist is centered on his subject are called *one*-point perspective drawings because all the converging lines meet at the same vanishing point, as in Vermeer's *View of Town* (Figure 5.2), where the

converging horizontal lines of the houses and lane in the foreground appear to meet below and to the left of the windmill. But note that the church and windmill, because they are positioned more parallel to the picture-plane, show little convergence of lines. Again, in Guardi's *View through an Archway* (Figure 5.8), the converging lines of the archway and floor lead us to a point on an unseen horizon line located below the edge of the large building that divides the archway's far opening, but the buildings in the background, *being parallel to our field of vision*, do not.

The meeting of converging lines will occur whether the forms are above, on, or below the horizon line, so long as the lines are parallel to each other, and with the ground-plane, as in Figure 5.9A. Note that the middle box, observed at eye-level, shows only one plane. This is the one parallel to our field of vision (or at a right angle to our line of sight), and it is comprised of four right angles. The other boxes show the same plane, but because these boxes are above and below the horizon line, we see the underside of the one above and the top of the one below.

But one-point perspective has an immediate limitation. If we wish now to surround the central box with two others—one far to the left and one far to the right and parallel with it—a dilemma arises. Indeed, it already exists in Figure 5.9A, but because the three boxes are so close together, it is hardly noticeable. Assuming all the boxes to be made of rectangular planes, there is only *one* position that will show a plane with four right angles: the eye-level position of one-point perspective. This is also the only position that will not show any of the sides of the boxes. But, seeing the sides of the two new boxes in Figure 5.9B, we recognize that the observer is no longer directly in front of them, but views them from oblique angles. But if the new boxes are turned enough to show a foreshortened view of their side plane, their front planes should no longer be seen straight on. The new boxes cannot show a three-quarter view of their *side* planes without similarly changing their *front* planes. If, then, the front planes of these two boxes are not centered on the observer, they must conform to the principle of convergence and show the horizontal

Figure 5.8

FRANCESCO GUARDI (1712–1793)

View through an Archway
Black crayon, pen, and wash on white paper.
34.2 x 28 cm.
The Metropolitan Museum of Art, Rogers Fund

A

B

C

Figure 5.9

117

lines of their front planes to incline toward vanishing points on the horizon line. The lines of the front plane of the box on the left will meet at a vanishing point to the left, those of the front plane of the box to the right will meet far to the right. These left and right vanishing points will be distant because the degree of inclination of the front planes (as shown in Figure 5.9C) is slight.

This "correction" has been made in Figure 5.9C, and the boxes on either side of the center one are no longer distorted. They are

Figure 5.10
MICHAEL MAZUR (1935–   )
View into Broadway (1971)
Pencil. 40 1/2 x 26 1/2 in.
Collection of Mr. and Mrs. William Marsteller

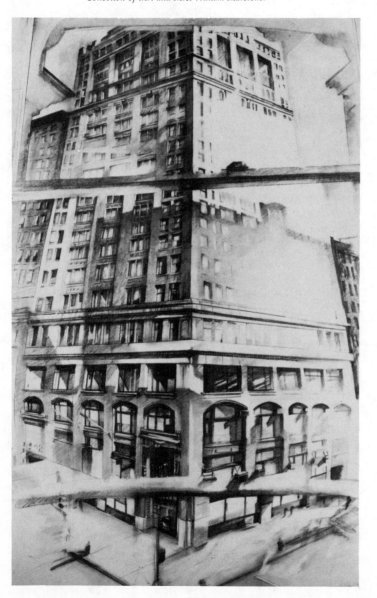

now "in perspective" but their alignment with the center box has been destroyed. In Figure 5.9B the three boxes line up in a row parallel to the observer, but at the cost of distorting the side boxes. Here the limits of projecting real volume and space onto a flat surface become apparent.

Because Vermeer's design theme (Figure 5.2) depends on the bold convergence of the lines of the houses and lane, especially on the right side, he chooses, on the far left, to contrast this thrust by treating the planes of the houses more nearly facing us as being parallel with the picture-plane. Thus, in selecting the "option" shown in Figure 5.9B over that of Figure 5.9C, he forsakes a degree of measurable fact in one place in order to amplify a dramatic spatial event in another.

Looking again at Figure 5.9C, we note that the side boxes, no longer centered on the observer, each possess *two* sets of converging lines that meet at two widely separated vanishing points. These boxes, unlike the center one or their counterparts in Figure 5.9B, are drawn in two-point perspective.

Whenever forms are parallel to the ground-plane but not to the observer, as for example, when we stand facing an inside or outside corner, not a side of a building, the lines of its two visible planes will appear to meet at two vanishing points on the horizon, as in Mazur's *View into Broadway* (Figure 5.10). Any number of forms, when parallel to the ground-plane but differing in their alignment to each other, as, for example, a floor strewn with boxes all upright but at various angles to each other, will each have its own two vanishing points on the horizon. Though an object like the folding screen in Figure 5.11 may have many parallel lines converging on many vanishing points, it is still regarded as being drawn in two-point perspective.

When forms are positioned at an angle to the ground-plane, their vanishing points will be above or below the horizon, as occurs in several instances in Figure 5.11. Note that the lines of the folding screen and the boxes denoting their verticality, whether or not they are actually at a right angle to the ground-plane, do not converge. In two-point perspective, lines parallel to the observer's field

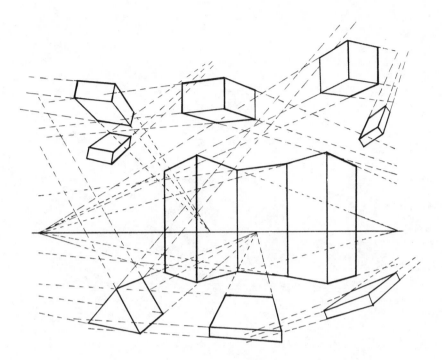

Figure 5.11

of vision (and hence, measurably parallel), as noted earlier, are drawn as true parallels.

But this is not the case when the vertical lines are very long, or when we look down upon a subject from a great height or look up from a low observation point to see a towering form such as a skyscraper. Then, the subject's *vertical* lines will appear to converge toward a vanishing point. When this is observed, a three-point perspective situation exists, as in Figures 5.7 and 5.10. Thus, three-point perspective occurs when the long axis of a form aims well above or below our eye-level. But note, in Figure 5.11, that one set of converging lines of the block in the upper left corner goes to the horizon line while the other set aims upward toward a vanishing point in the sky. This is the result of the block's particular angle in relation to the ground-plane. But because the vertical lines that define the block's side planes are not seen as converging, the block is regarded as drawn in two-point, not three-point perspective.

In both two- and three-point perspective the vanishing points should not be placed too close together. Crowding them produces forces and distorted forms, such as those in

Figure 5.12. Because of the unavoidable distortions in transposing real volume and space to a flat surface, most artists make subtle adjustments between conflicting perspective conditions such as exist between Figures 5.9B and 5.9C, thereby reducing and obscuring the evidence of distortion, as in Meryon's preparatory sketch (Figure 5.13). Here, neither the lines indicating rows of bricks on the arch nor those which we can extend from the tower and the buildings below come to common vanishing points. Many artists intentionally "go against" the convergence effect, to reduce the camera-like distortions that a strict adher-

Figure 5.12

Figure 5.13
CHARLES MERYON (1821–1868)
Study for Etching "La Pompe Notre Dame"
Pencil. 11 5/8 x 13 7/8 in.
Courtesy, Museum of Fine Arts, Boston

ence to perspective can sometimes cause. They purposely place a form's vanishing points extremely far apart, giving it a broad "frontality" that emphasizes its picture-plane condition (Figure 5.14).

In the following exercise, try to select views that will test your understanding of one-, two-, and three-point perspective.

exercise 5A

Draw in pencil on any suitable surface. Use a ruler and eraser freely on all but the last of the three drawings you will make.

drawing 1

Use two simple, block forms as models. Gift boxes, cartons, or children's large pasteboard building blocks are excellent, but any block-like objects will serve. These need not be cubes, but do avoid very long block forms. If possible, one or both of the forms should be open at one or both ends, permitting you to see inside. You will be drawing both forms as if they are semi-transparent. It is important to learn to see the angles of inside as well as outside lines.

These forms may be the same or they may differ in size, with neither being smaller than five nor larger than twelve inches in any direction.

Plan to cover a sheet of 18" × 24" paper with as many views of these two blocks together, in varying positions, as will conveniently fit on the page. Draw these considerably smaller than actual size, but avoid tiny drawings.

Arrange these forms in any way that offers a new combination for each sketch. Or, leaving the blocks in some arrangement, draw the different views you see as you move around them. You can place them next to each other at different angles, place one atop the other, or lean them against a support, balancing them on their corners. Draw them as they appear above, at, and below your eye-level. If the forms are light enough, they can be suspended from a doorjamb or otherwise held above eye-level.

Begin your drawing of each view in a free manner. Note first, where each form is in relation to the other and to your eye-level. Look for the shape-state of the planes. In doing so, you will see planes more objectively and be more aware of the direction of their lines. When your drawing has some rough relationship to the shape, scale, and location of the two forms, use a ruler to establish

120

Figure 5.14

DOMENICO CAMPAGNOLA (c. 1500–1552)

Buildings in a Rocky Landscape
Pen and ink. 6 1/16 x 7 3/4 in.
The Pierpont Morgan Library, New York

the right relationship of inclination between the lines. Should you wish to further strengthen the sense of lines moving toward common vanishing points, you can slightly increase the degree of convergence between them. Allow the lines to extend beyond the point of intersection with other lines when you see them as converging toward a vanishing point. As there are no visible horizon lines

to be drawn on this page, extend such lines only slightly beyond the form itself. These extensions help you to see their inclination better, as in Figure 5.15. Notice that many of the lines of the lower block are visible through the upper one. Assume the forms to be semi-transparent, allowing you to draw most of the unseen lines. Should a profusion of lines become confusing, draw those you do not

Figure 5.15

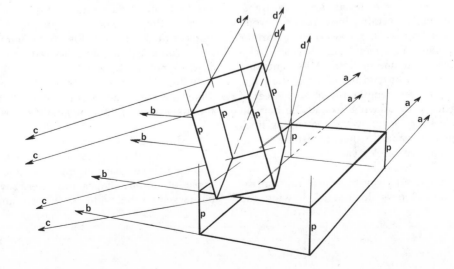

121

actually see only lightly, occasionally allowing some of these lines to disappear for a little distance along their paths. Use your eraser to clarify and adjust the drawing, and to lighten the imagined lines still further. Drawing the nearest segments of the lines you do see in heavier strokes also helps explain the location of the various lines in space.

In Figure 5.15 the two forms each show three groups of lines. Those marked *p* are parallel to the observer, despite the tilt to the left of those in the upper block. Lines *a* and *b* of the lower block and lines *c* and *d* of the upper one are not parallel to the observer and are, therefore, drawn in two-point perspective. There is no time limit for the various views you will draw on this page. When you have filled the entire page, go over each sketch to see if any of the forms seem distorted because the inclination of the lines is too extreme, or because they have gone awry. Look at these drawings again in a few days to see if you can locate the observer's position for each sketch, and if they "feel right."

drawing 2

This drawing is to be completely imaginative. Again, draw in pencil on a sheet of 18″ × 24″ paper. Turning the sheet vertically, divide it into three even sections. Starting with the topmost section, draw a horizontal line four inches from its base, dividing it in half. In the second section, draw a similar line two inches from its top. In the third section, draw a horizontal line two inches from its base. These three lines will represent, in each drawing, the horizon-eye-level line.

Starting with the *middle* section, draw three block-like forms that appear to "sit" on the ground-plane. Each should be drawn in two-point perspective at an angle differing from the other two. This will result in six different vanishing points. We saw in Figure 5.11 that forms parallel to the ground-plane, but not to each other, have their own vanishing points on the horizon line.

Again, assume the forms are semi-transparent and let the converging lines extend beyond the forms, this time all the way to their various vanishing points. You may find that a block's placement results in one or both of its vanishing points being located beyond the limits of the page. When this is the case, temporarily place a sheet of paper alongside your drawing, extend the horizon line, and, using a ruler, draw the converging lines onto this sheet of paper to their vanishing point. Be sure to keep each block's vanishing points well apart.

There is a second way by which you can establish the three blocks. Instead of drawing the

forms and adjusting their lines until they meet at their appropriate points on the horizon, you can begin by selecting a block's two vanishing points and draw two *diverging* lines from each in the general direction of your desired location for the block. The shape resulting from the intersecting of the four lines establishes the block's bottom plane. Elevating a vertical line at each point of intersection raises the four sides of the block. To locate the top plane of the block, again draw diverging lines from both vanishing points until they intersect the four verticals (and each other) at the desired height.

Whichever way you draw the three blocks, place them well away from the horizon line. They may, however, vary in their nearness to the viewer. These blocks, when completed, will be your "models" for the two remaining sections.

Using a ruler held vertically, locate the six vanishing points on the horizon lines of the first and third sections. In both sections, draw the three forms in the same relationship to the ground-plane (and to each other) as established in the middle section.

The differences in the location of the horizon line will make the blocks appear farther below the observer's position in the first section than in the third section. Depending on their height and position on the ground-plane, the upper portions of the blocks in the third section may rise above the horizon line.

When you have completed drawing the first and third sections, return to the center section and continue to develop it as if the blocks represented the geometrically "pure" state of houses. Add windows, doors, and anything else that would convert the original forms into houses. Place a simple landscape setting about them that may include streets, lampposts, trees, and fences. Keep these additions quite simple. Use converging lines to align windows, streets, etc. Then try to show how this landscape would look from different elevations by drawing the same objects in the same positions in the first and third sections. When completed, the three sections should show three different elevations of the houses and their environment.

You may find yourself faced with perspective matters not yet discussed. If so, return to this drawing at the completion of the chapter to see what new information you can apply to complete the three views of this imaginary scene.

drawing 3

Sit about two feet away from a small table upon which you have arranged some eight or nine books of various shapes and sizes. Several should be stacked on their sides at different angles, one or two can lean against the stacked books, while others can be placed at various angles upon the table top and may overhang it.

Study the subject to determine your horizon-eye-level line and lightly indicate this on a sheet of 18″ × 24″ paper, to be used horizontally. Do not use a ruler for this drawing and keep erasures to a minimum. Your attitude here is to use perspective as an aid to inquiries intended at uncovering gestural, structural, and tonal facts about the subject.

Begin gesturally and develop the drawing tonally. Search for positive and negative shapes, scale differences, and the relative location of the components to each other (you do not need to include all of the table). At every stage of the drawing's development refer to the eye-level line to help you align planes and forms. Note the angles of convergence of the edges of your subject's parts and, where books seem to "float," check on their diagonal lines to see if they terminate at the horizon line. Use, but do not merely rely on, perspective to assist your understanding of the arrangement of these forms in space. Now your goal is a drawing responsive to your subject's dynamic as well as structural condition. Not only must you insist on conveying the positions of all the forms in relation to each other and to you the observer-artist, but you must do so in graphic terms that reveal your sensitivity to the subject's moving energies, too.

PERSPECTIVE AND EXACT LOCATION

Occasionally, it is necessary to locate the middle of a square or rectangular plane turned away in some direction from the observer's line of sight. In Figure 5.16A, a square and rectangle are shown parallel to the observer. When diagonal lines are drawn from corner to corner in each, they intersect in the exact center, thus establishing the central location of the window in each shape. Drawing diagonal lines from corner to corner on foreshortened planes gives us their exact *perspective* center, enabling us to accurately locate the windows on them, as in Figure 5.16B.

Perspective provides a simple system for locating the position of evenly spaced forms such as trees or posts. To locate them, you draw the first member of a row of forms and, extending lines from its tip and base, incline these lines to meet at the desired vanishing point. Based on these lines, you draw the second member at the desired distance from the first. This first space interval establishes the size of all the spaces between the rest of the forms. Recall that the principle of relative distance demands that spaces between evenly spaced forms must diminish as they recede toward the horizon line. To locate the placement of the third member, first you draw a line from the vanishing point to the center of the first member, dividing it in half. Then you draw a diagonal line from the top of the first member through the point of intersection between the second member and the dividing line, continuing until it strikes the base line, as in Figure 5.17A. The third member is drawn at the point at which the diagonal line strikes the base line. This procedure is repeated to locate all subsequent members, as in Figure 5.17B.

There are many sophisticated extensions of these two suggestions for locating forms that provide exact mathematical and geometric results. But often these tend to inhibit rather than strengthen responsive drawings.

Figure 5.16

Figure 5.17

For those who wish to explore these more intricate applications of perspective, several useful source books are listed in the bibliography.

THE CIRCLE IN PERSPECTIVE

To see a circular shape, the observer must be parallel to its surface and centered on its limits. When totally foreshortened, the circular shape (or any other shape) will of course be reduced to a straight line, as in Figure 5.18. Viewed from any other angle, it appears as an ellipse-like shape, growing more narrow as it approaches total foreshortening.

Figure 5.18

If we bisect a true ellipse along its longer axis, it produces two equal halves. Bisecting a circle seen in perspective in this way produces a slightly fuller curve in the half nearest the observer (Figure 5.18). In drawing foreshortened circular forms it is important to remember that they are not seen as true ellipses—though sometimes referred to as such in this chapter.

The angle of any foreshortened circle is determined by its long axis. When such an elliptical shape is upright, its long axis will be vertical. When it is parallel with the ground-plane and centered on the observer, it is horizontal. All other positions will show the long axis as inclined to some degree.

In Figure 5.19 the long axis in each of the four ellipses is different. In A it is horizontal because, unlike B, it is centered on the observer. But both are parallel with the ground-plane. In C, it tilts away from a vertical position, matching the tilt of its box-like container. Many artists find it easier to place an ellipse (or any other curvilinear form) at the desired angle by first drawing such containers in the required position. Note that the vanishing points for C are above the horizon line, and for D, below it. Note, too, that the long and short axes of each of the four ellipses always form a right angle. This can be seen in E, where the line running through the curving cylinder represents the short axis of the ellipses shown.

To help establish the desired angle of an ellipse at one end of a cylinder form, such as

Figure 5.19

a wheel or column, begin by drawing the box-like container, as shown in Figure 5.20. Running a line through its center parallel with its tilt in space establishes the long axis of the container shown but the *short* axis of the ellipse. Drawing a line at a right angle (90 degrees) to the short axis establishes the oval's long axis. Circles in perspective offer no view from which sharp corners are visible, as in the wrongly drawn cylinder in Figure 5.20.

CAST SHADOWS

Linear perspective affects the shape and scale of cast shadows. When forms are illuminated by a nearby source of light such as a candle

(Figure 5.21), their cast shadows will radiate from a point at the base of the light source. To establish the length of a shadow cast under these conditions, you draw lines from the top of the light source, touching the top of the form and ending where these lines meet with lines drawn from the base of the light source, as in Figure 5.21. The lines emerging from the base of the light source represent the shape of the cast shadow. Here, the base of the light source acts like a vanishing point toward which the lines of the cast shadow converge.

When forms are illuminated by sunlight the radiating effect of the light rays is far less evident because of the great distance separating them from the light source. To establish the shape of a shadow cast by a vertical plane

Figure 5.20

Figure 5.21

Figure 5.22

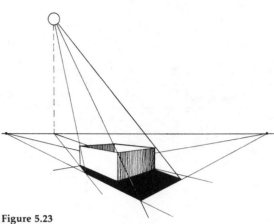

Figure 5.23

in sunlight, drop a vertical line from the position of the sun to the horizon line. This creates the vanishing point for the lines of the shadow (Figure 5.22). Two lines, drawn from the sun at an angle that touches the top corners of the plane and continue farther to intersect the radiating lines of the cast shadow, establish the shape, scale, and direction of the cast shadow. Using the plane's vanishing point to draw a line that touches both of these intersections "proves" the angle of the leading edge of the cast shadow.

To establish the shape of a shadow cast by a three-dimensional solid such as a block, follow the same general procedure. However, as shown in Figure 5.23, there are now *three* vanishing points that affect the cast shadow. The vanishing point of the shadow's lines dictates the direction of the block's shadow; the other two vanishing points and the sun's height determine the shadow's shape and scale. The irregular shape of the cast shadow in this illustration results from the block's height and position in relation to the sun.

Another Mazur drawing, *Ladder* (Figure 5.24), shows cast shadows resulting from a light source located high up and to our right. Note that Mazur does not overload these shadows with dark tones, nor does he call undue attention to them by sharply focused edges. To do either would risk a confusion between shadow and substance. This drawing serves as a good example of one way in which perspective can serve creative instincts. Mazur faithfully records the two-point perspective condition of the ladder and even tells us that he drew it from a position below the lowest step. But instead of emphasizing the subject's perspective state as the goal, or merely allow-

ing the rules of perspective to determine the image, he uses perspective selectively, omitting an occasional segment of cast shadow, widening or thinning down the shapes of shadows and ladder parts, and adjusting the

Figure 5.24
MICHAEL MAZUR (1935–   )
Ladder (1971)
Pencil. 40 x 26 in.
Courtesy, Terry Dintenfass, Inc., New York

location and clarity of some edges, thus creating an engaging abstract play of shapes, tones, and directions. Mazur even suggests an ineffable sense of mystery and expectancy.

FORESHORTENING

The real theme of this chapter is *foreshortening*. We have been discussing it all along. As noted earlier, foreshortening is a given condition of three-dimensional drawing; it is never absent in drawings of forms in space. The beginner who prefers to draw the "easier" side view of a model's head because the front view seems too difficult, must then draw that front view from a severely foreshortened angle as well as the full, parallel view of the side of the head. Not much has been gained. Though some subjects *do* offer a view from one position that is far more complex than other views, moving to a right angle view of a complicated subject only severely foreshortens and thus further complicates it.

Those parts of a three-dimensional form that recede into space at angles that permit us to see them always undergo two major changes. Their *length* and *width* are both diminished to some degree. But usually, *they do not diminish at the same rate*. As a form approaches total foreshortening its length diminishes at a faster rate than its width—its overall girth. Only with severely foreshortened views of subjects which possess

enormous length does the reduction in width keep pace with that of length. This differing rate of reduction is important. As an example, if we draw a foreshortened view of a leg (Figure 5.25), it is necessary to distinguish between the rapid "telescoping" of its length and the relatively minor reduction of its width, as in Figure 5.25A. Many beginners, perhaps subconsciously influenced by the severe reduction of a form's length, reduce its width far too much, as in Figure 5.25B.

But many beginners, finding oblique views of their subjects confusing, prefer instead straight on, or frontal, views. By placing himself squarely before a subject, as in the example of the model's head, the beginner hopes to avoid foreshortening. This, as we have seen, is impossible. When confronted by a foreshortening situation, he will often substitute remembered notions of the subject's forms for what he actually sees. He may *see* a foreshortened leg, but will draw it as if it were fully extended. Or, if he attempts to show its foreshortened state, he may diminish the leg's width, rather than its length, because he is more likely to note the reduction of the overall scale of the form than its foreshortened shape-state. Then, too, it is somehow easier for the beginner to accept a reduced scale for the leg than to alter its familiar outlines. Naturally, this tendency toward unintended frontality subsides as the student begins to shift from preconceived notions to perceptual comprehension.

Figure 5.25

A   B

Learning to see gestural expression and shapes are crucial first steps in perceptual comprehension. Seeing the measurable actualities of and between forms in space is another. These are not separate issues. We have seen that gesture and shape contribute to a fuller realization of a volume's structure and design. Here, we are examining perspective principles that can sensitize us to the structure *and* order of the parts that make up a subject.

Perspective more immediately applies to geometric solids. Applying its principles to a house or fence seems logical and manageable. Its equal presence in organic forms such as trees or the human figure is less evident and too often overlooked. But doing so risks los-

ing the sense of the artist's station point in relation to the subject, and increases the likelihood of perceptual errors going undetected. For example, it is helpful to know that if we are seated before a standing figure, we look *down* upon the tops of the feet, but *up* at the underside of the chin and nose. Knowing that our eye-level falls approximately at the figure's hips alerts us to an important relationship that exist between each part and our own position.

Perspective, then, helps organize complex organic subjects by providing us with a set of conditions to look for in even the most fluid and ornate subjects. Bernini, in his drawing *Sunrise* (Figure 5.26), although he shows few diagonals to suggest convergence,

Figure 5.26
GIOVANNI LORENZO BERNINI (1598–1680)
Sunrise
Pen and wash. 29.5 x 27.3 cm.
Kupferstichkabinett, Berlin (KdZ 15200)

Figure 5.27
PETER PAUL RUBENS (1577–1640)
Studies of Arms and Legs
Black chalk, touches of white chalk. 35 x 24 cm.
Boymans-van Beuningen Museum, Rotterdam

and treats his subject in a broad, painterly manner, convinces us of the perspective rightness of the clouds, water, and rock formations. His sound grasp of perspective enables him to incline the clouds, keep the surface of the sea level, and raise the rocks from it with only the subtlest of visual clues. Knowing that the most fanciful cloud or tree can be conceived of as temporarily reduced to its most suitably simple container permits us to better locate and understand its essential mass. Once the geometrically simple "stand in" has taken its position, and its scale, shape, and converging edges have been established, the development of its unique form particularities can be more easily stated.

In Rubens's drawing of arms and legs (Figure 5.27), the limbs have been drawn in a way that echoes their geometric core. Rubens favors cylindrical and ovoid form summaries, as is especially evident in the drawing of the foreshortened right lower leg. Notice how clearly Rubens orients each of the smaller form-units that comprise these limbs. In the drawing of the arms in the lower left corner he even distinguishes between the direction of the upper and lower segments of the man's left forearm.

The overlapping of one part by another often plays an important role in conveying the foreshortened state of one or more forms. In Figure 5.27 the clear overlap of the lower left

129

leg by the foot, and in turn, the lower leg's overlap of the upper leg leave no room for a misreading of the alignment of these parts. Again in the right foot, the overlap of the bones at the ankle by the protuberence of the heel, and *their* overlap of the forward part of the foot help us to understand the order of these parts in space.

When forms overlap, the nearer, or dominant one sometimes casts a weak shadow or causes a lessening of light upon the farther, or subordinate one, on that segment nearest to the dominant form, as in Figure 5.28A. The impression of volume is increased when values "underscore" the blocking of one form by another in this way. When forms lie close together on a plane in a way that makes it difficult to know which one is dominant at any one point, using values to darken the subordinate form near its neighbor helps to clarify their placement (Figure 5.28B). As with any device, unselective usage can make this tactic quickly degenerate into gimmickry. But it is a helpful step when other clues cannot "sort out" the dominant from the subordinate forms, or when we wish to emphasize a part.

The use of structural cross-section or cage-lines, or of other kinds of hatching is another means of providing clues about foreshortened forms. In Figure 5.29 the undulations of the lines convey the surface-state, their increasing closeness or delicacy, the sense of receding in space.

Even aerial perspective, generally reserved for subjects in deep space, as in Figure 5.30, can assist in conveying the spatial behavior of nearby forms, when used with great subtlety. Leonardo da Vinci, in his *Five Grotesque Heads* (see Figure 3.3), discreetly suggests the second head from the right as being less defined. Relative to the other figures the value range of this head is lessened, and there is less textural activity. Likewise Katzman's drawing (see Figure 4.28), although drawn in a very different manner, relies on aerial perspective devices to make the figure's far leg go back in space.

Relative distance and position can also help convey foreshortened views of independent forms. The decreasing space between trees, flowers, or figures arranged in some orderly pattern suggests space. The farther back in space such separations occur the more critical their position and scale become. A small misjudgment in the distance between two nearby forms is generally of little importance.

Figure 5.28

Figure 5.29

But the same degree of misjudgment between forms a mile or so away becomes a serious change in the scale of the distance between them. In a drawing showing a foreshortened view of a row of trees intended as equidistant, enlarging, or even only failing to reduce the distance between the last two trees, would show the last one as being a full city block away from its neighbor, when only a fraction of that distance was intended.

Thus, all nine principles of perspective can be present in the foreshortening of some forms, although the phenomena of convergence and overlap will always be dominant considerations. The more complex the form or the more severe the foreshortening, the more necessary these phenomena become in clarifying direction, scale, and location.

Because volume and space are inseparable qualities, the drawing of a fore-

Figure 5.30
CHOU CH'ÊN (16th Century)
The Northern Sea (detail)
Ink and slight color on silk. 11 3/16 x 53 1/4 in.
Nelson Gallery, Atkins Museum, Kansas City, Mo.

shortened form must be made as though we believed that the flat surface of the page does not exist, and that, like Alice going through the looking glass, we can reach in and touch, with our drawing instrument, a form located far away in space. Many artists, therefore, simultaneously develop the volume and the spatial field in which it exists. Leaving the space around a form (or between forms) as just the white of the paper sometimes tends to have a flattening effect on masses, the forms appearing somewhat pressed upon the page. Or, it may make some forms seem to hover above the plane of the page. Both of these problems are solved by lines and tones that establish a spatial cavity to receive them. Where such cavities are enclosed and thus shaped by other masses, perspective principles apply in the drawing of such "masses" of air.

In the following exercise, you will draw some foreshortened forms. As you go from simple to more complex ones, remember the nine ways in which perspective can help locate and construct both form *and* space.

exercise 5B

There are no time limits on any of the six parts in this exercise. The first part consists of invented forms, the remaining five will be drawn from observed subjects. The landscape drawings should be done from a locale that provides some forms in the far distance, but need not be a complex panoramic view. For the rest, use the human figure, either draped or nude, as your subject. If no model is available, make a still-life arrangement consisting of some of the following: pillows, purses, hats, boots, dolls, and houseplants. Here, the idea is to simulate some of the characteristics and forms of organic subjects. Any other objects that you feel would be consistent with this theme may, of course, be used. The still life should be fairly simple and should avoid more than a few angular or mechanical objects. However, if a choice of subjects is possible, use the figure, preferably nude or simply clad.

Use any medium or combination of media, and work in any scale you wish. However, avoid extremely small or large drawings.

drawing 1
Fill one half of the page with some seven to ten simple geometric forms such as cylinders, cones, half-spheres, and any other variations of such basically rounded forms. A few may, as in Figure 5.31, show straight or angular passages. Use your imagination freely, but avoid complex forms. The cylinders may bend, interlock, or develop variations in their thickness. However, their elliptical end planes must be shown at right angles to their bodies. Other forms may consist of several joined volumes, as in Figure 5.31.

Begin by "encasing" each invented form in a container, as in Figure 5.32, to help you control its direction and degree of foreshortening. Once you have roughed in a form's essential structure, erase

Figure 5.31

Figure 5.32

its encasing lines and develop it in structural lines whose hatchings further explain the form.

When you have completed the half-page, as in Figure 5.31A, draw each of the objects again on the other half of the page—as if you have moved a few feet to your right. Imagine how each of these would look if you changed your position in this way, and draw their new view. Although each form is now "seen" from this new angle, avoid any blocking of independent forms that would occur in such a shift of position. Therefore, draw each one independent of its position in relation to other forms; as floating free of the rest (Figure 5.31B).

drawing 2

Make two drawings of the same view of an observed landscape (or cityscape). In the first, try to create a sense of deep space by aerial as well as linear perspective devices. Using Vermeer's draw-

ing (Figure 5.2) as a rough guide, permit structures and spaces farther back in the spatial field to become less focused, less tonally contrasting, and less detailed. In the second drawing, and using Figure 5.3 as a rough guide, try to handle the same view more two-dimensionally. Deliberately flatten the image, but not at the expense of the clarity of the scene's essential order of the forms in space. Begin both by locating the horizon-eye-level line.

drawing 3

The model or still life used for this drawing will also be the subject for drawings 4 and 5. The subject should be placed atop a tall stool, desk, or other support higher that a household chair. If the figure is used, the pose should include crossed arms or legs, or otherwise show a variety of directions of the limbs. If you are drawing from the still life, arrange the components to offer a similar variety of directions. For this drawing, stand at an easel or any comparable support.

Study the subject until you understand the various directions of its major parts. Before you begin to draw, lightly indicate the horizon-eye-level line. Begin freely, drawing the forms of your subject *as if they are simple geometric solids*, as in Cambiaso's drawing (Figure 5.33), or as in Figure 5.34. The resulting drawing will, of course, look manikin-like, or, in the case of the still life, machine-tooled. But it should clearly show forms turned at various angles in space. As in Cambiaso's drawing, use some tones in the background to help create more solid forms and clearly established spatial cavities. Where possible, indicate the stool or other support, and perhaps some corner of the room.

Figure 5.33
LUCA CAMBIASO (1527–1585)
The Martyrdom of St. Lawrence
Pen and brown wash.
9 3/8 x 12 1/2 in.
National Gallery of Canada, Ottawa

drawing 4

With your subject in the same position, you are to work this time seated, in a chair, on a low stool, or even on the floor. Begin as you did the previous drawing, by noting the horizon-eye-level line. Though the pose has not changed, your lowered position will have altered all the relationships between the subject's parts. Noting these differences, again draw each form as reduced to a simple geometric state. But this time do so lightly, using as few lines as possible. Once you have established the direction, scale, and overlapping of these forms (which are best thought of now as transparent), continue by drawing upon them what you *do* see of the subject's surface actualities. That is, using the geometric forms as "armatures" that show each part's essential mass and direction, go on to develop the surface forms of your subject. If you find that some of these severely simplified forms are too remote from the surface-state of the parts they represent, develop such forms by stages. For example, instead of drawing the observed surface-forms of the head upon the block or egg form that represents it, "carve" the block or egg to make a few more broad planes that more nearly reflect the volume actualities of the observed head. This will help you locate some of the smaller forms upon the simplified form. Normally, it is not necessary to use such severely summarized masses as a basis for drawings in which structural solids are to be stressed (we examine that in Chapter Six), but here

it helps to more easily control the subject's perspective condition.

As you develop the simplified forms, do not bury them under many small details, but keep a strong undercurrent of the geometric "parent" evident in all the final forms, as in Figures 5.27 and 5.35. The rule here can be: "When in doubt, leave it out."

Check from time to time to see if you have subconsciously made a foreshortened form turn frontally. This sometimes happens when our attention shifts from a part's placement in space to its specific characteristics. Therefore, note especially the shape-state of strongly foreshortened parts.

Your goal here is to produce a drawing modelled mainly by structural lines that show convincing volumes in various positions in space as you saw them from your fixed position.

drawing 5

Rearrange the model or still life to create a strong foreshortening among many of the forms, as in Goodman's *Eileen on Beach Chair* (Figure 5.35). Locate yourself so that the subject is just a little below your eye-level in order to increase the telescoping of forms. Proceed to develop the forms as in the previous drawing, but here, as in Goodman's drawing, emphasize the shape-state of the parts, utilize cast shadows, and try for an interesting two-dimensional design of shapes, values, and textures. This last drawing can be regarded as

Figure 5.34

EYE LEVEL

EYE LEVEL

Figure 5.35

SIDNEY GOODMAN (1936–   )

Eileen on Beach Chair (1972)
Pencil. 15 x 10 1/2 in.
Courtesy, Terry Dintenfass, Inc., New York

135

a kind of summary of the topics covered in the previous chapters, as well as in this chapter. This being the case, consider gesture, shape, line, and value to be as important as perspective. Here, then, perspective no longer dominates but takes its place as one more set of considerations in helping you to "essay" your subject's inherent and potential qualities.

Should you find that any of these exercises are beyond your present level of control, work out the subject's perspective state in a preparatory sketch, and, using it as a guide, begin your exercise on another sheet of paper. You will find the preparatory analysis helps you to place and construct the forms better.

drawing 6
Select a newspaper or magazine photograph of several forms (they may range from boxes to buildings) arranged at different angles on a flat plane. Overlay the photo with tracing paper and, using a ruler, establish the horizon line and the major lines running from the forms to the several

vanishing points. When vanishing points lie beyond the boundaries of the photo, locate them by lines drawn onto sheets of paper affixed to either side of the photograph. Look for converging lines that lead to vanishing points above and below the horizon line, as in Figure 5.11.

PERSPECTIVE AS AN AGENT OF EXPRESSION

Perspective can contribute to expressive meanings by enabling the artist to draw a subject from the angle most evocative of its actions and character, and most compatible with the artist's feelings and intent. The view given in Sheeler's drawing (Figure 5.7) stimulates emotions about the scale and character of his subject. His use of three-point perspective helps us feel the building's towering elegance. Piranesi's turbulent drawing *Interior of a Prison* (Figure 5.36) shows a view that am-

Figure 5.36
GIOVANNI BATTISTA PIRANESI (1720–1778)
Interior of a Prison
Pen and wash over pencil. 25.6 x 18.9 cm.
Kunsthalle Hamburg

Figure 5.37
P. J. SAENREDAM (1597–1665)
St. Cunera Church, Rhenen
Pen and ink. 38.2 x 53.5 cm.
Rijksmuseum, Amsterdam

Figure 5.38
JACOPO TINTORETTO (1518–1594)
*Study of the Head from Michelangelo's
"Giuliano de Medici"*
Black and white chalk on toned paper (detail).
Rijksmuseum, Amsterdam

plifies the artist's fascination and dread of his subject. Here, as in Figure 3.20, Piranesi proves that perspective can be a tool of exciting expressive possibilities. In a very different mood, Saenredam's drawing (Figure 5.37) shows a hushed and serene interior. Although both drawings owe much of their expressive force to their handling—Piranesi's furious attack contrasting sharply with Saenredam's delicacy—Saenredam's view is as necessary to his expressive theme as Piranesi's more oblique view is to this theme. Likewise, the expressive mood of Tintoretto's drawing (Figure 5.38) is due in part to the bold foreshortening of the forms of the head. Perspective, then, as these drawings amply demonstrate, need not be thought of as the dry logic of structure and space, but as a fertile source of graphic invention.

We have seen that perspective is a given condition of three-dimensional drawing. It helps provide important information about masses in space, and furnishes the means by which masses can be ordered, clarified, and emphasized. Although sensitive visual perception would seem to make the study of perspective almost unnecessary, a firm grasp of its principles endows a drawing with that extra measure of authority and economy that the sensitive beholder recognizes as issuing from knowledge, not bravado or whimsey. Further, because responsive drawing may, for some artists, require considerable changes in what is observed, when such changes concern the relocation of volumes perspective is immediately involved. While linear perspective has its limits, it has important virtues—especially in helping us understand the condition of foreshortened forms. Its general influence promotes a sensitivity to the nature and behavior of forms in space, and the freedom to follow our responsive instincts, unhampered by the restrictions of ignorance.

CHAPTER SIX

VOLUME

the sculptural sense

A DEFINITION

A major consideration in each of the previous chapters was the fact of a subject's existence as volume in space. We saw, in examining gestural expression, shape, line, value, and perspective, that understanding each added to our means for understanding a subject's physical and behavioral nature in space. Such perceptions were shown to be fundamental to responsive drawing. This is not to suggest that responsive drawing need be primarily concerned with the impression of masses in space; our perceptual sensitivity and aesthetic inclinations, wherever they may lead, decide what role volume building will play. Rather, it is the crippling restrictions on graphic freedom that result from the inability to create convincing impressions of volume in space which make it necessary to develop the skills and insights that convey such impressions. Then, too, in failing to comprehend a subject's structural condition, we fail to uncover a rich source of dynamic activities. For, as we shall see, important organizational and ex-pressive themes are revealed by the structure and arrangement of forms.

In this chapter we will explore, and occasionally review, the various factors that can participate in conveying volume—not the outlining of volumes, not their surface effects, not vague suggestions of volumes, but the convincing impression of solid masses that occupy space, show their various constructional arrangements, and suggest their differing weights and surface characteristics.

Volumes can be represented in two ways. A drawing can describe a subject's outsides, its tonal and textural surface-state, or explain its structural nature, the way its parts are constructed, interjoined, and arranged in space. These are not mutually exclusive concerns, and many master drawings, both old and contemporary, exhibit forms whose inner and outer conditions are well understood and integrated. Some artists, such as Giacometti (see Figure 3.1) and de Gheyn (Figure 6.1) are almost exclusively preoccupied with structural matters. Some, such as Katzman (Figure 4.28) and Jacobo da Empoli (Figure 6.2) concentrate on surface conditions; while others, such as Goodman (Figure 5.35) and Rembrandt (Figure 6.3) emphasize the structural. But no artists of serious inventive worth can be cited who concentrate wholly on surface matters. This is hardly surprising, for no creative graphic results are possible without a comprehension of a subject's structural essentials, and these cannot be buried under surface detail.

In drawings that concentrate accurately but exclusively on the effects of light, texture, and atmosphere, a sense of volume similar to that in an ordinary snapshot of the subject can result. Such an overemphasis on surface characteristics tends to limit the impression of volume in the same way the photograph does. In both, the results are confined to the nature of the light's accidental behavior and the subject's superficial and occasionally volume-denying details.

But drawings that disclose a subject's constructional nature, the tensions and pressures within and among its parts, and its relationships of direction, shape, location, and scale, in fixing on the visual issues that we see manifest in all master drawings—making them come alive—are the more responsive and, hence, more creative works. It is this latter way of confronting the challenge of what we will call *structured volume* that we will examine here.

THREE BASIC APPROACHES TO STRUCTURED VOLUME

All volumes, as we saw in Chapter Two, can be transposed into flat or curved planes. Some subjects—jagged rocks, bureaus, books, or bananas—clearly disclose their planar construction. Whether simple or complex, their surfaces can be resolved into explicit planar divisions that give such objects great structural clarity. Other forms—bottles, apples, boulders, or animal and human forms, being less angular, show less clearly defined surface facets. The more smoothly rounded a subject's surfaces, the more arbitrarily intrusive it seems to translate them into planar divisions. The sphere, for example, would seem to defy planar analysis. But in drawings showing vol-

ume with emphatic clarity, evenly rounded forms are often shown as less smoothly rounded by flat or curved planes that abut at subtle angles, as in de Gheyn's *Three Gypsies* (Figure 6.1). As this drawing shows, such an approach, even when tonalities play a considerable role, often relies on the use of structural line-groupings.

A second approach to structured volume relies less on clearly defined abutments. Instead, the planar-state of forms, especially organic and curvasive ones, is shown by sensitive graduations of value, as in Jacobo da Empoli's *Young Man Seen from the Back* (Figure 6.2). Here the planes are more discreetly defined, their clarity conveyed more by tonal than by linear modelling.

A third approach, and one often showing strong calligraphic qualities, combines both tonal and linear drawing, as in Kokoschka's *Portrait of Mrs. Lanyi* (see Figure 1.15), Rembrandt's *Standing Male Nude* (Figure 6.3), and Carpeaux's *Study for Ugolino* (Figure 6.4).

De Gheyn constructs the folds of the robes by long convex or concave planes that abut with each other somewhat abruptly, suggesting pronounced changes in their direction. Despite these sudden and sometimes angular abutments, the forms are not stiff or mechanical but move in a decidedly rhythmic way. Note that de Gheyn models the forms by hatchings that partially encircle the terrain of convex and concave parts *on their darker sides*, thus suggesting a common light source falling from the left.

In da Empoli's drawing, gradual transitions of value explain the fusing of planes to create gently undulating, "caressed" surfaces. But, unlike de Gheyn, who permits unexplained (but implied) planes to be represented by the white of the paper, da Empoli insists on value-variations that show every nuance of change in the figure's surface-state. However, in the man's drape, the values are less blended, producing a bolder planar construction. This change in tactics from a tonal, to a more linear (and thus, more directional) treatment of the planes reflects da Empoli's interest in conveying the visual and textural differences of these forms. In this way da Empoli explains the volume of both without violating the dominant visual and textural differences

Figure 6.1

JACQUES DE GHEYN (1565–1629)

Three Gypsies
Pen and ink. 22.5 x 25.8 cm.
Courtesy of The Art Institute of Chicago
Gift of Mrs. Tiffany Blake

of either. Although both artists suggest an illuminating source, neither permits any part of their subject to be lost in shadow. Even though in da Empoli's drawing the man's back is in shadow, every form-unit is volumetrically clear. Likewise, the planar surfaces of the center figure in de Gheyn's drawing are visible even when they are shaded by the robe and arm.

Notice how both artists create a sense of spatial depth. Da Empoli uses a series of faint, curved lines to imply an area of space behind the figure. When we look at the figure we are not immediately aware that the background is comprised of lines, but we do sense space around the figure. The collective tone of these lines appears to go back in space for two reasons: first, because this tone, being darker

Figure 6.2
JACOBO DA EMPOLI (1551–1640)
Young Man, Seen from the Back
Red chalk. 16 x 10 5/6 in.
The Pierpont Morgan Library, New York

sight, and planes located at angles to strongly illuminated ones to be dropping back in space.

De Gheyn's solution for establishing spatial depth is simply to draw small, vague, cast shadows at the base of the figures, the obliquity of the shadows suggesting a ground-plane that extends behind the group.

Rembrandt, as mentioned earlier, uses both line and value to explore and explain structural character. In the broad and vigorous handling of the background, he relies mainly on line to establish the boundaries of planes, and to suggest some folds in the drape behind the figure's right side. A light tone that envelops over two-thirds of the background serves, as in da Empoli's drawing, to push the figure forward, and, in its several variations, creates the spatial cavity occupied by him. On the drawing's right side, bold cast shadows help explain the masses of the supporting pillow and the surface against which the figure stands. As the cast shadow descends, it "measures" the increasing divergence and advance of the figure's left leg from the nearby wall. In drawing the forms that make up the young man's figure, Rembrandt more evenly divides the roles of line and value to develop the volumes. Usually, short, structural hatchings define sudden changes in direction between planes, and washes of tone explain the more rounded forms or serve to push back large segments, such as the upper part of the supporting leg. Here, as in the de Gheyn and da Empoli drawings, illumination helps to explain, not obscure, the subject's structural character. Note that Rembrandt considers the tonal order and shape-state of the dark as well as the light areas. The dark areas are not merely "left" as a result of a concentration on forms in the light. Thus, a two-dimensional pattern of light and dark tones, and a concern for the structural conditions of forms in shadow, as well as in light, reveals two deliberately conceived systems of design and structure that interwork to activate the forms they describe.

Rembrandt often relies on broad planes to stand as summaries of several smaller ones, gaining the structural clarity and strength that such a succinct analysis provides. For example, a single faint tone describes a broad

than the figure's lightest areas of tone, seems to drop behind them, causing the figure to advance; second, because the lines of the background tone align themselves on either side of the figure, appearing to have passed behind it. Here the light tones of the figure seem to advance because we tend to regard small light tones upon a large dark field to be in front of the darker field. Usually, too, we assume planes turning away from our line of

Figure 6.3

REMBRANDT VAN RIJN (1606–1669)

Standing Male Figure
Pen and brown wash, heightened with white.
25.2 x 19.3 cm.
The British Museum, London

143

Figure 6.4
JEAN BAPTISTE CARPEAUX (1827–1875)
Study for Ugolino
Pen and gouache on brown paper.
24 1/2 x 18 7/8 in.
Courtesy of The Art Institute of Chicago
Joseph and Helen Regenstein Foundation

plane at the side of the head, bounded at the top and left side by the ridge of the cheekbone. To summarize the planar actualities of the side of the face, Rembrandt had to determine the general, overall direction of the planes in that area. Because no other overall changes in the direction of surfaces in that location were as strongly evident as that forming the ridge of the cheekbone, he chose this change as the demarcation line between those planes above and below it. Such incisive carving reveals a grasp of structural issues too often obscured in more detailed approaches.

Carpeaux's drawing, a study for a sculptural work, also combines tonal washes of grays and grays formed by line-groups, to more fully explore volume. Here there is the need to understand each part's structural essentials and the overall structural behavior of five interwoven figures. This makes the relatively less probing approach of de Gheyn's brief drawing, or da Empoli's somewhat naturalistic and thus not so aggressively analytical approach, unsuited to Carpeaux's purposes. These aim at understanding the major planes that form the parts of each figure; the spaces, or negative "masses" that result from the placement of the figures; the organizational and dynamic character of the group; and the way light plays across the forms from this view. By drawing on a toned surface and adding both light and dark tones, Carpeaux gains a further measure of control in modelling the forms. The results of such analytical approaches to volume as Rembrandt and Carpeaux utilize enables them to indicate structural, spatial, and even expressive qualities that would otherwise be lost.

To disregard the interlocking, directional behavior of a subject's planes weakens the impression of volume. Trying to convey the weighty substantiality of solids in space by copying their externals not only *re-presents* the subject's superficial and random properties— some of which actually obscure the essential nature of the volumes—but also records the subject's structural clues in their original state *as undeveloped potentialities*. The raw material is not analyzed and interpreted, but only re-presented as raw material.

As we have seen, there are a number of factors that participate in creating the convincing impression of structured volume. Whether it is general information about masses in space that result from the search for gestural expression, shape, line, or value, or the more specific information provided by the principles of perspective, or any of the other volume-revealing considerations already dis-

cussed, the sense of solid masses results from the *choices* and *changes* such concepts make possible. To establish volume it is always necessary to analyze, extract, and stress the measurable and dynamic qualities that define it, and subdue or omit observations that would weaken or obscure it.

In the energetic drawing by Delacroix, *Studies after Rubens's "Crucifixion"* (Figure 6.5), there are some extreme examples of just such extracts from some forms in a Rubens painting. We see these forms as both weighty and animated because Delacroix stresses these qualities. In making this sketch he knew what his interests and intentions were and, consequently, so do we.

This drawing, made not from nature but from a work of art in which the volumes of the original subject have already been interpreted and translated into visual terms, is a kind of double extraction. Perhaps that is

Figure 6.5
EUGÈNE DELACROIX (1798–1863)
Studies of Arms and Legs, after "The Crucifixion" by Rubens
Pen and sepia ink on buff paper. 21.7 x 35 cm.
Courtesy of The Art Institute of Chicago

what makes Delacroix's brief sketch appear to seize the very essence of the structural character of these human forms. Although Delacroix's spirited approach to drawing is quite different from Rubens's more sensuous one (see Figures 2.15 and 2.23), each in their own way builds powerful volumes from an excited involvement with the processes and concepts of structural *and* dynamic inquiry. For, just as gestural drawing includes (or develops into) a search for the subject's structural generalities, so must the structural analysis embrace considerations of the subject's actions and energies. To do otherwise too often results in drawings that are rather dry inventories of planar facts, unfertilized by feeling.

DIRECTION AND GEOMETRIC SUMMARY

The impression of structured volume, like most other goals in responsive drawing, is usually arrived at by working from generalities to specifics. The artist, like the sculptor, generally states the broader planes of his subject before the smaller ones. Indeed, neither one can know with any certainty just where smaller planes are to be located until the broad "parent" plane is established because, as we saw in Chapter Five, the smaller ones are always variations on the direction of the parent plane and depend on *its* position for their own.

This is especially evident when drawing forms that are naturally almost pure geometric volumes. But in complex forms the superficial

details of surface and texture can easily divert the unwary student from perceiving the direction of major planes or of entire masses. For example, few students are likely to overlook the basic planes and directions of an old stucco wall by any minor variations in its surface-state due to aging or an uneven application of stucco. However, as such variations increase in scale and frequency, the likelihood of disregarding the wall's position in space, as well as the major planes of which it is constructed, increases (Figure 6.6). When we consider the many volumetric complexities of subjects such as human figures or cityscapes, the need to understand each part's direction and those of its major planes becomes apparent.

There are, generally, two unfortunate results when a concern for details overrules the early establishment of a subject's position in space and the location of its major planes. First, because what is not perceived is only accidentally (and rarely) drawn in accordance with the subject's actualities, the probability of error in the part's direction, location, or proportions is very high. Second, beginning with details and permitting them to determine the whole, is, as we saw in Chapter One, a sequential, piecemeal process in which little particulars dominate or smother essential structural and dynamic conditions. It is the tail wagging the dog.

It also violates the way we see forms in nature. A form's volumetric character is not perceived by adding up its details. Rather, the details are seen secondarily as particular facts belonging to a volume whose general structure is understood. If, for example, we are asked to identify an object flashed on a screen for one-tenth of a second, we may recognize its general shape and structure, but we are not likely to have seen its details of surface change, texture, or illumination.

In drawings that include a considerable amount of volumetric or other detail, the major planes and masses must maintain their dominance over smaller ones. When their influence as basic planes and masses is neutralized by minor embellishments upon them, both the structure and the unity of the forms are seriously weakened.

The persistent influence of major planes and masses seen "through" the details is

Figure 6.6

A

B

Figure 6.7
MICHELANGELO BUONARROTI (1475–1564)
Seated Nude and Head Study
Black chalk. 24.3 x 18.3 cm.
Teylers Museum, Haarlem

readily sensed in Michelangelo's imposing study (Figure 6.7), and in an early Degas drawing (Figure 6.8). In these drawings, otherwise so different in mood and manner of execution, there are many similarities. But in neither do the parts "add up" to become the figure. Nor, in either drawing, do the parts of the figure result from an accumulation of details. Instead, the details are seen as subtle planar and tonal variations on the basic geometrical, directional, and tonal condition of these forms. They "well up" from the forms and "belong" to them.

Likewise, the position in space of the figures themselves do not result from their parts having been drawn separately. Seeing the figure's overall direction in space (note the search for the entire figure's direction in the begin-

ning few lines of a second nude in the Degas drawing), each artist was better able to locate the direction of arms, legs, etc. to it, and relate these parts to each other. In both drawings the parts are subordinate to the whole, and because they are drawn with an awareness to their relative location, scale, shape, and direction, rhythms and movements emerge that contribute to the unity of the whole. In both drawings we even sense the basic geometric core that underlies each of the smaller form-units which make up the figure's forms. And each of *these* is a convincing structural form with its own hierarchy of essentials and details, that has weight and occupies a specific direction in space. Note that neither artist relies much on smudges of tone to model the forms, but establishes the masses by subtle hatchings. These are more in-

147

Figure 6.8
EDGAR DEGAS (1834–1917)
Standing Nude
Pencil. 11 1/2 x 8 9/16 in.
Sterling and Francine Clark Art Institute,
Williamstown

volved with a tactile experiencing of the subject's terrain than with the effects of illumination. In these drawings, light's ability to reveal form is integrated with, but subordinate to, modelling based on the structural clarity of major planes and masses.

When a subject *is* comprised of many independent volumes, the danger of disregarding its overall mass is increased. If in the earlier example the wall were made of casually heaped fieldstone instead of stucco, a greater analytical effort would be required to conceive its overall mass as reducible to a simple volume-summary. The more the independent volumes that form a greater mass are

scattered, the more difficult it is to see their collective mass. The direction and essential mass of the tightly constructed wall (A) in Figure 6.9 is easier to see than in the wall formed by loosely piled stones (B).

Unlike the walls in Figure 6.6, which are both reducible to slender, vertical slabs inclined toward the horizon to the observer's right, only the tightly constructed wall in Figure 6.9 approximates a similar volume-summary. Although both walls in Figure 6.9 go in the same direction as those of Figure 6.6, the loosely constructed wall (B) is more accurately analyzed as a half-cylinder. Discerning a form's volume-summary is essential to its more specific devel-

Figure 6.9

opment. Leonardo da Vinci's drawing of stratified rocks (Figure 6.10) clearly shows his grasp
of the volume-summaries that unite the subject's many independent volumes. Indeed, it
seems that discovering such summaries is part
of this striking drawing's visual and expressive
theme.

In analyzing structure, then, the two basic perceptions of a subject's masses are its
main directions and volume-summaries. Both
require an effort to temporarily bypass lesser
planes and volumes to be seen—and much
depends on their being seen. Disregarding
such fundamental generalities will almost cer-

Figure 6.10
LEONARDO DA VINCI (1452–1519)
Outcrop of Stratified Rock
Pen over chalk. 18.5 x 26.8 cm.
Royal Collection, Windsor Castle

tainly compromise a volume's specifics. The more complex a subject's forms are, the greater the need to see such generalities first. There are three basic ways of approaching these simplifications.

Some artists begin by actually drawing the subject as reduced to volume-summaries such as those you made in Exercise 5B. However, such severe summaries are often felt to be too mechanical or too removed from the expressive character of most subjects. Therefore, many artists who begin by showing a subject's volume-summaries, arrive at simple geometric masses that are less extreme. They search for simplifications that clarify perspective, but still retain the major, and even some of the secondary, structural features, as in Cambiaso's drawing (Figure 5.33). Al-

Figure 6.11
PAUL CÉZANNE (1839–1906)
Study of a Nude Figure
Pen and wash. 25 x 19 1/4 in.
Fogg Art Museum, Harvard University
Gift of Mr. and Mrs. Justin K. Thannhauser

though the Cambiaso is a completed study, it is sometimes useful to establish such a stage of form simplification even when the volumes are to be more specifically developed. Unencumbered by many small planar changes, by texture or by the effects of illumination, perceptions concerning direction, scale, shape, or location can be more easily established. Making adjustments in such perceptions before the forms are developed further avoids the later more difficult changes that are so injurious to a drawing's spontaneity.

Other artists, like Cezanne (Figure 6.11), start by drawing only a few abbreviated hints about a subject's volumes in space, again somewhat simplified for the sake of clarity. This second approach is preferred by those who feel it is too restricting to divide the act of drawing into separate stages, or, that it is too strong and isolated an emphasis on structure outside the context of the subject's other potentialities for dynamic activity. Once established, these more briefly stated forms can be integrated, as they are developed, with other, nonstructural considerations. Sometimes, such condensed structural statements, reduced to the barest of visual clues, are intended as a drawing's final state. Polonsky, in his drawing *Head Study* (Figure 6.12), finds the perceptual acuity of such a demanding economy to be an exciting graphic challenge. The drawing's few lines and tones convey a surprising amount of structural information. We can read the structure around the eye and nose, can see the rise of the cheek caused by the ledge of the cheekbone, can sense the thickening of the brow, and how the hair is shaped on the head. Even the fullness of the lips and chin can be discerned. Here the artist's dense "screen" of intent stops all but the most necessary few marks. And, as we can see, each carries some structural information.

But Polonsky's main theme is not structure. Equally evident is an engaging abstract play of lines and tones that, in hinting at shapes as well as masses, and by their independent and energetic condition, rise to the surface where their assertive calligraphy provides a delicate pattern of rhythms and textures.

This second approach is also useful where the nature of some drawing media, as

Figure 6.12
ARTHUR POLONSKY (1925–   )
Head Study
Ink. 8 1/2 x 11 in. (1971)
Courtesy of the artist

for example, pen and ink or wax-based crayon make any extensive underdrawing impractical. Finally, this approach is practical where an artist's intention is toward simple and spontaneous images that exhibit penetrating structural knowledge. Because this approach places a higher priority on the economy of means, many of the volume-summaries must be conceived in the mind's eye, rather than worked out on the page, as is possible in the first approach.

Still other artists begin a drawing in the charged spirit of a direct attack—intending each line and tone as final. Although some changes and developments in the initial drawing usually take place, the intention, at least, is to state the total interpretation of

their subject in one spontaneous effort, responding to all of the visual and expressive motives and stimuli simultaneously. Here again, the volume-summary of parts must be understood not by feeling one's way to a solution while drawing, but before the part is drawn. Held in the mind's eye, it serves as a guide, as a kind of invisible scaffold upon which the form is built. Of course, envisioning the simple form-summary of an observed part while you draw its *final* form "over it" requires an ability to reason in visual terms. It is the ability to sort out its important (usually largest or visually dominating) directions, shapes, and planes from lesser ones to "see" what simple mass can be fairly claimed to underlie it.

Figure 6.13
JEAN-FRANCOIS MILLET (1814–1975)
Young Mother Preparing the Evening Meal
Pen and brown ink. 8 3/16 x 6 11/16 in.
National Gallery of Canada, Ottawa

Figure 6.14
MARIANNA PINEDA (19 –   )
Standing Male Figure, Back View
India ink, pen and brush. 18 x 22 in.
Courtesy of the artist

152

Millet's direct drawing (Figure 6.13) reveals his envisioned form-summaries. We can name the geometric mass underlying virtually every part, from the truncated cones of the cooking vessel to the cylinders, wedges, and blocks of the figures. Some form-units, while they do not conform to nameable geometric solids, are clearly legible, as in the woman's skirt where large interlocking forms are simple variants of spheres, cones, and cylinders. And, as in all master drawings, Millet's certainty about the rightness of his form-judgments is reflected in the conviction with which the parts are drawn.

Similarly, the forms in Pineda's forceful drawing (Figure 6.14), despite its urgency and turmoil, are established upon a "projection" of envisioned volume-summaries.

PLANAR ANALYSIS

All three approaches we have been discussing utilize an important process in the analysis of a form's structure, which holds that planes are the basic structural unit of volume building. And, while planes, in drawing as in painting, can be stated by value, line is the most frequently used element, its presence sensed even in the boundaries of value-shapes.

The process, therefore, uses line diagrammatically to run between *key structural points*, measuring the distances that separate them. These reference points occur on *and within* a form's boundaries. We find them at the junction between planes, as occurs on outer edges where the changing direction of an edge indicates the differing lengths of totally foreshortened planes, as in Figure 6.15A; or at the junction of inner edges that establish a plane's particular shape, as in Figure 6.15B. Here, schematic lines not only measure the distance between points along edges, but estimate distances between points on widely separated parts. For example, the lines running from the hat's brim to the cheek, and from the nose to the shoulder, measure the relative distances between these parts. Additionally, some lines establish true verticals and horizontals to serve as references for the various

Figure 6.15

angles of other lines and form-units, while other lines reduce observed curved boundaries to several straight line-segments (Figure 6.15C). Naturally enough, such a search for the relative length of planes and edge segments and their differing directions provides an important means for determining the location, shape, and scale of whole parts.

As in the case of volume-summaries (which this process so importantly assists), often such key structural points are not drawn, but held in mind as important cites, places where some change in the direction of an inner or outer edge marks a visually logical stop—and a structurally significant fact. As such points are found and the lines that connect them are drawn, planes emerge.

As noted in Chapter Three, such an analytical approach intellectually responds to the *principles* of the subject's structure, rather than to perceptions of textured, illuminated, or inherently toned surfaces. Often, drawings developed in this way, at least in their early stages, show forms as if they were transparent—the results of measurements that search out the width, depth, and axes of parts, as well as their lengths. Thus, as in Figure 6.15, a kind of skeletal framework of points and lines emerges that, in noting mainly the straight or simple C-curved paths between key points, creates simplified planes that "cut through" the surface complexities of a form (especially intricate organic ones). This helps the artist to establish the volume-summaries that organize even the most involved complex of forms. And, as we shall see later in this chapter (and in Chapter Eight), such a structural armature is important not only as a means of understanding a subject's architectural system, but as a helpful tool in discovering dynamic relationships as well.

But here, as with any visual process or convention, we should guard against the danger of regarding it as a universal cure-all. This important means for relating measurable matters, developed in the Renaissance and utilized, at least to *some* degree (often subconsciously) by all artists, can, if too exclusively pursued, overrule those dynamic responses that make drawings come alive. For the best drawings always disclose a fusion of facts and feelings, and to displace intuition and empathy with an intellectual examination of a sub-

ject's structural condition upsets the necessary and delicate balance between discipline and indulgence that gives master drawings their individual character and spirit.

Although some artists, like da Empoli, sometimes prefer to lessen attention to a subject's structural condition and to concentrate instead on a fuller exploration of light, local-tone, and texture, others, like Delacroix (Figure 6.16) and Jacques Villon (Figure 6.17) emphasize a planar simplification of volume, achieving a sculptural quality. In such drawing, volume-summaries, with few modifications, become final structural statements. The sculptural nature of this kind of bold modelling is especially evident in Villon's etching, which is in fact a work based on a

Figure 6.16
EUGÈNE DELACROIX (1798–1863)
Nude Woman
Pen and brown ink. 6 11/16 x 4 1/8 in.
Sterling and Francine Clark Institute, Williamstown

Figure 6.17
JACQUES VILLON (1875–1963)
Portrait of Baudelaire
Etching. 24 7/16 x 17 5/8 in.
Collection, The Museum of Modern Art, New York
Gift of Victor S. Riesenfeld

sculpture by his brother, Raymond Duchamp Villon. Here, the chin, a block-like form jutting out at almost a right angle to the thin, clearly defined plane under the lower lip, is typical of the incisive carving of the rest of the head. Note how the planar clarity of the nose, ear, forehead, and cheek rule out any misreading of these form-units.

Figure 6.17 illustrates another helpful device for conveying volumes in space: "stacking" volumes one upon the other to emphasize their relative locations in space. By drawing the head set upon a pedestal, which in turn is placed upon a flat surface, Villon provides clear, planar guides that help us understand the head's location to be well back of the picture-plane and at our eye-level. Here, as in the da Empoli drawing, the lines of the

background tone pass behind the head, adding to the impression of its existence in a spatial field.

Delacroix, using more curved than flat planes, draws the figure's forms as simplified masses that occupy clearly readable positions in space. For example, note the subtle difference in elevation between the left and right legs, and the differing axes of the upper arms. Like Villon, Delacroix explains the form's structural nature with great clarity. But his more sensual approach to volume sharply contrasts with Villon's more intellectual one.

A brief summary of the perceptions necessary in analyzing a subject's structural nature would be helpful here. We have already seen the importance of an early noting of the subject's gestural character, shape-state, inherent and accidental tonalities, and its perspective conditions, and have examined the possibilities for establishing these underlying states in line and tone.

Without a grasp of the subject's physical and dynamic gestures—of what it is *doing* at both the representational and abstract levels—we miss the necessary understanding of the subject's collective actions and purpose. And, as noted earlier, such a perceptual omission not only risks stilted drawings that seem made up of isolated units, it also results in missed insights concerning the subject's volume generalities, its important axes, shapes, and scale differences.

Without a deliberate examination of negative as well as positive shapes, countless misjudgments accumulate, each one causing the drawing to drift farther away from the actualities. And, because planes must be simultaneously understood as shapes, no useful understanding of structural conditions is possible without a search for shapes.

Without a study of the subject's tonalities, important structural clues are missed. Disregarding the subject's tonal facts also bypasses important representational and dynamic truths which both serve and stimulate structural understanding.

And without a sense of the perspective principles at work from our view of a subject, broad structural essentials are missed. We cannot begin to draw responsively unless we recognize the fixed relationship between ourselves and the subject.

As these basic perceptions are made, a general and *tentative* armature emerges that both holds and guides further structural (and plastic) observations and ideas. This necessary armature is regarded as tentative not only because further perceptions will be drawn over it, but because some of these perceptions may uncover ways in which the armature must be adjusted. Therefore, it is best to regard these first estimates and insights as exploratory and to state them economically in a light and fluid manner. Being approximations, they are almost always right in noting essentials, but frequently somewhat "off" in exact measurements of shape, scale, location, or direction. Yet without these preliminary probes, "near misses" and all, our subsequent estimates and judgments about the subject's structure *and spirit* are almost impossible to establish.

Such scaffolds prepare the way for further structural development in two important ways. First, any greater form, if it is to retain a sense of its basic volume-character and unity, requires its component parts, large and small, to be subordinate to it. Many otherwise admirable student drawings have suffered because a part "broke away" from its major form, as in, say, a figure drawing when a muscle is shown as a self-contained unit, isolated, and as visually attracting as its parent form. Or, when a few folds of a coat sleeve appear more important than, and compete with, the arm inside. Establishing the greater form first, increases its influence in the drawing's final state and helps to govern the visual power of its components.

Second, locating the directions of the greater planes and masses guides us in locating all smaller ones. If the subject is, for example, a hand, its mitten-like mass should be

Figure 6.18

known before the structural nature of its major subdivisions is considered. Seeing these should, in turn, precede the drawing of specifics—fingernails and skin folds (Figure 6.18). Reversing the visual order of showing smaller parts as belonging to larger ones isolates the specifics as ends in themselves, obscures the character of the greater volume, and destroys the unity of the drawing.

In forming such tentative frameworks, it is best to rely on diagrammatic and structural uses of line, as in the Degas study of a dancer (Figure 6.19). For, our interest here is in developing an efficient and economical means of stating the measurements necessary to establishing a subject's structural condition. While calligraphic and expressive line activities are intrinsic to responsive drawing, they are not,

Figure 6.19
EDGAR DEGAS (1834–1917)
Ballet Dancer in Position Facing Three-Quarters Front Graphite and crayon, heightened with white chalk, on pink paper. 41 x 28.6 cm.
Fogg Art Museum, Harvard University

strictly speaking, *directly* involved with measurement. Rather, they reflect our feelings about a subject's structure and spirit. And, while they may modify measurements, such qualities play no part in uncovering them. Even when the only line describing, say, a shore's curving edge is richly calligraphic, its length, axis, and position in the drawing are essentially diagrammatic properties of that line. Thus, whatever our temperamental disposition to line may be, in the early analysis of structural matters we must recognize its primary function to be investigatory.

THE JOINING OF PLANES AND VOLUMES

Any ambiguity of the direction of planes, or in their manner of joining to form volumes, creates ruptures in the continuity of the structural and spatial clarity of volumetric drawings. Although some structurally unexplained passages are often found in master drawings (Figures 6.1, 6.7, 6.13, 6.16), they are never the results of indecision or innocence. Sometimes such drawings are preparatory studies for works in other media, and the artist develops only those areas of the subject he wishes to study more fully. Often undeveloped passages serve compositional or expressive interests. The relative directness of drawing compared to painting and sculpture, and the relative simplicity of means, makes it far more suited to spontaneous, bold, and brief explorations and declarations. The results of such direct drawings are sometimes more intimate and revealing of an artist's judgments, feelings, and intent than those of his more formal works. Also, they are more free of the deadening effects of a completeness that conveys the "polished" at the expense of the spontaneous.

In master drawings that stress volumes in space, undeveloped areas often serve as passive foils for other areas that stand out as crescendos of structural emphasis. In this way, the weight and sculptural strength of stressed passages take on greater visual and expressive meaning. In such master drawings, unexplained passages, when consciously left, are intended; when subconsciously left, are

necessary. But they are never perceptual failings or oversights.

Nor are such unexplained areas *wholly* without volumetric clues. In Figure 6.13, Millet provides strong hints about the surface-state of the woman's arms, back, and skirt by the shapes of the planes and the nature of the contours surrounding these "empty" passages. In Delacroix's drawing (Figure 6.16), the differing directions between the figure's right thigh and hip is clear, though no line or tone marks the end of one part and the beginning of the other. The change in direction is suggested, as in the Millet drawing, by structural lines explaining the tilt and shape of the nearby planes. Some of the appeal of these two drawings comes from our realization that so much is being indicated by so little. Both are good examples of how much economy is possible in structural drawing. Note that, although both are pen-and-ink drawings, we can find, especially in the Millet, lighter, schematic lines along inner and outer contours and at junctions between planes; evidence of the preliminary framework.

But for the student the sculptural attitude toward forms should be tested through the experience of working from a subject's broader planes and masses to those smaller ones that clarify specific volume-characteristics of its parts. In doing so, care must be taken to select only those small planar surface changes that are most informing of a part's smaller form-units. Just as in drawing major planes and masses, small ones are clarified by seeing *their* direction, shape, and location, summarizing their volumetric character, and explaining, by lines and tones, the way they join with other parts. The scale of a part or plane, then, should not affect the way it is perceived or developed. The planes of a pebble, blossom, or eyelid are as deserving of structural analysis as are those of a mountain, tree, or man.

It is helpful to think of every joining of planes or volumes, large or small, as interlocking, clasping, impacting, or fusing. The clarity and conviction with which unions are drawn requires more than sensitive perceptual skill. It demands *felt* responses to the ways they join. Although the drawings reproduced in this chapter are highly individual in temperament and intent, they all reveal the artist's feelings about the nature of the unions between planes and masses. Hence, seeing the relative scale, location, direction, and essential shape-state or mass of every plane or form is necessary to the clarity of their various joinings, but feeling the gentle or driving energy behind such joinings invests a drawing with the dynamic character of the subject's structure.

The gestural characteristics of such unions are limitless. They may suggest slow, subtle movements, as in the way the column of the young man's neck in da Empoli's drawing (Figure 6.2) seems to lift gracefully from deep between the shoulder masses that ap-

pear to part and allow its rise. Or they may seem fast and forceful, as in the interlaced race of folds around the young man's waist. They may be given to variously gradual fusions, as in Degas' figure drawing (Figure 6.8), or to sudden abutments of planes and wedge-like interlockings of form-units, as in Carpeaux's drawing (Figure 6.4), and Villon's etching (Figure 6.17). They may be frenzied couplings, as in Delacroix's drawing (Figure 6.5), or rhythmic, as in Leonardo da Vinci's (Figure 6.10). Often, the nature of form-joinings eludes any verbal description.

Pearlstein, in his drawing of two nudes (Figure 6.20), emphasizes the boundaries and unions between form-units by dotted lines,

Figure 6.20
PHILIP PEARLSTEIN (1924–   )
Two Seated Nudes
Wash drawing. 22 x 30 in.
Courtesy, Allan Frumkin Gallery, New York

solid lines, and washes of tone. Note the artist's sensitivity to subtle joinings, such as occur in both torsos. Note, too, how seldom line and tone describe the same edge. Unlike some student drawings in line and tone where every value is encircled by line—as if tones alone cannot establish shapes and edges—here, almost always, either line or tone is used alone.

Another aspect of structure to be considered concerns inner or hidden supports. Some subjects such as human or other living forms, buildings, furniture, or even a log pile are constructed of parts which support and other parts which are supported. These form arrangements create tensions and pressures between the parts of such subjects. Some of these forces are actual, some are implied. When a subject's forms are supported by, suspended from, or attached to an inner skeletal framework such as a human or other skeleton, or when naturally limp materials like cloth or leather are supported by solid masses beneath them, there is real tension and pressure between the visibly "held" and the inner "holder."

In such constructions, the supporting structure, whether skeletal or solid, is sometimes stable, as when a cube supports a cloth draped over it. Removing the cloth does not affect the cube's construction or behavior. Other constructions depend on mutual support among the parts. Two poles holding up a pup tent are themselves held in place by the balanced weight and tensions of its canvas cover, stretched taut when stakes are driven into the ground at each of its four corners. Removing any of these stakes affects the balance of forces and collapses the tent's shape. Both the cloth-covered cube and the tent's framework prevent the collapse of the covering material. But in the case of the tent, the elastic nature of the covering material and the balanced tensions upon it help to contain and support the framework. The human figure's construction is of the latter kind. Its inner supports and outer suspensions assist and restrain each other.

In such subjects the forces of weight and tension—the burdens of support and containment—create folds, bulges, and sags that disclose the strain, resistance, and pressure between the holder and the held. To infuse a drawing with the power to convey the *feel* as well as the *look* of such force and counterforce, the artist must empathize with the struggle between the inner and outer parts of his subject, must feel the weight and strivings of the parts. The force of gravity is an important participant in the struggle between the parts. Supporting frameworks, in addition to the tensions and pressures between themselves and the material they support, also resist the force of gravity upon themselves and the supported material. The sagging and taut folds, the bulges and hollows of inner supported subjects, and the folds and bulges resulting from parts pressed against each other express the struggle within the subject and between it and gravitational pull.

The pressure upon the right shoulder of the figure in Michelangelo's drawing (Figure 6.7), the straining of the bones and muscles of the shoulder and the chest against the thin container of skin, the pressure of the heavy upper body upon the midsection—these are more than accurately noted observations. They are deeply felt responses to the actualities of the figure's structural character—intensified to express the artist's feelings about the drama of the powerful struggle of physical forces within and upon the figure. Likewise, in Delacroix's sketches from a Rubens painting, bone, muscle, and skin all strain, press, and resist each other to achieve a balance of forces. The knee bone of the figure's raised left leg, at the far left of the drawing, is barely constrained by the taut skin covering it. The lower leg drives up hard against the upper, which swells with bulging muscles that tell of the pressure upon them. At the drawing's far right, the bone at the elbow shows the strain of the arm's burden—of its being forced down while it strains to support its load. These actions strike us as highly charged because Delacroix (and Rubens) felt their force, and intensified it.

Empathic responses to the ways in which planes and masses join, and to those generated by a subject's inner and outer structure and weight, help endow a drawing with a "life" that is the graphic equivalent to those qualities seen and felt in living subjects. But such responses are not restricted to organic forms only. Draped fabrics, rock and ice formations, architectural structures, furniture, utensils and tools of various kinds, and numerous other inorganic subjects often suggest some or all of these energies to some degree. Although some of these subjects have inner supports and others do not, the character of their masses can suggest the kinds of union, tension, resistance, and pressure conveyed by

living things, as in the rocks and clouds in Figure 6.10, or in the chair and plant holder in Figure 6.21.

Whether the subject is the human figure or some rock slabs, and whether the energies are actual or inferred, the artist must feel the force of their structural activities as "meant" or necessary—as obligatory actions inherent in the subject's construction. To the extent

Figure 6.21
NATHAN GOLDSTEIN (1927–   )
Mother and Child
Pen, brush and sepia ink. 15 x 16 in.
Collection of Drs. Arje and Elizabeth Latz,
Kiryat Ono, Israel

that we can identify with these actions, our expressive involvement deepens, urging more incisive and direct drawing solutions. Again, responses concerned with the measurable actualities of shape, scale, directions, etc., will record important physical facts, but a sensitivity to the animation and vitality of union, support, containment, and gravity that issue from or affect the subject are necessary to convey the energies inherent in its structural character.

That such energies can come alive in inanimate objects can be seen in Goodman's *Wrapped Still Life* (Figure 6.22). The force with which the table's edges seem to push against the drape, and the drape's own harsh, planar

facets create tensions and rhythms that activate what might otherwise be a dull subject. Indeed, the artist, in emphasizing the structure of the forms and the strong light falling upon them, creates a sense of expectancy and dread.

Pontormo's drawing *Striding Nude* (Figure 6.23) suggests the energies that drive planes and volumes into strong unions, and those issuing from pressures and stresses between inner and outer parts. Note how the volumes around the shoulders, knees, and ankles insert and clasp each other with hard intent. The planes abut with vigorous certainty, enacting the forceful energy of the interlockings among the form-units they produce.

Figure 6.22
SIDNEY GOODMAN (1936–   )
Wrapped Still Life (1970)
Charcoal. 29 3/4 x 36 1/2 in.
Courtesy, Terry Dintenfass, Inc., New York

The skeletal framework emerges from deep within the figure to press against the containing surfaces at the ankles, knees, elbows, and at several places on the torso, creating firm anchors against which the muscles strain. The entire figure seems to vibrate with the activity of forms pressing, straining, and resisting.

Pontormo's interest in such energies is apparent in the way he suggests gestural "ripples" of motion that course through the figure, and lesser ones that move between the parts. These actions are further strengthened by showing some volumes as elongated—as if they are being stretched between fixed points. Such attenuations serve to exaggerate the graceful flow of the forms by stressing rhythmic patterns of growth and diminution among them. Just as Pontormo causes small form-units to rise from, swell, and subside back into larger forms, so major volumes, like the torso, right arm, and right leg suggest a pattern of moving, changing masses. In the right leg, for example, the volume begins at the ankle, swells at the calf and, beginning to subside, is overtaken by the clasping tendons of the upper leg. These, in turn, expand and merge to form one swelling, tubular mass which suddenly erupts into a still greater volume by the addition of the buttock, part of the pelvic area, and some muscles of the lower torso. We see the right leg and hip as *one* volume springing up from the ankle with some velocity, swelling, subsiding, and finally implanting itself deep within the torso. Its last identifiable ripples reach as far as the figure's rib cage.

THE DESIGN OF VOLUMES IN SPACE

Pontormo's interest in structural energy does more than make good use of a subject's clues for its gesturally expressive potentialities. By intensifying them he clarifies another important category of response: the sense of volumes as related by a comprehensible order or plan—a system of abstract affinities. Chapter Eight will further explore the design of volumes, but here it is necessary to grasp something of the basic nature of ordered patterns among volumes, and of the necessity for such order in responsive drawing. There are a

Figure 6.23

JACOPO DA PONTORMO (1494–1556)
Striding Nude
Red and black chalk, heightened with white chalk.
16 x 8 7/8 in.
The Pierpont Morgan Library, New York

number of structural factors that can help extract this sense of order between volumes, whether the volumes comprise a figure, landscape, or still life.

Similarities and contrasts of scale, direction, shape, value, texture, and manner of handling and of form-joinings, as well as the distribution of parts within a spatial arena all contribute to establishing a system of order among volumes. Especially does the distribution of masses, the various ways they overlap and interlock provide strong relationships among volumes. Hence, when Pontormo stresses structural energies coursing through the figure, he also contributes to the sense of its abstract, dynamic actions and patterns.

This is so because sensitivity to a subject's structural condition is largely an awareness of relationships based on similarities and contrasts of scale, direction, location, and shape. The rhythms and affinities these relationships uncover help convey the subject's volume-design. To the extent that an artist wishes to strengthen the sense of volumes as unified by an overall system of associations, *usually based on movement*, he will stress the

Figure 6.24
EDGAR DEGAS (1834–1917)
After the Bath
Charcoal. 13 7/8 x 10 in.
Sterling and Francine Clark Institute, Williamstown

visual bonds between the parts of his subject—the "alikeness" between unlike things—*and* their collective gestural behavior. For example, Pontormo's frequent use of straight lines to define passages of the contours causes these segments to "call" to each other, even when they are separated by great distances in the drawing, as are the straight lines that describe the spinal furrow and the feet. And such kinships reinforce movement-energies.

Conversely, sensitivity to the rhythms and actions in a subject's forms helps discover structural facts. For, in responding to the "rush" and "resistance" of parts, our attention is drawn to the state of the planes and masses that produce such actions. Did Pontormo first see the dynamic or the structural aspects of the right leg—or both simultaneously? It is impossible to say. What is evident in his drawing, however, is his awareness that both of these qualities *are* the leg. Measurement alone can never make forms come alive, any more than empathy can. These two considerations, the mechanics and the dynamics of volumetric structure are interlaced considerations. Both are necessary in apprehending the potentialities for expressive order in nature.

Without the visual links and harmonies among the drawing's marks, and among the forms they produce, even representational content suffers. For whatever subject we may happen to select, it *is* a subject because we see it as having a set of related conditions separate from other forms surrounding it—as having at least a raw unity and spirit. Disregarding the abstract associations by which its unity and spirit can be extracted and enhanced results in works in which even the subject's raw order is broken down—works that are no more than representations of isolated and discordant details, or, even if structurally readable, that lack cohesion and character.

Degas, in his drawing *After the Bath* (Figure 6.24), shows a strong interest in the design of volumes. Although the model's forms must have described something like the action of the drawing's forms, it is evident that Degas extracted and strengthened the continuity of their flow. They rise from the bottom of the page as three simple shapes

Figure 6.25
DOMENIC CRETARA (1946–   )
Reclining Woman Reading
Red chalk and oil wash. 14 x 17 in.
Courtesy of the artist

that become three volumes as they move upward, united in a vigorous curving action continued and intensified by the forms of the upper body. The energy generated by the figure's forms sweeping to the right seems to have an "escape" in the hair that ripples down in a way that answers their rising thrust.

Degas' responses to his subject's volumes, united in a curving motion, is conveyed by virtually every available means. He accents the similarity between the shape and scale of the left leg and two parts of the nearby towel. Note that the lighter of the two shapes of the towel strongly resembles the left leg upside down, while the other towel shape imitates the movement and direction of the leg and the contour of its right side. Degas' use of structural hatchings made of thick, bold, charcoal strokes, introduces a texture that further unites the volumes. He holds his darkest values in reserve while the curving action mounts, and commits them in the curve's "crescendo" in the head and hair—the two forms that, in descending, are in contrast with the rising of the others. Thus, values also help explain the plastic action of the forms. Degas' stressing of the figure as comprised of twin halves, and his treatment of the volumes as somewhat tubular gives additional unity and force to the figure's forms. Note how emphatically he overlaps the lower part of the head with the right shoulder, and how powerfully the right hand is forced into the towel.

Again, in Cretara's drawing *Reclining Woman, Reading* (Figure 6.25), a sound structural knowledge and a keen dynamic sensibility combine to create an image that is alive at both its representational and abstract levels. Here, too, structural insights uncover dynamic actions and vice versa.

Whether we emphasize the structure of volumes or their designed flow, both considerations must be understood as interrelated aspects of any form. Without the energies that structural conditions provide, volumes are dead bulk; without the dynamic energies that move among the marks, they are discomposed as well.

In the following exercise, a series of drawings will stress the material discussed in this chapter. As you first look at your subject,

most of its perspective, planes, system of support, the forces that drive them, and the subject's overall design potentialities may not be at all apparent. After all, you are looking for many things, and many of them are elusive and subtle. Their presence is better discovered by searching with an empathic as well as an analytical eye.

exercise 6A

There are seven drawings in this exercise section. For the first five, use an easily erasable medium such as vine charcoal sticks or a 5B or 6B graphite pencil, on any suitable surface. For the sixth drawing, use only pen and ink. There are no restrictions on media for the last drawing. Again, avoid tiny drawings.

Here, your attention must focus on the structural facts and forces of your subject: on its measurements and relationships of length, scale, shape, direction, location, value, edge, and on the rhythms and movements of its masses. In fact, your involvement in discerning these qualities should be so exclusive that the resulting drawings will be something of a surprising byproduct of your experience in responding to the constructional, relational, and gestural aspects of your subject. The real value of these drawings is more in the quality of the realizations and insights they provide than in their successful accomplishment on the page. In responsive drawing, as in the development of any other ability, concept and experience precede successful usage. Here then, you must, strange as it may seem, concentrate on this new kind of searching, rather than on results.

drawing 1
Collect seven or eight small objects of a simple volumetric nature. Books, boxes, cups, bowls or anything else that is basically box-like, cylindrical, etc., are usable, but need not be severely geometrical in form. Fruits and vegetables, shoes, shells, even rocks, will do. Cover some of these with a thin fabric such as cotton or jersey. Some of the objects may be partially uncovered. Place the remaining objects upon the fabric, amongst the fully or partially hidden objects beneath it. Arrange all the objects in ways that reveal something of the forms of the hidden ones and that create strong protrusions, hollows, sagging and taut folds, and overlaps. The tensions and pressures produced will be roughly similar to those on the surfaces of subjects formed around skeletal frames. The overall arrangement should not be an

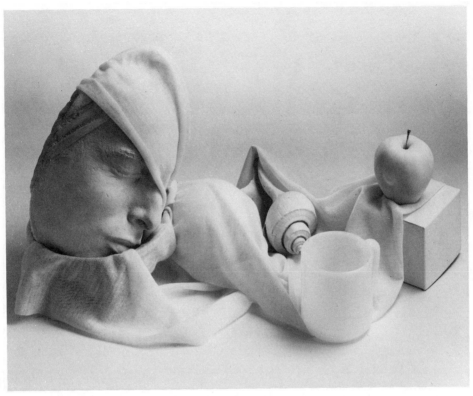

Figure 6.26

extended, rambling one, but somewhat compacted, as in Figure 6.26.

This is a twenty-five minute drawing. In the first five minutes draw in a schematic and investigatory way to establish a preliminary structural framework. That is, broaden your gestural approach to include a greater emphasis on establishing the subject's main directions, shapes, scale relationships, and volume summaries. To do this, you must disregard all surface effects of light and texture, and all small details, *including minor planar conditions.* Avoid making this merely a contour drawing, but "get inside" a form's boundaries to define major planar joinings. Here, you will draw edges in a simplified way, measuring the lengths between pronounced changes in direction, noting only prominent turnings and angles. This five-minute phase has the general character and goal of gesture drawing, but it attempts to measure, however broadly, the subject's major structural actualities. It is somewhat similar in concept to that of Exercise 5B in the previous chapter. There, the need to clarify and stress foreshortening, overlap, convergence, etc., led us to draw the simplest available geometric volume a part could be reduced to without losing its basic volume character. Thus, a head became a block *or* cylinder, because a visual case exists for either as an acceptable geometric core form. Here, such extreme generality is not desirable. Although the clarity of the subject's foreshortenings, overlaps, etc., is just as important in this drawing as in Exercise 5B, clarity now should not be gained at the expense of the general structural spirit, as well as character of the subject's parts. Grasping the essentials of the subject's action and structure in the first five minutes is important to the development of the volumes in the remaining twenty minutes.

Figure 6.27 suggests a degree of gestural and structural summary, and of a stress on directions that the arrangement in Figure 6.26 could be reduced to. Note the use of structural hatchings to suggest some major planes, and the diagrammatic lines feeling out both solid mass and spatial areas. Note, too, the emphasis on pressures, tensions, and weight, and on the rhythms and movements between the parts.

This illustration should not influence you to emulate its particular characteristics—its handwriting. It is not intended in a how-to-do-it sense, but as an example of a serviceable degree of development of the subject's forms and forces in the five-minute phase. It *is* intended to suggest a degree of emphasis on direction, volume summary, and the energies of structural and plastic forces, specific enough to establish important aspects of

Figure 6.27

the subject's major masses, and general enough to be free of lesser—and for the moment—complicating ones. To summarize in a more sweeping way produces generalities too removed from measurable actualities, and restricts responses to the structural and dynamic energies. To draw the arrangement in a much less generalized way than that suggested in Figure 6.27 risks missing some basic observations having to do with direction and essential mass, as well as with relationships of scale and location, and the energies that flow between the parts. Drawings that do not grasp the subject's pattern of volumes in space cannot become fully organized.

In this five-minute phase, your goal is to extract from the arrangement the simplified nature of its various volumes and their relationship to each other, and to convey the dynamic forces that move among them. Your attention, then, should focus as much on seeing and feeling the kinships between parts as on analyzing them separately. Look for independent parts that may share a common direction, scale, or value by comparing such angles, sizes, and tones with those of parts placed far from as well as near to each other. Stress the strongest pressures and tensions, and call forward the subject's overall design theme—the rhythmic order of its parts.

This phase of the drawing is limited to five minutes for the same reason that the gestural drawings in Chapter One were held to even briefer limits. It encourages a search for essentials before particulars.

In the second part of this drawing, the emphasis should shift to an analysis of the shape, scale, angle, and location of smaller planes—those which explain the various surface irregularities of the subject's components and any substantial volume variations formed by their unions. Even here, however, you should distinguish between those smaller, or *secondary planes* that advance your explanation of a part's structure, and those which, because of their tiny scale—such as the hundreds of small planes in an extremely wrinkled cloth—merely crowd the drawing with unimportant, "busy" details. When a surface is comprised of such tiny planes, most artists draw only a few here and there to imply their presence throughout the object. Drawing them all often weakens a form's volumetric clarity, which is conveyed by the primary and secondary planes, not by the multitude of tiny ones.

Beginning anywhere on the drawing, compare any generalized volume with its original in the arrangement. If the generalized volume represents a rather geometrically simple object such as a book or cup, you may find little to add to your initial observations. Instead you may want to adjust its direction, scale, or contour. If it represents a complex and irregular object such as a pillow (Figure 6.28A), it will require the addition of its secondary planes to convey its unique structural and expressive character (Figure 6.28B).

In the case of a volume formed around and enclosing a space, as, for example, a cup, consider this enclosed space as a "negative" volume. Instead of having it result from observations of the cup's solid parts, study the space as one more measurable component of the cup. Seen directly, its direction, scale, and shape requirements may warrant changes in your drawing of the cup's solid parts.

Now you are more precisely clarifying the subject's physical facts, moving energies, and overall rhythmic order. Try to keep a balanced attitude to all three considerations. Becoming too in-

Figure 6.28

A

B

tellectually engrossed in the technicalities of a complex joining of planes or form-units may result in correct but cold passages in the drawing. Conversely, overreacting to the gestural character of such a union may produce frenzied ambiguities. And, considering both the structural and dynamic behavior of a particular union to the exclusion of its relationship to the rest of the drawing's forms may break the continuity of the design.

Here, we should consider a common error in placement. Sometimes two adjacent objects are drawn so close that an overhead view would show them to be interpenetrated. Be sure that you allow enough room for the bodies of closely placed objects. Although your drawing of any volume stops at its contours, your ability to believe in the existence of its unseen back must be strong enough to prevent the invasion of one solid by another.

As you draw, try to feel the heaviness of the objects and the "determined" resistance of the fabric-supporting solids. Thinking of the fabric as sopping wet helps to respond to its surrender to the pull of gravity. This also helps explain the form of the objects covered by the fabric.

As the drawing develops, refer to the principles of perspective to prove or help clarify any part of the drawing that seems troublesome. In fact, perspective considerations have been an influence throughout the drawing. Now, a concentrated examination of relative distance, scale, and convergence, and any other perspective consideration dealt with in Chapter Five can help you adjust some faulty or confusing passages.

drawing 2

You have thirty-five minutes for the second drawing. This time, select three or four of the objects used in the first drawing and place them inside a cloth container, such as a laundry bag or pillowcase. Tie the container at the top with a rope long enough to tie onto some overhead support such as a rafter or pipe, enabling the container to hang free. As you draw, notice the folds caused by the weight of the container pulling against its restraining rope. At the top of the container they will be extremely pronounced. Lower down, the objects inside it will press against the fabric, revealing parts of their form. Try to stress this struggle between the container and its restrainer, and between the container and the objects inside.

Again, begin the drawing with a five-minute analytical-gestural search for direction, location, shape, scale, etc. Again, establish a preliminary armature based on the subject's essential structure and action.

In the remaining thirty minutes, spread your attention over the entire subject, advancing it together. Here, be especially insistent on showing the pressures and tensions between the parts of the subject. Do not hesitate to make moderate adjustments to help intensify these forces — to exaggerate the weight of the objects and the pliancy of the container. Here, too, search for the abstract energies — the rhythms and movements — that organize the subject into a system of visually related forms, each of which participates in the structural *and* design activities.

drawing 3

This, too, is a thirty-five minute drawing. This time, the human figure, preferably nude, should be used. If a draped figure is used, the attire should be simple and should not cause complex folds or billowing shapes. Again, begin with a five-minute analytical-gestural drawing. The forms should be simplified enough to help you establish the foreshortening of forms with some ease.

In the first drawing of this exercise, the independent nature of the objects helped you to understand their volume better. The objects were rather simple in their construction, and establishing their generalized volume-state was correspondingly simple. Now the subject is composed of complex organic forms, rooted in the central form of the torso — a single, extended system of inner-supported masses. Pose the model to avoid complicated overlappings of the limbs. This helps maintain your awareness of its continuity — its oneness. Therefore, a simple standing or reclining pose is most suitable.

In such less compacted poses the forms are seen as flowing into one another. For example, there is no one place on a leg where we can see the ankle as ending and the lower leg beginning with sausage-link clarity. Instead, there is an interlaced, almost braided system of bone, tendon, and muscle, producing transitional planar passages. Sometimes these planes are subtle and fluid (Figure 6.8); sometimes they erupt from the surface forming clearly carved volume variations (Figure 6.7). Often, these transitional planar "avenues" can be traced for long distances above and below a joining of parts, adding to the flow of the forms. As your drawing continues beyond the five-minute phase, try to see the several planes and the volumes they form, that explain these transitions. Their visibility is partly due to the yielding, pliant character of the skin, which, like the fabric, will collapse unless supported by a framework. As the inner system of bone, tendon, muscle, and fatty tissue interact, their forms, pressed against the elastic skin, like the objects in the suspended container, reveal their support function and some of their volume by the amount of pressure they exert on the figure's surfaces.

In the remaining thirty minutes, try to see and feel the subject's structural behavior as having its origins deep inside, the result of forms and forces that press against the figure's interior walls. As before, first establish the secondary planes and then consider the smaller ones. Use only those smaller planes necessary to explain the important structural characteristics of the figure's forms. Such a restriction usually reveals how much the impression of structured volume is carried by the primary and secondary planes. Often, only a few smaller planes are required, or, as in Delacroix's drawing *Nude Woman* (Figure 6.16), desired. Looking at this drawing we know that the artist has omitted many of the planes of the female figure, but nowhere are we left with blank, flat areas. The figure's "topography" is readable everywhere. Here, the volumes owe much of their sculptural strength to Delacroix's emphasis upon those larger planes that denote important changes in the direction of a volume's surface. Such bold, selective carving of large forms by large planes itself gives volumes power and impact. It *is* impressive when so little can express so much. This is not to suggest that your drawing should stop at this degree of volume-revealing information. Delacroix did because he felt this drawing fulfilled his purpose at its present stage. His goals were realized. What *is* suggested by the example of this drawing is the inadvisability of stopping short of this degree of volume building, to build such volumes by their larger planes, and to avoid the enticements of little details as ends in themselves.

drawing 4

This drawing will take one hour. Use only a segment of the figure for your subject. It can be an arm, leg, torso, or head, from any challenging view of the form, as in Figures 6.29 and 6.30. Draw large — a little over actual size. Again, begin with an analytical-gestural search for the volume fundamentals described earlier. This time, however, take as much time as you need to establish these broad generalities. Now you have about twice as much time as you had for the previous drawing in which to draw considerably less of the figure. This will permit you to include many of the smaller planar changes that would ordinarily be omitted in drawings limited to less time, or to a smaller scale. In closing in on a part of the former whole, you will find that what are small planes in drawings of the segment as part of the entire figure, here are elevated to the status of primary and secondary planes. As in the previous drawings, these should, of course, be developed first.

The longer drawing time allows you to make a more probing study of quite small structural details. As you begin to include these, be sure to

Figure 6.29
BARTOLOMEO PASSAROTTI (1529–1592)
Studies of an Arm
Chalk.
Courtesy, Museum of Fine Arts, Boston
Gift of Henry P. Rossiter

keep them subordinate to the larger planes and masses. You may want to explain all the small volumetric activity, as in Figure 6.29, or show it as all but absorbed by the major mass, as in Figure 6.30. Whichever way you develop the drawing, remember to search out the structure by working from the general to the specific, and to show the unity of a major mass regardless of the amount of planar change in its terrain. Here, as in the previous drawings, look for the pressures and tensions between the holder and the held, for the way in which parts join, and for the design of the segment—the continuity among its parts. Avoid involvements with illumination where it does not help explain volume, and use direction-informing hatchings to show the various tilts of the planes, as in Figure 6.29. Notice that the hatchings in Figure 6.30 all move in the same direction. Here, surface

changes are conveyed by the variations in their density and in their value. Although such line variations do explain the subject's terrain, changing the direction of lines to correspond to the direction of the planes they describe is an important aid in explaining the subject's surface-state.

Your goal here is to develop a drawing so structurally clear and convincing that a sculptor could use it as a guide for sculptural work and never be confused in understanding the general structural volume or the various planar changes on its surfaces.

drawing 5
This drawing is limited to fifteen minutes. Pose the model in some animated position. There is no time limit for establishing the broad volume generalities. You may, if you choose, attac˪

Figure 6.30
Follower of LEONARDO DA VINCI
Head of a Woman
Metalpoint on greenish prepared paper.
5 7/8 x 4 7/8 in.
Sterling and Francine Clark Institute,
Williamstown

directly, intending each mark as part of your final statement. In this case, begin in a gestural way, as described in Chapter One. Whether or not you employ an underdrawing stage, continue to stress the major planes and masses first.

In the previous four drawings, establishing a preliminary structural and dynamic scaffold permitted you to develop your drawings in the knowledge that all early explorations were tentative—that they would largely be absorbed and altered by later drawing. Here, should you choose to work directly, every mark must respond to the subject with feeling and decisiveness. Instead of emphasizing analysis first and "conclusions" later, in direct drawing these considerations are parts of the same percept and the same action.

You may find that the reduced time demands a more energetic and broader approach to your subject. This can assist rather than restrict your grasp of the essentials. Figures 6.23, 6.24, and 6.25 show the kinds of energy and excitement such a spontaneous approach can reveal. This is knowledgeable simplicity, not empty flourish. Your

drawing, too, should aim for volume in simple, sculptural terms. And it should convey the structural and abstract energies that make it more than just bulk.

drawing 6

Using pen and ink (a ball-point pen will also work well here) and using Leonardo da Vinci's drawing (Figure 6.10) as a rough guide, make a drawing no smaller than 18″ × 22″ of some rock formations. Your "models" can be any two or three interesting stones or pebbles. Arrange them in a good light and proceed to draw large enough to fill the page. Because drawing in pen and ink to develop the structure of complex forms you have no preconceived notions about takes time, there is no time limit on this drawing. This being the case, you might want to make your rock formation more permanent by gluing the stones to a stiff support. As in the previous drawing, preliminary underdrawing must be held to a minimum, for erasures are not possible. Your drawing is to carry the clarification of the rock's terrain further than da Vinci does. His drawing is an investigatory probe; yours is to be an extended realization of the subject's forms, and of the *light* and *textures* upon it. The challenge here is not only to build solid volumes using a medium that restricts underdrawing and erasures, but to construct them well enough to show the surface effects of local-tone, light, and texture without being buried or flattened under such surface detail. Keeping such surface changes from obscuring the forms will demand a strong grasp of each part's structure, and the discipline to keep retinal impressions from overruling structural ones.

drawing 7

This drawing allows you a great deal of free choice. *You* set the time limit, determine how much time, if any, to use for a preparatory stage, and select both the subject and the medium. Although the figure is an excellent subject for this largely self-directed drawing, you may want to apply the concepts and procedures you have been practicing in this section to a landscape, animal form, interior, or other subject.

You will even decide whether constructing volume is to be a dominant or supporting theme of this drawing. Your goal is to regard what you now know about volume building more as a tool (albeit an important one) of responsive drawing, and use it here as your interests require. Whether it will be central to your drawing's theme or subdued by other visual interests should now depend on your

first, generalized responses to your subject—let the subject suggest the means and even the medium. But, however subordinated the role of volume may be in this exercise, and however subjectively you state the forms, none should be ambiguously drawn or discordant in the drawing.

Creating the impression of convincing structured volume is both a demanding perceptual challenge and an emotional experience. It calls for an understanding (and inter-working) of gesture, line, shape, value, perspective, and the ability to feel a subject's structural and dynamic energies, as well as measure its actualities of scale, location, direction, and length. It is the quality of the negotiations among these considerations that determines the quality of the resulting volumes. By knowing what is involved in creating volumes we also know what is involved in subduing them. In this way, our control of the images we make is expanded.

The necessity for, and logic of, the concepts and processes discussed in this chapter become more evident the more you confront the challenge of creating convincing volumes. Not because they convince as a *system*, but as an *approach*. These concepts and processes require and deserve your patience and tireless efforts to see, feel, and know volume.

CHAPTER SEVEN

MEDIA AND MATERIALS

the tools of drawing

A DEFINITION

For the responsive artist, the substances that produce the lines and tones of drawing—the *media*—and the papers and boards that receive them—the *surfaces* or *supports*—simultaneously carry and influence his responses and thus are important in the forming of his works.

The beginning student may be amazed at how many kinds of drawing media are available at the larger art stores. Much of this apparent variety is often the same media, stocked in various brands. Fifteen or more India inks may be displayed, representing no more than three or four distinctly different kinds, made by as many manufacturers. Also, there are the various specialized media and materials for the graphic designer. Although some of these can be used for any kind of drawing, the student can disregard the more exotic paraphernalia of the advertising artist.

This still leaves a wide variety of drawing media. But the beginner need not immediately experiment with many. Considering the virtually endless combinations of media

and surfaces, it would be practically impossible to explore the entire range of available supplies. Nor should one go to the other extreme and remain indifferent. Because both an indifference to media and a compulsive search for "the right one" are unsound attitudes, the student should develop an interest in exploring media, but should recognize that, while they can significantly aid, they cannot invent creative solutions. The best guides in the investigation of additional media are the student's own needs and curiosity, as his studies progress.

Some order can be made of the varieties of media by recognizing that they are all applied to a surface either by adhesion or intromission. The adhesive media are the dry, or *abrasive media*, applied by rubbing off particles onto the grain, or *tooth*, of the surface. The intromissive media are the wet, or *fluid media*. These have pigment particles suspended in a holding agent, or *binder*, and water. Applied in a liquid state, the pigment, binder, and water are absorbed in quantities that depend on the porous nature of the sup-

174

port. The water evaporates, but the binder dries among the fibers of the support, holding the pigment particles in place.

Every medium has its intrinsic characteristics and technical limits. Some, such as a hard graphite pencil, have pronounced characteristics and definite limits. Others, like brush and ink, have an almost limitless ability to change character, and answer virtually every graphic demand.

Although every medium is distinct in its character and range of usage, the graphic possibilities of each can never be fully exhausted. In an age of media proliferation that includes plastics, film, neon, and power-driven works, the common "lead," or graphite pencil is still capable of new uses. Because a medium reflects the user's sensitivity to it as well as his judgments about its graphic function, some new accents of usage are always possible. If the user is "blind" to a medium's nature and range, or influenced by the way others have used it, his responses will be poorly or derivatively expressed. But if he finds the medium compatible with his intent, and if his creative themes are original, that is, *genuinely* personal, his rapport with the medium can create still another unique use of it. There can be as many original uses of a medium as there are inventive artists for whom its nature is congenial and stimulating. Although the technical limits of a medium cannot be appealed, the scope of its behavior within these limits is bounded only by the artist's sensitivity to the medium and by his creative wit.

The first time we manipulate a new tool or medium, we experiment with it in various ways that interest us. If we are given to slow, deliberate statements, or fast, impulsive ones, we want to know if it is responsive to such demands. By such exploration we learn how the medium *feels*—literally. The heft of the instrument, the drag or flow of dry or wet media, the overall tactile nature of its properties are important considerations. We test its behavior in maneuvers we have required of other media to make comparisons. We try to learn its character and consider its potentialities. These manipulations are instructive. They not only tell us what a medium or tool is like, they tell us something about our overall attitude and interests—what we are looking for in a medium or tool is a clue to how we want to draw.

A medium's range and nature can influence the artist's tactics. He is not likely to draw a cloud formation with pen and ink in the same way he would with charcoal. Artist's tend to use a medium's strengths and avoid forcing it to do what it cannot do well. Congenial media will stimulate and extend our range of responses, but do not determine them. Thus, the medium does influence but should never dominate a drawing's imagery.

A versatility with a wide number of media is convenient and useful, but such a pursuit must not be overstressed. Picasso is equally at home with pen and ink, chalk, crayon, and a number of other media. But Holbein, Ingres, and many others used only one or two media to produce most of their drawings. What is important is how well a medium assists our expression. The medium used in every instance should be one that the artist feels a rapport with for its aptness—an intuitive sense of its compatibility—with his intent, and with the nature of the subject.

But a word of caution. Any new medium deserves more than a brief trial. All media require time and repeated use to comprehend and control. During a period of exploration, it *is* helpful to see how others have used a medium, to gain some idea of its range. In the case of the graphite pencil, one can look at drawings by artists as different in temperament and approach as Ingres (Figure 3.32), Degas (Figure 6.8), Cézanne (Figure 6.11), Eilshemius (Figure 7.1), and Klee (Figure 7.2), to see how flexible a tool it is.

Sometimes, a medium may work poorly on one kind of surface but should not be rejected until other kinds of paper have been tried. At times, the problems with a medium are traceable to the scale of the drawings. Sometimes, pen and ink appears weak in drawings of large dimensions, and charcoal seems too broad and textured in a small drawing area. In general, the student should experiment freely for a few months with a medium before deciding about its suitability to his needs. He should occasionally combine media and work against, as well as with, their characteristics. He should use them in drawings of various sizes, for various purposes.

Figure 7.1
LOUIS M. EILSHEMIUS (1864–1942)
Old Saw Mill (1959)
Pencil. 11.5 x 15.3 cm.
Courtesy of Amherst College, Mass.
Gift of Mr. Roy R. Neuberger

Our first, unfavorable reactions to a material may survive the period of exploration—but they may not. It is not uncommon for many beginners to prefer "neat" media such as the harder degrees of graphite or charcoal pencils, which have the additional "advantage" of being more or less erasable. Other media, such as conté crayons or brush and ink, are bolder, broader media and cannot be erased. Do not reject an unfamiliar medium because of its bold or permanent nature. It can help guide you away from minor niceties and toward major essentials. Usually, the stronger, more animated results of such media are soon recognized by the student concerned with analysis and expression, rather than exposition and polish.

We should realize that the medium has too often been blamed for shortcomings of perception *and* conception. Although after an adequate period of trial we may wisely set aside a particular medium as unsuited to our needs, we must always guard against rejecting one because it has not solved perceptual or creative problems. As noted earlier, a compatible medium *will* stimulate invention—*will* ease and enhance expression—but cannot itself *provide* perceptions or directly contribute concepts. The medium is an integral part of the graphic message, but not the message itself.

Beginning with the cave artists, who discovered painting and drawing possibilities in natural chalks and clay, artists have always shown ingenuity in adapting any material that suggested potential as a medium or tool. The need to create certain textural, tonal, or color effects, or to improvise when art supplies were unavailable, has stimulated the invention of many tools and materials in use today. The first painting knife may well have been an artist's palette scraper, used in a moment when a heavy impasto was needed. For years, soft bread was used as a charcoal eraser. Crumpled paper dabbed with ink, watercolor, or opaque paint produced interesting results, and this is now a common practice. Fingers were probably man's first "brushes," and there are few artists who do not add or adjust a tone or line in this way.

Finding himself without a pen or brush, an artist may apply ink or paint with a twig, a cotton swab, sponge, matchstick, or any one of a score or more of adaptable applicators. When the medium itself was unavailable, coffee or tea have been used, as has food coloring, iodine, and similar staining liquids. Al-

most any substance that can make a mark, and any surface that can receive it may serve as drawing materials. Sometimes tools and media discovered in an emergency situation, or in free experiment, have become favored media for some artists. One contemporary watercolorist of note for years regularly used Mercurochrome to produce golden reds, and executed his works on common shelf paper. Too often, however, as in this case, such innovations lack permanence or adequate control.

The abrasive media in common usage can be grouped into four general divisions: the several kinds of charcoal-based media; graphite, with clay or carbon mixtures; the several kinds of chalks; and the fatty-based crayons. The fluid media include: waterproof and washable inks; transparent watercolors; and the several more or less opaque water-based paints. Sometimes thinned oil paint is also used as a drawing medium—a practice of long standing.

Figure 7.2
PAUL KLEE (1879–1940)
Trees behind Rocks
Pencil. 8 1/4 x 13 in.
The Solomon R. Guggenheim Museum

Figure 7.3
HONORÉ DAUMIER (1808–1879)
Connoisseurs
Watercolor, charcoal and pencil.
10 1/4 x 7 5/8 in.
The Cleveland Museum of Art,
Dudley P. Allen Fund

Often dry and wet media are intermixed. In Daumier's *Connoisseurs* (Figure 7.3), graphite pencil, charcoal, and watercolor washes are used. Mixed-media drawings often result from the structural and expressive needs of the moment. If, as a drawing develops, the artist finds that new creative possibilities suggested by the subject or the emerging image warrant a change in strategy, he will use whatever additional media are then required.

Sometimes an artist's strategy must necessarily include several media. Daumier's drawing seems to be one of these. Here, the soft, vague charcoal lines appear as a first, gestural underdrawing, as can be seen by the preliminary indications of a figure on the far left. Graphite lines delineate the forms more specifi-

cally, and watercolor washes convey the local tones and the broad modelling of the forms. Note the integration of the media; the drawing has no sizable segment expressed by only one medium. Each is active everywhere.

Unless media and materials are technically or chemically incompatible, they can be combined in any way that offers a solution to our desired goals. "Rules" for using the various media have often presented unnecessary barriers to creative expression. Many of these prescriptions for usage grew up around those procedures that direct the user toward a medium's most natural characteristics, or which have proven successful in the past. For example, some artists still insist that the use of watercolors must be limited to transparent washes. To include opaque passages is considered an illegitimate or impure use of the medium. But such a peremptory view stands in the way of an objective evaluation of works that disregard this "rule." Whether opaque passages help or hurt a watercolor drawing must be decided on its merits as a visual system of expressive order, not on its conformity to established codes of usage. Such codes, begun as well-intentioned suggestions, sometimes have, over the years, hardened into unquestioned policies that are, in the light of subsequent aesthetic attitudes, no longer supportable. Today the justification for the use of any medium or combination of media can only be found in the artistic worth of the work in question.

Because successful drawings always disclose a happy union of their meaning and the means used, every great drawing is a virtuoso performance of the medium used. But placing the emphasis on a display of technical facility shifts the emphasis in drawing from analysis and expression to deliberate performance. Drawings then become not the result of an artist's interpretation of nature, but a show of skill in manipulating tools. When such clever usage becomes his primary objective, then a drawing's *real* subject has become the exhibit of an artist's facility with materials—a dubious goal.

THE ABRASIVE MEDIA

The common *stick*, or *vine charcoal* (Figure 7.4), possibly used in prehistoric times, continues to be a popular medium. Stick charcoal is simply carbonized wood. Usually of willow, beech, or vine branches, the longer they are allowed to carbonize in a sealed chamber, the softer the charcoal sticks become, producing darker lines and tones. Because charcoal has no holding, or adhesive agent—no binder, it is an especially *friable* material; that is, it can be very easily crushed into a powder. It depends, as do most abrasive media, on a surface that has a tooth, however fine or rough. By rubbing charcoal (or any abrasive medium) across such a roughened surface, minute particles are filed away and lodge among the hills and valleys of the paper's surface (Figure 7.5).

Being extremely friable, stick charcoal needs only light pressure to mark a surface. Its particles are not usually embedded deeply into a paper's grain, and erase or dust off easily.

Figure 7.4
Charcoal and chalk media. From left to right: compressed charcoal stick, soft chalk, conté crayon, hard chalk, sanguine red conté crayon, soft charcoal block, and white conté crayon. At bottom, stick charcoal.

Figure 7.5
Bold, heavy strokes drive charcoal stick particles into the "valleys" of a paper's surface texture. Light strokes deposit the particles only on the "hilltops."

Charcoal can be repeatedly erased and reworked. It can, when sharpened on a sandpaper block, produce quite delicate lines. When used on its side, stick charcoal makes bold, broad tones. Because of its easy application and removal, and its wide range of effects, it has been used for centuries to make the preparatory drawings that underlie many oil paintings. Such drawings, when they are developed to the desired degree, can easily be isolated by spraying with a weak solution of shellac or lacquer, called *fixative*, or the draw-

Figure 7.6
PIET MONDRIAN (1872–1944)
Chrysanthemum
Charcoal. 24 3/4 x 15 1/8 in.
Smith College Museum of Art

ing can simply be dusted away as the painting develops. For all these reasons, too, around the beginning of the nineteenth century charcoal became the standard drawing medium in the European art academies. Its easy handling made stick charcoal an especially popular medium for making sustained, closely observed studies.

Although charcoal was and continues to be used for final drawings, its fragile hold on the paper, until fixed, makes it difficult to retain dark tones upon the page, or avoid smearing. The unwary student who sneezes toward a drawing heavily laden with charcoal may find his drawing suddenly faded, the particles "exploded" on the page. Fixing the drawing prevents this, but then erasure becomes almost impossible. One solution to the problem is to use fixative as the drawing progresses, at stages when there are not likely to be any subsequent changes of major tones or lines. Fixative does not prevent additional drawing over fixed areas. In fact, fixing helps produce darker tones because the earlier charcoal layers, now encased in the fixing material, form a new, firm tooth and can hold new charcoal particles better.

Although stick charcoal's tonal range does not extend as far as the rich black possible with chalks and crayons, it permits a wide enough range for most drawing purposes and styles. It can be used for subtle tonal and line drawing, as in Figures 7.6 and 7.7, or for bold, brooding ones, such as Hopper's study (Figure 7.8), especially when a good quality of soft charcoal is used on an intensely white surface. Unlike most of the other abrasive media, which can hold on surfaces with a very fine tooth, stick charcoal's weak holding power will fail on such smooth surfaces. Even some of the smoother types of newsprint paper do not take charcoal well.

Compressed charcoal, made by pulverizing charcoal, adding a binding agent, and compressing it into small cylinders or square-sided sticks, produces richer dark tones, has good holding power, and is less easily erased than stick charcoal. Charcoal in this form is sometimes regarded as black chalk. Manufactured in varying degrees of softness, its character is controlled by the amount of binder added. The hardest compressed charcoal sticks

Figure 7.7
HENRI DE TOULOUSE-LAUTREC (1864–1901)
The Model Nizzavona
Charcoal. 61 x 47 cm.
Courtesy of The Art Institute of Chicago

Figure 7.8
EDWARD HOPPER (1882–1967)
Sketch for "Manhattan Bridge Loop"
Charcoal. 6 x 11 in.
Addison Gallery of American Art, Andover, Mass.

181

Figure 7.9
HANS HOLBEIN, the Younger (1497–1543)
Cécily Heron
Natural black chalk. 15 x 11 1/8 in.
Royal Collection, Windsor Castle

though this can provide handsome results (Figure 7.11), it can have inhibiting effects on the handling of large drawings. It is generally used for works of a small scale, or in conjunction with the broader charcoal media when linear or tonal statements of a more precise nature are required.

All members of the charcoal family are intermixable and frequently used together. Compressed charcoal is often used to deepen values and add accents to stick charcoal drawings. Charcoal media work well with water-based ones in mixed media combinations, as in Figure 7.3.

The term *chalk* has been freely applied to a wide variety of friable media, including those of a fatty-based composition. Originally, the term referred to the natural chalks, now rarely available. Today, the differences between various types of manufactured chalks that are a mixture of dry pigments and non-fatty binders, are hard to define. With black chalks, even the line dividing them from compressed charcoal is hardly discernible. Pulverized charcoal is just one of several dry pigments used in the manufacture of some chalks. It is difficult to group types of chalks because of the many possible combinations of

have some of the characteristics of the natural black chalks in use from the fifteenth century to the nineteenth century, when good quality natural black chalks became less available. Formed of various colored earths, minerals, and carbon mixtures, natural chalks were available in black and several shades of brown and earth red. Most natural black chalks (Figure 7.9) seem to smear less and permit a precision not as easily attainable with the softer, manufactured chalks.

Compressed charcoal, available in various degrees of softness, is also manufactured in pencil form, and referred to as *charcoal* or *carbon pencils* (Figure 7.10). Fashioned into slender "leads," it is also sold in packets, for use in holders.

The thin lines possible with a charcoal pencil allow for a more delicate line use. Al-

Figure 7.10
Chalks in pencil form. From left to right: white conté crayon pencil, compressed charcoal pencil with string for exposing additional chalk, sanguine red conté crayon pencil, mechanical holder with thin chalk sticks, hard compressed charcoal pencil, mechanical holder with broad chalk stick.

Figure 7.11
PABLO PICASSO (1881–1974)
The Donkey Driver
Carbon pencil. 10 5/16 x 7 7/8 in.
The Cleveland Museum of Art
Leonard C. Hanna, Jr. Collection

pigments, binders, and other additives, and the particular formulas of the various manufacturers. The term *pastel* has come to be associated with the great variety of colored chalks; but black pastel is generally made of ivory-black pigment (charred bone), gum arabic, ball clay, and, sometimes, other materials often found in other types of black chalk.

Harder to classify are those chalks that have a slightly waxy binder but are, in use, much closer to the more friable chalks than to crayons. All chalks can be erased to some degree, but those having a waxy base are far less erasable. The popular conté crayon is such a medium. Its slightly fatty, smooth flow (especially pronounced in the sanguine, or

earth red, color), still retains some of the look and feel of the more erasable, drier chalks. Conté crayon seems to bridge the division between chalks and the family of waxy-based media called *crayons* (see Figures 2.10, 4.25, and 4.37).

Chalks range from the very soft and "painterly" ones (as used in Figure 4.28), to those of quite hard consistency that require some pressure to produce dark tones (see Figure 2.23). Because of the various types and colors of chalks available, the student should experiment with several. Their differences in behavior are often subtle, and any type of chalk is capable of quite differing effects when used on papers of various grains. To-

Figure 7.12
JEAN HONORÉ FRAGONARD (1732–1806)
Woman Standing with Hand on Hip
Red chalk. 15 3/4 x 9 3/4 in.
Fogg Art Museum, Harvard University
Bequest of Meta and Paul J. Sachs

day, an excellent choice of blacks, browns, grays, earth reds, and white is available, as are other colors.

Fragonard's drawing (Figure 7.12) in red chalk shows a sensitive understanding of the broad, painterly qualities that the softer chalks are capable of. Fragonard utilizes chalk's capacity for suggesting light, establishing planes, and conveying strong calligraphic statements. The rich texture of soft manufactured chalks is apparent in Degas' *Jockey on a Rearing Horse* (Figure 7.13). Their rugged power lends itself well to such bold statements. Whistler's study for an etching (Figure 7.14) shows the mellow dark tones that chalk can produce. Note that the artist achieves these subtle tonal harmonies by hatched lines, and that the blending of chalk tones, so favored by the beginner, is seldom relied on in the chalk drawings of old or contemporary masters, although the fusing of tones can be an effective tactic, as Ipousteguy's drawing shows (see Figure 2.10).

Chalks are often used in combination with other media. Moore's drawing of miners (Figure 7.15) is a mixed media work in black,

Figure 7.13
EDGAR DEGAS (1834–1917)
Jockey on a Rearing Horse
Black, olive and light green chalk.
9 1/4 x 14 1/4 in.
Sterling and Francine Clark Institute,
Williamstown

Figure 7.14
JAMES McNEILL WHISTLER (1834–1903)
Study for "Weary"
Black chalk. 9 5/8 x 6 7/8 in.
Sterling and Francine Clark Art Institute, Williamstown

Figure 7.15
HENRY MOORE (1898–   )
Miners at Work on a Coal Face
Black chalk, pen and ink with gray wash,
heightened with white chalk and body color.
Surface scratching and yellow and brown chalk.
13 1/8 x 21 3/8 in.
Whitworth Art Gallery, University of Manchester

brown, tan, yellow, and white chalks, pen and ink, gray washes of ink, and with some surface scratching to reveal lower layers of tone and color. Here, the chalk's texture is revealed by the rough tooth of the paper, the repeated applications of chalk, the scratching through, and the use of washes, which settle in the valleys of the surface, darkening them and leaving the chalk-covered hills lighter.

As in the case of chalks, there is a wide range of wax or other fatty-based crayons available, from those of a rather dry, chalk-like nature to the greasy and viscous ones, not unlike children's crayons. The type of binder used in the manufacture of crayon media determines the degree of viscosity. Those, like conté crayon, that retain some chalk-like characteristics, usually contain soap, ball clay, and sometimes, small amounts of beeswax. The

most greasy ones contain high amounts of wax and tallow. Most crayon media are available in stick and pencil form (Figure 7.16), and are available in a wide assortment of colors. Some can be dissolved in turpentine, providing painterly effects, and are compatible with oil paints.

Toulouse-Lautrec's drawing (see Figure 1.7) well illustrates the flowing, linear freedom possible with crayon. Picasso's *Head of a Young Man* (Figure 7.17) shows the rich blacks and the sharp focus of crayon lines. These tend to exceed even the strong darks and clarity of chalk lines. Because of the adhesive strength of the binder, crayon is almost impossible to remove from the page. For the same reason, the blending of tones is not possible. Tones must be achieved by hatching, as in Figure 7.17. Many artists are attracted to

Figure 7.16

Crayon media. From left to right: carpenter's marking crayon, black crayon pencil, white crayon pencil with string for exposing additional crayon, black litho crayon pencil with string, mechanical holder with soft crayon "lead," sanguine red crayon pencil, sepia crayon pencil, and square stock of litho crayon.

crayon's sharp, rich lines, and to the challenge of its permanence which, like pen and ink, demands resolute decisions and handling.

One group of fatty-based materials was developed for use in the graphic process of lithography (Figure 2.13). Black lithography crayons and pencils (a waxy-based ink called *tusche* is also available) come in varying degrees of softness but are, as a group, more fatty than most other crayons. They are a versatile and popular medium for both short and sustained drawings.

Because the fatty-based media do not require fixative and do not smear in the sketchbook, they are a useful medium for drawing out of doors. But their water-resisting binders make them less compatible in certain mixed-media combinations.

Perhaps the most familiar writing and drawing tool in use today is the *graphite pencil* (Figure 7.18), erroneously called a lead pencil. The confusion in terms probably resulted from the common, earlier use of the various metallic styluses, of which lead and lead-alloy metals were the most popular with the general public.

The use of lead, or lead and tin mixtures had the important advantage of not requiring a specially prepared surface to write on—usually a lead white base—as was necessary when silver, gold, brass, and other metals were used. This made lead a more popular material for writing and record-keeping purposes. But many artists often preferred the other metals, especially silver, because of the darker lines that resulted through oxidization (see Figure 6.30).

Although similar to graphite lines, metalpoint lines (usually silverpoint) are lighter, are not erasable, and cannot vary in width or value. While excellent for delicate drawings of a small scale that do not depend on such

Figure 7.17
PABLO PICASSO (1881–1974)
Head of a Young Man (1923)
Grease crayon. 62.1 x 47.4 cm.
Courtesy of The Brooklyn Museum

Figure 7.18
Graphite media. From top, counterclockwise: graphite pencil in pencil extender, thick graphite "lead" in double-ended extender made to hold any wide abrasive medium, an 8B graphite pencil, mechanical pencil holder for thin "leads," pencil made of graphite-carbon mixture (for very dense, black lines), flat graphite pencil, and broad, square-sided graphite block.

variations of line, metalpoint drawing has been largely superseded by the modern graphite pencil.

Graphite pencils are available in over twenty degrees of softness. The harder pencils usually carry an H designation, plus a number indicating the degree of hardness. The 1H pencil is the least hard of this group, the 9H the hardest. The softer pencils are marked B, and the higher the number the softer and darker the pencil. These extend up to 8B. There are three pencil grades between the two categories, usually marked (from softer to harder): F, HB, and H. All the hard pencils can produce lines similar to the fine lines of the metalpoint instruments. The various degrees are determined by the mixtures of graphite and clay. The softest pencils contain some carbon. The more clay present in the mixture, the harder and lighter the line. The more carbon present, the darker the lines.

Like the slender compressed charcoal sticks, graphite "leads" are available for use in mechanical holders, and in flat-sided sticks or blocks (Figure 7.18). The many degrees of graphite available provide a versatile range of linear and tonal possibilities. The beginner too often strains the range of a single pencil. It is of course unnecessary to have the entire range, but some four or five degrees of softness are sometimes needed in extended tonal drawings (Figure 7.19). A good, all-purpose selection might be: 3H, HB, 2B, 5B, and 8B.

Figure 7.19
ANDREW WYETH (1917–   )
Beckie King
Pencil. 28 1/2 x 34 in.
Dallas Museum of Fine Arts
Gift of Mr. Everett L. DeGoyler

Figure 7.20
SIDNEY GOODMAN (1936–   )
Dead Figure
Pencil. 23 x 29 in. (1973)
Collection, Moravian College

Although the harder degrees are omitted here, some surfaces (and styles) may require their use. In general, though, their limited value range and hard, fine lines too often promote a tight, timid result. The softer pencils can still give great exactitude, and more tonal range than the hard ones (Figure 7.20).

If one's choice were limited to a single pencil, a 2B or 3B would serve most needs the best, unless the drawing was to be large scale, in which case a 4B or 5B would be more useful. Bonheur (Figure 7.21) uses a single soft pencil to establish the delicate nuances and bold accents of her subject. Note the range of fine to heavy lines.

Although graphite is easily blended, most artists prefer the texture and freshness of massed graphite lines (Figure 7.22). Graphite's easy erasability (less so in the very hardest and softest degrees) leads many students to overwork their drawings. Graphite's freshness is fragile and easily lost. Extensive erasure, blending, and reworking of tones and edges causes an unpleasant shiny, "tired" surface.

Graphite is a frequent participant in mixed-media works (Figures 7.3 and 7.23). Its

Figure 7.21
ROSA BONHEUR (1822–1899)
Bull Resting
Pencil. 11 3/4 x 17 1/4 in.
Sterling and Francine Clark Art Institute, Williamstown

Figure 7.22
RACHEL CARNEGIE (1901–
Study of Back and Shoulders
Pencil. 5 1/4 x 4 in.
Courtesy, Museum of Fine Arts, Boston
Gift of George P. Gardner

Figure 7.23

PHILIP EVERGOOD (1901–1972)

Girl in Brocade Chemise (1964)
Pencil, crayon, brush, ink. 24 1/4 x 19 1/4 in.
Collection of Mr. and Mrs. Joseph Akston

ability to be used in faint wisps or powerful accents, its easy application over layers of almost any other medium, and its pleasing character as a dry "counterpoint" to wet media make it a versatile member of almost any combination of media. Graphite can even be made to function as a fluid medium by washing over the layers of the material with turpentine.

THE FLUID MEDIA

Whatever their differences, all dry media, because of the friction of the abrasive process, are slower to produce a line or tone. Whereas an energetic calligraphy in chalk or graphite involves some effort, the absence of resistance in applying wet media makes this group harder to control. The chalk or pencil may have to be prodded along; the pen or brush must be restrained.

The designation *pen and ink* is sometimes freely applied to drawings made with tools other than, or in addition to, the pen. Twigs or sticks of various kinds, especially balsa wood; feathers used as brushes; sponges, rolled paper, even cocktail stirrers or eye droppers, and other unlikely objects have been used to produce certain textural and linear characteristics. Although the wide selection of available pens meets nearly every kind of graphic demand, it is instructive to explore new means of using ink.

Some innovations, such as string dipped in ink, may lack the control necessary to keep the tool from dominating a drawing's development, and harm rather than help it. Others, such as raking the thumbnail or a stick across a toothbrush dipped in ink, while difficult to control, are sometimes helpful, especially for producing various textural effects. Any drawing instrument can lead to mannered habits and a fascination with unusual or superficial surface effects. The user must decide whether a particular tool serves or masters him.

Ink, applied with brush or pen, was used as a drawing and writing medium in most ancient cultures. It retained its popularity in the West even after the introduction of manufactured chalks, crayons, and graphite, and continues to be one of the most appealing and adaptable of drawing media. Ink has the ability to produce strong or subtle value-contrasts; it can be used with painterly force or delicate finesse; its range of linear, tonal, and textural characteristics is virtually endless. Because of its great versatility, ink has been a favorite drawing medium in almost every age and culture, for a variety of expressive or stylistic purposes.

Today, many kinds of inks in many colors (including white) are available for many uses. There are inks made of dye solutions for use in ball-point pens; there are the traditional fountain-pen inks and inks made especially for etching, lithography, and for the commercial printing industry, as well as the several kinds of ink used for drawing. Inks may be transparent or opaque (when used full strength), waterproof or water-soluble, and come in liquid, paste, or solid form.

One of the oldest and most versatile inks is the Oriental *sumi* ink. Made of carbon and a water-soluble binder, it is formed into small blocks which are rubbed on a slate inkstone containing a small amount of water, to produce either a paste or liquid, depending on the ratio of pigment to water. Sumi ink is now also available in liquid and paste forms, as well as the traditional cake form. In a liquid state it produces a rich, black line as good as the best of the contemporary inks (whether water-soluble or waterproof) and better than some (Figure 7.24).

Another early drawing ink, *sepia*, is olive-brown in color, and is made of the inky substance from the sacs of squid and cuttlefish. An ink called sepia is available today, but many manufacturers do not use the original material. One brand, Pelikan Drawing Inks, makes a particularly handsome, waterproof sepia ink that is a blackish-brown at full strength, produces various shades of olive-brown through the middle values, and golden-tans in the lighter washes. Being transparent in the lighter values, it is especially adaptable to wash drawings (see Figure 2.17). Like another early ink, *bistre*, yellowish-brown in color, sepia ink was and is favored for its suggestions of color. Bistre ink is not available commercially.*

---

*For those interested in making bistre and other inks, I recommend James Watrous, *The Craft of Old Master Drawings* (Madison: University of Wisconsin Press, 1957).

Figure 7.24

Late Kamakura Period (ca. 1200)

White-Robed Kannon from Kozan-Ji Temple
Brush and ink. 36 x 17 3/4 in.
The Cleveland Museum of Art
Purchase, John L. Severance Fund

India ink is a generic term for a contemporary drawing ink, usually made of carbon or lampblack pigment, and a shellac binder which renders the finished drawing waterproof. It tends to have a heavier consistency, a more velvety feel, than most black water-soluble inks because of the solids in its composition. Because of these solids and the shellac, the user must from time to time scrape or

wash from his instrument the dried ink which accumulates during usage. At the end of a drawing session, all instruments that have been in contact with India ink must be thoroughly washed with soap and water. Should it be necessary, India ink solvents are available. A wide selection of brands offers several densities of India ink for various purposes. All produce dense blacks and all are excellent drawing inks.

Although India ink can be diluted for tonal washes, these usually appear granular when compared to similar sumi ink washes. Also, India ink washes often end in rather abrupt shapes when compared to the more feathered edges of a sumi wash. However, the paper used, the manner and instrument of application, and the density of the wash all affect the appearance of any ink wash.

Less frequently associated with drawing are transparent *watercolors*, in cake, tube, or liquid form. Of particular interest to the draughtsman are the blacks, the many browns (including bistre and sepia), and the various earth reds. Although other colors are sometimes used, these are more compatible with the inks described above. Watercolors are often used in conjunction with inks and other media, as well as for tonal and linear drawing with a brush.

Watercolors are made of dry pigment and gum arabic. Additionally, those in tube form contain an ingredient such as glycerin to retard their drying out in the tube and to help dissolve the paint in water. Liquid watercolors are usually made of dyes, or dyes added to pigment. Often they are described as *concentrates*, and such colors *do* have very strong tinting power. But the permanence of many of these colors is doubtful. Some of those in cake form contain an agent that retards their drying out in storage. Others (usually the less expensive brands) do not.

The composition of watercolors does not easily permit their application in heavy layers—at least not over large areas. Watercolors can be made opaque by the addition of any water-based white paint. The one most often used is called *Chinese white*. When watercolors are used in this way, the medium is referred to as *gouache*. Several manufacturers offer gouache paints in tube or pan form. In full strength, gouache colors are strong in hue, but when thinned with water the washes appear clouded and dull.

Lampblack watercolor (Figure 4.19) is similar in its characteristics to sumi ink and is compatible with it and other carbon inks. Often it is used to lay in washes of tone over India ink lines, which, of course, will not dissolve and spread on the page. *Ivory black* is a cooler, bluish-black, and when used alongside warmer blacks, imparts a subtle note of color to a drawing's tones.

Although the liquid watercolors can be used for pen drawing, the tube and cake forms are not normally thinned out for use in this way. The process of diluting them is a tedious one, and their faster drying properties make their use with pens difficult. When strong, colorful lines are desired, colored inks (though many are of questionable permanence) produce fresher lines of richer hues. When heavy layers of paint are desired, opaque water-based media such as gouache, casein, tempera, and acrylic paints should be used.

Casein is a strong binder made from the curd of milk. Because of its brittleness, gum and other additives are combined with it and the dry pigments to produce a more flexible paint film. Even so, casein is too brittle to use on any but the heaviest of paper supports. It is the most opaque water-based paint available and surrenders this quality with reluctance. When used transparently it handles poorly and produces washes of a mottled and clouded appearance. As an opaque paint, its matte finish and excellent brushing properties are suited to large, bold drawing, and make it a desirable component in mixed-media combinations with the drier abrasive media and others of a matte nature. When dry, the paint film is insoluble. Because of its powerful opacity, casein white is sometimes used to cover over unwanted lines and tones in other media. If subsequent drawing is to be applied over thin washes of casein, the clouded quality of such washes may matter far less than the rather pleasant tooth and good receptivity to both abrasive and fluid media that casein provides.

The term *tempera* has been freely applied to many water-based paints. Today, it is often used to describe poster paint, but some manufacturers offer a tubed tempera paint that behaves somewhat like casein but has the advantage of producing clearer washes. Its composition is not unlike that of gouache, but it differs in being a more viscous paint, capable of being more heavily applied over larger areas. Like casein, it is rather brittle when dry and must be used on stiff supports to avoid cracking. Manufactured temperas should not be confused with *egg-tempera*, a medium popular between the twelfth and fifteenth centuries (and currently enjoying a renewal of interest), which uses raw egg yolk as a binder with dry pigments. Because it spoils quickly in storage, egg-tempera is not available commercially.*

Acrylic paints, a fairly recent addition to the media now available, uses a synthetic resin as a binder. This imparts a remarkable pliancy to the paint film that prevents cracking. Somewhat less opaque than casein and tempera, it nevertheless can be applied heavily enough to achieve total opacity. Acrylic paint is extremely fast-drying. This makes it necessary, while working, to place brushes temporarily not in use in a container of water. Left lying on the palette, the paint will dry on the brush within minutes. Dried acrylic paint is insoluble in water, and is difficult to remove from the palette. Its stubborn resistance to soap and water makes it necessary to thoroughly wash brushes immediately after use. Should the need arise, an acrylic solvent is now available. Most manufacturers also offer an acrylic extender for thinning the paint. This can be purchased in either a matte or glossy form, allowing the artist to control the degree of reflectivity of the painted surface. This material can, when added to casein or tempera paint, impart some additional pliancy to these paints, broadening their range of use and character.

Acrylics can be applied more heavily than either casein or tempera paints with little danger of their cracking or peeling. Unlike any other water-based paint, acrylic paint films can be drawn upon with pen and ink

---

*For those interested in making egg-tempera and other paints, a most useful source is the succinct and accurate text by Reed Kay, *The Painter's Guide to Studio Methods and Materials* (Garden City, N. Y.: Doubleday & Company, Inc., 1972).

without the ink spreading, blotting, or mixing with the paint, and with no danger of the paint chipping off. This is so because the synthetic binder forms an impenetrable shield that permits no other absorbable medium to enter. However, for the same reason, no other wet medium, including oil paint, can physically bond with an acrylic paint film. They can adhere to its surface but cannot penetrate it for a firmer hold. Available in a wide range of colors, acrylic paints have a rich vibrancy that is retained in the thinnest washes.

Some of the media we have been discussing are generally associated with painting rather than with drawing materials. However, it is impossible to say just where drawing ends and painting begins. Cézanne's *Study of a Nude Figure* (see Figure 6.11) is clearly a drawing, although it has transparent washes in several colors. Likewise, Moore's *Miners at Work*, despite its color is not a painting. Nor is color the only criterion. Constable's wash-drawing (Figure 7.25) in sepia ink is monochromatic, but seems to possess painterly qualities.

It is sometimes impossible to say whether a particular work is a drawing or a painting because no clear demarcation line between these two broad categories can be found. This is a natural result of the imperative of freedom in creativity. The freedom to pursue any system of expressive order ex-

Figure 7.25
JOHN CONSTABLE (1776–1837)
Stoke by Nayland
Brush and sepia ink. 12.7 x 18.5 cm.
Victoria and Albert Museum, London

tends to the free choice of tactical means. When the responsive demands of an artist require that he use materials and processes usually associated with painting (Figure 7.26) in a work which, in other respects, appears to be a drawing, no particular rule has been violated. To insist on precise boundaries to keep these media categories from overlapping would be as partisan and limiting as those codes which proscribe a medium's usage. Although most drawings *do* omit color, *are* small in scale, *are* made on paper supports, and *do* tend to emphasize line, there are no compelling reasons for accepting these traditional characteristics as fixed barriers.

Therefore, the several paints discussed here should be considered as additional ways to increase our options in drawing. Oil paints are omitted here only because the addition of a medium requiring its own thinner, varnishes, oils, etc., would complicate the mixed-media possibilities and restrictions. But drawing in oils, or combining oil paint with other drawing media is a common practice of long standing (Figure 7.27). The use of paints in drawing tends to promote a broader, often more daring approach on a larger scale, which can act as a healthy corrective for those who tend to make tiny drawings in a timid manner.

Figure 7.26
HENRI DE TOULOUSE-LAUTREC (1864–1901)
The Dog
Oil on cardboard. 61 x 63.5 cm.
Toulouse-Lautrec Museum, Albi

Figure 7.27
DOMENIC CRETARA (1946–   )
Seated Nude Figure
Sepia chalk and oil washes. 14 x 18 in.
Courtesy of the artist

THE DRAWING INSTRUMENTS

Most of the abrasive media, except for the thin and fragile compressed charcoal, crayon, and graphite leads, do not normally require any mechanical implements or holders. However, some artists prefer holders or extenders for all the abrasive media, to permit them to stand farther back from large drawings, or to extend the drawing life of a medium worn too short to be comfortably held in the hand (Figure 7.18).

Some mention has already been made of the many improvised drawing tools that can be used with inks or paints. In this section we will examine the various pens and brushes designed for use with these media.

PENS

Probably the oldest instrument for applying ink is the *reed pen*. Found at many river banks and marshes, the tubular reeds are cut to a comfortable length, and sharpened to a point at one or both ends. Splitting the shaft at the point provides a steadier ink flow and a slightly more flexible point (Figure 7.28). The reed pen with its thick, tubular body naturally produces broad, "plain spoken" lines. Although quite thin lines are possible if the pen is sharpened to a fine point, the fibers of fine points wear away or break down quickly. Even the blunt point wears away after a short period of drawing and needs to be recut. Also, some ink is taken up into the pen's tip through capillary action in the fibers, making the point rather spongy after about twenty minutes of drawing. It should be set aside to dry. Many artists use two or three reed pens, in rotation.

But the reed's ability to take up ink in its fibers has one useful advantage. When the pen is fully charged, the lines will, of course, be dark and dense. But as the ink is used up, it can be forced from the fibers by increased pressure on the pen, and can produce variously toned lines (see Figure 1.8). These can be extremely light and dry-looking, making possible very delicate tonal and color nuances.

Reed pens do not work well for long or complex curvasive lines. Their ink flow is

Figure 7.28
Cutting a reed pen. Using a sharp blade, make a 45-degree cut (A). A second cut (B) is then made at a more oblique angle than the first. Sharpen to a dull point, as in C. On the back, with a nail or pin, drive a hole through the wall of the reed. Using a knife blade, slit from hole down to the end of the reed, as in D.

usually too heavy to sustain such lines. Nor do they, except when fully charged, glide along the surface easily. The user feels a decided friction between the pen and paper, and may tend, therefore, to make slower, shorter lines with a reed pen than with any other. Many artists consider these restrictions as a challenge that encourages a concise and vigorous approach to drawing, instead of clever facility (Figure 7.29).

Some localities provide sturdy reeds from which pens can easily be made. Art stores offer bamboo reed pens, sometimes with a brush at one end. Reed pens work well on most surfaces, but their character is best revealed on surfaces with a moderate to rough tooth. Very smooth papers may promote a heavy flow of ink that is hard to control.

The *quill pen*, which was popular until the introduction of the steel pen, is made from the heavier pinion feathers of the goose, crow, or swan. Unlike the reed pen, it is light to hold and requires almost no pressure to use. The thin tubular wall of the feather (a horn-like substance) allows a much finer and more flexible point to be cut. Because it glides easily over even the roughest grained paper, the point does not wear away as fast as the reed's. Like the reed pen—and for the same

Figure 7.29
VINCENT VAN GOGH (1853–1890)
Tree in a Meadow
Charcoal under ink with reed pen.
48.8 x 61.3 cm.
Courtesy of the Art Institute of Chicago

reasons—the quill pen is split up the middle, as shown in Figure 7.30.

The quill pen responds to the slightest inflections of the hand. It produces extended fine lines or lines that can be varied in width by changing the pressure on the pen. The quill's flexible point can ride the hills and valleys of a rough-grained paper better than the modern steel pen, which is more likely to tear through the paper, causing the ink to spatter (Figure 7.31). The quill's tip can be shaped to suit the user. Cut at an oblique angle, it produces a script-like line as the pen is turned in different ways. Cut with a blunt point, it can produce some of the effects of the reed pen (Figure 7.32). Uncommon in most art stores, goose quills can be obtained from meat markets, farms, and some novelty shops. Crow and swan quills perform about as well, but are much harder to obtain.

The quill provides a delicate and ornamental counterpoint to the reed's blunt, terse statements. In Rembrandt's *Cottage Beside a Canal* (Figure 7.33), the bolder reed lines can be seen in the drawing of the boat, deck, and in parts of the building. It also seems to have been used—in the lighter, drier state—to suggest the thatched roofs. The quill lines appear in the drawing of the foliage and the contour

of the rise in front of the central house, and dart around in curvilinear sweeps on various depictive "duties."

The steel pen appeared in the early 1800's. Providing several degrees of flexibility and styles for use in a holder, it quickly superseded the reed and quill pens because of

Figure 7.30
Cutting a quill pen. Make the same two angled cuts as for a reed pen (Figure 7.28). To split the point, press thumbnail down hard at the point where slit is to end (about 3/4" from tip of quill), and forcing a brush handle into quill opening, press upward toward the thumb (D). The quill will not split beyond the point where the thumbnail presses against the quill. Sharpen the point to the desired angle and degree of fineness (E).

199

Figure 7.31
Differences in pen lines on a rough-surfaced paper. The lines in A were made with a reed pen; those in B with a quill pen; and those in C with a steel crow-quill pen. Note the splatters in C when the steel pen is used to make the same kinds of lines at those in A and B.

several advantages. Their uniform manufacture insures the availability of a particular type; they usually hold more ink; they never need sharpening; and they can produce sharper, cleaner lines than either of their precursers, as Figure 7.34 indicates.

Today, the wide assortment available ranges from extremely flexible pens that produce lines varying in width from an almost invisible thread of ink to over one-eighth of an inch thick, to stiff pens that make uniform lines of mechanical exactness. Some pens are made for use with a holder, others are made to fit into a fountain pen (Figure 7.35).

Despite these advantages, many steel pens lack the warm, animated character of the

Figure 7.32
REMBRANDT VAN RIJN (1606–1669)
Jan Cornelius Sylvius, Preacher
Reed and quill pens and ink. 13.3 x 12.2 cm.
National Gallery of Art, Washington, D. C.
Rosenwald Collection

Figure 7.33
REMBRANDT VAN RIJN (1606–1669)
Cottage beside a Canal
Pen and wash. 15 x 24.8 cm.
Courtesy of The Art Institute of Chicago

reed and quill pens. Few will function as well on the rough-grained papers that so well suit the reed and quill pens. These older instruments make a more sensitive union with such surfaces. That is, they are more affected by, and accommodating to, the paper's terrain than most steel pens. The stiffer steel pens make their own flat road on rough paper, denting it as they move, thus losing the tactile and visual benefits of interplay between the tool and the terrain. The more flexible pens are more apt to become entangled in the fibers of such papers and splatter.

The wide selection of steel pens and types of paper, and the differing needs of the user, make it impossible to recommend specific combinations of pen and paper. In general, moderately flexible steel pens—on papers of a moderate tooth and absorbency—can ap-

proximate much of the character of the earlier quill pen. On smoother papers, and when precise or fine lines, or delicate hatching is required, the steel pen's free-flowing, incisive character has no equal (see Figures 3.25 and 7.34).

The several kinds of drawing pens designed to use drawing inks are a most convenient drawing tool because they hold a generous ink supply and can be easily carried about (Figure 7.35). Many are made to take a wide assortment of treaded nibs—which allows the user to change the kind of point being used. Those used with water-soluble inks work quite well if thoroughly washed every few weeks. Another type of drawing pen, for use with India ink, is more prone to clogging, but again, periodic cleaning will keep it functioning. A completely trouble-free India ink pen may not exist because of the drying properties of permanent inks, but several durable and versatile ones are available. Some have the helpful feature of interchangeable nibs, and offer a wide range of drawing and technical drawing nibs.

Still another type of fountain pen is often used for technical or mechanical drawing purposes, or where a line's width must be unchanging. These have stylus-like nibs, made for use with water-soluble inks. The near uniformity of the lines has an etching-like qual-

ity, unlike any other kind of pen line (Figure 7.36). These instruments also take interchangeable nibs in several line widths.

The *ball-point pen* is another serviceable addition to the range of drawing media. Its very limited line variation and the relative weakness of the black ink, compared to carbon blacks, are considered disadvantages by some artists. Others enjoy the "clouds" of almost invisible lines that hatchings with a fine-point ball-point pen make possible. On hard surfaces its easy flow and maneuver-

Figure 7.35
Some pens. Clockwise, starting at bottom: Goose-quill pen, crow-quill steel pen, Japanese reed pen with squirrel-hair brush at opposite end (brush retracts into handle when not in use), felt-tip pen, stylus type fountain pen for use with washable inks, and India ink fountain pen with nib that lowers into barrel when not in use.

Figure 7.36

ability (it cannot spatter) are excellent for producing intricate linear delicacies.

The artist's felt-tipped fountain pen, a recent development, allows for interchangeable nibs and uses a special dye-based ink, available in several colors. The best pens allow the artist to continue to feed the ink, or to let it run dry, producing effects not unlike the reed pen (Figure 7.37).

Nylon-tipped pens are useful for some drawing purposes and are favored by those who like a bold, quick-maneuvering line. Their line variety is limited and is incapable of the fineness possible with most other pens.

Figure 7.37
HAROLD ALTMAN (1924–
Matriarch
Felt pen. 16 1/2 x 20 in.
Philadelphia Museum of Art

Even those claimed to make fine lines are heavy compared to all but the felt-tipped pens.

BRUSHES

There are two basic types of artist's brushes: the stiff, coarse-haired *bristle* brush—generally hog bristles, but also of nylon "hairs" (for painting in acrylics); and the soft-haired brush made of various animal furs—especially sable and squirrel (Figure 7.38).

The term *sable* is sometimes applied to any soft-haired brush, which can be confusing. When selecting a sable brush, be sure it *is* sable. The best sable brushes, generally called *red sable*, have a golden-reddish color and are very springy and resilient. Less expensive "sable" brushes may contain squirrel hair, which is less lively in use.

Bristle brushes are used for painting and drawing with any wet medium, but their use with transparent watercolors is rare. When used on paper, one must avoid too vigorous scrubbing movements because the stiff

Figure 7.38
Some brushes. Clockwise, from bottom: portable sable brush with cover which serves to extend handle when in use, French quill brush taped to a stick, number 2 round bristle, flat red sable, number 5 filbert bristle, Japanese squirrel-hair brush, portable fountain brush, number 4 round red sable, large flat red sable with a beveled handle tip for incising lines and removing paint, common paste brush of nylon "hairs."

bristles will damage the surface—unless the paper has been previously prepared with a foundation coat of paint, called a *priming*.

There are several classifications of bristle brushes, determined by shape. *Flats* and *brights* are square-ended brushes, usually available in eighteen sizes, differing only in the somewhat greater length of the flats. *Filberts* are rounded at the ends and fuller in body. *Rounds* are rather long, have pointed tips, and round bodies. Both are available in twelve sizes. Bristle brushes are sized according to a scale from 1 (smallest) to 18 (largest). Other stiff-haired brushes sometimes used include the stencil brush, helpful in producing certain textural effects, and the common house-painting brush, for preparing surfaces and for very broad washes.

When used with opaque paints, bristle brushes are stiff enough to push their way through heavy concentrations of paint without splaying out, becoming bogged down, or wearing away quickly, as any soft-haired brush will. The round bristle brush works well as a line instrument when used with thinned paint or ink.

But for drawing, the soft-haired brushes have always been preferred. Made from hairs of various animals, these come in a large selection of shapes and sizes. In the Orient, where the brush is also a writing tool, the hairs commonly used are goat, rabbit, and badger. Wolf and horse hair is also used for larger, stiffer brushes, as is hog bristle. For writing and drawing purposes the hairs are set into a bamboo shaft, the hairs coming to a point when wetted. Some larger brushes are set into wooden handles. The beautiful calligraphic results possible with the Oriental brushes have long attracted Western artists. Softer and somewhat less springy than the sable brush, they work best when held at a right angle to the paper. Very slight pressure is required for the release of ink. The variety of line possible with the Oriental brush rivals that of the best round sable brushes.

The round sable is one of the most versatile of brushes for drawing in ink and watercolor. It also works well with casein or tempera, especially when these are slightly thinned, but like all soft-haired brushes, it performs poorly with acrylics. This medium must be applied with a stiff brush, preferably of nylon.

Sable brushes come with short handles, more often used for drawing with ink or watercolor, and long handles, for use in easel painting. Their sizes commonly range from the tiny 000, less than $1/40$ of an inch wide, to size 12, which is almost $1/2$ inch wide. Some manufacturers offer even larger sizes. Because the larger round sable brushes ably do any work the smaller ones can—sometimes better—it is best to buy fewer but larger brushes. A good, all-purpose selection might be sizes 2, 4, 6, 9, and 12. Good quality round sables—even the largest ones—can produce lines finer than those of any steel pen.

Besides the round sable, there are full-bodied oval-shaped sables, and another group of flat, square-ended ones. Both are designed for broader handling—the largest ones for brushing in large washes of tone, or for wetting the paper.

Brushes in all shapes and sizes are available in squirrel hair, camel hair, or in mixtures of various hairs that possess some of the qualities of the expensive sable ones. Other brushes used in drawing are the group called *quill brushes.* These are long, round squirrel-hair brushes intended for lettering and various decorative purposes. Their longer bodies and pointed ends allow for very delicate drawing.

Many other types of brushes are available in a wide selection of shapes, sizes, and materials, for use in sign writing, lettering, or other special painting functions.

As brushes wear down they can be assigned other duties. It is hard to imagine a worn brush that cannot be used in some way. In fact, brushes often wear down to shapes that suit an artist's purpose better than new ones. The wear and tear with use ages a brush in a healthy way. But letting brushes dry without washing them thoroughly, or standing brushes—especially soft-haired ones—upright in containers of water, can damage them so they are useless. With proper care the delicate and expensive sables can last for many years.

Brushes are fast-moving tools that require steady practice to control. In the case of the soft-haired brushes, their sensitive re-sponses record the slightest hesitations and idiosyncratic behavior of the user's hand. Once familiarity is gained, a limitless range of abstract and depictive nuance becomes possible.

THE SUITABLE SUPPORT

The character of the surface drawn upon also helps form the image. As the artist transfers his responses to the paper, its submission or resistance to a particular medium—the paper's tooth, absorbency, and tactile properties—influence the artist's tactics and even the expressive nature of the work itself. The beginner seldom reflects on a paper's physical composition, weight, absorbency, or surface character, although he is sometimes amazed at a particular paper's influence on his drawing. He may also be amazed by the many kinds of paper in the art stores. Some are permanent papers that will not yellow and crumble with age; others will begin to darken and fall apart in a year or two. Some can take rough handling; others are quite fragile. Each has certain uses, some quite specialized, others are adaptable to a variety of uses and media.

The most permanent papers—usually the toughest and most capable of accepting a wide range of media—are made of linen rag. They are also the most expensive, particularly the handmade papers. The least permanent papers are made of wood pulp, untreated by any chemical preservatives.

Papers are classified according to weight and surface character. The figures designating a paper's weight refer to the weight of five hundred sheets, called a *ream.* Thus, a 30-pound paper is one that weighs thirty pounds per ream. Newsprint, the paper used in the publication of newspapers, is a 30- to 35-pound paper. Some of the heavier papers, those used primarily for watercolor painting but also very well suited to drawing, weigh up to four hundred pounds a ream and are nearly as stiff as cardboard.

Rag papers are classified into three basic types:

1. *Hotpressed.* These are the hard-surfaced, smooth, and sometimes even glossy papers; best suited to pen and ink drawing of an exact or delicate kind, and wash drawings that do not require repeated overpainting of tones. Hotpressed rag is the least absorbent of the three types.

2. *Coldpressed.* These papers have a moderate tooth and absorbency, accept all media well, and are the most frequently used. They vary somewhat according to the manufacturers' formula, but it is hard to find a coldpressed paper that is not an appealing surface for drawing.

3. *Rough.* The papers with the most pronounced tooth, they are least accommodating to fine or exact pen-and-ink drawing, although some artists enjoy working on such surfaces. They give ink and watercolor washes a brilliance and sparkle not possible with other surfaces.

Rag papers are sold in single sheets and blocks. The sheets in the blocks are attached on all four sides in order to flatten out any buckling that may occur when water-based media are used. Water by itself, or as part of ink or thinned paint, swells the fibers, causing ripples in the paper. Although not generally noticeable in pen-and-ink drawings unless the lines are densely massed on a lightweight paper, not much water is necessary to cause ripples on most papers. The heavier the paper, the more water it can tolerate before buckling. Papers lighter than 140 pounds will buckle even with a quite restricted use of water. Papers of 200 pounds or more will not buckle no matter how wet.

To prevent buckling, the paper should be soaked for a few minutes, and then secured to a stiff board such as particle board by taping it on all four sides with a gummed tape. If a second paper is similarly stretched on the back of the board, warping of the board is less likely, and a second sheet is ready for use.

For extensive use of opaque paints, only the heaviest papers or paperboards should be used. Unless, like illustration board, such supports are faced with drawing or watercolor paper, they may require priming to provide a more receptive tooth to hold the paint, and to reduce absorbency. An acrylic *gesso*, or primer, designed as a base for paints, makes a good surface for both wet and dry media.

Illustration board is available in the three surface designations for rag papers. These boards are made of an inexpensive backing of pulpboard, upon which is mounted a thin sheet of drawing or watercolor paper. Some are made with all-rag surfaces. The Strathmore Paper Company markets an illustration board faced on both sides by an all-rag paper. The completed drawing can be stripped from the illustration board. Thus, the Strathmore board is really two illustration boards in one.

Oriental papers have a distinctive absorbent character. Often called rice paper, they are actually made from the inner bark fibers of a mulberry plant. Oriental papers contain none of the clay additives of many Western papers that reduce absorbency, and are, therefore, far more absorbent and more prone to blotting. Often used in the graphic process of woodcut printing, such papers offer an unusual receptivity to sumi ink washes and brush drawing.

The term *bond* refers to a wide assortment of papers often used for writing and typing purposes. Bond papers vary in weight from thirteen to thirty-five pounds, and in surface from the slick to the moderately grained. They may be made either of woodpulp, rag, or various mixtures of both. All are excellent for pen or pencil drawing, and those manufactured for general drawing purposes are receptive to most media. But, their light weight makes extensive use of water-based media impractical.

Many drawing pads and sketchbooks do not identify the papers' ingredients. Advertised as "white drawing paper," or "all-purpose drawing paper," many are like bond papers in character. Most are heavier, being between thirty and fifty pounds, or more. Their qualities vary according to their price. At their best, they are made of 100 percent rag materials.

A serviceable paper for practice drawings with dry media is newsprint paper, mentioned earlier. It is an impermanent paper of a warm, light gray tone and can be either smooth or moderately rough. The rough-toothed paper has a more interesting character and is generally heavier. It is especially receptive to conté crayon and compressed charcoal.

Bristol and *vellum* are heavyweight papers, often made of woodpulp, but available in the all-rag state. Of postcard weight, they offer fine surfaces for pen and ink, brush and ink, and graphite. Often sold in pads of various sizes, they are a most serviceable paper for almost any medium. These papers are usually treated with preservatives and chemically whitened. They are tough papers; all are long-lasting, and many are permanent. The bristol paper has a hard, glossy surface and may take the softer abrasive media less well than vellum, which has a slight tooth.

Charcoal paper, usually between sixty and seventy pounds, is a fairly substantial paper, capable of the rough treatment that drawings in charcoal, chalks, and the other dry media often entail. Its rough tooth and tough "skin" takes erasures well. These papers always have some rag content, and the best are 100 percent rag. It is available in various light colors as well as white.

Tracing paper is a semi-transparent, lightweight paper used for drawing or for developing a drawing placed beneath it. It is sometimes useful to place a sheet of tracing paper over a work in progress, to experiment with drawing ideas, or to check on the design and structure of a drawing in progress, by tracing its main characteristics and, by turning the tracing paper over, see the drawing reversed. Changes can be made on the tracing paper and easily transferred to the original drawing.

There are, of course, many other types of paper suitable for drawing. The various kinds used in the printing of etchings and lithographs; the common kraft, or wrapping paper; cameo paper, especially suited to graphite; and even papers recently developed of spun glass, plastic, and re-cycled paper-products—all serve various drawing interests and needs.

At first the student need not extensively explore types of paper or drawing media and their tools. A deep concern with the materials of drawing may, in the beginning, cause an overdependence on their powers. The more we know, the more we demand of ourselves and our materials. The exploration of new media, tools, and surfaces tends to expand as the limits of familiar materials become restrictive, and as our understanding and curiosity expand.

For the beginner, a serviceable selection of papers could include: an 18″ × 22″ pad of rough-toothed newsprint paper; an 18″ × 22″ pad of any good grade of bond or other white drawing paper; a medium-sized pad of bristol or vellum paper (11″ × 14″ or 12″ × 16″); several large sheets of charcoal paper, of which one or two may be colored; and several sheets of the heavier, coldpressed, all-rag papers. A sketchbook, not smaller than 8½″ × 11″, but preferably larger, is also basic.

For the student the sketchbook should be, as it is for many artists, a kind of private visual journal. It is also a portable studio, a

Figure 7.39
THÉODORE GÉRICAULT (1791–1824)
Study of Horses
Pencil. 17.4 x 23.2 cm.
Courtesy of The Art Institute of Chicago.

place for private speculations and experiments. With no one looking on, we try things we would hesitate to try in a classroom, or on a large drawing pad, which feels more public. The sketchbook is a place to experiment with whatever interests us in the subject, in the processes of drawing, or in ourselves. It is a useful tool in developing a better grasp of our strengths and susceptibilities, and for exploring the world around us (Figures 7.29 and 7.39).

One convenient form of the sketchbook permits the user to fill it with any combination of papers and to remove completed drawings. Surprisingly, this kind is not normally

Figure 7.40
Filling a spring-binder sketchbook. Any combination of drawing papers are cut to size and placed in the inner folder. Covers are folded backward, as in A, the folder is inserted and covers released. This type of sketchbook has the additional advantage of lying flat when open, as in B.

A

B

found in the art stores, but in the larger stationary stores. These are called *spring binders* and are available in several sizes. In effect, it is a permanent, spring-operated book cover, filled and changed as needed (Figure 7.40).

MIXED MEDIA

As noted earlier, some mixed-media drawings are planned and others evolve from the interactions between the artist, the subject, the emerging drawing, and the limits of the medium in use. When planned, the media should be necessary to a work's expressive meaning. They should not be combined for mere caprice, or for a show of technical facility as ends in themselves. Earlier too, it was pointed out that limitations on the use of media imposed by custom or tradition are unnecessary restrictions. These two extreme attitudes about media—freewheeling show, or unquestioning obedience to past practices—both intrude on the quality of responses that extract and intensify a subject's meanings. If, in Émile Zola's words, "art is life seen through a temperament," then it is the quality of our responses to the subject, and not our attitudes of play or duty toward the materials of drawing through which nature—life—is interpreted.

For some artists a medium's limits are an exciting challenge. Some notable artists have achieved deeply expressive results in a single medium. Such artists accept the medium's limits (not the man-made "rules" concerning it) as if they were working in a form such as a sonnet in poetry, or a sonata in music. For them, part of the challenge in drawing is to see how much a particular medium can be made to do. This is a valid and even praiseworthy goal, as long as it does not stifle responses that cannot be expressed by the medium in use.

The student should also try to explore and push each medium to its limits; and he must be slow to decide its limits have been reached. He should use it in every possible way and on a variety of surfaces before turning to other media. How a medium behaves— what it will and will not do—affects our drawing and stimulates meaningful innovations in the medium's use. But, when certain visual or expressive intentions demand more than a medium can give, other media should be utilized.

As mentioned earlier, any combinations of media and materials can be used except those incompatible for chemical or technical reasons. Acrylic paints cause some inks to curdle when mixed with them; casein paint on thin supports will promptly crack; oil paint can rot the fibers of unprimed papers; charcoal media and some chalks drawn upon dense layers of graphite will not adhere; ink lines drawn upon any dried water-based

paint except acrylics will spread and blot. There are other incompatible mixtures. Unfortunately, most are learned the hard way. Often only two or three media are used in mixed-media combinations. Considering what any one medium can do, to use more than three suggests inexperience more than need.

The thick brush strokes in Bageris's *Infanta—after Velasquez* (Figure 7.41), interacting with the lean, fast-moving graphite lines, are basic to the drawing's enigmatic theme. Lines or paint strokes alone could not convey the overlapping, darting, "hide and seek" quality that the artist's responses to the Velasquez

Figure 7.41
JOHN BAGERIS (1924–   )
Infanta—after Velázquez
Tempera and pencil. 11 1/4 x 14 in.
Collection of Lucy G. Stone

Figure 7.42
LYONEL FEININGER (1871–1956)
Block Houses
.Pen and ink, black and gold wash. 11 1/2 x 18 1/2 in.
Courtesy, Museum of Fine Arts, Boston
Gift of John S. Newberry, Jr.

painting demanded. This interplay between thick and thin, fast and slow, and the drawing's overall shimmering immediacy conveys the impression of the Infanta forming and fading. The way we are teased by the forms welling up and subsiding into the background's light values is part of the artist's interpretive aim. Here, the choice of media and the way they are used is not arbitrary; it is essential.

Similarly, Feininger's drawing *Block Houses* (Figure 7.42), in chalk and black and gold washes, economically conveys the fusion of a group of houses with their cloud-like surroundings. Applied to a wet surface, the washes blend into each other, their softness contrasting with the rough chalk lines. Here again, the choice of media is necessary to the artist's intent.

The possible combinations of media, tools, and surfaces are almost endless. Any group exhibition of drawings shows a wide variety of mixed media. Some are unusual combinations, such as: lithographic crayons and ink with watercolor on colored paper; brown wax-based pencil and sepia ink; casein, graphite, and conté crayon; fatty-based crayon, turpentine (as the crayon's thinner), and ink; white chalk and white ink on black paper; and white acrylic, compressed charcoal, and sepia washes on gray paper. Others are familiar combinations such as ink or graphite and watercolor washes, or charcoal and ink. Some combinations are not of mixed media, but instruments, as in Whistler's gentle drawing of a seated woman (Figure 7.43). Here, the light and dark tones in the woman's head, the tone of her shawl, and the light tones in the background and on the chair are broadly brushed in with ink washes that contrast with the ink lines. These tones soften the figure, and hold the drawing together. Whistler could have achieved most of these results with just the pen, but not the contrasts of wet and dry passages, of actual and optical grays, or the splashy treatment of the woman's left arm.

Experiencing the feel of a medium, instrument, or surface is best accomplished in the act of drawing itself, but some free exploration helps you to become familiar with many characteristics, limits, and combinations you might not otherwise encounter, and which can play important roles in your subsequent drawings. The following exercise is intended as a general approach to the study of these matters.

exercise 7A

Here, you will use only a few media, surfaces, and tools. The several experiments described suggest a style of media exploration adaptable to the study of virtually any medium, tool, and surface. Even so, possibilities for extensive exploration are too numerous to examine here, but the several offered below should point the way to fuller experimentation.

For these three drawings you require the following papers: one sheet of bristol paper (or any comparably smooth surface) approximately 14″ × 20″; one sheet of 18″ × 22″ white charcoal paper, the heavier the weight, the better; and one coldpressed or medium-toothed illustration board, 20″ × 30″

In addition, you will need:

stick charcoal, soft or medium
6B graphite pencil
black wax-based pencil or crayon
black acrylic paint
black water-soluble ink
white acrylic paint
Chinese white paint
a fine, flexible steel pen, and holder
number 4, round, soft-hair brush, preferably
  sable
number 5, flat, bristle or nylon brush
number 3, round, bristle brush
a graphite eraser

Before beginning, get somewhat familiar with these materials by free manipulations. On some scraps of paper, preferably of different types, draw with these media in any way that interests you. Try to feel their differing tactile characteristics. To fully appreciate their differences, alternate media and tools every few minutes.

Do not attempt to draw anything in particular during this manipulation period. Just try to observe their differences in touch and handling. Draw long lines and strokes. As you do, change the pressure on the tool to feel the kind of response it makes. Pens and brushes will react more to changes in pressure than abrasive media, but all show the effects of such pressure—each differently. Try erasing some charcoal, pencil, and crayon lines. Cross-hatch with each medium, going from dense hatchings to open ones. Draw the smallest circle possible with each. Write your name with each. At this stage it is not necessary to mix the media, but

Figure 7.43
JAMES McNEILL WHISTLER (1834–1903)
Study of Mrs. Philip
Pen and wash. 5 1/8 x 3 5/8 in.
Courtesy, Museum of Fine Arts, Boston
Helen and Alice Colburn Fund

it is often hard *not* to experiment with one medium over another. Let your curiosity guide you.

These first few experimental efforts are important. Just playing with these materials is instructive play. You will have already made some judgments about them.

drawing 1

Divide the sheet of charcoal paper into four even, horizontal parts, and three vertical ones, making twelve divisions, as in Figure 7.44. In box 1A, use the 6B pencil to draw an even tone of approximately a 50 percent gray. Drawing lines adjacent to each other should produce an optical gray that needs no smudging. But here, it will be instructive to blend one-half of the lines in the box, to study the effects on value and texture. Do the same with the stick charcoal in box 2A, also blending the lines in half of it. You may find the blended halves have changed value. Rework them until each matches the tone of its other half. In 3A, using the wax-based medium, again establish exactly the same value as now appears in 1A and 2A. Here, you will not be able to blend extensively, if at all, nor erase, and this should be borne in mind when you try to match the value of the first two boxes.

When you have filled all three boxes, use these media freely to draw additional lines in these boxes. For example, you should use charcoal and crayon in 1A, and so on. These new lines may intermix with each other as well as with the original lines in any given box. Some mixtures will work better than others. Note that the order in which they are drawn is important. Graphite may do well over charcoal, but charcoal may do poorly over graphite. It depends in part on how much the paper fibers have been filled. Continue to add (or erase) lines in any order. You can even try to scrape some of the crayon off with a penknife, and rebuild the tone of 3A with a combination of these media. Use your imagination freely. The original medium of each box may be partially or completely covered by such additional drawing. Now you may wish to draw some simple form or texture in each, or try to establish some gradual transitions in value with differing mixtures. Continue until you cannot think of any other combinations or drawing tests to put these media to.

In 1B, using graphite, start with the darkest tone the pencil can produce, and gradually lighten it as the tone moves across the box from left to right, ending just short of the box's edge, leaving a bit of the white paper on the far right side. This should be a very gradual value change. Rework until the dark on the left appears to fade away at an even rate, and end just short of the right side of the box. Do the same with 2B, using charcoal, and in 3B, with crayon. Do not erase to establish these graduations of tone. Notice the differences in the value and texture of the three dark areas, and that each medium requires a decidedly different handling to produce the tonal change from dark to light.

In 1C, make a tonal drawing of any simple object, such as an apple, shoe, mitten, etc., using the 6B pencil. Draw the same object, from the same view, in 2C using charcoal, and again in 3C with crayon. Again, note the differences in handling required. Because the 6B pencil cannot produce darks as easily as the crayon, more pressure is required. Because the crayon so easily produces strong darks, less pressure must be used for the lighter tones. Because stick charcoal is a soft tool that tends to make heavy lines, small details are not as easily drawn as with the other two media. Take advantage of what each medium offers. If crayon produces stronger darks, use them to show a more dramatic range of values. If charcoal can be manipulated on the page in ways that the other media cannot, do so to extract from the subject qualities that charcoal can state by these manipulations, including smudging and erasing. If graphite can state details with more precision, use this to explain smaller planes and tones. Let the limits and characteristics of the media guide your tactics.

Leave the bottom D row blank. You will complete these boxes after the next drawing.

drawing 2

Using the bristol paper or its equivalent, again divide it as in Figure 7.44. In 1A, draw a gray tone of about 50 percent, using pen and ink. The lines can go in any direction or be crosshatched. In 2A, draw the same value with the sable brush, and ink diluted in water. Again, use hatched or cross-hatched lines only, *but fill only one half of box 2A*. In the other half, use the number 5 bristle brush and undiluted ink to match the value in 2A as follows: dip only the tip of the bristle

Figure 7.44

brush in the ink, and, with light back-and-forth brushing on a scrap of nonabsorbent paper, remove almost all the ink from the brush. When the brush is almost dry, it will produce a stroke of very fine, black lines that can be brushed into the other half of 2A, producing an optical gray. Naturally, this should be practiced first on a scrap of paper similar to bristol. This process is called *dry-brush*, and can be seen in the paintings of the Flemish primitives as well as in many tonal brush drawings (Figure 4.19). The brush strokes of fine lines so produced look somewhat like chalk strokes. They permit a gradual building up of values (Figure 7.45). This can also be done with soft-hair brushes and ink, or thinly diluted paints, but acrylic is less adaptable to dry-brush handling than other paints. You may wish to use this manner of application later in this second drawing.

In 3A, mix ink and Chinese white with enough water to allow for easy brushing, and apply the 50 percent gray tone by using any of the three brushes. This should be an opaque layer of paint, but a quite thin one. Now, as in Drawing 1, rework these boxes in any way you wish, mixing media to produce volumes, textures, and tonalities.

In 1B, use pen and ink to make the same kind of tonal change as in Drawing 1. Do the same with brush and ink in 2B, *after* you have moistened the box with clear water applied with a clean brush. This will make the ink spread. The more water, the more the ink will spread—and the harder it will be to control. Therefore, do not lay in any washes until the area is only faintly damp. If a segment becomes too dark, a clean soft-hair brush can pick up much of the tone while it is still wet. In 3B, draw the same kind of value transition, using opaque mixtures of Chinese white and ink.

Figure 7.45
Examples of drybrush. The strokes in A were made with a bristle brush; those in B, with an Oriental squirrel-hair brush.

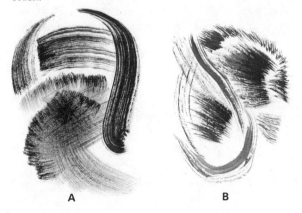

A   B

This time, use only the sable brush, and draw fine lines with the thinnest opaque mixture. If the mixture is the correct consistency, the paint should easily glide upon the page with no sense of "drag." Dry-brush will work well here.

In 1C, using pen and ink any way you wish, make a tonal drawing of any simple object. Using brush and water, draw the same object in 2C. This can be done in the wet-in-wet manner used in 2B, or in any combination of wet and dry brush strokes. In 3C, the same subject should be drawn in any opaque manner with ink and Chinese white. The experience of the first two rows should help you decide how you wish to handle these three drawings in the C row. Again, leave the D row blank.

Now return to the D row of Drawing 1. In 1D, using brush and ink and Chinese white, try to *imitate* the drawing in 1C exactly. That is, your drawing in 1D should look as if it had been done with the 6B pencil. In 2D, use brush and ink (and water if needed) to reproduce the drawing in 2C exactly. Again, try to imitate the medium used in 2C. In 3D, use only pen and ink to reproduce the drawing in 3C. If you are working with other students, drawings can be exchanged at this point, so that you can try to reproduce someone else's row of C drawings.

When the D row of Drawing 1 has been completed, return to the D row of Drawing 2. Again, drawings can be exchanged. Now, use only the crayon to reproduce the drawing (and the medium) of 1C of Drawing 2, use only the charcoal to do the same with the drawing in 2C, and the 6B pencil for the one in 3C.

In both sets of drawings in the D rows, you are straining the media by trying to get them to imitate each other. In most cases you can only get close to the original texture and character, but it may surprise you to see *how* close.

In Drawings 1 and 2, you experimented with the various media and materials and tried to feel and see their character, strengths, and limits. You worked within those limits, taking advantage of their strengths, and finally, worked against their limits, forcing them to "become" another medium. It is this full testing of a medium's range that provides us with a sense of its nature, its range, and its potentialities.

drawing 3

Turning the illustration board vertically, divide it into three horizontal sections of ten inches each. Divide it vertically in half (Figure 7.46). Using black acrylic, the number 5 flat bristle brush, and water, make a gradual tonal change from black to white, allowing the white board to be visible on

Figure 7.46

the far right side of 1A, as in the earlier tonal changes. Thus, as the tone lightens, you will use less paint and more water. In 2A, do the same, but use both black and white acrylics, keeping the paint film opaque. When completed, both should be smooth graduations of tone. This will be less easily accomplished in 1A. Once they have dried, dark areas cannot be removed. Therefore, adjustments in 1A must be made quickly. Here, it is best to start with the lightest tones and work toward the darks on the left. If, after drying, 1A or 2A need further tonal adjusting, use both Chinese and acrylic white to touch up, and notice the better covering power when these paints are mixed. After completion, use these two boxes for any further experiments with any of the other media.

Use 1B as an area in which to experiment on this new surface with all of the media you used in Drawings 1 and 2. In 2B, wet the illustration board lightly with clean water. When just slightly damp, lay in a thin, semi-opaque wash of 50 percent gray. When this has dried, use both of your bristle brushes however you wish to draw any simple object in black and white acrylic. In 1C, using black acrylic, any or all of your three brushes, and water, lay in the volume-summary of another observed object. This should be done within five minutes. Continue to develop the drawing in any one of the abrasive media used earlier. In 2C, using any combination of these media, but omitting acrylics, and any tools except brushes, try to duplicate the drawing in 2B exactly. In place of brushes, you can use your fingers, rolled up paper, cotton swabs, sponges, etc. You may want to try duplicating 2B with abrasive media alone—perhaps using only charcoal.

In the preceding exercises you have explored some materials by going with and against their character. This of course does not exhaust the possibilities. Acrylics can be used to imitate the various abrasive media; one combination of media can be made to imitate another; different surfaces would affect the behavior of both media and tools; different tools would affect the media, and so on. The possibilities are virtually endless.

At the beginning, it is better to probe a few media and materials and go deeper. Here, a suggested approach for the study of any medium, tool, or surface is offered to help you when you seek them out. Although all our materials continue to reveal their nature as we use them, the few hours spent in testing, forcing, probing—in discovering—can provide an understanding that may only come in bits and pieces over a long period of time. It may be years before a student tries to mix—in one drawing—casein, ink, and chalks, only to find the combination works better than anything else he has tried for establishing the images he intends. But if, when first encountering caseins, he takes the time to experiment, he can learn this sooner.

The media and materials of drawing are the physical agents of our intentions. They do not themselves discover or invent, but they *do* suggest. To understand these suggestions we have to learn to understand and respect our tools. One without the other will not yet produce control.

In the act of responsive drawing, our media and materials either help or hurt our interpretive efforts. They serve us well if we know them well—but they are never neutral.

CHAPTER EIGHT

VISUAL ISSUES

the forming of order

A DEFINITION

We have seen that responsive drawing concerns *what* is drawn and *how* it is drawn, and that these considerations are interdependent. Each mark on the page does two things: it helps define a subject's structural and spatial characteristics, and by its physical properties, conveys a particular kind of dynamic meaning. This meaning can be thought of as embracing both energy and mood—the marks produce *expressive actions*. Furthermore by their interactions, that is, by the way the lines and tones relate and affect each other, they create the visual associations and forces that give a drawing its own pattern of abstract order, its expressive character, and, consequently, its aesthetic worth. To expand an earlier observation about line, *all* the marks that constitute a drawing *define, act,* and *interact.* Each mark is a part of the drawing's organizational and emotive condition.

This chapter concentrates on those factors that influence a drawing's organizational aspects—its abstract and compositional de-

sign. But, because each mark simultaneously affects a drawing's visual and expressive meanings, to separate a drawing's organization from its expression risks distorting our understanding of both. Nevertheless we have separated these factors temporarily, focussing upon the visual in this chapter and the expressive in the next, in order to help clarify our understanding of each, and deepen our realization of their interrelated nature.

Some cultures have always understood drawings as systems of *design*. The single Italian term *disegno* describes both drawing and design, as does the French *dessin*. In fact, it is impossible to regard any drawing as *only* descriptive, even when nothing more was intended. Seeing and sensing the relationships and forces generated by the lines and tones is unavoidable. Design is intrinsic to any collection of marks, and is thus a given condition of drawing. How well integrated the marks are determines the quality of the design.

In a good design the marks produce affinities, contrasts, and energies that convey a sense of balance, of equilibrium between its

215

parts, and between them and the page. Additionally, all of the design's components—its lines, shapes, tones, textures, and masses—have strong interacting bonds of dependence and association that create an overall sense of oneness, or *unity*. But both of these conditions can exist in very dull drawings. A drawing of a brick wall or a Venetian blind, unless the overall sameness is relieved by some variety, is boring. A drawing's stability and unity must emerge from the stimulating action of contrasts, as well as the union of similarities. We need diversity as an antidote to monotony. General principles in art are best approached cautiously, but it seems safe to assume that whatever else art is or may be, it will never allow disorder or boredom as goals. In drawings where stability and unity are achieved by interesting contrasts, similarities, and energies, we sense their order to be *necessary; any* change will destroy their organizational resolution.

RELATIONSHIPS AND ENERGIES

The preceding chapters examined the measurable relationships of shape, placement, length, scale, direction, value, and mass, in order to learn to more objectively see and inventively state volume and space. In doing so we touched briefly on design considerations concerning rhythm, movement, and continuity among a subject's parts. In this section we will expand our investigation of design to include other kinds of energies that emerge from these relationships, and to consider the balanced distribution of the subject's parts within the bounded limits of the page in ways that engage the entire page.

We have seen that all of a drawing's marks must be made of *line* or *value*, and that these in turn form the several graphic factors of *shape, volume and space*, and *texture*. All of the visual issues that concern a drawing's design result from the behavior of these five basic factors. They are collectively called *visual elements* (another visual element, color, being incidental to the essentials of drawing, is here omitted). To discuss the relational possibilities that can occur in a drawing's design, we will need to examine these elements fur-

ther. As we do, remember that the term "element" refers to anything from a line or tone to the mass of a house. Remember too that, unlike the visible relationships between elements, the various abstract or plastic (and emotive) energies that these relationships generate are themselves invisible. We only sense or intuit them.

The possibilities for relationships based on similarity or contrast between the elements are limitless. In fact, in the best drawings the visual activities of the elements seem capable of endless interactions. Great drawings are never "used up." Relationships can be obvious or extremely subtle. Each element in a drawing participates in at least a few, and sometimes many, different visual associations, producing different visual forces. These forces are as varied as the relationships that create them. Being so much a matter of intuited impressions, they elude verbal descriptions of more than their general kind of behavior.

Relationships are always based on comparisons of some kind, but depend on contrasts to be effective. A shape may be large in relation to the page—its scale is *similar* to that of the page—but will appear even larger if it is seen in *contrast* to smaller shapes upon the page. Likewise, we do not usually regard a white sheet of paper as being bright, we regard it as blank. Not until dark tones appear on the page does its tone have any quality of light or any other visual meaning. Where everything is bright, nothing is.

A single vertical line drawn on a page creates a contrast with the "emptiness" of the page. The line is unlike any other part of the paper (though it is similar in direction to the vertical borders of the page). When a second line is drawn parallel to the first, an obvious similarity exists between them. Two more lines, drawn at right angles to the first pair, are like them as lines, but contrasting in their position. If the four lines form a square, they are related to the page *and* to each other by the shape they make (Figure 8.1). Thus, elements can show contrast on one level of relationship and similarity on another. When, as in Figure 8.1, similarities overpower contrasts the result is boredom. When contrasts overpower similarities, the result is chaos. A successful design must avoid both of these extremes. Its contrasts may

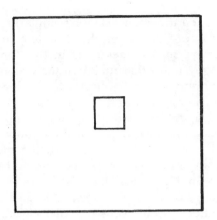

Figure 8.1

threaten but should never succeed in destroying balance and unity. The artist must organize confronting contrasts into some greater system of order.

Although unlimited in their visual interactions, relationships among the elements can be roughly sorted into twelve discernibly different categories. These categories of relational activity and some of the energies they generate are as follows.

1. line. The similarities and contrasts arising from their direction, length, weight and value, location, handling (or character), and their straight or curved nature, as in Figure 8.2. Note that some lines, despite their contrasting lengths, directions, weights, etc., relate by in-

Figure 8.2

tersecting, location, or through other similarities. Note, too, that similar lines can contrast in other ways, as in their weight or handling.

2. direction. The sense of movement or of striving for change, as when like or unlike elements relate because of a discernible continuity of their positions on the picture-plane or in the pictorial field. Direction is also sensed when similarities of length, shape, value, scale, or texture among various elements cause us to recognize common directions among them. Such elements seem to move in various straight or curved paths, and even suggest their speed. Elements can "amble" along or can convey powerful velocity. The more unlike elements in a direction are, the weaker and slower the sense of movement; the greater their similarities, the stronger their directional thrust. For example, note the strong fan-like energy of the long lines in Figure 8.2, and the weaker directional energy that unites the shorter straight and curved lines at the bottom of the drawing.

All elements except shapes and masses whose boundaries are equidistant from their centers, such as squares and spheres, are *inherently* directional. This being the case, directional cues, and the movement energies they generate, *pervade all other relationships.* Thus, visual associations based on direction, and the sense of moving forces at work in a drawing (and in the observed or envisioned subject) are at the heart of any system of visual order. The importance in recognizing the dominance of directional relationships cannot be overstated. Just as directional forces activate the lines in Figure 8.2, so can we see them at work in the following illustrations of relationships among the elements, and in *all* drawings.

3. scale. The similarities or contrasts of size between like or unlike elements. When other visual factors are alike or in balance, the larger of two elements will dominate the smaller one. For a strong sense of dominance to occur, the larger elements must relate clearly with those they dominate, as in Figure 8.3, where the scale differences between the houses, and between the trees, are more evident than the similarities of scale between the

Figure 8.3

large house and tree, or the small house and tree. But note that, in sharing long, vertical axes and chevron-like endings at their tops, all four units relate by directional cues (including the horizontal direction of their alignment).

4. shape. The similarities or contrasts of shape between elements. In Figure 8.4, the elements form one set of relationships based on shape-character, another based on scale, and still another on moving energies. Because all planes, masses, and interspaces have shape, it is important to be aware of the shape-groupings that form in any drawing.

5. value. The similarities or contrasts of value between elements. In Figure 8.5, the elements, in addition to relationships based on scale,

shape, and direction, relate by similarities and contrasts of value. Note that in doing so, new directional forces emerge, as in the "line" of light gray tones that runs obliquely along the lower right side of the illustration. Value is an important agent of unity. As a comparison between Figures 8.4 and 8.5 shows, value, when added to line drawings, can profoundly affect visual groupings of elements on the picture-plane and in the spatial field of depth. For example, in Figure 8.4, the small block in the drawing's center can be seen as located either behind or in front of the irregular block in the lower center of the design; in Figure 8.5, it appears to fall behind the irregular shape, now a block. When used for purposes of illuminating forms, values by bathing them, whatever the intricacies and differences of the forms, unite them by darkening the sides turned away from the light. Each form is affected by the light in the same way. And, in casting shadows on neighbors, dissimilar forms share the tonal bonds created by the light.

6. rhythm. The sense of a regulated pattern of movement or visual occurrences between like or unlike elements. Rhythm can be thought of as a kind of visual meter, a system of moving or pulsating activities among the elements, or among their properties of scale, location, or direction. And, like a musical meter, such relationships occur within some pattern of

Figure 8.4

Figure 8.5

rigid or loose intervals. Like directional relationships, the presence of rhythmic ones can be sensed throughout the best drawings, where every line and tone, and every one of the forms, textures, or spaces they produce is a member of one or more rhythmic systems. Often, rhythms are sensed most among elements repeating a similar movement or interval. The more often such activities are repeated, the stronger the sense of rhythm. Whether they are moving or "beat" rhythms, the sense of rhythm is one of the stronger forces in unifying a drawing, weaving together many otherwise weakly related elements. When, as in Rembrandt's *Saskia Asleep in Bed* (Figure 8.6), strong rhythmic and directional forces are combined, intense movement energies course through a drawing, enveloping and uniting every part.

7. texture. The similarities or contrasts of textures, whether of a tactile or media-induced nature, between like or unlike elements. In Figure 8.7, dots unite walls, flowers, grasses, and fields. Additionally, Van Gogh uses the reed pen to make broad, short, jabbing strokes which invest each shape, mass, and value with a common pattern of marks. Textures can create passages of surface activity that give other, more "restful" passages, greater meaning. Notice in this drawing how the dense concentrations of texture in the

Figure 8.6
REMBRANDT VAN RIJN (1606–1669)
Saskia Asleep in Bed
Brush, pen, bistre ink. 13.7 x 20.3 cm.
Ashmolean Museum, Oxford

Figure 8.7
VINCENT VAN GOGH (1853–1890)
Montmajour
Reed pen and ink. 48.5 x 59 cm.
Rijksmuseum, Amsterdam

foreground give the more simply stated boulders a stronger sense of weight and mass, and the sky a greater tranquility.

8. location and proximity. When like or unlike elements are seen as belonging together because they occupy positions equally near or far from the center of the page, or when unlike elements are yet more alike than surrounding ones. Both of these conditions are seen in Figure 8.8. Delacroix relates the archway and the door beyond it to the large door and the figure on the right by centering each segment in its half of the page, and by surrounding these concentrations of small

shapes, values, and forms by large, light shapes, values, and forms. In a drawing of forms as unlike as leaves, locks, and cups, they will appear related if encompassed by forms, spaces, shapes, or values unlike any in the cluster. It is difficult to overcome the unity of dense groupings. We cannot see an apple in a bowl of fruit as separate from the rest. However, through other relational forces, and by relating the apple with a symmetrically located form or tone, it can be made to join with elements far across the page (Figure 8.9). When elements are very close to each other or to a border of the page they produce a sense of striving toward contact, toward the completion of the suggested action. This is called *closure*, and is a compelling force. It is impossible to disregard the circular "shape" a ring of dots suggests. Although no line delineates the circle, we sense its presence.

9. handling, or character. The similarities and contrasts of elements because of the artist's use of the medium and his forceful or delicate manner of graphic expression. By changes in the handling, two otherwise similar lines, shapes, or tones can be made to contrast. Conversely, in a drawing where everything is broadly suggested and the medium's charac-

teristics are pronounced, two or more elements, even located far apart on the page, may relate if they are more delicately handled and more precisely stated. In Figure 8.10, Wyeth's changes in handling, from sweeping, gestural generalities to precise enunciations, create strong associations between parts of the drawing that would be absent in a detailed execution of every part.

10. visual weight. The degree of visual importance or impact on the design of elements *on the picture-plane.* Visual weight is determined mainly by an element's location on the page, by its contrast to other elements in the

Figure 8.8
EUGÈNE DELACROIX (1798–1863)
Arab at the Door of His House
Watercolor. 10.8 x 14.5 cm.
Rijksmuseum, Amsterdam

Figure 8.9

Figure 8.10
ANDREW WYETH (1917–
Turkey Buzzard
Pencil. 17 3/4 x 23 3/4 in.
Courtesy, Museum of Fine Arts, Boston
Bequest of Maxim Karolik

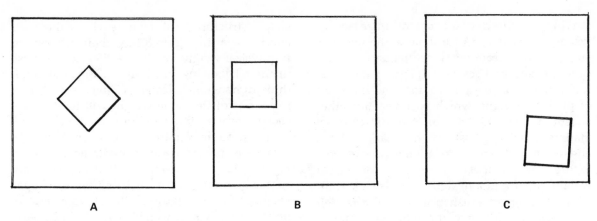

Figure 8.11

drawing, and by its inherent directional energies. Although an element's directional energy (or, in the case of a volume, its suggested physical weight) strongly influences its visual weight, an element's visual weight is to a considerable degree independent of these factors. And while the visual weights in a design generally tend, like physical weight, to balance by a sensed pulling downward to the left and right of an imagined fulcrum, they *can* suggest movement in any direction. For example, in Figure 8.8, the unit comprised of the large door and the man, in "reaching" for a point at the top of the page, seem to "fall" up, rather than down. This is especially pronounced in the man's upper body, where its overall wedge-like shape and dark tones strive obliquely upward. Again, on the left, the archway and the shapes within it seem upward-, not downward-bound.

That the visual weight of an element will vary with its location on the picture-plane can be seen by comparing Figure 8.1 with the three variations in Figure 8.11. In Figure 8.1, the centrally placed square seems balanced within its frame. Here, balance is not so much a state of absolute rest as it is a neutralization of "invisible" forces that move between the square and the boundaries of the picture-plane. We sense a strong alignment between the parallel lines, and between the corners of the square and the frame. The square seems suspended in its position because of "magnetic" forces acting with equal energy on all sides. Here, the square is not weightless, but its visual force is controlled—it does not upset

equilibrium. In Figure 8.11A, the sense of balance, while still strong, is of a more tenuous nature—the square is less securely held in check. This is so partly because the total configuration *and* the forces at work are more complex, and partly because a diamond shape is inherently more active than a square, offering diagonal lines everywhere, instead of the more stable verticals and horizontals of the square. In Figure 8.11B, the square takes on more visual weight; there is an increased degree of tension, a need for balance between it and the frame. The square strives for centrality *and* for union with the left vertical side of the frame. Nor is the frame entirely passive. We sense it "pulling" the square towards the left. Here, the square has more visual impact, is of more arresting attraction to the viewer, because its condition is more unresolved. In Figure 8.11C, the visual weight of the square is even greater. This is the result of three conditions: the square is now nearer to two edges of the frame, thus increasing the force of closure; it is positioned at an ambiguous angle, not quite upright nor obviously tilted, creating an even greater "wish" in the viewer for some simpler alignment; and it is located at the far lower right corner of the frame, the area where all elements will seem heaviest. It is not altogether clear why this last fact is so, but Gestalt psychologists have shown this to be the case.* As these examples indicate, a

*See Rudolf Arnheim, *Art and Visual Perception* (Berkeley and Los Angeles:University of California Press, 1969), Chapter 1.

striving for directed movement increases as visual weight does. Additionally, the energies emerging here from relationships based on location, shape, and scale also play a part in determining visual weight, as does the influence of physical weight, which is never altogether absent in evaluations of two-dimensional matters. Indeed, visual weight is affected by, and in turn affects, *all* relational phenomena. Figure 8.6 provides an example of visual weight at work in a design. The visual weight of the two broad brushstrokes on the far left help balance and vary the otherwise largely horizontal configuration. Although these strokes suggest a curtain, their main function is to add visual weight on the left, to keep the configuration from tipping into the lower right corner. To appreciate the phenomenon oᶠ elements weighing more on the right than the left side of a picture-plane, hold this drawing up to a mirror and note how the figure, the bedding, and the broad brush strokes of the curtain and the wall rush toward the lower right corner, destroying the drawing's balance on the page. The avoidance of heavy visual or physical weight on the right side can be noted in most of the drawings reproduced in this book.

11. physical weight. The contrasts and similarities of forms based on their structural nature and their suggested or known weight. For example, given two forms similar in scale,

shape, structure, and value, such as the vase and hammer in Figure 8.12A, their differences in physical weight will cause them to contrast in their balancing functions in the drawing's three-dimensional design. Conversely, differing forms of the same weight will tend to associate through this similarity, as the rock and hammer do in Figure 8.12B. A more stable balance of physical weight exists here than in Figure 8.12A. However, note that Figure 8.12A succeeds more in its distribution of visual weight, whereas Figure 8.12B suffers a serious imbalance of visual weights.

All drawings of volumes in space convey a sense of gravity at work among the forms, but a form's physical weight can be considerably increased or decreased by its visual weight in the design. Thus, a form's position in the pictorial field is a factor in establishing both its two- and three-dimensional role in the design. That each type of weight can modify the other can be seen by holding Figure 8.12 up to a mirror. Now Figure 8.12B seems less unbalanced by visual weight, and Figure 8.12A seems less unbalanced by physical weight. The suggested or known physical weight of recognizable forms, being an important modifier of visual weight, can greatly affect a drawing's overall design.

In Goya's powerful drawing (Figure 8.13), the physical weight of the suspended figure (made even heavier by the visual weight that results from the figure's isolation

Figure 8.12

Figure 8.13

FRANCISCO DE GOYA (1746–1828)

Torture by the Strappado
Sepia wash. 20.5 x 14.3 cm.
Courtesy of The Hispanic Society of America

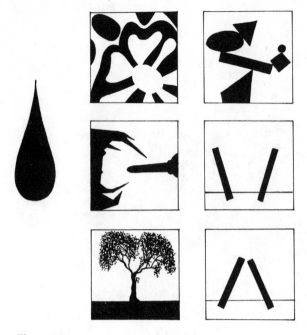

Figure 8.14

against the background and by the forceful diagonal thrusts of the shapes) is necessary to the balance of masses in the design. Were the figure to be replaced by a bundle of similarly shaped and toned drapery, the design would be far too weighted on the right side. Indeed, as it is, there is a greater physical weight on the right side. But Goya's increase of the victim's total pictorial weight compensates for this. Additionally, by stressing the upward movement of the wedge-like "super" shape of all the forms on the drawing's right side, Goya causes the visual weight of these forms to be directed up, further decreasing the physical weight on the right side.

As this example suggests, the forms in a drawing must make visual sense at both the two- and three-dimensional levels, and at their depictive and abstract levels. While it is absurd (if more humane) to torture a bundle of draperies, it is equally (if less evidently) absurd to defeat a drawing's psychological and social message by destroying its balance on the page. For, when our attention is diverted by a basic imbalance in what we are looking at, the particular activities of the scene are less important, and even less understandable.

12. tension. When two or more elements, or parts of the same element, opposed or attracting in some way, suggest a sense of impending ac-

tion or change. The elements participating in tension often share strong similarities in other respects, but seem poised and about to attack or pull away from each other. Elements in tension suggest an "awareness" of each other. Although opposition is often their basic stance, they always suggest a magnetic attraction. This dual relationship makes elements in tension seem to pulsate. Often, the members of such a relationship are roughly equal in their visual importance in the design. Tension can be sensed between elements nearby or far from each other, and between confronting groups of elements. Tension is also sensed between elements that seem to support or unbalance each other, or when elements are engaged in contrasting relationships, such as opposing directions. Tension is possible between parts of a single element, as, for example, the tension we sense in the heavy, rounded bottom of a waterdrop shape. There is tension inherent in diagonal lines and complex shapes, in elements that almost touch, and in ambiguities between figure and ground shapes (Figure 8.14).

As these twelve categories suggest, elements are always engaged in multiple relationships. For example, an association between two values must necessarily extend to include their *shape* relationship, and these shapes of tone have *location, scale, direction,* and *visual weight,* are *handled* in a certain way, etc. A drawing's balance and unity depend on the artist's ability to *sense* and control these relational bonds. For, after the first few marks of a drawing, the relational possibilities, growing by geometric progression, are too many to be seen; they must be sensed. The artist is guided toward equilibrium and unity by an overall sensitivity to a drawing's "rightness" of balance and cohesion—as much a matter of intuition as of intellect. As with all other aspects of responsive drawing, designs are formed by facts *and* feelings.

THE CONFIGURATION AND THE PAGE

When the artist begins to draw, relational energies begin among the elements and between them and the page. These relationships exist as two- and three-dimensional events simultaneously. Sometimes, two-dimensional relationships "work" with the drawing's design on the picture-plane, but conflict with three-dimensional meanings, and vice versa. For example, the eight shapes in Figure 8.15A relate in a balanced, unified way. There is a gradual progression in their scale; their several directions and abutments offer interesting variety; and the design of the two larger shapes embracing six smaller ones form a discernible theme. But, regarded as blocks in space, the abutments between their planes and the borders of the spatial field, as well as the abutment between the blocks, weaken the impression of volumes in space. Such tangential connections make it difficult to know which of the blocks is ahead of the other, or which is larger.

The six small shapes in Figure 8.15B are, from the standpoint of two-dimensional design, too small to relate to the large shape of the picture-plane. Instead of the interaction between *all* the shapes, as in Figure 8.15A, here the little shapes form two isolated clusters, and the shape of the picture-plane remains passive. Additionally, the tension and direction between the two clusters of shapes creates a diagonal "tug" that disturbs the vertical-horizontal orientation of the picture-plane. For, the first diagonal direction in a drawing, unlike vertical and horizontal directions which always run parallel to two of the picture-plane's boundaries, is obviously

"alone." There are no "friendly" directions to relate with. Therefore, diagonals are usually counterbalanced by other diagonals, as in Figure 8.15A, where sets of oblique lines cancel each other's movements.

In Figure 8.15B, no good compositional end is served by the placement of such small volumes in so large a field of space, but the blocks *are* clearly presented as forms in space. Additionally, the sense of weight adds a second force. Acting somewhat as a counterforce, the pull of gravity starts a downward tug. This "promise" of a downward movement of the blocks, especially of the one on the right, seems to lessen the imbalance between the blocks and the page. If we turn this illustration on its side, the sense of gravity, plus the forces of direction and tension, unite to create an even stronger diagonal pull. Seen right-side-up again, we sense the moderating effect of physical weight on the diagonal position of the blocks.

Although responsive drawings always convey some impression of the third dimension, they are formed by flat lines and tones upon a bounded, flat surface. Their design as two-dimensional facts must be compatible with their three-dimensional impressions. These facts and impressions must be complemental—must work with each other and with the shape of the page.

Many drawings are quick sketchbook notations, or brief, preliminary investigations. Such spontaneous, on-the-spot efforts generally try to capture a subject's essential character and action, study some particular structural or textural aspect of its forms, or serve as a preliminary design strategy for a work in another medium. We have seen examples in Figures 1.6, 2.20, 3.5, 7.29, and 8.10. Often, such sketches are not intended to be integrated with the page. Even here, though, an intuitive sense of balance between configuration and page, of the influence on the thing drawn by the shape of the surface, causes subconscious decisions about the placement of the configuration (or the several independent studies) on the page.

It is clear from Raphael's page of sketches (Figure 8.16) that the artist is absorbed in examining the volume of a draped figure and some hands, and not (intention-

Figure 8.15

Figure 8.16
RAPHAEL (1483–1520)
Study for the Parnassus
Pen and ink. 34.3 x 24.2 cm.
The British Museum, London

Figure 8.17
THÉODORE GÉRICAULT (1791–1824)
Pencil sketches of Carabinieri, Heads of Horses
Pencil. 17.4 x 23.2 cm.
Courtesy of The Art Institute of Chicago

ally) concerned with a balanced arrangement of forms on the page. Even so, it is difficult to imagine redesigning this group of studies into some better pattern. Each independent segment is placed with a sensitive regard for the others. Similarly, Géricault's sketches of mounted soldiers and heads of horses (Figure 8.17) are drawn as independent studies but, by their location and rhythmic kinships, show an overall harmony and balance on the page. Both the Raphael and Géricault drawings are, however unintentionally, well-designed works. But other drawings, although they may not fill the page, *do* intend an interrelational bond between the configuration and the page. Such drawings are unlike the usually more formal compositions of paintings or drawings that engage the entire picture-plane. They are conceived (or resolved) as arrangements of forms in spatial environments that depend on, but do not touch, the limits of a page to make sense as a design.

In such drawings, visual issues actively involve the entire page. The outer zones of drawings that do not extend to the limits of the page may be empty of drawing marks, but not of visual meaning. They always have shape, scale, and value, convey direction, and are similar to, or in contrast with, various parts of the configuration. They are always part of the drawing's design. These "empty" areas influence the configurations *representational dynamics*, that is, what the things depicted do as actions (falling, running, bending, etc.), and what the *visual and expressive dynamics*, the abstract design and emotive energies do as actions. These figural and plastic actions and expressions together, are called a drawing's *content* (see Chapter Eleven).

Because so many responsive drawings are spontaneous, brief, and image-oriented, artists often use such a design strategy. It permits a strong concentration on the subject. Often, the surrounding, empty area of the page acts as a "shock absorber" against which the drawing's forces are turned back upon themselves to start the cycle of moving actions over again. Then, too, this strategy allows a fuller concentration of responsive powers on the subject than when they are divided between it and demands of a full-scale com-

positional scheme. This does not mean that such drawings are less united with the page than are those which fill it entirely. It means only that the encircling, undrawn area is assigned the less active, but no less important, role of containing and modifying the dynamics of the configuration.

In Rembrandt's *The Mummers* (Figure 8.18), the configuration is well within the limits of the page, but strongly interrelated with its shape and scale. The drawing "opens up" in several places to admit the surrounding empty area of the page, physically fusing with it. The frequent reappearance of the white page within the drawn areas helps unite them. But the strongest bond between the configuration and the page exists in the organizational dependence they have for each other.

Near the drawing's exact center, the hand holding the reins marks the center of an expanding burst of lines, shapes, and tones of such power that we sense its radiating force in the hat, collar, elbow, leg, and reins of the figure on the left. This force is continued in the neck and chest of the horse, and in the lines near the man on the right. The release of such explosive energies warrants the thick, surrounding buffer of space (Figure 8.19A). We can sense an "implosion" too. The empty area absorbs the "shock waves" and sends them back again. These sensations keep alternating as we look at the page. Both the drawn and empty areas contribute to, and share, these pulsations.

Had Rembrandt continued to draw the entire horse, the empty area would have been cut in two, destroying the surrounding buffer and weakening the radiating force as well. Had he made this drawing on a larger sheet of paper, the impact of the explosive pattern would have been greatly reduced and the subject overwhelmed by the scale of the empty area. No "echoes" would return from the limits of the page, because they would be beyond the range of the drawing's energies, and thus, no visual interplay between the drawn and empty areas would exist. The configuration would be isolated in a sea of paper.

Every type of relational activity is present in this drawing. We see how powerfully line and direction are used, and how they

Figure 8.18
REMBRANDT VAN RIJN (1606–1669)
The Mummers
Pen and ink with wash. 21.2 x 15.3 cm.
The Pierpont Morgan Library

230

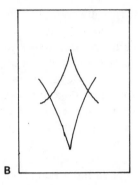

A   B

Figure 8.19

pervade the entire composition. The rhythm of the many directional "spokes," radiating from the drawing's center owes much to line, and to those invisible "lines" of force that relationships of direction produce. An almost equally powerful visual theme that also moves through the drawing is generated by other directions, rhythms, and tensions (Figure 8.19B).

In Figure 8.18, beginning with the near man's lower leg, a vertical movement spreads left and right in a fan-like manner. The angle of the near man's lower arm, and the repeated lines of his waistcoat convey one half of the fan's spread; the other half is carried by the lines in the far man's coat, by the several brush strokes defining the horse's mane, and by the lines of the background near the man on the right. This fan-like action creates one tension between its two halves, and another between it and the inverted V-shaped counterforce formed by the directions of the sword and the reins. The V shape is reinforced by some lines in the near man's saddle, and some of the lines between the leg and the reins. Tensions between the various lines and brush strokes of the horse make these marks seem to attract each other. These tensions, and the sense of closure between the marks, help us to "see" the largely nonexistent animal. The proximity of the two figures, and the dominant dark value between them, unite the men into one great diamond-like shape that is centrally balanced on the page in the same tenuous and provocative way as the diamond shape in Figure 8.11A. Visual and physical weight are also centrally balanced in this design. Note that Rembrandt reduces the physical weight of the horse's neck and head, lest

the weight of so large a mass undo the drawing's equilibrium. Rembrandt's handwriting—its consistent, animated energy—further reinforces the power of the actions described above, and helps to unite the drawing. The resulting balance, involving every component, can be tested by covering any segment of the drawn area by a small scrap of paper, or by surrounding the boundaries of the drawing with a frame of white paper, or by reducing the size of the drawing by seeing it through a dark mat, cut smaller than the present measurements of the drawing. Doing any of these things will destroy the drawing's stability.

These are only *some* of the drawing's relational activities. There are many more. Indeed, each of the marks has some function that contributes to the drawing's organization and unity. As we have stated, each defines, acts, and interacts.

Beginning students often question whether an artist consciously intends each of the force-producing relationships in a drawing. They doubt that the drawing's dynamics always represent deliberate judgments, and suspect that many of the relationships pointed out in a particular drawing never entered the artist's mind—and they are right! It was observed earlier that after a drawing is well under way, there are just too many bonds of association, too many abstract actions for the artist to see and consciously control, and that the drawing's resolution depends on intuition as much as intellect.

This holds true for an examination of any particular drawing. As we study other drawing strategies in this chapter, we should remember that any analysis of a design reveals only some of its relational activities (probably those reflecting the analyst's own instincts about organization)—and that many of these may well reflect the artist's intuitive impulses *and subconscious interest.* For, the content of any drawing contains certain intangibles that express the artist's personality and philosophy that are not only subconscious, but resistant to any attempts by the artist to free himself of them.

Also, we must recognize that even if a drawing's relational life *could* be fully and objectively known, a key if impalpable ingredient would still be missing. This mysterious "something" certainly concerns a drawing's design and expression, but is not limited to them. It is a quality that permeates the drawing, transforming the means into active meanings. If we regard responsive drawings as graphic equivalents of living organisms, then whatever gives the graphic organism "life" is as mysterious as those powers that animate and sustain living things in nature. Therefore, intellectual dissection can no more determine this "something plus" that separates art from competence than the character of a person can be learned by surgery.

What *can* be learned about the relational activities that form a drawing's design strategy makes analyzing drawings an important source of information and insight. Although the beginner rightly senses that drawing is not a wholly conscious activity, a more pertinent question would be: are these relationships really present? In the analysis of Figure 8.18, the several relationships and forces discussed occur too consistently, are too

critically established, and too self-evident to be mere chance or exaggerated claims on their effects. Moreover, the absence of visual discords and non sequiturs—of elements *not* engaged in the several actions discussed, or not otherwise contributing to the drawings order—is, again, beyond chance. Whatever an artist's personal "formula" between reason and instinct may be, the fact remains that in great drawings a great many questions and needs have been well answered.

Although very different in style, mood, and subject, Diaz de la Peña's drawing *Landscape* (Figure 8.20), shows a use of the empty areas of the page similar to that in Rembrandt's drawing. Here, a "ground burst" of radiating directions spreads out on the horizontal plane of the field as well as on the picture-plane, and almost fades away at the edges of the page, retaining the encircling, single shape of the rest of the page. Again, the plan is the use of the outer portions of the page as a force-absorbing belt of space. The trees, rising from the center of the burst, take

Figure 8.20
NARCISSE VIRGILE DIAZ DE LA PEÑA (1807–1876)
Landscape
Black chalk. 6 x 11 in.
Sterling and Francine Clark Art Institute, Williamstown

Figure 8.21
KENNETH CALLAHAN (1906–   )
Summer Bug
Sumi ink. 23 1/16 x 35 1/4 in.
Worcester Art Museum, Worcester, Mass.

on more contrasting force from it. But, unlike the vigorous energy in Rembrandt's drawing, the forces in Diaz de la Peña's are more muffled. The horizontally located configuration, the pronounced texture of the chalk medium, the restricted value-range, and the soft edges of the forms make this a quiet design, compatible with the subject's restful mood. The surrounding space, especially that above the landscape, reducing and absorbing the configuration's energies, helps to suggest the drawing's pastoral nature.

The surrounding buffer in Callahan's drawing *Summer Bug* (Figure 8.21), does have some light washes of tone near the insect, but again, the space serves to contain and contrast with the actions generated by the configuration. A sense of the bug's slowly moving legs is conveyed by the rhythms between them.

Callahan uses the visual weight and dominance of the dark tone on the last segment of the bug's body to counterbalance the physical weight and downward tilt of the form, and by this single, strong contrast, to heighten the drawing's fragile delicacy.

While the Diaz and Callahan drawings are widely divergent in subject, time, and aesthetic persuasion, they share a similar design strategy. The encircling of a horizontal image by white space, an overall gentle handling, pronounced textures, energies radiating from a central point in the image, and darker tones surrounding a white core at its center are tactics common to both works.

A somewhat similar abstract theme organizes still another kind of subject in Cretara's *Sleeping Woman* (Figure 8.22). Here again, an encircling buffer of space "fits" the configura-

Figure 8.22
DOMENIC CRETARA (1946–   )
Sleeping Woman
Red chalk. 14 x 18 in.
Courtesy of the artist

tion's moving energies, emerging mainly from the center of the image. Again, dark tones encircle a white core, and, like the tree in the Diaz de la Peña drawing and the lower body of the bug in the Callahan, a single dark tone in the hair gives the drawing a gentler air, tonal variety, and needed visual weight on the right. But in the Cretara, forceful lines and shapes, such as those throughout the torso and pillows, give the drawing a more vigorous and spontaneous spirit.

As these examples show, drawings of differing subjects can utilize a common design plan which gives them a kind of family resemblance. Drawings of the same or similar subjects, even when a common set of abstract patterns are used, can also be markedly contrasting. This can be seen by comparing two drawings by Hokusai and Rodin (Figures 8.23 and 8.24). Both use a broad "pedestal" of curvilinear lines, shapes, and volumes to support the animated behavior of their subject; both emphasize the rhythms of drapery and figure; and both shape the configuration into a rough C-shaped curve (reversed in Hokusai).

Hokusai places the figure to the right of the page, while Rodin places it almost centrally. These differences in location are due mainly to the tilt and actions of the figures. In Hokusai's drawing, the extended material at

Figure 8.23
KATSUSHIKA HOKUSAI (1760–1849)
A Maid Preparing to Dust
Brush and ink. 12½ x 9 in.
Freer Gallery of Art, Washington, D. C.

ground shapes echo the triangular shape of the woman's drape.

In addition to these nuances of differences in the same basic design theme, these two drawings differ in far more obvious ways, chief among them being a linear versus a tonal basis of expression.

Perhaps artists do not always consciously consider the design of the configuration on the page, especially in drawings of a brief, exploratory nature. However, it is universally recognized that once an artist's initial responses are translated into marks upon the page, they in turn stimulate responses to the organizational needs of the evolving drawing within the limits of the pictorial field, including the latter as a consideration in shaping the design. Whatever dynamic themes combine to begin a drawing, its realization is

Figure 8.24
AUGUSTE RODIN (1840–1917)
Nude
Pencil and watercolor. 17 5/8 x 12 1/2 in.
Courtesy of The Art Institute of Chicago

the top and the swirling robe at the bottom of the page swerve abruptly from the figure's nearly vertical direction to move forcefully to the left. Had the artist placed the figure to the right, it would have left a very large pocket of empty space on the left, out of scale with the other shapes on the page, and crowding the figure unnecessarily to the right. Her slight leftward tilt also permits Hokusai to place the figure near the right side. Were she exactly vertical, there would be too much weight and attention on the right.

Rodin's design of the figure, though there is not a single vertical line in the drawing, taken collectively is vertical. Placing the image nearer to the right side would upset the drawing's balance on the page; moving it to the left would make the background shapes monotonously alike. Notice that the back-influenced by the visual events resulting from the size and shape of the page, as well as the visual nature of the emerging image and the characteristics of the medium used. Although these drawings do not fill the page, they *use* the page as an active part of the design and not merely as a blank area, unrelated to the configuration.

Other themes require other solutions. Often, as in painting, artists draw to the borders of the page. This is frequently the case when an artist's initial interests in a subject concern its potentialities for a unique design arrangement. That is, their attraction is stimulated by anticipating an interaction of subject and page that will result in a composition compatible with their interests in the subject's character or condition. Although all responsive artists regard as interdependent the subject and the design system it suggests, artists vary widely as to which of these receives primary emphasis.

If we compare Figure 5.14 with Figure 3.2, we see that Campagnola's primary interest is in the subject, and Toulouse-Lautrec's is in the drawing's design. Although neither artist emphasizes one consideration to the neglect of the other, the difference in their responses to each is evident. For Campagnola the balance between directions, the contrasts and tensions between elements, and the rhythmic play between straight and curved edges are subdued. The forces are there, the drawing functions as a handsome system of order, but the design is below the surface—an intangible presence of pattern. In Lautrec's drawing the directions, contrasts, and rhythms are pronounced. As with all good designs, neither drawing can be cropped or added to without destroying its balance and unity.

Hopper's drawing *Burlesque Theatre, Times Square* (Figure 8.25) conveys an even-handed interest in both considerations. He captures the massive scale and baroque flavor of the theatre—we sense its spacious interior and false grandeur. But Hopper is equally interested in the forces that convey these qualities as visual events in their own right.

Many of the drawing's parts are designed to suspend at oblique angles from the centrally located columns that curve to the left and right near the top of the page. To the columns' left, the theatre boxes tilt down toward the left; to the columns' right, the curtains and stage tilt down toward the right. Together, these tilted forms—and the shapes, lines, and values that comprise them—act like chevron marks across the page. These oblique directions and the rising, double-arching vertical action that counters them is the drawing's basic design plan. The design works with the shape of the page, and is as much a part of the drawing's content as the page is part of the design.

Hopper's use of bold contrasts of direction, value, and rhythms intensifies the tensions between the obliquely suspended forms. Note that Hopper increases the visual weight on the drawing's left to compensate for our tendency to sense things on the right as being heavier. Note, too, that some of the force of the various directional thrusts gains momentum from Hopper's consistently loose, energetic handling of the charcoal.

Most artists turn to drawing to state linear rather than tonal ideas, and to explore and note down essential actions and edges, usually with pointed instruments. Perhaps that is why direction and rhythm are two of the more important relational forces in depicting and designing. To more fully experience direction and rhythm at work within and among a drawing's parts, it will be helpful to analyze a few of the drawings in this book by making some drawings that extract these relationships.

exercise 8A

In a three-phase progression, you will make three drawings on separate sheets of tracing paper, using any soft graphite pencil and a colored chalk or crayon pencil. There is no time limit on these analyses, but you should try not to spend much more than fifteen minutes on each phase per drawing. Select any three of the drawings reproduced in this book that show strong directional and rhythmic actions.

first phase
Using the colored pencil, draw the directional activities first. This is done by placing a sheet of

Figure 8.25
EDWARD HOPPER (1882–1967)
Burlesque Theatre, Times Square
Charcoal. 30.2 x 22.5 cm.
Corcoran Gallery of Art, Washington, D. C.

tracing paper over each drawing and selecting those straight, curved, or undulating directional actions that you regard to be the major ones—those having the most evident impact and energy. Begin by searching for those directed actions that unite parts of forms, unite interspaces and parts, and even the lines, shapes, and tones that form them. Depending on the drawings you have selected, these directed movements may correspond to the axes of forms, shapes, values, or textures. They may also be along the edges of any of these (but be careful not to turn your analysis into a contour drawing only), or may be found in a more "pure" state in the route of independent lines. When several forms, shapes, interspaces, etc., appear to con-

tinue a direction, even though such like or unlike units may be separated in the drawing, your directional lines should continue from one to the other without stopping, as in Figure 8.26. In the drawings you are analyzing, such directional movement is felt as energy. You are making these energies visible. Therefore, try to feel the force of these moving energies. Although you are looking for directions that continue between larger units, you may find that directions first seen as independent ones join up with the flow of others. When a direction is conveyed by a form's edge, do not copy the contour, but draw its *general* character, its moving action. As in gestural drawing, seek out the drawing's main movements.

Figure 8.26

When you feel you have established each drawing's major system of directional forces, using the graphite pencil, begin to extract its rhythms. As mentioned earlier, the sense of rhythm occurs as repeated movements or as "beats." As with all relationships, those based on rhythm can exist between any of the elements. Unlike the major directional forces that require strong or extended actions to have compositional significance, flowing rhythms are often built up by repetitions of smaller directions among the elements, as well as among the major ones. "Beat" rhythms are generally seen in the spaced reappearance of any element. Sometimes, both kinds of rhythm will be present in the same formations, as in Guardi's *A Venetian Scene* (Figure 8.27). Here, the figures offer a system of fence-like vertical directions that relate with other short vertical movements throughout the drawing to create a rhythm of up-and-down motions that animates the scene. Additionally, a "cadence" of small, dark and light value "beats" moves across the figures, as does a moving rhythm of wriggling lines. Notice that, collectively, the figures also form the strongest directional force in the drawing.

As you analyze each of the three drawings for rhythm, you can expect to be shunted onto a directional track now and then. Flowing rhythms frequently merge with directional actions because both are concerned with movement, as can be seen in Figure 8.28, where rhythms and directions cannot easily be sorted out. But, because a drawing's

Figure 8.27
FRANCESCO GUARDI (1712–1793)
A Venetian Scene
Pen and wash. 2 15/16 x 7 5/8 in.
Fogg Art Museum, Harvard University
Charles A. Loeser Bequest

pattern of directions is made up of *major* movement actions and its pattern of rhythms generally of lesser ones, we might regard the system of undulating edges of the forms in Figure 8.28 as rhythmic actions, but the axes of the forms as directional ones. Keep the lines and tones representing rhythms general and simple, as in the analysis of the rhythms of Pascin's drawing in Figure 8.29.

Because you have been using two different sheets of paper, by placing this second analysis over the first it is easy to see which parts of the drawing emit both kinds of forces. There may be a few passages of a drawing that do not provide much of either force. Such segments may have other relational functions, and will be relatively dormant as carriers of directional or rhythmic action.

third phase

Now, with the reproduction nearby as your model, place a third sheet of tracing paper over the two analyses, enabling you to see both, and, using a graphite pencil, begin to copy the reproduction. It will not matter that you may be using a medium different from that of the original. You need not go on to make an accurate copy of the drawing, but just far enough to "flesh out" the forms around your extracts of the drawing's directional and rhythmic patterns. As you do, note the interrelated nature of the drawing's "what"—its figurative matter (arms, torsos, trees, drapes, etc.), with these two aspects of the drawing's "how"— its abstract design. In the best drawings, all of the elements that form the image form the design. No lines and tones are used *only* for depictive or dy-

Figure 8.28
EGON SCHIELE (1890–1918)
Two Girls Embracing
Charcoal. 18 1/8 x 11 5/8 in.
Dial Collection, Worcester Art Museum

Figure 8.29
JULES PASCIN (1885–1930)
Girl in an Armchair
Charcoal, some yellow chalk. 55.9 x 43.1 cm.
Collection of The Newark Museum

namic purposes. Your goal in the third phase is to produce a version of the original that permits its directional and rhythmic qualities to be more in evidence. Therefore, redraw any of those lines or tones from either of the first two analyses which will help strengthen these moving actions in your "copy."

When you have completed these analyses, compare them with the three drawings you selected. Often the lines and tones of an analysis form a balanced composition, revealing some of the artist's design strategy. They also indicate something about each artist's visual (and expressive) interests, and suggest the quantity and vigor of such forces necessary to create the kinds of moving actions these drawings possess.

For an additional, helpful exercise, analyze some of your own drawings this way. You will probably find that strengthening or adding the interweaving, animating, and unifying qualities of direction and rhythm will improve your drawings.

Analyzing the drawings of master artists for these, or any other relational patterns, such as those based on value, shape, or texture, helps us to more fully understand the necessary union between the perceptual and conceptual aspects of drawing. Two common hazards of such analyses are the assumptions that all of the artist's responses to his *constant* subject and his *evolving* drawing are conscious and deliberate, whereas we have seen that many are essentially intuitive actions; and that such analyses fully explain a drawing—or an artist. However, not until we have experienced the existence of such forces as universal, integral, and inescapable participants in the act of drawing, will a sensitivity to bonds of visual association become a largely subconscious and intuitive part of our comprehension and response.

THE ELEMENTS AS AGENTS OF DESIGN

The central theme of this chapter is that the quality of a drawing's design and the visual dynamics that express it are never expendable niceties but fundamental to its meaning and worth as a creative, visual statement. If we regard a drawing's design as the artist's strategy for organizing his visual and expressive responses, then the relational behavior of the elements can be regarded as the tactical means used to effect that strategy. And, as we have seen, relationships begin with the first few marks. Perhaps that is why so many gifted artists, even in the briefest of preparatory notations, not only intuitively organize independently drawn sketches into some pattern on the page, but reveal an awareness of each mark as being a unit of energy. They seem unable to regard a line or tone as "exempt" from some kind of relational function, nor can they accept the imbalance and randomness that inevitably result from unrelated segments. The sensitive artist reacts to visual disorder with anxiety-producing tensions. Such drawings simply do not "feel right." When stability and unity are achieved, there is a release of tension. Drawings developed without an organizational strategy, however intuitive and general, always disclose a kind of wandering, a lack of visual bearing or purpose. When an overall strategy is absent, the interrelating and unifying activities of the elements are absent. Whatever else such drawings may convey, disharmony and ambiguity are always parts of the message.

In this section we will examine a group of drawings that provide opportunities to consider some of the elements' design activities not yet discussed, or only touched on earlier. As previously noted, their possibilities for visual associations and activities are unlimited. But, seeing some of the ways in which they relate and act may stimulate the search for others.

Ingres' *Study for Drapery* (Figure 8.30) reveals his sensitivity to two- and three-dimensional matters at the same time. We are as aware of the structural nature of these forms as of the swirl of black, gray, and white shapes forming them. They are simultaneously seen as planes and shapes. Ingres' main strategy is to organize the drawing by stressing the animated and voluptuous swirls by rhythms that result from repetitions of line and shape. Many lines, some of them really thin shadows, follow the same routes, each adding force to directions and rhythms. Most of the drawing's variously toned shapes are strongly related to the lines in their action. Note that a majority of them are variations of a boomerang shape. They range from narrow V-shapes to very open, rounded V's. Most of these below the horizontal midline are placed right-side-up; above the midline, most are inverted. The more we examine the drawing, the more evident it is that almost every line, shape, and tone is a variation of the boomerang idea. The main thrust of the volume—where it seems headed—is toward the lower right corner of the page. Ingres has built up quite an energetic sense of visual and physical weight moving in that direction. He checks its action by the strong tension at the knotted section on the drawing's left side, and by the largest concentration of dark tones in the drawing, below the knot, in the lower left. This "tug-of-war" between the pulling to the left by the knot and the dark tones on one side, and the movement of heavy volume straining to the right on the other, creates a balance based on the most tenuous resolution of forces. The drawing is continuously in motion. It no sooner achieves its balance then it is set going again. Note how the five or six thick shadow-lines in the lower right and center swing up toward the drape's knot to help "return" the energy to its source. Note, too, that the most inclusive shape we can find, the one that takes in almost every mark on the page, is again a large, almost page-filling boomerang shape. The elements of line, shape, value, and volume all function at the three levels referred to earlier. Each, in addition to depicting the drape, reinforces the drape's behavior by various dynamic actions, and finally, functions in some organizational way.

How very different from Ingres' spirited image is Sheeler's *Barn Abstraction* (Figure 8.31). Here, there is a firmly stabilized balance of forces. The image is formal and deliberate.

Figure 8.30
DOMINIQUE INGRES (1780–1867)
Study for drapery
Black crayon. 12 x 9 13/16 in.
The Metropolitan Museum of Art, Rogers Fund

242

Each mark counts. The design depends on a system of interdicting vertical and horizontal lines and shapes of an almost mechanical nature. The impression of volume is subdued, being conveyed more by overlapping shapes than by any other structure-building measure. There is movement here, but of a restrained and stately kind. Even the textures, variations on the density of massed lines, move across the page in three deliberate steps, and the rhythm's movements and beats are in slow staccato. The plane of the page itself moves subtly back and forth, suggesting a sense of deep space above the buildings, becoming the facing planes of the buildings' walls and then moving forward to become the foreground— without a mark being drawn *in* the sky, *on* the walls, or *upon* the foreground. Openings in the roof and walls, and around both sides of the grouped buildings enable the surface of the page to imply these different spatial func-

tions. Note that the drawing's stability is partly due to the roughly equal energies between vertical and horizontal directions. The largest building, which is on the right and contains the visually heaviest black shape, does not tip the drawing to the right. Balance is achieved by the directional thrust and visual weight of the long "overhang" of the lower buildings on the left, "urged on" by the wedge-like shape's direction and diagonal edge. This diagonal, being the only *drawn* one in the design, possesses a strong attracting power. Other, *implied* diagonals are sensed in the staggered location of the roofs, in the base line of the building on the far left, and in one of the roof lines.

In this deceptively simple-looking drawing, all the elements are engaged. Each helps advance the "weaving" of the vertical and horizontal directions into a stable design. All of the basic kinds of relationship are also

Figure 8.31
CHARLES SHEELER (1883–1965)
Barn Abstraction
Black conté crayon. 14 1/8 x 19 1/2 in.
Philadelphia Museum of Art

here. Direction, visual weight, texture, location, and rhythm have already been mentioned, and the play between lines, values, and shapes implied. Sheeler utilizes scale differences for purposes of harmony, contrast, and balance, and by his patient and certain handling of the marks, further strengthens the drawing's cohesive properties. Tensions work between various value-shapes and between the drawing's two largest segments, separated by the vertical line running to the left of the large black shape. Even physical weight has a role in this design, for, despite the two-dimensional nature of the buildings, we understand them as heavy masses whose weights are also in balance when we regard the same vertical line as the fulcrum of a scale.

Sheeler, whose drawings are so frequently concerned with the design of convincing volumes and spatial depth (See Figures 4.37 and 5.7), seems to be reminding us here that drawing is not sculpture, that the dominance of three-dimensional impressions in a drawing is a graphic option, not a fixed responsibility. Although, no matter what our aesthetic persuasion may be, no form whose essential structure eludes us can be successfully drawn, it is an artist's intent that determines whether this structure will be fully explained or largely disguised. There should be no barriers blocking the way of responses that intensify a subject's essential meanings to us.

It is interesting to compare Sheeler's drawing with Tiepolo's *A Group of Farm Buildings* (Figure 8.32). Here, volume is a more active element. Its physical weight counterbalances the design's overall tilt to the lower left. Notice Tiepolo's use of value to create tonal accents of white within the grays of the buildings. These do more than strengthen

Figure 8.32
GIOVANNI BATTISTA TIEPOLO (1696–1770)
A Group of Farm Buildings
Pen and bistre wash. 6 3/8 x 10 1/4 in.
Fogg Art Museum, Harvard University
Gift of Denman W. Ross

Figure 8.33
WILLIAM T. WILEY (1937–   )
Novato (1974)
Watercolor. 9 x 12 1/4 in.
Courtesy, Allan Frumkin Gallery, New York

structural clarity; they add tonal variety to the design, and by their contrasting value (but similar shape) give the darker pitched roof more emphasis in its balancing function by providing small, counter-shapes against which the roof's bold scale, value, and texture have more visual meaning.

Unlike Sheeler, who uses the elements for a balanced awareness of the drawing's two- and three-dimensional life, Tiepolo relies on every element mainly to convey volume—but each does have a two-dimensional function. Note again, that the strongest concentration of line, value, and texture fall just where their combined direction, shape, and scale are most needed—in the pitched roof.

In still another drawing of buildings, Wiley's *Novato* (Figure 8.33) seems to avoid a clear commitment to either two- or three-dimensional clarity. Unlike Sheeler and Tiepolo, who rely strongly on closed shapes, strong directions, and tonal clarity, Wiley utilizes textures of all sorts to purposely impede both volumetric *and* flat readings of the image. Instead of being invited in to move among structures in space, or to judge and feel the behavior of elements on the picture-plane, we are held at a distance by contradicting visual cues and "clouds" of texture. These planned ambiguities guide us toward what the artist intends us to see: the *whole* panoramic view and the *total* page, and at the

Figure 8.34
PABLO PICASSO (1881–1974)
Three Female Nudes Dancing
Pen and ink. 13 7/8 x 10 3/8 in.
Copyright SPADEM 1972 by French Reproduction Rights, Inc.

same time. Note how the artist's use of textures that describe foliage merge with those resulting from the paper's rough tooth and the artist's vigorous handling of the materials.

Picasso's *Three Female Nudes Dancing* (Figure 8.34) shows an interesting example of the "dual life" that the element of line is capable of. By drawing these figures in unconnected, rhythmic lines, Picasso calls our attention to an abstract harmony among the lines that is almost independent of their depictive relation. Despite their unconnected mode the lines still suggest volume. But the shapes and planes that build these volumes are hinted at, rather than plainly declared, while the dynamic character of the lines is plainly declared, instead of hinted at. This is not to suggest that these two conditions of the lines is weakly presented or confused, but rather that Picasso's plan requires such teasing sugges-

tions, and that, in fact, these two themes are engagingly interdependent. There is the *exact* degree of volume present to convey Picasso's linear motive: the simultaneous life of a line as an edge in space, and as a line on paper. This idea is supported by the function of the paper's surface which, as in Sheeler's drawing, occupies several depth levels at the same time that it continues to exist as picture-plane. This dual impression of the second and third dimension (and of figural and abstract states of order) is further enhanced by the fact that there is not a single enclosed shape in the drawing. Just as we begin to sense several "shapes" forming masses, the openings between the lines remind us that we are looking at ink lines on a flat, bounded, surface. But the moment we register that fact, the lines begin to make shapes, planes, and forms again. In this way Picasso creates a tensional life between the lines that merely descriptive lines cannot produce. This abstract and depictive play of line, or any other element, is always present to some degree as part of the intended or subconscious theme of all good drawings.

In Picasso's drawing, as in Sheeler's and Wiley's, the dual life of the image is evenly advanced. Were the lines less or more descriptive, the balance between "in-and-out" space and "surface" space would be weakened, and the abstract tensions lessened. As it is, we react to the behavior of the lines as Picasso meant them to function.

However, making the impression of volumes in spatial depth clearer does not have to diminish a drawing's two-dimensional life. If its two-dimensional design is "forward" enough, if the elements always advance both considerations, a drawing can, as we saw in Chapter Six, give a strong, simultaneous sense of volumes in space and of elements on a page.

In the drawing by Wen Cheng, *Cypress and Rock* (Figure 8.35) we can read the drawing's line, shape, value, and texture as flat occupants on the picture-plane *and* as forms in space. Here, there is no mark that fails to depict, act, and interact. Again, the theme is an explosive eruption that spreads out from the center of the configuration's base. Note

Figure 8.35
WEN CHÊNG-MING (1470–1559)
Cypress and Rock
Brush and ink. 19 1/4 x 10 1/4 in.
Nelson Gallery, Atkins Museum, Kansas City, Mo.

the clarity of the negative white shapes, and the strong rhythms activating every part of the drawing. The artist places the main thrust of the forms to the left of the page, countering the configuration's location on the right.

A similar strategy is used by Degas in his drawing *Three Dancers* (Figure 8.36). Located in the lower right, the figures are balanced on the page by their united, powerful thrust to the left. The visual and physical weight of the dancer in the foreground, and the direction of the bench she is seated on, act as additional counterbalancing factors. Note that the other two dancers "run off" the page. This snapshot treatment has the effect of making us more aware of their shape-state than we might otherwise be. And Degas uses shape to reinforce our sense of the second dimension. His emphasis on heavy contours intensifies their shape-state and the force of their leftward movement. This repeated use of heavy lines also serves as a unifying rhythm. Note how all the limbs stand out—a pattern of arcs moving to the left.

In another Degas drawing, a preparatory sketch for a portrait of Emily Duranty (Figure 8.37), stabilizing the heavy oblique mass in the lower right becomes the artist's major organizational task. Degas uses the longest vertical line in the drawing, the upright support of the lower bookcase, to "spearhead" the downward movement of the other vertical lines and shapes on the left, anchoring the bookshelves to the left instead of the right side of the page. The converging lines of the bookshelves (and the several leftward-leaning books) also help the surge to the left, countering the weight of the pile of books and papers in the foreground. Note how Degas uses value to bridge the space between the forms in the foreground and background, and how broadly he suggests the differing angles and forms of the books, which, in their line, value, texture, and scale differences form several interesting relational patterns.

Although Tintoretto's study (Figure 8.38) preceeds Degas' by several centuries and is very different in subject and treatment, there is a similar compositional solution to the

247

Figure 8.36
EDGAR DEGAS (1834–1917)
Three Dancers
Crayon and pastel. 23 3/4 x 18 1/8 in.
Courtesy, Museum of Fine Arts, Boston
Bequest of John T. Spaulding

Figure 8.37
EDGAR DEGAS (1834–1917)
Bookshelves in Duranty's Library
Charcoal, heightened with white chalk.
46.9 x 30.5 cm.
The Metropolitan Museum of Art
Rogers Fund, 1918.

Figure 8.38
JACOPO TINTORETTO (1518–1594)
Study of the Head from Michelangelo's
"Giuliano de Medici"
Black and white on toned paper. 37.4 x 27 cm.
Rijksmuseum, Amsterdam

problem of great physical weight on the right side. Like Degas, Tintoretto counters the weight by strong visual weight on the opposite side of the page, expressed here by the downward plunge of the large dark tone of the throat. Further, as in Figure 8.36, there is an emphasis on picture-plane activities by making parts of the head run off the page, and, as in Picasso's drawing, on stressing the directional relationships among the lines by leaving many unconnected. Here, the configuration's two- and three-dimensional qualities enhance each other. The dynamic energies released by the elements strengthen the power and grace of the forms, and the design "hid-

den" among the structural essentials of the forms trigger vigorous dynamic activities.

Schiele's *Portrait of Marie Schiele* (Figure 8.39) is a daring fusion of figural and abstract meanings. To call forward the harmonious play of the planes, patterns, and rhythms of the forms shown, the artist simply omits the torso. In doing so he amplifies the abstract actions among the elements. And these shapes, lines, textures, and tones, in their animated and tactile properties, and in their collective encircling action, reveal the artist's sympathetic feelings for the sitter, his wife. "Tender" and "tough" lines and tones become the graphic equivalents to the hard and

249

Figure 8.39
EGON SCHIELE (1890–1918)
Portrait of Maria Schiele
Black chalk.
Albertina Museum, Vienna

soft surfaces in the subject, and serpentine lines suggest sensual undertones. Schiele, in finding engaging, graphic solutions to these form-revealing lines and tones, not only reinforces his representational message, but invents a fresh and provocative "treat" of visual themes and variations that has aesthetic worth in its own right.

In Diebenkorn's drawing of a reclining figure (Figure 8.40) value-shapes are the main elements in establishing the forms and the design. Again, we are made aware of the multiple activities of the elements, and of their bold, two-dimensional life. The sense of volume is sometimes strikingly convincing, especially in the figure, by a great economy of

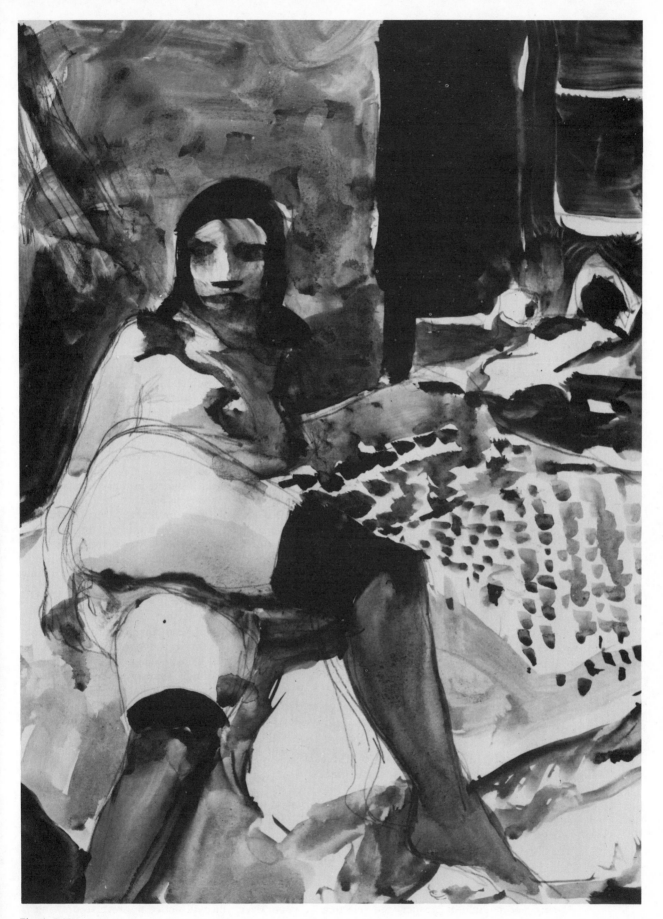

Figure 8.40
RICHARD DIEBENKORN (1922–   )
Untitled 1962(?)
Ink and wash on paper. 17 x 12 3/8 in.
San Francisco Museum of Modern Art, Purchase

means and without any lessening of vigorous dynamic actions among the elements. In the figure's upper body the lines, values, and shapes defining the forms of the head, shoulder, and breasts also enact a handsome abstract event that strongly supports figural meanings. The large, white, diamond shape of the figure in contrasting with the large, black rectangle in the upper right area of the drawing poses a seemingly irreconcilable difference. But these contrasting shapes are related by their scale, their participation in directional forces forming a large X that extends from corner to corner on the page, and even by their polarity in an otherwise textured and largely gray field of smaller shapes. Then, too, their differences are overcome by their respective visual weight function in the design. Neither is stabilized on the picture-plane without the other's counterbalancing action. They are also, and importantly, related in their representational function, each clarifying the other's position in the spatial field of the room. Finally, these two shapes relate by a sameness in their handling, and by black and white shape-"envoys" that encircle each of these large segments. And, by appearing elsewhere in the design, these small tonal "shards" weave all the other elements together. As in all good designs, the arrangement of the elements here is *necessary*, not haphazard.

A survey of the drawings in this book will show that the elements of every one exist on the several levels discussed. The two- and three-dimensional design of each is not the result of chance. Each tries to contain and resolve the energies within it, and in each, representational and dynamic meanings reveal an interworking accord that makes them come alive.

The following exercise consists of brief suggestions for challenging your sense of balance and unity through the way you use the elements' ability to depict, act, and interact.

exercise 8B

drawing 1

Using any medium and paper, and selecting any subject, make a drawing that is contained well within the limits of the page, as in Figures 8.18

through 8.24. Begin by making a light gesture drawing that stresses the subject's overall directional and rhythmic forces. Seeing these actions, decide on a design strategy that will utilize them. At least some of what you have extracted from the subject's actions and forms already represents a kind of subconscious design strategy. You have stressed certain relationships that another artist drawing the same view might not stress. He might find another system of directional and rhythmic associations that reflect *his* interpretation of the subject's arrangement. But seeing what energies have emerged from *your* responses to the subject, decide how they might best function as a major theme for your subsequent interpretation of the subject's forms and the drawing's balance and unity. As you draw, think about the role of the encircling space of the picture-plane. How far can the configuration spread on the page before its forces are too strong to be contained by the outer regions of the surface? Is there too much space? Does the image merely float on the page, leaving its empty areas unengaged? Are the shapes of the picture-plane actually part of your drawing's design? Does the image seem too heavy on one side, or seem to form a large, unanswered diagonal "supershape" on the page? In this drawing (and in those which follow) try to utilize the various kinds of relationships discussed earlier. It may be that a particular segment of your drawing requires a contrast (or sameness) of handling, scale, value, or visual weight to make it compatible with the rest of the design, or to have it strengthen or subdue another part of the design.

drawing 2

Select one of your directional analyses from Exercise 8A (or make another from one of the drawings in this book). Using the analysis as the basis for your design strategy, arrange a still life that reenacts the same general directional actions. For example, in Rembrandt's drawing (Figure 8.18) the explosive spread of its directed energies and its second directional theme discussed earlier should guide your placement of the components of the still life. Your completed drawing should suggest the same directional actions as the original drawing's design. Where possible, use the same medium, and even try to approach a similar handling of the materials.

drawing 3

Using tracing paper, carefully trace the major linear and tonal aspects of the Toulouse-Lautrec drawing *Equestrienne* (Figure 8.41). Turning your paper over, you will notice the reverse drawing is no longer balanced on the page. The drawing now seems to rush down toward the lower right corner.

Figure 8.41
HENRI DE TOULOUSE-LAUTREC (1864–1901)
Equestrienne
Crayon. 19 1/4 x 12 3/8 in.
Museum of Art, Rhode Island School of Design, Providence

Taking any liberties you wish, make any necessary changes, additions, or deletions that you feel will balance the drawing and maintain its unity. If you wish, transfer the reversed view to a more durable paper before you begin to rework it.

drawing 4

Arrange any subject in a way that you feel suggests an interesting design plan for a *horizontal* format. The drawing should fill the page, as in Figures 5.14 or 8.40. Intentionally place a heavy object where it will appear in the drawing's lower right side, then counterbalance it by any combination of the basic types of relationship discussed earlier.

drawing 5

Without changing the subject or your view of the subject used in the previous drawing, draw it again to make an equally good design in a *vertical* format. Now, you may need to increase or decrease the scale of the image on your page to help you develop a workable composition. Again, the physically heavy part should be located in the troublesome lower right.

drawing 6

Using line only, make a drawing that is just as active two-dimensionally as it is three-dimensionally, as in Figure 8.34.

drawing 7

Using any black chalk, make a drawing in which line, tone, and texture are as active two-dimensionally as they are three-dimensionally, as in Figure 8.39.

drawing 8

Using only brush and ink (thinned with water as necessary) make a tonal drawing that is as active two-dimensionally as it is three-dimensionally, as in Figure 8.40.

drawing 9

Using Figure 8.30 as a rough guide, arrange a drape in any way that suggests an interesting theme of directions, rhythms, shapes, and values. Working large (perhaps 24″ × 30″ or so), make a bold, twenty-minute drawing that stresses both the drape's structure and those dynamic energies that suggest the drape's limp weight, as well as its resolution on the page.

drawing 10

Select any drawing in this book that has a vertical format, and, taking any liberties you wish with its forms, make a drawing that redesigns the image to work in a horizontal format.

In this examination of visual issues we saw that each mark adds a unit of energy to the drawing's depictive and dynamic meanings, and that the resulting configuration's design is dependent in part on the dimensions of the page. To disregard these fundamental *given* conditions of drawing prevents our seeing the means by which an image's order and unity are achieved and its representational content is clarified and strengthened. But self-consciously planning the visual behavior of each mark is, as noted earlier, impossible. Both judgments and feelings must negotiate the drawing's final form. The exploration of force-producing relationships can extend the responsive options we can call on in developing this final form. A drawing's visual resolution as a system of expressive order is as much the result of subconscious knowledge and need as of intentional strategy. A study of the visual means that can stimulate such knowledge, need, and strategy, informs both our intellect and our intuition.

To broaden the options of both is essential because our responses to the relational life of the elements on the page involves the same kind of comprehension that determines our responses to the subject. Expanding our understanding of drawings as designs expands our perceptual skills and interests. It also adds to the range of expression of those intangibles of temperament and idiosyncrasy that meet the last requirement of a good drawing: the sense of a genuinely personal—and thus, a genuinely original—view of what it was about a subject that made us draw it.

CHAPTER NINE

EXPRESSIVE ISSUES

the forming of meaning

A DEFINITION

A common thread running through the previous chapters is the view that responsive drawings are formed as much by intuition and feeling as by intellectual motive and analysis. We *need* as much as *want* to draw in a certain way. And even our conscious, intellectual intentions, our wish to make certain visual inquiries and order systems, are themselves shaped in part by intuitive knowing and need.

We might therefore further define responsive drawing as the *personal* ordering of perceptions. *What* and *how well* we draw is determined by the quality of our responses to both the visual and expressive conditions in the subject *and* in the emerging drawing, and by the character of our temperamental and creative attitudes and concepts. For some artists these concepts may be mainly concerned with visual considerations; for others, with expressive ones. But our *total* interest in a subject is always concerned, to some degree, with both. Some concepts affect the way we see the subject. Other concepts are influenced

by the subject's effect on *them*. And still others affect, and are in turn affected by, the changing states of the emerging drawing. Hence, we bring certain perceptual and personal concepts to, and gain others from, each drawing. In responsive drawing, perception and conception are interdependent and mutually supporting considerations, and consequently, so are the design and expressive aspects of the resulting works.

As noted in Chapter Eight, to separate the deeply interrelated issues of organization and expression risks the misunderstanding that they are independent, whereas in fact every mark added to a drawing adds to its expression as well as to its design. In the previous chapter our attention focused on the ways elements and relational energies shape and animate designs. Here we will explore how elements and energies convey feelings and moods. But we should bear in mind that the same relational forces which organize also express.

Like the predominantly expressive lines examined in Chapter Three, *all* the elements can convey predominantly emotive themes—

not only by what they depict, but through their inherent nature. That is, they can express at the figural and dynamic levels simultaneously. Expressively motivated lines, values, shapes, etc., can be sensual, reserved, aggressive, sportive; they can create relationships with other elements that stress such expressive qualities throughout the drawing. A drawing's expressive character, its emotive theme, like its design strategy, is produced through the relational behavior of the elements, beginning with the very first marks. Therefore, to the responsive artist, whether a drawing's dominant theme is order or ex-

Figure 9.1
PAUL CÉZANNE (1839–1906)
Sketchbook page 21 (recto)
Pencil. 12.5 x 22.3 cm.
Courtesy of The Art Institute of Chicago

pression, neither theme can have universal meaning except in the presence of the other. For him, these are fundamentally interworking concepts.

But expression should not be understood as willful or arbitrary emotion. Genuine expressive meanings are not sought out at all, but come as a natural by-product of a genuine empathy with a subject's form and content. Nor must expression be understood only as passion. Expressive qualities can be contemplative and delicate.

Cézanne's sketch of a man's head (Figure 9.1) is primarily concerned with the analysis and organization of volumes through a selective use of planes. Structural interests are dominant. But the search for, and the satisfaction in the discovery of structural keys to an economical realization of the subject's volumes is a major source of Cézanne's excitation—and the lines express this. The authority and earnest nature of the lines reveal both the artist's depth of commitment to his visual theme of inquiry *and* his feelings about it.

Guercino's *Head of a Man* (Figure 9.2) is not visually less active than Cézanne's. Indeed, the drawing in the head has something of the same interest in planar construction, but it is more expressively forceful. Here, the lines and tones endow the man's character with some of their own energetic power. But Guercino's expressive interests are not limited to psychological or humanistic matters alone. He calls our attention to the similarities of the curvasive actions of the collar and hair by a bold calligraphy that organizes as it expresses, and even continues such lines into the background. The cumulative energy of so many swirling lines cannot be read with the calm that is possible in viewing the Cézanne drawing. Guercino succeeds in conveying his felt impressions of the subject, but he is equally successful in creating a field of strong visual and expressive energies. The man *and* the marks that depict him both express strength, authority, and intensity. The drawing's design supports its expressive theme.

Whether our drawings are dominantly visual or expressive, or whether these considerations receive somewhat equal attention is also determined by the nature of our perceptual and conceptual interests. For Rem-

Figure 9.2
GUERCINO (1591–1666)
Head of a Man
Pen, brown ink wash.
13.7 x 15.2 cm.
The Metropolitan Museum of Art
Harris Brisbane Dick Fund

brandt, design and expression are not only inextricably fused considerations—they are almost always equally active properties of each form he draws. His drawing *Young Woman at Her Toilet* (Figure 9.3) strongly conveys his equal interest in order and empathy.

Visually, the alternating light and dark tones that splash across the page, by their contrasts, movements, and tensions, produce a bold design. The oblique direction of the two figures is countered by the direction of the two large, dark masses of tone, subtly repeated in the seated woman's folded arms, in some of the folds in her skirt, and in the sloping shoulders of both figures. Radial energies beginning in the hand of the seated figure seem to give the flower-like shape of her configuration the power to "hold off" the enclosing dark tones. The similarity between the positions of the arms of both women, and the slashing, downward brush strokes at their waists, unify and animate the two figures while, in becoming lost among the dark tones on the right and in adding visual weight to

the left side, they unify and animate the drawing. Note how the light tones, flowing down through both figures toward the lower right corner, enter the foreground and sweep to the left, rising along the left side the page to begin the cycle of action again. This is not a placid design. Its overall stability is based on barely contained forces of considerable power.

Expressively, the design is no less powerful. The energies creating the visual activities are, of course, themselves expressive forces. But there is another emotive quality that pervades this drawing. An ordinary domestic scene is here transformed by an atmosphere of expectancy. The light does not merely illuminate the women, it dignifies them, giving their forms and actions an indefinable grace and importance. This almost spiritual presence is created as much by the nature and behavior of the elements as by the depictive matter. The sudden shock of value contrasts, the bold sonority of the tonal shapes, the controlled turbulence of the lines, and the sweep-

Figure 9.3
REMBRANDT VAN RIJN (1606–1669)
Young Woman at Her Toilet
Pen, ink and wash. 23.8 x 18.4 cm.
Albertina Museum, Vienna

ing directions result from Rembrandt's intuition and empathy. A largely subconscious need and knowledge led him to believe that such harmonies and contrasts, at play among such forms, could generate just such a transcendental mood.

The reciprocity between the plastic and expressive dynamics of drawing can be seen even in our reliance on expressive terms for describing visual issues (as in Chapter Eight, and in our foregoing analysis of Figure 9.3), while expressive themes are conveyed by describing the visual behavior of the elements. To better understand the expressive nature of the elements, let us examine each of them in several moods.

258

THE ELEMENTS AS AGENTS OF EXPRESSION

line. Although the expressive use of line has already been discussed, it will be helpful here to see some clearly different expressive states of this key element. In Figure 9.4, the five groups of line shown, while not representative of its entire expressive range, do demonstrate some general types of expressive line. Group A are patient, earnest, and searching lines. As in Pascin's drawing (Figure 3.13), they are often sensual and tactile. Group B are bold, energetic lines. Sometimes playful, sensual, or urgent, they are always fast-moving, even frenzied, as in Van Gogh's drawing (Figure 3.29), or Guercino's (Figure 9.2). The harsh, slashing lines in Group C are always aggressive, often explosive. Sometimes, as in Matisse's drawing (Figure 4.24), their thickness and the density of their clashing assaults on each other form tones. Group D are gentle, caressing lines. Not as slow and precise as Group A, or as animated as Group B, they move gracefully, as in Picasso's drawing (Figure 3.15), or in the late Kamakura Period drawing (Figure 7.24). Group E are relatively mechanical and businesslike, but always suggest certainty. They can be cold, as in Sheeler (Figure 8.31), delicate, as in Saenredam (Figure 5.37), or show a surprising energy and warmth, as in Papo and Goodman (Figures 3.6 and 3.26).

But few drawings are restricted to only one kind of expressing line. As noted in Chapter Three, a line begun in one emotive mode can end in another. For example, note the differing kinds of line in Figure 9.3, and

those which change character as they move. Of course, any kind of line can be used to enhance expressive meanings. Depending on the context in which a line occurs, even a short, straight line can evoke powerful expressive meaning. In Kollwitz's drawing *Woman Seated with Folded Hands* (Figure 9.5), the slight, short, charcoal stroke depicting the woman's mouth more eloquently reveals the woman's purse-lipped, introspective mood than any extensive rendering of the lips could. The "knife-slit" nature of the line intensifies the artist's expressive intent. It not only depicts the gesture, it enacts it.

The Kollwitz's drawing also conveys its mood through shapes and values that evoke feelings. The black cast shadow that "overshadows" the rest of the drawing is not large, dark, and unfocused by chance. Its dominance in the drawing is expressively necessary. Kollwitz seems to suggest it as a symbol of tragedy. Our universal apprehension of dark, unknown, ghost-like shapes and forms are awakened by the shadow. Kollwitz blurs its sharply defined and blackest segment with an outer dark tone, further suggesting an apparition-like presence in shadow. The woman's right shoulder, almost lost in shadow, seems to be caressed by the broad strokes of dark tones that fuse the woman to the cast shadow. All of the drawing's shapes, and the lines that define their edges, flow toward the shadow as if attracted to it by some force. Only the folded hands, their stark whiteness contrasting with the shadow, seem free of this attraction. This directed movement, whether supplied by the artist's intellect or intuition, was

Figure 9.4

A   B   C   D   E

Figure 9.5
KÄTHE KOLLWITZ (1867–1945)
Woman Seated with Folded Hands
Charcoal. 24 1/2 x 18 3/4 in.
Courtesy, Museum of Fine Arts, Boston
Helen and Alice Colburn Fund

utilized because its action seemed necessary to the drawing's expressive meaning. To adapt an old saying: "Expressive need (like love) finds a way."

In this drawing the relational energies of the elements, their differences of scale, weight, and location, and their various directional, rhythmic, and tensional forces are in strong alliance with the artist's expressive goal. Directions and moving rhythms leading from all parts of the figure to the cast shadow's "head" amplify the opposing direction of the woman's gaze—a countering action

as necessary to the drawing's design as to its mood. The sense of the woman's fragility, relative to the massive dark shadow, adds strength to the emotive force of both, while the ambiguity and tension in their respective substantiality and in their value contrasts are equally necessary to the drawing's order and emotive tenor.

shape. Like line, shapes conform to general types. In Chapter Two, we saw that all shapes can be finally grouped into two basic categories: geometric and organic. But these cate-

Figure 9.6

gories are too general in discussing expressive uses. Figure 9.6 shows five groupings that typify the most frequently used shapes. Those of Group A are stately; when oriented on vertical and horizontal axes they are stable shapes that suggest a dignified or calm air, as in Seurat's drawing (Figure 4.25). In Group B the shapes are active, agitated, and rather complex. Sometimes their action is strongly directional, but often it is largely contained within the animated behavior of the shape itself. Rembrandt's and Guardi's drawings (Figures 4.13 and 8.27) show the intense activity of this type. The shapes of Group C are rhythmic and undulating in their movements. They may suggest fast motion, as in Renoir's drawing (Figure 2.20), or, when more convoluted, slow movement, as in Schiele's drawing (Figure 8.28). The angular, jagged shapes of Group D are usually active, even explosively so, as in Schiele's drawing (Figure 3.14), or Wen Cheng-Ming's drawing (Figure 8.35). Group E are relatively stable shapes, and suggest slow or weak movement. They have a rather firm, dependable feel, as conveyed in Holbein's and Picasso's drawings (Figures 7.9 and 7.17).

As in the case of line, all shapes are emotive, including those that combine differing type characteristics. In Seligman's drawing *Caterpillar* (Figure 9.7), undulating and angular shapes struggle and resist each other, but are united by the design's rhythmic strength. The absence of sudden or extreme value changes and the precise, restrained handling suggest a quiet contest rather than a dramatic struggle. As this example indicates, some of a drawing's expressive character is revealed by the nature of the shapes, and some by their collective behavior.

We should recognize that shapes, or any of the other elements, may complement or conflict with a drawing's representational dynamics—the action and character of its identifiable forms. Where the things depicted are to be understood as stilled, as, for example, in a drawing of a sleeping figure, the presence of many shapes such as those in Groups B, C, or D of Figure 9.6 would work against the sense of stationary forms. Those in Groups A and D would tend to support such a stable and arrested state of motion.

The four arrangements in Figure 9.8 show some of the limitless possibilities for shapes' expressive activity. Those in A move toward a common point in the design, as in the Kollwitz drawing (Figure 9.5). In B, the upper, active shape appears about to attack the placid one below, while the shapes in C seem to strain toward each other. Notice the sense of tension at the point of impending contact in these arrangements. In B and C there is also tension between the shapes themselves. We experience a back-and-forth recognition of each shape's situation. The shapes in D unite in a circular movement around the page. Shapes engaged in such rotating actions can generate strong emotive energies, as in Ingres' drawing (Figure 8.30), or in Munch's lithograph *Self-Portrait with a Cigarette* (Figure 9.9).

volume. The expressive nature of volumes is revealed by their weight and scale, by their physical characteristics which, like those of

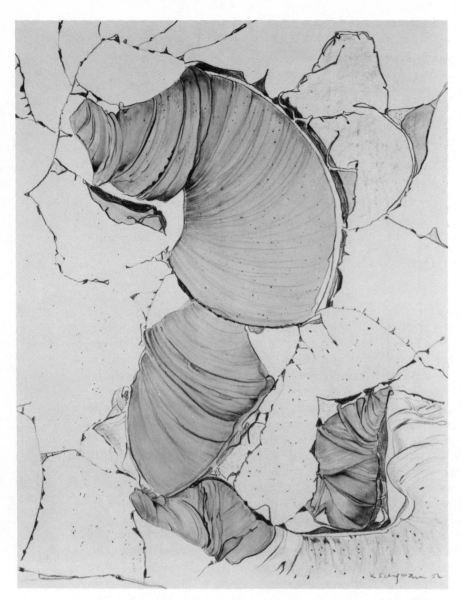

Figure 9.7
KURT SELIGMAN (1900–   )
Caterpillar
Varnish, black crayon and wash. 28 x 22 in.
Fogg Art Museum, Harvard University
Bequest of Meta and Paul J. Sachs

line or shape, range from the placid and stilled to the aggressive and active, and by the nature of their interaction with other volumes. In Figure 9.10, the types of volumes in A (and the shape-state of the planes that form them) combine in a balanced arrangement of great stability. In B the same volumes, rearranged, create tensions and instability. Masses possessing complex contours, such as those in Leonardo da Vinci's drawing (Figure 3.3),

Figure 9.8

A   B   C   D

262

Figure 9.9
EDVARD MUNCH (1863–1944)
Self-Portrait with a Cigarette
Lithograph. 22 1/8 x 18 in.
Dial Collection, Worcester Art Museum

seem more animated and intense than those with more simple contours, such as those in Watteau (Figure 4.26), or Goya (Figure 9.11). Like the volumes in the Watteau, gently rounded forms, especially when they are simple and delicately modelled, can express gentleness or quietude. When more angular in nature, and especially when harshly carved, they suggest more aggressive states.

The volumes in Lebrun's drawing *Kneeling and Standing Figures* (Figure 9.12) behave somewhat like those in Groups A and B of Figure 9.10. Compare the relative stability of the figure on the left with the tumbling forms of the figure on the right. In this provocative drawing, Lebrun uses sharp, slashing lines, brooding tones, slow-moving shapes, and ponderous volumes, each of which contrib-

utes to the drawing's haunting atmosphere of both coarse and spiritual forces. But it is the strange floating quality of these heavy forms that is most provocative. This becomes evident by turning the drawing upside-down. When the volume is less convincing, the drawing's overall mood is somewhat lessened.

Lessening the impression of physical weight and structure can itself be an ex-

Figure 9.10

Figure 9.11
FRANCISCO DE GOYA (1746–1828)
Peasant Carrying Woman
Sepia wash. 20.5 x 14.3 cm.
Courtesy of The Hispanic Society of America

pressively powerful tactic. In Mazur's drawing *Study for "Closed Ward Number 12"* (Figure 9.13), the skeletal-like volumes of the figure and the chair are sometimes left open to fuse with other parts of each other and the page, dulling the impression of volume. The resulting angular "shards" of harsh and torn shapes, their clashing directions, and their overall pattern of angularity, as well as the intense light and cruel shadows they produce, suggest at the dynamic level the same desolate mood conveyed by the depictive content.

Again, in Polonsky's monoprint *Child with Rat* (Figure 9.14), dulling the subject's

structural facts sharpens its expressive tenor. Here, the psychological contrast of a pensive boy nestling a giant and somewhat agitated rat in his arms is intensified by the artist's gentle treatment of the child's forms, and his more urgent handling of the rat. The elements that form the boy all suggest stability and graceful rhythms. In the rat, the elements, especially texture, and the relational energies, especially those based on directions and physical and visual weights, suggest unrest. To have unselectively emphasized the structure of each of the subject's forms would have diminished the drawing's enigmatic mood,

264

Figure 9.12
RICO LEBRUN (1900–1964)
Kneeling and Standing Figures
Brush and ink.
27 9/16 x 39 1/2 in.
Philadelphia Museum of Art, Purchased: The Harrison Fund

which gains more from these quiet and subtle dynamic forces than it could from a more reportorial approach to this dream-like image.

But a volume's weight can be a powerful expressive force. We are not usually consciously aware of the force of gravitational pull unless we sense its absence, or when it suggests danger. Vespignani relies on our appreciation of the meaning of its force in his drawing *Hanged Man* (Figure 9.15). The artist does not abuse our sensibilities by emphasizing the victim's agony, or by an exaggerated impression of heavy volume. Here, to our relief, volume is somewhat subdued. The

implications of its weight are clear enough. Instead of a sensational description of one man's execution, Vespignani asks us to consider the indignity and tragedy of Man as a thing. Here, the expressive meaning points to Man's universal inhumanity. The victim's isolated, labelled, and broken body is felt as an obscene violation, a precious loss rather than a repellent sight.

Vespignani intentionally keeps the divisions of the page simple. There is even some ambiguity between the second and third dimensional state of the background. This has the effect of frustrating our wish to concen-

Figure 9.13
MICHAEL MAZUR (1935–   )
Study for "Closed Ward Number 12"
Brown wash, brush, pen and ink. 16 3/4 x 13 1/8 in.
Collection, The Museum of Modern Art, New York
Gift of Mrs. Bertram Smith

trate our attention elsewhere on the page; only the figure provides a visually logical and "comfortable" haven (and thus, an additional irony). The absence of a single white tone casts a gloomy pall over the entire scene, its stillness conveyed by the simple, block-like character of the design's large divisions. The most active movement is in the oblique edge of the shadow, pulled away like a curtain. The figure's overall light tone, and the thin dark tones upon and around it, in being both lighter and darker than any other tone in the drawing, further isolate the figure and call our attention to it. Vespignani contrasts the simple purity of the man's forms with the clothing's tangled state, and with the harsh, scarred and lettered poster. The awful stillness of the figure is intensified further by this contrasting activity of the lines, shapes, values, and textures upon it.

Figure 9.14
ARTHUR POLONSKY (1925–   )
Child with Rat
Monotype. 9 x 12 in.
Courtesy of the artist.

Figure 9.15
RENZO VESPIGNANI (1924–
Hanged Man (1949)
Pen, brush, and ink. 15 7/8 x 7 1/4 in.
Collection, The Museum of Modern Art, New York. Purchase.

texture. Textures too carry expressive meanings. The possible kinds of textural activity in drawing are unlimited, but all can be divided into two basic categories: the controlled and sometimes regularly patterned textures; and the more active and usually unregulated ones. The textures in Sheeler's drawing (Figure 8.31) are an example of the regulated kind; the strident texture of the lines and tones of the seventeenth-century Venetian drawing (Figure 4.1), is an example of the loose and active kind. As the textures in these two drawings show, each is consistent with, and contributes to, the emotional tenor of the rest of the drawing. But, as we saw in Vespignani's drawing, textures that contrast with a drawing's psychological tone can also provide important expressive meaning.

In Chapter Four, textures in nature were seen to be any kind of discernible grouping or repetition of colors, values, shapes, or volumes, or any distinguishing characteristics of a form or a spatial area. Here, we must include the textures that media produce—the rough grain of chalk or crayon, the fused stains of ink washes, etc. and, as in Figure 4.1, the textures formed by a matrix of shapes, lines, values, and volumes on the drawn page.

The textural life of volumes can be highly expressive, as in Leonardo da Vinci's drawing of stratified rock (Figure 6.10). The expressive role of a medium's texture can be seen in another da Vinci drawing *A Storm over a Mountain and a Valley* (Figure 9.16). Here, the chalk's rough texture helps to suggest the charged atmosphere. The rugged grain of the chalk's particles envelops the components of this panoramic scene in tones that unify them and evoke the feel as well as the look of a rainstorm.

Leonardo utilizes the expressive power of textures throughout the drawing in creating its tumultuous mood. He divides the page into four horizontal bands of differing textures. First, the storm clouds' churning turbulence is in marked contrast to the straight lines of the rain that form the second band of texture. Below this, a generalized impression of the distant town is suggested by the short vertical and horizontal lines, by the trees, and by lines describing the letter C at various angles. Finally, the looser, complex texture formed by the circular lines, structural hatch-

Figure 9.16

LEONARDO DA VINCI (1452–1519)

A Storm over a Mountain and a Valley
Red chalk. 19.9 x 15 cm.
Royal Collection, Windsor Castle

Figure 9.17

HYMAN BLOOM (1913–)

Forest Number 1 (1971)
Pen and ink. 23 1/2 x 18 1/2 in.
Collection of Mrs. Sophie Goldberg

ings, long and rhythmic curved lines, and small, block-like forms, conveys the impression of the rolling hills of the foreground. Except for the texture that represents the town, all are loose and active. The drawing's turbulent mood is emphasized by the top and bottom bands of texture. Both suggest strong curvilinear movements that "bracket" the area of the storm, adding dynamic pressures to meteorological ones.

When a medium's own texture is compatible with the textures it describes, emotive force is increased. In Bloom's drawing, *Forest #1* (Figure 9.17), the naturally fine lines and small interspaces of dense pen-and-ink hatchings are in accord with the artist's emphasis on the texture of leaves, bark, and branches. The mysterious mood of the forest, enhanced by the stress on its wild, dense web of flora is further amplified by the dense and vigorous web of the lines themselves. But note that Bloom orders this "disordered" scene. Subtle patterns of large and small, light and dark, simple and complex, and straight and curved segments provide harmonies and contrasts that, by their overall balance and unity, keep the image from being only a record of random forest growth. And, by subtle modifications of some textures, tones, and forms, the artist suggests some barely discernible hints of strange forms hidden among the shadows and branches. These passages add to the sense of the forest's forbidding but enchanting mood.

value. We have seen value's power as an agent of expression in most of the drawings in this chapter. Values are bolder and more charged with energy when drawn with abrupt changes between them, as in Mazur's drawing

Figure 9.18
ALBRECHT DÜRER (1471–1528)
Hands in Adoration
Black and white tempera on blue paper.
29 x 19.7 cm.
Albertina Museum, Vienna

(Figure 9.13). They evoke more dramatic or brooding moods when such changes involve large areas of dark tones, as in the Rembrandt or Bloom drawings (Figures 9.3 and 9.17), or when forms emerge from dark backgrounds, as in Lebrun's (Figure 9.12). When a drawing's overall tones are light, as in Cézanne's (Figure 9.1), or when the values change by gentle graduations, as in Dürer's *Hands in Adoration* (Figure 9.18), they are usually less bold or active. Gradual value progressions such as those in Dürer's drawing, by their subtle nuances of change, suggest a calmer mood. Note that the great clarity of the structure of these hands is suggested by tones made of dark *and light* hatched lines. In addition to their incisive structural use, these lines build gradually to a crescendo of light on the lower part of the left hand and sleeve. This tonal control enhances the drawing's evocation of the spiritual.

Again, in Courbet's *Landscape* (Figure 9.19), intensity of light has dramatic impact. The value variations are gradual, but the framing of a large square of light tones by the darker trees and their cast shadows makes the light on the trees and field within this frame radiate an intense glow.

Just the opposite tonal arrangement is used by Goya in *Al Mercado* (Figure 9.20), but the child's upturned face is made to radiate light by the surrounding dark tones. The virtual absence of moderating gray tones gives this drawing an air of intensity and drama. Here the shapes match the values in boldness, adding to the drawing's sense of expectancy.

Figure 9.19
GUSTAVE COURBET (1819–1877)
Landscape
Black chalk. 19 x 30.5 cm.
Boymans-Van Beuningen Museum, Rotterdam

Figure 9.20
FRANCISCO DE GOYA (1746–1828)
Al Mercado
Brush and wash. 20 x 14 cm.
Prado Museum, Madrid

OTHER FACTORS OF EXPRESSION

The medium always participates in a drawing's expressive character. It does so by its intrinsic traits and by the way it is used. But the same medium can augment many kinds of emotive meaning. In Chapter Seven, we saw that the intrinsic characteristics and the limits of most media permit a wide range of use. Still, depending on the expressive theme, some media will be more adaptable to the artist's intentions than others.

The selection of a medium should be based on its congeniality to the intended expressive mode. Lebrun, in his drawing of two figures (Figure 9.12), might have achieved similar results with chalks, but it is obvious why he did not use graphite or pen and ink. In Flaxman's drawing (Figure 9.21) the soft graphite (on a rough surface) allows a quiet delicacy of line and tone that echoes the subject's quiet delicacy. Flaxman uses graphite's dry, granular character to produce wool-like lines that enhance the drawing's gentle

Figure 9.21

JOHN FLAXMAN (1755–1826)

Woman Seated on the Floor
Pencil. 5 1/8 x 3 1/8 in.
Courtesy, Museum of Fine Arts, Boston
Gift of Rowland-Burdon Muller and Wm. A. Sargent Fund

Figure 9.22

MICHAEL MULLEN (19 –   )

Study for Sculpture (1960)
Pencil. 5 1/8 x 11 1/8 in.
Collection, The Museum of Modern Art, New York
Ethel R. Scull Fund

274

mood. But the same medium, in Mullen's *Study for Sculpture* (Figure 9.22), is used to support a powerful and threatening image. Unlike Flaxman's drawing, its angular shapes, sudden value changes, strong directions, and machine-like volumes all suggest aggressive action—and Mullen's use of graphite adds to their collective expression. Here, graphite's granular quality produces an abrasive texture and a clouded atmosphere that imply something of the drawing's menacing temper. Note how Mullen uses erasures as a means of creating fast, slashing tones and lost edges.

In Figure 9.22 Mullen uses another device to intensify meaning: *distortion*. This term should be understood not only in its dictionary definition, "to twist out of shape or change the appearance of," but also in the broader sense of any kind of intentional exaggeration of a subject's proportions or properties by addition, deletion, etc. To some extent,

all responsive drawings can be regarded as "distortions" of the subjects they depict. Not only because, as we saw in Chapter Five, the transposing of real volume and space into marks on a flat surface makes some distortion unavoidable, but because responsive drawing is a process of selection, of relating, omitting, stressing, and otherwise "essaying"—interpreting—the subject's actualities. But the term is generally applied to pronounced changes in a subject's proportions, surfaces, or other physical characteristics, or in its perspective, illumination, or clarity. The figure in Mullen's drawing, or those in Lebrun's, would be regarded as distorted, but the figures in the Rembrandt or Goya drawings (Figures 9.3, 9.11, and 9.20) would not.

Mullen's treatment of the figure's head distorts it into a threatening, mask-like form. The arms and legs are reduced to hard, tubular volumes; hands and feet almost disappear;

Figure 9.23
JOHN BAGERIS (1924–   )
Two Figures (1960)
Gouache, ink, and graphite. 12 x 18 in.
Collection of the artist

the torso is reshaped into a heavy "battering ram." Such distortions are, of course, very effective intensifiers of human forms and can all too easily be carried to absurd or even comical degrees. But Mullen's distortions produce forms that are inherently threatening. Because this is so, the drawing continues to convey aggressive action even when it is turned upside-down.

Any of a subject's measurable or emotive aspects can be distorted. In the Mullen drawing, the proportions, perspective, values, and clarity of human forms are all affected by the artist's expressive theme, but the forms are still volumetrically logical and human-like. This begins to be less the case in Bageris's, *Two Seated Figures* (Figure 9.23). Bageris carries the distortion of human forms to the brink of disintegration. Furious brush strokes lash and wind upon the forms, reshaping them into expressions of convulsive energy. But more than enough survives this highly subjective interpretation to permit us to identify with these two figures, and thus, to be caught up in the image's frenzied temper.

A very different kind of distortion occurs in Tchelitchew's drawing *Tree into Hand and Foot with Children* (Figure 9.24). Here, distortions not only add to, they constitute most of, the drawing's expressive message. In this richly imaginative drawing, the "realistic" metamorphosis of a tree into human form is, of course, impossible without resorting to distortions. But the artist does not only depend on figurative content to convey the drawing's ominous tone. The expressive nature of the elements contribute almost as much to its emotive force as do the figurative surprises they produce. This drawing, too, carries its meanings in the inherent nature of the marks, as can be seen by turning the drawing upside-down. Now, even with the figurative clues impeded, the drawing's spidery, brooding mood can be sensed in the elements, in their relational activities, and in the character of the handling.

ADDITIONAL EXAMPLES OF EXPRESSIVE RESPONSE

The possibilities for expression in drawing are unlimited. Not only does every responsive artist tend toward some general personal style of expression, but in each of his successful drawings some original variant on the possibilities for expression occurs. The several expressive themes and strategies that follow are offered here as helpful examples from the un-limited possibilities available to the searching, sensitive artist. Exploring some of the vast possibilities for conveying such meanings en-courages a more daring employment of the elements, the medium, and of our uncensored impressions.

Sometimes distortions are so well in-tegrated or subtle that we are not always aware of them. But the emotive power of such subtle amplifications can be considerable. Manet, in his drawing *A Man on Crutches* (Figure 9.25), only slightly exaggerates the fig-ure's bulk by subtly stressing the balloon-like nature of the sleeves and coat. These rounded forms seem even fuller and more weighty by their contrast with the rather weak-looking and spindly crutches. Manet's emphasis on the figure's bulk gives added meaning to the empty space alongside the figure's right leg. The artist shrewdly guides our attention to this space by using a 'roughly symmetrical pose and view. Because we see two roughly even halves of the figure, two arms, and two crutches, only the missing leg upsets the com-pletion of this simple system of paired forms. Additionally, the figure is located on the page where the missing leg would have occupied the picture-plane's central vertical axis—the most stable and balanced vertical position possible.

In the context of the broad, loose han-dling of Guardi's *Architectural Capriccio* (Fig-ure 9.26), the highly distorted figures in the drawing's lower left corner, and those on the landing and staircase higher up, seem per-fectly "correct," and expressively, they *are*. Closer examination shows that all the forms are only generalized, very free suggestions—pillars do not reach their bases; ledges, stairs, balustrades, and walls wander out of align-ment or disappear altogether; shadows start and stop suddenly; the drawing's perspective seems in places to go awry. But this *consistent* instability in the structure of the scene's forms creates an animated, excited air. Guardi, using splashes of tone and a darting, nervous line, adds to this mood by trans-forming what we know to be hard, archi-tectural forms into vibrating, gestural ones. Spirited "ripples" of energy move among the forms, changing inert structures into almost

organic ones. Note how the differing ex-pressive goals affect Manet's and Guardi's use of brush and ink.

In Delacroix's *Forepart of a Lion* (Figure 9.27), the artist's interest in the structured vol-ume of the lion is shared with an appreciation of the animal's self-assured air of power. Delacroix amplifies the lion's physical weight and strength by simplifying and thickening the volumes of the animal's mane and head, and by arranging their contours to form a continuous, massive, block of volume. The mane is drawn by bold structural lines, most

Figure 9.25
ÉDOUARD MANET (1832–1883)
A Man on Crutches
Brush, black ink, and tan wash. 27.1 x 19.7 cm.
Metropolitan Museum of Art
Harris Brisbane Dick Fund, 1948

Figure 9.26
FRANCESCO GUARDI (1712–1793)
Architectural Capriccio
Brush and wash. 7 x 5 1/8 in.
Victoria and Albert Museum, London

Figure 9.27
EUGÈNE DELACROIX (1798–1863)
Forepart of a Lion
Black crayon. 2.55 x 2.5 cm.
The Art Museum, Princeton University

278

of which are placed more or less vertically, further increasing the sense of heavy mass. To suggest even more weight, the lion's mane is shown as quite dark throughout, and darker still in its lower parts. The feel of great weight is so convincing that we sense the strain on the sturdy legs. Note how the assertive handling of the black crayon echoes the subject's temperament. Note, too, that Delacroix locates the animal in such a way as to prevent the head's contact with the right side of the page, and to permit the legs to fall to the left of the format's vertical center, thereby offsetting the physical weight on the right by visual weight on the left.

The influence of our expressive interests upon our treatment of volume is interest-

ingly revealed in comparing Guardi's "softening" of geometric, inert volumes, and Delacroix's "hardening" of organic ones. This is clearly evident in Delacroix's block-like treatment of the mane and head, and in the squared-off contour of the lion's face. Guardi's expressive intent would have been stifled by solid, stable forms; but Delacroix's is enhanced by it.

That differing expressive meanings affect an artist's perceptions and line of "attack," is clearly demonstrated by two Kollwitz drawings. In her *Losbruch (Black Anna)* (Figure 9.28), an exploratory sketch of a figure for a group of striking miners, the artist's need to convey the woman's anger and excitement leads her to a use of line not unlike Guardi's

Figure 9.28
KÄTHE KOLLWITZ (1867–1945)
Losbruch (Black Anna)
Charcoal. 51.3 x 38 cm.
Kunsthalle Bremen

Figure 9.29
KÄTHE KOLLWITZ (1867–1945)
Home Worker
Charcoal. 16 x 22 1/2 in.
Los Angeles County Museum of Art
Graphic Arts Council Fund

in its emphasis on gestural energies. Here, too, shapes and forms are left open, and tones are not restricted to the boundaries established by lines. But in her drawing *Home Worker* (Figure 9.29), the artist's expressive interests concern the limp weight of the weary worker, collapsed in sleep at his table. Now Kollwitz approaches the subject in a manner not unlike Delacroix's treatment. Again, structural lines, block-like masses, and bold, tonal modelling help suggest the artist's emotive theme.

In Daumier's drawing *The Lawyer* (Figure 9.30), shapes and masses are simplified, but not to increase the sense of weighty mass. Here they cause a steady *lessening* of volume,

as we read the drawing from top to bottom. In fact, covering the top half of the drawing shows the remainder quite without any suggestion of structured mass. Instead, the lower half of the image seems to suggest torn, ruffled, value-shapes. The further up we look, the more volume develops until finally, in the head, structured volume is strongly conveyed.

By making the figure's shoulders and head the most convincingly three-dimensional of the drawing's forms, by placing the strongest value contrasts here, and by the provocative, somewhat caricatured expression of the face, as well as by the animated quality of the lines and tones that produce it, Daumier fixes our attention on this part of the drawing. The

280

broader, lighter, and flatter character of the drawing's lower half contributes to the crescendo of attention upon the lawyer's malicious smile, and the drawing's loose, energetic behavior helps to convey the impression of his movement. Although we do not see his legs, the figure's overall tilt, and the "windblown" nature of the shapes and tones suggest that he is walking quickly. Notice that the head, although its structure is more fully developed than that of any other part, is no less vigorously drawn.

As this drawing demonstrates, the consistency of commitment to a particular expressive attitude, partly reflected in a drawing's handling, is important. In the best drawings, the artist always sustains his expressive intent. Deviating from it makes the drawing's design as well as its expression self-contradictory.

Another drawing by Daumier, *The Song* (Figure 9.31), shows a consistency of intent sustained throughout a more extensively developed work. As in the previous drawing, facial features (and the body of the centrally placed figure) are slightly caricatured. Here, contrasts of value are intensified, creating a strong light that plays across the group, boldly sculpting the forms as it gives them a sense of dramatic importance. Daumier deletes all extraneous detail. The clothing and hands of the figures are broadly stated—even the heads are simplified toward the back of each, away from the expressive features of their faces. The background is simply a darkened spatial container for the group. The facial features are developed with a strong interest in the details of careworn folds and wrinkles. Daumier's sympathetic treatment of these weathered faces, temporarily enlivened by drink, suggests that the group's impromptu song is as sudden and as temporary as the intense light is to the darkened scene—that the usual state of both is more somber.

Note how the artist combines light and dark tones with clear and vague edges to help guide us to areas of emphasis. Notice also how the thick, rounded character of the forms, whether of a body or a finger, is everywhere the same. Even the volume-summary of the group itself forms a monumental, rounded,

half-sphere, its curved upper edge conveyed by the arc of the heads.

Daumier's mastery of facial expressions is evident in these four faces. The lines and tone of each not only model form, they also enact the gestures that animate these faces. Note especially the pulling action of the eyebrows and folds of the forehead of the man on the far right. There is not a line or tone that does not convey the drinking action. The

Figure 9.30
HONORÉ DAUMIER (1808–1879)
The Lawyer
Black chalk, pen and wash. 20.7 x 13.9 cm.
Boymans-Van Beuningen Museum, Rotterdam

Figure 9.31
HONORÉ DAUMIER (1808–1879)
The Song
Black chalk, pen and black ink, grey wash, and
watercolor. 9 5/16 x 10 7/16 in.
Sterling and Francine Clark Art Institute, Williamstown

shapes, forms, and directions of the head
even suggest the movement of the head back-
wards. Such eloquently expressed human actions do not emerge merely from patient scrutiny, but from perceptions guided by
humanistic interests.

As Daumier's drawing indicates, light
can be a strong agent of expression. Rembrandt's mastery of light's emotive force is
evident in his brush drawing *Girl Sleeping*

(Figure 9.32). Despite the spontaneous and
largely linear handling, Rembrandt's profound
grasp of structure enables him to suggest
planes turned toward and away from a strong
light source, falling from the upper left side.
The unusual intensity of this light, especially
when seen against the retreating dark tone in
the upper left corner, suggests a supernatural
presence. The brush strokes appear to hover
between a linear and tonal role, their spirited

abstract energies transforming the girl and her bed into swaying, restless lines and shapes that contradict her passive state. This contrast between her inaction and the driving energy of the elements also suggests that the forms are being acted on by some force.

Lorrain's study of a man climbing a tree (Figure 9.33), stresses scale differences and a sense of movement to evoke the quiet drama of a figure climbing to a great height. The difference between the size of the man and the tree is emphasized by the artist's selection of a view far enough back to include the entire tree. Also, considering the size of the leaves, it appears the artist has somewhat reduced

the scale of the man to the tree. Lorrain evinces the windblown movements of the leaves and branches by the harmonious rhythm of the bell-shaped forms of the leaf-clumps. Other movements are implied by oblique hatchings alongside and upon the trunk that the man is climbing, and upon the mass of leaves to the man's right. Though hardly intense or powerfully dramatic, Lorrain's drawing is not less successful in conveying its expressive mood than others we have discussed. The scale and grandeur of the tree, the sense of its gentle swaying motion, and the underplayed human challenge is supported by a graceful, easy handwriting, and

Figure 9.32
REMBRANDT VAN RIJN (1606–1669)
Girl Sleeping
Brush and wash. 24.5 x 20.3 cm.
British Museum, London

Figure 9.33
CLAUDE LORRAIN (1600–1682)
Study of a Tall Tree with a Man Climbing It
Pen and brown ink. 11 1/8 x 8 5/8 in.
National Gallery of Canada, Ottawa

the consistent avoidance of strong value contrasts.

A different emotive theme emerges from Grosz's *Trees, Wellfleet, Cape Cod* (Figure 9.34). The rugged forms and tortuous movements of the trunks and branches; the occasional silhouettes, shaded areas, and gray tones of the pine needles and grasses; even the misty tone of the page—all allude to a plaintive melancholy.

Although in examining these drawings we have been concentrating on expressive factors, it must by now be evident that the artist's design and expressive interests are

deeply interlaced matters, and that any drawing action generally involves both considerations. However, recognizing the differences between selections and changes based on visual issues and those which serve expression, helps us to better govern and integrate both kinds of response.

The drawing exercises that follow are intended to help you experience the role of the elements, of media, and of distortion in conveying expressive meanings.

exercise 9A

Genuinely felt responses to a subject cannot often be summoned on demand, and there is no really adequate substitute for such expressive sensations. The best test of the ability to freely utilize expressive factors must occur in drawings of subjects that strongly engage your feelings. But, here, by aiming pairs of drawings toward clearly opposed expressive goals, you may, if you can invest these goals with some degree of meaning, begin to experience new attitudes toward the uses of the elements, your media, and the devices of distortion or exaggeration.

There are no time limits on any of the following drawings. Except for the first four drawings, you can use any medium (or combination) you wish, on any suitable supports, of any desired size or shape. Because of a medium's influence on a drawing's emotive nature it is advisable to vary these, but in each drawing the primary consideration in selecting a medium should be its compatibility with your expressive goal.

drawings 1 and 2

Using a nude model (or one simply clad) as your subject, make two drawings of the same pose, from the same position. In Drawing 1, use pen and ink and any suitable paper about 10″ × 14″. Your expressive goal is to depict the model as passive, at rest. Try to convey a sense of tranquility and stillness. Here (and in *all* of the drawings in Exercise 9A), consider an overall design strategy before you begin to draw what you feel will stress your meaning. Because expression is conveyed by the elements as well as the character of the forms they produce, think about their use before getting started. A tentative, general plan should of course be based as much as possible on responses to the subject. In all of the drawings from the model, the subject should include his or her immediate environment. Once you begin, however, do not feel bound by any prior strategy, but let any visual or

Figure 9.34

GEORGE GROSZ (1893–1959)

Trees, Wellfleet, Cape Cod
Charcoal, ink and watercolor. 19 5/8 x 15 3/8 in.
The Cleveland Museum of Art, John L. Severance Fund

expressive events or opportunities suggest a new plan for achieving your expressive goal.

In Drawing 2, use any friable black chalk, the softer the better, and any suitable paper, approximately 18″ × 22″. Now, your expressive goal is to depict the model as powerful, aggressive, and active. Again, consider a general approach before you begin.

Having just selected very different qualities from the same view of the same pose, you will of course have to search for those actualities or potentialities that will serve this new goal. In this admittedly arbitrary search for clues to support expressive themes that the model may not easily suggest, you can more fully appreciate the many choices possible in the "raw material." The more you study the forms and consider what choices and changes would help convey your expressive theme, the more they will appear. It is obviously helpful to pose the model in a way that will suggest some possibilities for either of these opposing goals.

In neither of these drawings should you force the medium to go against its inherent characteristics. Also, do not, in these first two drawings, rely on bold distortions. Indeed, try to avoid any but the most essential exaggerations, and keep these restricted to minor adjustments. As you begin to *feel* an expressive intent, subtle exaggerations will occur without your awareness. These unbidden changes are at this stage far more preferable to any deliberate changes on your part. In general, drastic distortions make subsequent responses to a subject more difficult because the constant subject and the evolving drawing pull farther and farther apart.

drawings 3 and 4

Select a new pose that will again allow some possibilities for the two opposing expressive goals of Drawings 1 and 2. This time, exchange media and try to make Drawing 3, using chalk, convey gentle passivity, and Drawing 4, using pen and ink, aggressive power. With this exhange of media, new possibilities and restrictions occur, requiring new strategies and perceptions. Again, distortions should be few and minor.

drawings 5 and 6

Place the model in a new pose that offers some possibilities for depicting it as transfigured into a wraith, or cloud-like form in Drawing 5, and into a machine-like form in Drawing 6.

In Drawing 5, show the model as being almost weightless. You may want to regard the forms as somewhat translucent and ethereal. Here,

you can either extend this mirage-like image to include the figure's environment, or use the substantiality of the surrounding forms as a contrast to those of the ghost-like figure. In Drawing 6, using the same pose, try to regard the model as robot-like. You want to evince the sense of the figure's heavy weight and unyielding rigidity.

In this pair of drawings, distortions can become bolder, but should be stimulated by the model's forms and grow from them as exaggerations of observed actualities, rather than being tacked on arbitrarily to the image. For example, in suggesting the model as transformed into a machine, you may logically want to exaggerate the various interlocking unions of the forms (especially at the joints) to suggest machine-like fittings, or simplify forms into more severely "tooled" forms, but deciding to add gears and shafts here and there is not invention stimulated by observed potentiality, but by prior concepts about what machines should look like.

drawings 7 and 8

Pose the model in a standing position that displays some rhythmic movements. In Drawing 7, *subtly* suggest that the forms are made of some soft, wax-like material that has just begun to melt. Here, distortions are built into the situation, but should be employed with some finesse. Try to feel the pull of gravity straining the softening, projecting or supporting limbs, how they have begun to yield to their own weight, their form beginning to alter. *Make these masses structurally convincing.*

In Drawing 8, use the same pose to subtly suggest the figure has begun to be transformed into a tree. Try to believe that this is actually happening, *must* happen; it will help you make inventive changes stimulated by the figures' folds, tendons, and muscles, rather than by memory. Be sure that these changes occur gradually. Again, structural clarity, *especially* in the passages where "metamorphosis" is in progress, is important.

drawings 9 and 10

Make both drawings from the same view of a landscape. In Drawing 9, convey the scene as forbidding, mysterious, or dangerous. In Drawing 10, the same scene should suggest a peaceful, welcoming mood. This time, resist *any* tendencies towards obvious distortions of the proportions, perspective, or contours. That is, try to record the subject's physical forms with a reasonable degree of objectivity. Rely instead on your use of the elements, especially value, and your handling of the media to convey your intent. This will influence the physical state of the forms anyway, but here the selections and changes you make should result from utilizing line, value, texture, and the other elements to express your meaning, rather than from pronounced additions, deletions, or other drastic changes in the subject's actualities.

drawings 11 and 12

Make two drawings of the same view of a simple still-life arrangement. In Drawing 11, suggest a serene and monumental air; in Drawing 12, a feeling of turbulence and action. Here, emphasize two-dimensional activities as much as three-dimensional ones. Rely on shapes rather than on extensively modelled forms; and on relational energies such as rhythmic, directional, and tensional ones, rather than on drastic distortions. However, do not hesitate to make whatever deletions, additions, and distortions you feel are necessary to amplify your expressive themes.

In this chapter we have emphasized examples by artists who are strongly expressive in order to more easily identify the expressive factors at work. But it is really impossible to imagine a drawing without some expressive meaning. This may be subconscious and unintentional in some; in others, the desire to express may be held in check to help unselectively duplicate a subject's surfaces. But this restriction is itself expressive of holding back intuitions and feelings that permit the fullest realization of a subect's essential character and mood. Such drawings often reveal the absence of the artist's satisfaction in released feelings in the act of drawing. In still other drawings, expressive meanings, left disregarded, make their emotive themes confused and contradictory. They reveal an aimlessness of meaning, a wandering of purpose. There are drawings that are largely bravado—bold flourishes that convey little form or feeling—and drawings that are evasive, timid, or uncertain. All these characteristics are expressions of their authors.

All drawings reveal something of the artist as an individual: his or her greatness or smallness of character, wit and resourcefulness, view of what is worthwhile ("value judgments"), and philosophy of life. To disregard *the given condition* of expression as part of a drawing's content dissipates forces that could endow our drawings with greater meaning, impact, and life.

CHAPTER TEN

ENVISIONED IMAGES

improvisations of form

A DEFINITION

As with any other language, the ability to communicate in visual terms requires a sound knowledge of vocabulary. For this reason the main theme of this book concerns the broadening of our powers of perception and response to the world we encounter around us. But, just as written communications can relate not only to things witnessed but also to things envisioned or remembered, so visual communications can tell of the responsive artist's encounters with the people, landscapes, and spectors of his imagination. In this chapter we will briefly examine a crucial but often overlooked consideration in the creation of imaginary images, namely, the importance of *insight*. The dictionary defines insight as "the ability to see and understand clearly the inner nature of things, especially by intuition." Applied to drawing, this means the ability to penetrate analytically and to become involved empathically with the subject. For, in choosing to turn inward for our subjects, we encounter even greater structural and dynamic challenges than when we draw in the presence of our subject.

Unlike the model, landscape, or still life before us—its masses rich in nature's inventive structural variants and innovations, bathed by form-revealing light, and yielding to unhurried inquiry—the forms of our imagination are vague and illusive. They shift and change while we consider them. And because of the demands and opportunities in the emerging work, they continue to change while we draw them. All the more reason, then, to be able to follow their permutations, or those we order; to be able to seize upon their essential structure and spirit from the shifting and shadowy stage of our imagination.

For the beginner, contending with the perceptual challenges of drawing the subjects placed before him, it would seem that the greater complexities involved in the realization of imagined or remembered forms are simply beyond his ability. And so they are, if his first attempts are figures, forests, or any other kind of complex form arrangements. Indeed, drawing such subjects from imagination is, for many mature artists, an extremely demanding challenge, just as Drawings 1 and 2 of Exercise 5B were probably among the most difficult tests of form-realization for the reader. But in drawing *simple* forms such as the block, the sphere, and the cone, we "prove" our ability to understand the structural nature of the masses that underlie all forms, and are more likely to recognize their presence, in variously interjoined combinations, as the form-summaries of observed subjects. Once we *can* draw simple form-concepts it is easy to combine them to produce more complex solids, as in Figure 10.1.

This ability is of the greatest importance for two reasons. First, because we cannot draw a form whose structure we do not understand, the more skill we develop in the invention of forms based on combinations of simple solids the easier it becomes to decipher, clarify, and even alter the complex forms of our observed subjects. Second, without the structural understanding that comes from a wide variety of experiences with inventing structurally lucid forms, our ability to create envisioned images is severely restricted. After all, because the forms in our envisioned drawings are *ours*, are products and permutations of our past visual experiences, they

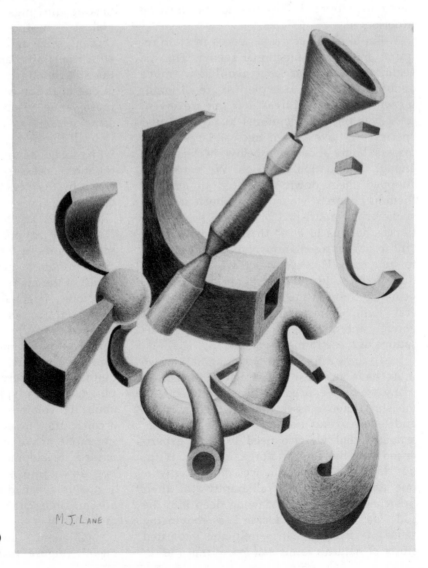

Figure 10.1
MARY-JO LANE
Masses in Space (Student drawing)
Graphite. 14 x 17 in.

are necessarily limited to the structural experiences we have had with the forms of our inner as well as outer world. Conceiving forms we have never encountered in our daily lives (at least, not in the combinations we may desire) is the stuff that imaginary images are made of, but we cannot draw those we cannot visually conceive.

Nor is the problem in invented imagery one of structure only. For the responsive artist it is equally important to "see" the gestural nature of his inner vision, and to sense its dynamic conditions. Here again, the artist's stockpile of earlier visual and expressive experiences, gathered from nature's limitless supply of relational and emotive possibilities, serves as his main resource of engaging dynamic inventions. Forces, like forms, must be experienced.

But to have such experiences in store requires more than functional seeing. That is, seeing forms as obstacles to avoid as we move about in space. For example, we are all familiar with a variety of trees but can we invent one, even one that conforms to no particular species? To have known trees as large, fixed, masses, larger above than below, is clearly not enough information to go on. We may have chopped them down, decorated or climbed them as children; we may have been scraped, sheltered, or nourished by them. These experiences help us to *know* trees in ways important to our representations, but do not help us to *draw* trees. However much we may admire their grand scale and color, their changing appearance through the seasons, and their general form characteristics, this is not yet enough information to serve our improvisations of these forms.

To draw a tree from our imagination, we must have analyzed the structural nature of many trees. We need to have explored and measured their masses, studied their surfaces and textures, and noted how their forms are arranged. But we also need to have experienced their dynamic and organic forces. Without deeply felt remembrances of their rhythmic energies, of the "calligraphy" of their branches, of their roots clawing deep into the soil, we cannot call forward a convincing sense of "treeness." It is from the dedicated study of nature's forms *and* forces that the responsive artist's fund of structural and dynamic insights are nourished.

To appreciate how these insights can be developed and used, we will examine some invented images. In studying these drawings, notice that the artists consistently apply the same processes and disciplines as for drawings made from observed subjects.

APPLYING GESTURAL INSIGHTS

Many of the drawings in this chapter are preparatory sketches. Artists confronted with major undertakings in another medium have often approached their envisioned subject by making drawings that, in exploring the general state of the intended work's form and content, seize on certain large moving actions, structural traits, and relational patterns from the still indefinite image. A gestural "attack" is one of the most effective means of snaring these vague, visual notions, and for much the same reasons as discussed in Chapter One. Indeed, the more clouded our "inner screen" is, its image as uncertain as it is provocative, the more necessary it is to get at the idea's essence by the penetrating nature of a gestural approach.

Reni does this in his *Allegory of the Dawn, The Aurora* (Figure 10.2). The artist's initial efforts go toward laying hold of the image's overall gestural behavior: a most active whorl of the many lines on the left converging to a long, diagonal movement to the format's upper right corner. Reni's interest in the plastic actions of the intended work outstrip his concern for its masses. Yet the volume-informing contours, the curved hatchings that define the drapery, and the somewhat simplified masses suggest his first judgments about the volumes of the intended work. Such a concentration on sheer energy, as an opening probe, makes it far less likely that an extended development of such an image will bog down into a dull cataloging of isolated segments, for its directed actions and rhythms are an integral part of the compositional order.

Guercino's gestural approach in his *Four Figures* (Figure 10.3) takes on the additional

Figure 10.2
GUIDO RENI (1575–1642)
Allegory of the Dawn, The Aurora
Pen, brush and ink over chalk drawing. 12.5 x 25.7 cm.
Albertina Museum, Vienna

consideration of illumination. By doing so, he includes an important influence on the final work's dynamic character. Value, as we have seen, is a potent graphic force. As in Reni's drawing, the primary goal is the establishment of at least the principal characteristics of the actions of his subject and of the elements themselves. No doubt a painting based on such a broadly stated sketch would find the splashes of tone modified, the volumes more defined, and subtler relational activities developed. But its overall pattern of forms and forces, established at the outset, would, as in the previous example, promote a strong system of expressive order. What is of interest in both of these drawings is that the artists elect to approach their subject, not by a patient solving of each part's final form, but by a scanning of its principal dynamic properties.

Too often the student drawing an imagined subject will revert to a tedious, peacemeal approach to his subject, "finishing" each segment before moving on to the next. And he may do so long after he would no longer

consider drawing an observed subject in that way. This may occur for several reasons. First, there is the anxiety-producing *fact* of being responsible for the realization of forms he does not actually see. In the absence of real forms to draw, his attention is divided between first inventing and holding an image steady in his mind's eyes, and then trying to react to its salient characteristics. Unable to hold on to the entire subject, he settles for a conscientious description of parts. And, unless he does have an adequate store of prior visual experiences with such parts, those he summons up to work from are going to offer meager graphic fare. Indeed, some of the most gifted artists on occasion show a slight lessening of inventive daring in their envisioned works, when compared to those made in the presence of their subject.

Second, without the forms before him, the student, fearing his imagined subject will elude him, feels impelled to pin it down, piece by piece. But the results here are no more likely to succeed than when observed forms are described in sequence.

Figure 10.3
GUERCINO (1591–1666)
Four Figures
Pen and brown ink and brown wash. 8 x 10 3/8 in.
Cooper-Hewitt Museum of Design, Smithsonian Institution, New York

And third, the student's struggle with the difficulties of form-realization make it all the harder to take on the search for unifying relationships and energies. But those given bonds and forces in nature must, of course, be sensed in those subjects he invents.

In concentrating on gestural expression at the outset, Reni and Barbieri advance their imagined image's overall behavior and mood. In this way each establishes an expressive armature that holds the image alive in the artist's mind, and augments both the drawing's design and emotive force.

APPLYING STRUCTURAL INSIGHTS

As we saw in Chapter One, a gestural approach naturally leads to more complex structural and dynamic considerations. The artist's emphasis, in gradually shifting from a sensual–schematic exploration of what the forms are doing, to what they look like, also moves from an emphasis on the subject's inner energies, to an emphasis on the volumetric nature of its outer surfaces. Most artists form their envisioned images in the same way.

In Poussin's *The Nurture of the Infant Jupiter* (Figure 10.4), the gestural drawing still dominates, but the artist has gone on to establish some general structural judgments and to enlarge upon the drawing's compositional order. In the drawing on and around the figures and the goat, Poussin begins to establish a few broad planes and shadows, and to rework edges, giving substance to these forms and suggesting the space among them. Organizationally, a pattern of undulating rhythms, straight and curved forms, textured and "plain" passages, fast and slow directional movements, and a low, triangular grouping of the forms in the foreground "flesh out" the gestural "skeleton."

Poussin reminds us here that whether we are confronting observed or envisioned subjects, drawing involves both discipline and release. Discipline moderates the animated expression of the forms, especially of the branches and masses of leaves, insisting on structural essentials and a rhythmic rap-

port among them; release energizes the schematic lines that construct masses and establish tone, giving them the same sense of urgency as the more calligraphic lines.

Similar in spirit to the Poussin, Guercino's *St. Domenic Kneeling before the Madonna and Child* (Figure 10.5), carries the fleshing out process farther by a vigorous but more precise and detailed structural development that enlists the effects of light falling across the forms. The gestural underdrawing, still visible, lets us see how Guercino uses it as a guide and how he builds upon it.

It is most unlikely that the convincing substantiality and presence of these figures, or the harmonious rhythms that course between them were very sharply focused in the artist's mind as he began this drawing. Rather, it is probable that only a rough visual idea, a plan, having more to do with the broader generalities of their postures, posi-

Figure 10.4
NICOLAS POUSSIN (1594–1665)
The Nurture of the Infant Jupiter
Pen and brown ink. 17.4 x 24.1 cm.
Stockholm National Museum, 2438/1863

Figure 10.5
GUERCINO (1591–1666)
St. Domenic Kneeling before the Madonna and Child
Pen, sepia ink, washes of tone.
27.2 x 20.7 cm.
Albertina Museum, Vienna

tions, and overall design, and certainly with their emotive meaning first stimulated the gestural attack. Indeed, the gesture drawing probably reflected about as much as Guercino's vision provided. Only after the subject's essential masses and movements were roughed in on the page, did the artist turn to the challenge of developing the forms *and* further strengthening the drawing's organizational and expressive themes.

Invented images rarely exist in the mind fully formed down to the last detail, waiting only to be transferred to the page. Typically, it is not until the artist has loosely established the all-embracing but unspecified essentials on the page—generalities assembled from his total structural resources—that he begins to call on his knowledge of the specific forms of the intended image.

As we saw in Chapter Three, structure is a dominant consideration for some artists. It does not surprise us that the drawings of Michelangelo and Cézanne are formed, almost from the start, out of inquiries concerning length, plane, mass, location, and space, for structure plays an important role in their major efforts in other media. For them, gestural considerations accompany a search for their subject's fundamental structural and spatial conditions, rather than the other way around. But that such an approach is utilized by artists whose paintings do not stress the constructional interjoining of every plane and form-unit, and who are especially insistent on such a structural approach when drawing from their imagination, may strike us as unexpected. However, recall that for the responsive artist, even when structural considerations are not to play a major role in a work, a sound understanding of the subject's masses is essential to his interpretation of them, for whatever creative purpose. All the more reason then, when the artist must invent, interpret, and integrate all the forms, to extract the envisioned subject's salient architectural features.

Raphael does this in his *Two Riders* (Figure 10.6), where gestural and structural interests harmoniously interwork to bring the artist's vision of monumental and fluent forms to the page. The massed lines that define broad, dark, planes, and the volume-informing contours are simultaneously engaged in establishing powerful masses and graceful movements that embody the graphic and temperamental gist of Raphael's invention and intent.

Again, in Papo's imaginary theme (Figure 10.7), architectural considerations are at least as important as gestural ones. As this

Figure 10.6
RAPHAEL (1483–1520)
Two Riders
Red chalk. 28.6 x 20.3 cm.
Albertina Museum, Vienna

Figure 10.7
ISO PAPO (1925–   )
Figures Seated under Trees
Sepia, pen and ink. 8 1/2 x 11 in.
Courtesy of the artist

drawing indicates, whether the subject is observed or imagined, many engaging dynamic solutions are stimulated by structural insights (compare with Figure 3.6). The energetic actions emerging from the artist's "web" of spirited lines create movements and tensions that animate the forms as they construct them, giving emotive force to the artist's deeply experienced inner vision.

The expressive force of the dynamics that issue from a fascination with structure is amplified when structural relationships exist between massive constructs in a large spatial field. Piranesi, in his *Fantastic Interior* (Figure 10.8), gives his imagination free play to build monumental forms that call to each other across vast spaces. And here, as in the previous examples, analysis and empathy com-

Figure 10.8
GIOVANNI BATTISTA PIRANESI (1720–1778)
Fantastic Interior
Pen and brown wash over chalk. 4 3/4 x 7 in.
National Gallery of Canada, Ottawa.

bine to embrace the vision's essential nature, not its details.

APPLYING DYNAMIC INSIGHTS

As Annibale Carracci's page of sketches demonstrates (Figure 10.9), for many artists even the most preliminary exploration of an envisioned theme is conceived of as a system of expressive order. Each of these visual ideas is composed in its own format and considered for its balance and rhythms as well as for its masses and figurative theme. In some, even the basic value distribution is established, and all show the rudiments of relational activities to be developed. For example, in the large, central drawing, Carracci contrasts the shadowed figure in the foreground with the illuminated state of the mother and child, and reinforces their importance by the radiating nature of the foliage be-

hind them. And, in the group of three seated figures in the lower right, boldly curvasive, S-shaped movements animate and unite the group. Notice, in the several figures only just begun, how Carracci searches first for their gestural character and then turns to the construction of their masses. Contours, the student's favorite means, are more firmly established here only *after* the artist has found actions, relationships, and masses that attract his interest.

A similar *gesture-to-structure-to-contour* process guides Ricci's drawing *Achilles Gives Hector's Dead Body to Priam* (Figure 10.10). This is not to suggest that in certain passages the order may not be altered. But in the main, firm, final contours are "asked to wait" until the gestural search, gradually evolving into a simultaneous development of the drawing's figurative actions, dynamic actions, and masses collectively determine not only where each edge must be, but how they will be stated, and what their relative importance will be in the design. We can, then, understand the process of many responsive artists as proceeding according to the following diagram:

And, as has been observed, when the subject is the indeterminate product of our imagination, such an approach, in fixing first on a vision's essential nature, is most suited to its veiled and elusive character.

A further observation on that point: even in contour drawings in which a single, deliberate, and continuous line conveys the image, a form of this process is at work. In such cases a kind of "mental gesture drawing" that goes on to take account of the subject's masses, and abstract and figurative actions, precedes the drawing of the line. The line then records the results of this process, which has gone on in the mind's eye; the line "traces" the mind's contour judgments.

But when, as in Ricci's preparatory work, an extensively developed and tonal drawing is desired, the forming image must evolve by stages. The student whose goal is a drawing

Figure 10.9
ANNIBALE CARRACCI (1560–1609)
Page of studies
Pen and bistre ink. 20.5 x 27.2 cm.
Rijksmuseum, Amsterdam

Figure 10.10
SEBASTIANO RICCI (1659–1734)
Achilles Gives Hector's Dead Body to Priam
Pen and bistre ink, heightened with white lead, on tan
paper. 22.4 x 31.1 cm.
Albertina Museum, Vienna

of comparable structural and relational complexities, and who proceeds to draw completed segments in sequence, or who concentrates on structural matters only, risks producing a wooden and disunified image in which organizational and measurable inconsistencies create distressing dissonances.

Just as Ricci's ability to recall familiar forms and invent others is based on earlier analytical and responsive involvements with various forms, so is his repertoire of organizational and expressive tactics the harvest of earlier involvements with the forces that govern systems of expressive order. That the artist can call to mind the forms necessary to de-

pict the fallen Hector is one thing; that he can compose them in a way that has compelling dynamic and humanistic meaning, is another.

Rembrandt's envisioned images are among the most moving and original works in the history of drawing. Endowed with profound philosophical and creative insights, his drawings are at once moving human documents and astonishing graphic inventions. More than penetrating structural and organizational solutions are at work in his *The Holy Family in the Carpenter's Workshop* (Figure 10.11). Rembrandt also brings to this image his mastery of light, his ability to make value relationships evoke powerful abstract and

Figure 10.11
REMBRANDT VAN RIJN (1609–1669)
The Holy Family in the Carpenter's Workshop
Pen and bistre ink. 18.4 x 24.6 cm.
The British Museum, London

psychological events, a skill developed from his many encounters with light's behavior in his portraits and landscapes. Again, we cannot envision what we have not experienced in our responsive involvements with nature.

Rembrandt's pictorial emphasis of Mary and the infant Jesus, unlike Carricci's solution of surrounding the figures with subtly radiating forms, is achieved by the almost blinding light that comes through the window directly above the figures. This light attains a supernatural brilliance, in part because of the room's sonorous shadows that seem strangely unaffected by it. The room's persistent dark tones are expressed by painterly washes of ink that are in accord with the lines' rugged

vitality, and activate areas that other artists might have stated as only dark. Note especially how important the two pulsating, dark tones on either side of the window are to both the design and expression, and how the bold and vibrant reed-pen lines hold up under the drawing's overall dark tones.

But some envisioned images, such as Bresdin's *The Crevasse* (Figure 10.12), are intended as final statements. When this is the case, the earlier gestural drawing, though it is often overlaid by subsequent drawing, is often, as here, visible in places. More important, however, is its influence on the subsequent drawing. Had Bresdin simply begun at one end of the blank page and drawn each part in turn, there would not be the complex relational play between shapes, rhythms, values, and textures, nor the majestic eruptions of form they create. In imaginary images, where anything may appear, the temptation to create fantastic configurations sometimes leads the unwary into volume formations that are beyond their ability to explain. But intricate volumes in complex interjoinings with others, as occur in Bresdin's drawing, become more manageable when we remember that they are still only unusual juxtapositions of a handful of basic geometric masses.

Lest it appear that anyone drawing invented images is under an obligation to be es-

pecially explicit in explaining structure, it should be noted again that drawing is not sculpture, and that the degree of volume-clarity in drawings made either from imagination or observation is determined by the artist. What is important in either case is the artist's *comprehension* of the forms he means to draw. Of course, some responsive drawings do contain passages in which volume and space impressions are subdued or intentionally ambiguous.

Indeed, the emotive force of Bloom's large drawing *On the Astral Plane: Beelzebub* (Figure 10.13) is intensified by the lessening of form-clarity in the drawing's upper half. Rather than represent the indescribable evil of

Figure 10.12
RODOLPHE BRESDIN (1822–1885)
The Crevasse (1860)
Pen and ink. 21.2 x 15.8 cm.
Courtesy of The Art Institute of Chicago

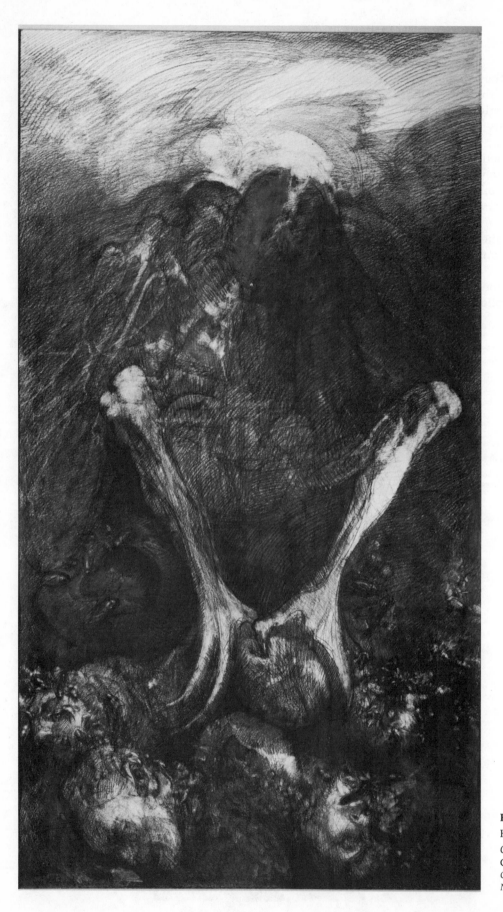

Figure 10.13
HYMAN BLOOM (1913–   )
On the Astral Plane: Beelzebub (1966)
Charcoal, 64 x 36 in.
Courtesy of Terry Dintenfass, Inc.,
New York

the devil-form and in order to more effectively express its ghoulish activity, the artist
"holds back" in the drawing's upper part, allowing our imaginations to participate. But,
where Bloom intends for us to consider the
symbolism of his imagery, convincingly structured forms emerge.

But the artist has planned for more than
solid volumes in a well-established spatial
field. He devises a somewhat symmetrical and
even restful design, keeps its forms contained
within the format, avoids harsh changes in
value or bold directional forces, and envelops
the configuration in dark and gently graduated values. In short, Bloom creates a stilled,
brooding configuration, against which the
strong diagonal thrusts and the sudden light
intensity of the two clawing limbs have more
expressive impact.

In addition to the intentional structural
ambiguities noted earlier, and the ones that
result from such a dark and muffled configuration, there are other, psychological ones.
The artist equivocates between the horrible
and the beautiful. The light at the top may be
a sunrise or an inferno; the insects crawling
over the disembodied heads seem flower-like;
and even the creature's limbs, drawn with
sympathetic appreciation of their sinewy
strength and their rugged structure, seem to
both attract and repel us. The more we examine this provocative work, the more we find
the same profound interworking of structural
and dynamic qualities to be seen in the artist's drawings from nature (Figure 9.17).

Again, in Redon's *The Captive Pegasus*
(Figure 10.14), large segments of the drawing are
not structurally explained. But, where masses
come into the strangely selective light, their
form shows the results of sound analytical understanding. And, as in the two previous examples, the selection and arrangement of unusual combinations of forms is made to seem
more plausible by the artist's conviction in
his vision, in its graphic and symbolic worth;
and by the knowledgeable construction and
ordering of forms that the artist's fund of perceptual insights provides.

The unity of this drawing is especially
strong. The shapes, values, and volumes, the
overall design scheme, and the emotive tone

Figure 10.14
ODILON REDON (1840–1916)
The Captive Pegasus
Lithograph. 13 3/8 x 11 5/8 in.
The Museum of Modern Art, New York
Lillie P. Bliss Collection

are all bold and direct. Elements associate and
contrast emphatically, moving actions are
powerful and balanced, and the drawing's
mood is sustained throughout by both the nature of the dynamic actions and the fervor of
the artist's handling.

This chapter does not attempt to be a
survey of imaginative drawing. Rather, its
purpose is to alert the reader to the need for
the same high degree of analytical and empathic
involvement that sound, responsive drawing of
observed subjects demands. The following exercise is designed to both test and guide your
ability to call on these structural and dynamic
skills in drawing envisioned images.

Figure 10.15

exercise 10A

Except where noted, the following seven drawings have no restrictions of media, size, or time.

drawing 1

Using Figures 10.1 and 10.15 as rough guides, and using graphite on a bristol or vellum paper approximately 14″ × 17″, draw several complex forms by interjoinings and fusions of simple geometric volumes. Although you will find it useful to select a light source for this tonal drawing, do not feel restricted to it when consistency would leave the structure of certain parts poorly explained. Instead, adopt another light source for such passages. In general, your goal here should be form-clarity. A sense of illumination is decidedly a secondary consideration in this drawing.

drawing 2

Using the same materials and attempting the same degree of form-clarity, draw a number of everyday objects whose forms you are familiar with and can "see" in your mind's eye. For example, an empty spool of thread, a simple container or cup, an apple, a pencil, and a spoon would make a useful combination of form challenges. Assume these forms to be tumbling about in space. You may want to draw some of the forms from several views, or overlap them, but do not allow them to run off the page. Because you are interested in a convincing impression of volumes in space, avoid an overconcern with textural effects or other minor surface detail.

drawing 3

Select any two objects that are different in form and function, and have one of them "metamorphose" into the other. For example, have a hand become a tree branch as it approaches the forearm. Or, turn a shoe into a hammer or a horn. The combinations are of course limitless, but again, avoid objects that are overly rich in texture or whose structure you are not certain of. In fact, you might very well make this drawing with the objects now before you, because you will be inventing the transitional passage between the two forms. This area of change from one form into another should be *gradual*. Now you must decide what changes would occur as one form gradually adapts and gradually flows into the other. Your goal is to explain, through convincing structural changes, how one object altered its form to become the other.

drawing 4

Using Piranesi's drawing (Figure 10.8) as a rough guide, invent your own fantastic interior.

drawing 5

Select any religious, mythological, or social theme and make three or four brief, preliminary sketches that explore differing compositional and structural arrangements. Draw at least one of these in a long, vertical format. Select the one you prefer and, after making further preparatory sketches, working from observed figures, draperies, landscapes, etc. as necessary, go on to make an extended drawing in which you may refer to all your preparatory sketches, but to nothing else.

drawing 6

Using Bresdin's drawing (Figure 10.12) as a rough guide, invent your own fantastic rocky landscape.

drawing 7

Select any reproduction in this book and draw your own version of the scene. Within moderate limits you may add or omit various forms. It is not necessary here to work in the manner of the artist whose drawing you are re-designing, nor is it necessary to make drastic changes from the original. Perhaps taking a slightly different view of the subject is all that you will need to provide you with a new set of relationships and forms. However, you should use similar materials, where this is possible.

For some artists (and they include some of the greatest) the process of drawing (and that of painting) can only begin with the stimulus provided by an observed subject. For them envisioned subjects hold little interest. Other artists (of equal stature) believe that we cannot draw anything really well until we can create good drawings of at least some of the things we envision. Whichever view we hold, it is clear that the *discipline* of inventing forms can only improve our responses to those we observe. For, just as we learn about nature's rich, inventive store of structural and dynamic phenomena by a sensitive study of the world around us, so do we learn about ourselves, our creative strengths, susceptibilities, and needs, when we work from imagination. The best drawings, whether observed or envisioned, come from those artists who know nature and themselves best.

But for those of us who find satisfaction and significance in the improvisation of forms and events, the need to understand how nature constructs and orders is essential. Redon had this in mind when he observed, in a letter to a friend, "There is a kind of drawing which the imagination has liberated from any concern with the details of reality in order to allow it to serve freely for the representation of things conceived. . . . No one can deny me the merit of having given the illusion of life to my most unreal creations. My whole originality, therefore, consists in having made improbable beings live humanly according to the laws of the probable, by as far as possible putting the logic of the visible at the service of the invisible."*

*Quoted in *Artists on Art*, ed. Robert Goldwater and Marco Treves (New York: Pantheon Books, 1972), p. 361.

CHAPTER ELEVEN

PATHOLOGIES
OF DRAWING

some symptoms and defects

A DEFINITION

A responsive drawing reflects the graphic equivalent of certain qualities in the subject which the artist considers essential to his creative interests. It also reflects his felt judgments about the expressive design of these qualities within the fixed boundaries of the page. Together, these objective and subjective responses to the subject's "what" and "how" create a system of expressive order that can be thought of as a graphic "organism," one whose structural and dynamic conditions convey a sense of "life" within and among the marks. Like living organisms, graphic ones depend on an efficient, interrelated functioning of their parts for life. They can be organizationally and expressively "healthy," or "suffer" various disorders that weaken and impede their effectiveness.

To regard drawings as organisms that roughly parallel some of the qualities and frailties of living organisms permits a useful analogy. It helps us better understand how important the relational condition of all of a

drawing's components is to its artistic well-being. It also helps us apply the same analytical honesty to our examination of the results that the act of drawing itself demands. We expect "diagnostic" objectivity when examining any organism's soundness. In fact, one of an art teacher's essential skills is just this ability to analyze a student's work objectively in order to suggest ways by which the student can better comprehend and manifest what are to him important stimuli in the subject. Such constructive analysis, and not coaching in formula solutions or in established schemas, is the art teacher's primary responsibility. Total objectivity in evaluation is not possible, involving, as it must, the teacher's own aesthetic persuasion and temperament. But the conscientious teacher whose purpose is enlightenment, not indoctrination, strives (like all good therapists) to be objective. The teacher whose evaluation is directed less at a drawing's particular weaknesses and strengths than toward its general aesthetic thrust, and whose advice refers to stylistic directions outside of the drawing under examination, is not unlike the doctor who prescribes aspirin no matter what the patient's disorder.

Instructors do encounter drawings that show an almost total innocence of the fundamentals of perception, organization, and expression. In such cases, the teacher should be less concerned with analyzing and correcting each symptom, or with salvaging the student's general approach, however unique, than with curing the problem itself. One does not help the visually illiterate by directing their interest toward a particular aesthetic ideology. The teacher's task is to turn such students away from essentially non-visual concepts that make perceptual, organizational, and expressive failure certain.

We are all limited by the quality of our perceptual comprehension, and by the kinds of responses they stimulate. The beginner's comprehension and range of response will expand greatly as his analytical and empathic understanding develop. If he is developing his skills with little or no professional guidance (and some great artists such as Rembrandt, Cézanne, and Van Gogh had little formal training), the experiences and insights that expand ability must come through his own efforts to study drawings, to continuously make drawings, to learn about the materials and the history of drawing, and to sustain his commitment to drawing during those inevitable periods of little forward progress. If the student is in a program of art study, some, perhaps much, of his ability will reflect good instructional guidance. But, like the student working on his own, the responsibility for his artistic growth is, finally, his own. It is developed through the same initiative to search out his own experiences, information, and interpretations. During the period of study and certainly afterwards, both the self-taught and those receiving formal instruction must continue to develop their own creative sensibilities and diagnostic skills.

In a formal art program the student's creative goals can be more sharply formed, and he has greater opportunities to develop the ability to analyze his work, to uncover and correct the factors that hinder him from achieving these goals. The abrasive exchange of ideas between the art student, his fellow-students, and teacher, and the teacher's own excited involvement in art help stimulate the formulation of good creative attitudes and challenges. Too often, the student working alone cannot discriminate between the *processes* of drawing, which are universal; and the *techniques* of drawing, which are personal. Without the guidance of a knowledgeable teacher to help him overcome fundamental perceptual and technical hurdles, the student may lose much valuable time developing superficial, expository skills instead of analytical, responsive ones.

Both types of student can benefit from studying the drawings of every period and culture, with a view to grasping the universal principles and considerations of artists as far removed in time and culture as cave artists and contemporary ones. All responsive drawings, whether of observed or envisioned subjects, show a profound grasp of structural and dynamic matters, an integration of expression and order, and a compelling economy and authority. But these drawings should be studied primarily as manifestations of various creative sensibilities rather than as sources of skillful techniques to emulate.

An artist's personal "recipe" for drawing is not altogether freely chosen. Part of what motivates the way we draw is determined by our instinctive need to have certain undefinable qualities present in the drawing. Such intuitive and idiosyncratic needs are as insistent as they are intangible. Though we cannot point to the places in a drawing where they manifest themselves, we reject those of our drawings in which these qualities are absent. These unique and necessary conditions are rooted in our subconscious reason and need, and though they cannot be measured, analyzed, or altered, they permeate a drawing. Examples of great drawings demonstrate the artist's acceptance and utilization of these intuitive needs. In such drawings we sense that the artist has accepted himself—an act as necessary in art as in life.

But students or artists whose drawings are heavily influenced by other artists may largely mask these qualities of self because they are "speaking" in another's "voice." If these intangibles that reveal an original presence are stifled in their drawings, whatever else the drawings may have gained through such influences and borrowings, they will lack a natural conviction and spirit. These intangibles cannot themselves make a drawing great, but their absence rules out greatness. The serious "malady" of the follower, then, is twofold: in denying his *self*-participation he smothers vital original meanings; and, as with all followers, he stays *behind* the admired artist in both concepts and inquiries, producing dull variations of great themes. But, more of this, later.

Let us now examine some specific "ailments" of drawings. The more we learn about graphic defects—how systems of expressive order fail—the more we can do to avoid such pitfalls and to diagnose a problem when it is present.

Figure 11.1
JEAN FRANCOIS MILLET (1814–1875)
Shepherdess Knitting
Crayon. 13 7/8 x 8 7/8 in.
Courtesy, Museum of Fine Arts, Boston

There is a danger here, however. Absolute perfection is an impossible goal and we should not pursue it. It is wrong to assume that a drawing has failed because one part or one aspect of it is faulty. There is no individual without some blemish or flaw, nor is even the greatest drawing flawless. Many fine works show some minor waverings in organizational or expressive continuity, or some minor discrepency in perception or handling. The wonder is not that a drawing can be great despite its imperfections, but that so much eloquence and strength is ever achieved with so few flaws. In fact, works of art are incredibly durable, even when quite pronounced problems exist.

As an example, in Millet's drawing *Shepherdess Knitting* (Figure 11.1), the position of the figure's right foot is difficult to understand. We are provided with no clues that explain how it came to be located on the figure's left side, or why it is placed at so marked an angle. *In the context of the drawing's overall structural and spatial clarity*, this appears to be an inconsistency. Additionally, the dark form at the figure's left shoulder, in being somewhat independently stated, seems unaccountably dark and isolated. In relation to the representational "pace" of the rest of the drawing, the dark form seems only a weakly integrated member of the design. The several lines from the top of the page to the head seem to define a tree's edge, but their collective tone brings the lines forward where they can also be interpreted as descending into the figure's head. Despite these ambiguous passages, the drawing's gentle charm, and the seemingly effortless way in which Millet conveys the forms and character of the shepherdess are impressive qualities.

The durability of a work of art can also be seen in the fragments of drawings, paintings, and sculptures from antiquity. The expressive order of many of these is so much a part of every segment that even surprisingly small fragments seem able to overcome the absence of the rest of the work to convey aesthetic meanings.

The following examination of common defects in responsive drawing is grouped into three categories: perceptual, organizational, and expressive. Throughout the discussion we should bear in mind that what may be a failing in the context of one drawing may be a vital function in another. More often than not, a response is right or wrong *in relation to the nature of the rest of the drawing*, and not in relation to any established conventions. What follows, then, is based not on any particular aesthetic ideology, but rather on the universal aesthetic principles of balance and unity of a drawing's representational and dynamic conditions.

Hence, a truck too small for the road, a road too large for the house, and a house too far from the man entering it are errors in scale and placement only in a drawing where most other relationships of scale and location objectively reflect the various sizes and positions observed in the subject. Conversely, in the context of drawings that intend *themes* of scale and placement distortions, a few, arbitrary areas of objective denotation (unless they provided a secondary theme, a pattern of accuracies) would appear in conflict with the rest of the drawing. Likewise, *random* structural ambiguities in the context of structural clarity, a solitary, "unanswered" diagonal thrust in a design based on vertical and horizontal axes, *or any other break in a drawing's type of design, expression, or handling* can be understood as damaging to the function of these factors and to the unity of the drawing.

PERCEPTUAL DEFECTS

Learning to see the measurable actualities, to analyze and relate a subject's essential shapes, values, masses, etc., is of course, the basic skill. Quite simply, we cannot draw the forms we cannot understand. Seeing the generalities before specifics, sorting the gestural and structural essentials from the superficial, being receptive to relational matters of every sort, and feeling the weight, strain, and energies among the parts (and among the marks that make them) are insights fundamental to any serious degree of growth as an artist. The following perceptual defects are among the most frequent and vexing:

1. weakness in all measurable matters. A poor sense of scale relationships (proportion),

Figure 11.2

placement, direction, or shape-state awareness is generally the result of a sequential assembly of parts, and of the failure to recognize the need for demanding, analytical inquiries regarding any and all measurable factors. It also indicates a weak grasp of the need for relating activities in one part of a drawing to those in another, perhaps distant, part. Often, especially in figure drawings, the forms will steadily decrease in scale from the top toward the bottom of the configuration, revealing no regard for relating the scale of parts, or for searching out the subject's gestural character (Figure 11.2A). This is sometimes the result of the student "crowding" his drawing. Many such discrepencies can be more easily seen if a greater distance separates the hand and the eye. This "broad-spectrum" weakness signifies a basic visual illiteracy that requires the careful study of the issues dealt with in Chapters One through Six.

2. conflicting perspectives. A common result of sequential assembly, this defect is symptomatic of a disregard for relating the positions in space of all the drawing's forms, and of the need to perceive the angle of their axes as well as their edges. When forms have been subjected to a probing search for their structural essentials, and when observations are "proved" by testing them against perspective principles, such defects are far more easily avoided. Failure to do so can result in any of

Figure 11.3
WILLIAM HOGARTH (1697–1764)
Satire on False Perspective
Engraving. 14 x 18 in.
Courtesy, Museum of Fine Arts, Boston
Harvey D. Parker Fund

the strange relationships shown in Hogarth's engraving *Satire on False Perspective* (Figure 11.3), the frontispiece to Kirby's book *Perspective*.

3. overload of details. Again, often a symptom of sequential assembly, this problem indicates an inability to analyze and extract the subject's essential directions, planes, and masses. Such an exclusive concentration upon surface effects generally smothers volumetric clues, thus destroying the very masses whose surfaces are so painstakingly examined. Usually, an overabundance of detail and a scarcity of convincingly structured volume go together, suggesting that scrutiny, not analysis, is at work.

4. parts isolated from the whole. This defect reveals a failure to consider the relative vi-

sual impact of form-units to the large mass of which they are parts. When small forms or parts receive more attention than the larger volume they constitute, such small segments conflict rather than accord with the large volume. The resulting isolation of such parts reveals an inability to establish a visual hierarchy among the drawing's major forms and those small forms and form-units of which they are comprised. In Figure 11.4, the eyes, nose, and mouth are more fully realized forms than the head as a whole, of which they are parts. However, the strong rhythmic energy in every segment of the drawing considerably helps to subdue the discrepency between the strongly modelled features and the weakly stated head and neck. Sometimes, as we saw in Chapter Eight, such studies of particular forms are preparatory notes for a work in another me-

310

dium (as is the case here). Even so, the fullest understanding of the nature of a larger volume's small parts is better achieved in the context of their structural and organizational relationships to it.

5. unconvincing volumes. When not due to an overemphasis on surface detail or a weak grasp of structural matters, a weak sense of volume is often the result of timid or confused modelling. A weak range of values, often only a few, small, light tones, sometimes diminishes the impression of volume, as occurs when a photograph is removed too early from the developing tray. Sometimes, having established the subject's structural essentials, the artist fails to maintain or develop it, and turns instead to various effects of illumination or texture, giving rise to conflicting clues by hatchings or tones that run counter to a form's structure, or disregard it altogether. Volumes also suffer when pronounced, continuous con-

Figure 11.5
CLAUDE LORRAIN (1600–1682)
A Herd of Cattle
Pencil, sanguine and wash. 4 3/16 x 7 in.
Courtesy, Museum of Fine Arts, Boston

tours, by their strong visual impact, "overrule" subtle inner modelling, converting forms into shapes. Sometimes, too, volumes are drawn in positions that would have them occupy the same space (Figure 11.2B). That this can occur in the works of gifted artists is seen in Figure 11.5, where parts of the two cows at the far right seem to exist in the same space. Here, too, the placement of the cow at the top of the page makes it appear to be standing on the back of the large cow in the foreground.

6. monotonous outlines. This weakness stems from the belief that only lines describing the limits of forms or parts can adequately convey a subject's volumetric character. The reluctance to leave the "safety" of the delineating edge to model the interior of a form makes some of these drawings look ghost-like. Usually, when interior modelling does occur, the use of single lines to suggest subtle changes in terrain, as occurs in a figure, produces "scars" on the white shape of the interior, rather than an impression of undulating surfaces. Such drawings reveal a fear or confusion about the use of tonalities to help establish edges and model form. But we should not confuse an inability to let go of line with the intentional use of it, as in Picasso's drawing of three dancing nudes (see Figure 8.34).

Figure 11.4
AUGUSTUS JOHN (1878–1961)
Head of a Young Woman
Pencil. 16 x 12 13/16 in.
Courtesy, Museum of Fine Arts, Boston
Helen and Alice Colburn Fund

7. stiff or wooden drawing. This suggests an overcautiousness about error and a disregard for gestural and rhythmic considerations. Ironically, the concern over making mistakes, the fear of "matching" energies in the subject by energies in the drawing, and the dread of making changes—of making a mess—have probably ruined more drawings than anything else. Fear is virtually certain to result in drawings that suffer the grave defect of stilted, dead forms. In responsive drawing there is safety only in perception, analysis, and uninhibited response. Here, caution is dangerous. Wooden drawing often results from an overconcern with surface detail at the expense of a subject's essential structure and spirit. Sometimes stiff form also occurs as a result of an overuse of straight lines and hard, right angles, often to the exclusion of all curved lines, as is seen in some mannered techniques.

8. tonal "anemia". This defect occurs in tonal drawings when there is a fear of using dark tones, especially over large areas, even though a drawing's volumes, composition, or expression require them. Often the forms in such drawings are defined by outlines, making what little tone there is seem even less necessary. Beginning tonal drawings on a toned surface (either a tinted paper or one that is given a coating of charcoal or graphite) is useful in overcoming a reluctance to use bold, dark, values.

9. formula solutions. When remembered clichés replace responses to any of a subject's actualities, the results are trite. There is a failure to respond because of disinterest in various parts of the subject, an inability to visually comprehend them, or a preference for familiar solutions. Such drawings do not seem convincingly in touch with nature. In part, they are not. When habit displaces analysis, formula displaces experience.

10. breezy mannerisms. These are usually false flourishes that imitate the economical, authoritative, and always multiply-engaged lines and tones of master artists. Drawings suffering from this defect usually convey little or nothing more about a subject than loose and poorly understood generalities. Often

symptomatic of a superficial grasp of perceptual skills, such drawings are often ambiguous about volume and space, design, and expression. At best, they are interesting "promissory notes," at worst, and more frequently, they are merely flashy pretensions.

To discover perceptual defects in our drawings we must be willing to go back and look for any measurable discrepancies that we did not recognize during the act of drawing. We must also apply evaluative criteria when examining *any* perceptual attitude or habit that hinders objective analysis.

In the excited involvement with the many interlaced factors of response to the subject and to the evolving drawing, one can easily overlook a scale relationship, or misjudge an angle, or make some inadvertent change. Viewed later, unintentional exaggerations of scale, value, etc., are often glaringly evident; but overworked, monotonous outlines, formula solutions, or an overload of details will remain as "invisible" defects unless they are examined critically. Such perceptual defects are certain to recur in subsequent drawings unless we objectively examine the concepts and procedures of our overall approach to drawing. The ability to analyze a subject's measurable actualities, and to recognize the symptoms that indicate faulty procedures and judgments is necessary *for any kind of graphic goal.* How we perceive is not the same as what we do about our perceptions. In analyzing the perceptual defects of our drawings and working to overcome them we also gain insights into our general approach that lead to artistic and even personal growth.

ORGANIZATIONAL DEFECTS

The way we order our responses reveals our aesthetic and temperamental interests. It reflects our understanding of the relational possibilities in the subject, and of the relational life of the marks that constitute our drawing. Sound perceptual skills require sound organizational sensitivity if they are to have any creative worth. The following are some of the organizational defects most often encountered.

Some are easy to spot, some are insidious and subtle, all diminish a drawing's design and consequently, its meaning.

1. labored drawings. Often this results from the fussy embellishment of parts with unnecessary details and "finish," isolating and reducing their relational activity. The problem is sometimes due to a poor choice of medium, where numerous attempts to force a medium to react to the artist's needs causes a general loss of spontaneity. Sometimes there is an almost obsessional concentration on some particular organizational or expressive theme so overbearing that the drawing's overall economy, spontaneity, and unity are weakened. Labored drawings often result from an overemphasis on representational considerations. Such drawings reveal a high degree of accurate depiction—of illustrative fact—not a high degree of dynamic life. Responsive drawings are complete when they cannot be made more visually and expressively exciting and succinct. "Finish," in the sense of photographic naturalism, is often *the finish* of a drawing's relational, abstract life. Accurate representation and inventive graphic design are *not* mutually exclusive, but the more thoroughly objective a drawing's imagery becomes, the greater the demands on our ability to organize the marks that make such images.

2. redundancy. The use of lines and tones for the same function in a single volume suggests a mistrust of values to convey the impression of volume without the aid of a final, encompassing line. This can be seen in Figure 11.6A. Although line and tone may work together in many ways, using both to say the same thing usually destroys a drawing's overall freshness, economy, *and* impression of volume. The duplicative behavior of line and tone is more confusing than clarifying because the role of each is obscured by the presence of the other. Note that 11.6B is more convincingly volumetric.

3. random lines and tones. This problem usually occurs when there is no general strategy for the roles of line and tone in a drawing. In such drawings, some parts may be depicted by line only, other parts by tones, and still others by various combinations of line and tone. Although variations in their use are often desirable and necessary (see Rembrandt, Figure 6.3), extreme differences that lack any compelling visual or expressive purpose, make it appear that two or more unrelated attitudes are at work in the same drawing (Figure 11.7). Such an erratic use of line and tone suggests a confusion or innocence about visual issues, goals, or both.

4. ostentatious facility. When adroit cleverness in the use of media, or deft expository devices are dominant goals, we face the problem of ostentatious facility. Although facility, that is, inventive and masterly control, is a desirable quality, drawings in which cleverness of execution is primary appear to be performances for approval rather than acts of graphic necessity. Such drawings often disclose only a passing interest in dynamic considerations, and a fascination with deft solutions to figurative illusions. When facility makes a drawing a system of clever representational mannerisms, instead of articulating an

Figure 11.6

Figure 11.7

organized and penetrating interpretation of nature, the drawing becomes illustrative rather than pictorial, exhibition rather than experience.

5. lack of unifying movements. This suggests a sequential approach. Completing parts in a piecemeal manner seldom permits their being woven together by directional and rhythmic forces that provide continuity between forms. The stilted results of a disregard for the moving energies that course through any group of forms may also stem from a concentration on the structural nature of small forms, to the exclusion of an awareness of their collective gestural, rhythmic, character.

6. random shifts between the second and third dimension. Like any other inconsistency, such shifts indicate the absence of an overall dynamic theme—an uncertainty about

the drawing's purpose or goal. Many drawings do have transitions of emphasis between two- and three-dimensional matters, as in Alcalay (Figure 5.3) and Diebenkorn (Figure 8.40), where integrated shifts in emphasis occur between events on the picture-plane and events among forms in space. But the random coming and going of volumetric and spatial clarity indicates a disregard for the fundamental need to hold to one frame of reference—one "voice"—in a drawing. When elements in one part of a drawing convey masses and space, and those in another do not, there must be some comprehensive design strategy that embraces and unites these parts. Burgess, in his *Double Interior* (Figure 11.8), places the emphasis on two-dimensional considerations but maintains an integrated and ordered "pace" to the reoccurring presence of volumes in space.

Figure 11.8
RICHARD BURGESS (1914–1946)
Double Interior
Graphite pencil. 12 x 16 in.
Courtesy private collection

Figure 11.9

7. random placement of the configuration on the page. This defect suggests an indifference to the format's effect on the image. We have seen that a drawing's design consists of the configuration *and* the page. The impact on the viewer of a visually illogical placement of the configuration often overrides the drawing's intended impact. In Figure 11.9, the active dark shape in A overwhelms the several white shapes and seems crammed into the picture-plane, straining for release. The same shape in B appears less active, and not at all crammed in. In fact, it appears somewhat isolated in so large a field of space. In C, it has been located in a position on the picture-plane that creates imbalance. Besides destroying the equilibrium of the design of the page, this can sometimes weaken the overall nature of the configuration. An image that is itself stable, if placed badly on the page, becomes part of an unstable design. An incompatible relationship between the configuration and the page sometimes occurs in the work of capable artists. In Vigée-Lebrun's drawing *Study of a Woman* (Figure 11.10), the lack of "breathing space" around the figure, especially at the top, where the head touches the edge of the page, produces a slightly claustrophobic state in what is otherwise an excellent drawing (although the drawing may have been cropped by another hand at a later date).

8. the divided drawing. This results from strong divisions of the page by lines, values, forms, or directional forces which isolate one part of a drawing from the rest, destroying the unity of the design. But such divisions,

when they are offset by other forces in the design that weave them together, are a frequent device in drawing. In Cheruy's drawing of a church interior (Figure 11.11), the columns on the far right cut the drawing vertically. But they are joined to the rest of the drawing in

Figure 11.10
ÉLISABETH VIGÉE-LEBRUN (1755–1842)
Study of a Woman
Red chalk. 9 1/2 x 6 in.
Courtesy, Museum of Fine Arts, Boston

Figure 11.11
GERMAINE ROUGET CHERUY (1896–   )
Vezelay, La Madeleine — The Nave
Ink on Japanese paper. 12 1/4 x 17 in.
Fogg Art Museum, Harvard University
Gift of E. W. Forbes

several ways. One of the strongest connections is the unseen but clearly suggested
arch spanning the interspace between them
and the center group of pillars. The similarity
of value and texture between the two massive
pillar groups, and their relationship to a third
group on the left, as well as to the smaller pillars and arches behind them, all form strong
visual bonds of association. When a section is
unintentionally severed from the rest of a
drawing, the two parts can be strongly joined
through direction, rhythm, value, and texture,
as in Cheruy's drawing, or by placing one or
more forms in a position that crosses the
boundary to join the parts together.

9. imbalance. This defect results from the visually uneven placement, direction, density,
weight, scale, or value of the elements, and of
the forms and spaces they create. It often results from such an exclusive concern with a
drawing's representational aspects that its intrinsic visual issues go unheeded. Balance is
partly guided by intuitive reason, but cannot
be consciously ignored. The artist's design
plan should include a tentative judgment
about the scale and placement of the configuration on the page that will assist the drawing's balance.

To create a balanced drawing, the artist
must cancel out visual forces that cause the

Figure 11.12

force on one side of the drawing with a similar force on the other side, as in Figure 11.12A. This *symmetrical* solution, if too evenly established, can be rigidly formal and obvious. But when used subtly, it is a dependable way of producing equilibrium. In Rembrandt's *A Cottage among Trees* (Figure 11.13), and Villon's *Study for Farmyard, Cany sur Thérain* (Figure 11.14), balance is achieved through roughly symmetrical forms and forces. In both, a gentle curve, horizontally oriented and cresting near the drawing's center, describes the contour of the foreground's shape. In both, the curve's crest is the location of a strong mass that acts as a fulcrum for the rest of the drawing's masses, and in both, the masses flanking the central one, bear a strong resemblance to it. Rembrandt continues the symmetrical system in the fences and in the horizon, making them quite similar to their

design to appear to be falling or crowding to one side, or that give any other impressions of unresolved instabilities among its parts. There are two basic ways of cancelling out such forces. One way is to answer a strong

Figure 11.13
REMBRANDT VAN RIJN (1606–1669)
A Cottage among Trees
Pen and bistre. 6 3/4 x 10 7/8 in.
The Metropolitan Museum of Art
H. O. Havemeyer Collection

Figure 11.14
JACQUES VILLON (1875–1963)
Study for Farmyard, Cany-sur-Thérain
Pen and ink. 6 3/8 x 9 3/4 in.
Print Department, Boston Public Library

counterparts across the page. Villon repeats the diagonal lines in the sky with the lines in the foreground.

A second way to cancel out strong visual forces is to answer them with different but equally strong forces, as in Figure 11.12B. This is an asymmetrical solution. Asymmetry, being the more prevalent state in nature and offering unlimited design possibilities, more frequently occurs in responsive drawings, as a glance at the drawings in the book show. In Ingres' *View of St. Peter's in Rome* (Figure 11.15), the placement of the cathedral to the left of center—its great facade and dome producing the strongest vertical movement in the drawing—is answered by the encircling sweep of the buildings, and by the pronounced curve of the roofed colonnade in the foreground. The single vertical direction of the obelisk on the right adds its energy to the drawing's balance, and serves as a unifying echo of the vertical forces of the cathedral.

As we saw in Chapter One, a gestural approach gives the artist an overview of the drawing's general compositional nature and needs. In many drawings where imbalance occurs, the failure to establish the design's basic gestural premise prevents their balanced realization.

10. the generalized drawing. When the artist is in doubt about how to realize some of the smaller, more specific aspects of the subject and the design, the result may be a generalized drawing. Often students establish quite handsome drawings of the subject's generalities and a good, equally generalized design, but seem unable to apply or sustain the attitudes and commitment that brought these broad states about in establishing the drawing's smaller structural and dynamic conditions. Of course, many artists intend a simply stated image that avoids specificities, and some of the best drawings show an impressive economy; but all are *concise* rather than general. They may be simply stated, but they are rich in visual and expressive meaning.

By contrast, the generalized drawing only suggests possibilities and hints at conclusions. Its simplicities are vague and seem more like uncertain assumptions than convincing assertions. Some students (and artists) make simple and general drawings in admiration of the economy of master drawings—and some do bear a superficial similarity to such drawings. But it is perceptual and organizational sensitivity and not simplicity for its own sake that leads to concise drawing. These sensitivities are expanded by making drawings that probe and establish conclusions about small as well as major forms and forces and their balanced resolution on the page.

Certainly, not all student drawings need be extensively developed to include a host of specific observations. But students need to develop the ability to state any specific detail or relationship to overcome *unselective* generality. They should, from time to time, reinforce the experience of applying the same degree of analysis and empathy to smaller events that is given to major ones. This is important for another reason. Just as the search for the essential structure and spirit of a subject's differing parts helps the student to see

Figure 11.15
DOMINIQUE INGRES (1780–1867)
View of St. Peter's in Rome
Graphite pencil. 33 x 49 cm.
Courtesy of The Art Institute of Chicago

similarities between them, in drawing the smaller forms and actions he comes to see the subtle differences between similar parts and energies. For example, while it would, at the outset, be important to see the similarity of form and direction between say, the twigs of a branch and the fingers of a hand holding it, it is also important, later in the drawing, to be able to show the differences between each twig and between each finger. Ironically, the insights that come from perceiving a subject's smaller actualities and actions, and controlling them in a system of expressive order, is the fastest and surest way to meaningful economy.

EXPRESSIVE DEFECTS

Although perception, organization, and expression are interdependent considerations, the expression of our genuinely personal responses to a subject's plastic and representational meanings is the fundamental role of these considerations. Drawings in which our own expressive responses are stifled or disregarded, or fail to touch on important facts and inferences about the subject, are either expressively evasive, confused, or derivative. The following expressive defects are some of the ways in which feelings fail to participate in the responsive process.

1. expressive reticence or blandness. This weakness suggests an over-concern with depictive "correctness" or inhibitions toward the intuitive and emotive responses that influence perceptions. But, as observed in Chapter Nine, even this reticence is expressive. The beholder senses a restraining of impulses that both empathy and intuitive knowledge demand. If the artist does not risk

Figure 11.16
Anonymous (Dutch or German School)
Study of Ten Hands
Pen and brown ink. 7⅞ x 12⅛ in.
National Gallery of Canada, Ottawa

Figure 11.17
PETER PAUL RUBENS (1577–1640)
Study of Cows
Pen and ink. 34 x 52.2 cm.
The British Museum, London

commitment to his responses at their deepest level, the drawing reveals the hesitancy and constraint.

All art teachers are familiar with the student who makes conscientiously observed or invented drawings that carefully avoid responses to the subject's dynamic potentialities. At one time the art academies insisted on just this kind of disciplined concentration on measurable matters. It constituted the main and sometimes only area of perceptual awareness. But such drawings often appear leaden, lifeless. Drawings that avoid the dynamic energies that create the graphic equivalent of life *are* lifeless.

Here, it will be helpful to compare two highly representational drawings. They show the differences in attitude and result between an almost exclusively reportorial approach and one that utilizes expressive impulses. The anonymous Dutch or German School *Study of Ten Hands* (Figure 11.16), shows a great concentration on the observed state of the terrain in each part, with little concern for the gestural, rhythmic flow within or between them. Each finger is drawn with hardly a clue to its participation with others in forming greater

units of form—or as engaged in pointing, gripping, or supporting *actions*. In almost every instance, there is no convincing impression that the arms really continue inside the sleeves. For all the concentration on individual volumes, many volume relationships do not convince. For example, in the middle drawing on the far left the structural means by which the forearm interlocks with the hand is unclear. Although the surfaces of these hands are explicit, the general structure, weight, power, and expressive character of the hands are not. They "describe" various acts of exertion, but they do not "enact" them. The artist is skillful. Many of the small folds and veins are deftly stated, and in some passages the drapery-like character of the skin, moving over bone, tendon, and muscle, is effective. Some hands, such as those of the bottom row (especially the one at the far left) do begin to "live." But the artist's basic theme is the scrutiny of small forms, too often at the expense of the large ones. A clue to the artist's thinking occurs in the beginning stage of the pointing hand in the upper right corner of the page. It is already a carefully delineated record of the outlines of the forms. Nowhere

321

can we find a gestural or analytical line. Nowhere do lines express movement or energy. The artist concentrates on shapes rather than masses.

Compare this beginning state with the early stage portions in Rubens's drawing, *Study of Cows* (Figure 11.17). A different kind of sensibility is at work here. In the upper left and right corners of the page, and even in the more developed drawings in the lower right, lines search for the actions, tensions, and *masses* of the forms *at the outset*. In these beginning stages, Rubens is not concerned with careful delineation (although he is equally interested in understanding shape-actualities), but with the *feel* of the forms' movements and with their essential constructional nature. The benefits to both the structural and expressive clarity of the forms is evident in the drawing of the large animals. The artist's response to their ponderous bulk and weight, their slow movements, and to the powerful pressures and tensions created by the inner structural forms supporting and straining against the walls of the supported hide, creates convincing, living images of visual and expressive significance. All this is more than the result of scrutiny—it is the result of perceptions selected, altered, and ordered by feelings and intuitions as well as intellect.

It is feelings and intuitions, too, that causes Rubens to select (perhaps subconsciously) an overall design that fans out toward the beholder, with strong, curved movements sweeping to the left and right. Note the great clarity of the forms. Heavy, interlocking, but rhythmically related masses, and hatchings that move sensually upon the changing "topography" of the forms, convey Rubens's profound understanding of the masses. These qualities, like the design itself, are strong, deliberate, and graceful. Compare Rubens's design with that of Figure 11.16. Again, there is a kind of restrained quality to the arrangement of the arms and hands. They form an overall checkerboard pattern, somewhat mechanical and dull. Unlike the design of the Rubens drawing, which evokes something of the behavior and character of the animals, this design seems unrelated to the character of the subject.

In another comparison, this time with a sketch of two hands by Agostino Carracci (Figure 11.18), we find more spirit and force in this sketch than in the hands of Figure 11.16, despite their more thoroughly explored surfaces. While Figure 11.18 is only a rough exploration and Figure 11.16 an extended study, the sketch is more responsive to structural matters than the study is to expressive ones.

In drawings that are expressively inhibited, more than the frank expression of felt responses is absent. They appear diminished in the clarity and force of their representational meanings as well. With human forms especially, a failure to support representational actions and energies by abstract ones deadens the figurative results.*

2. the literary or illustrative look. When the artist is concerned more with storytelling, or with conveying a message (whether social, political, historical, or religious) through a drawing's figurative matter, rather than with creating a system of expressive design, the illustrative look occurs. Any storytelling message can be a valid property of any drawing (see Figures 3.12, 9.15, 9.29), but should never reduce the creative depth of a work.

Whether or not it does diminish aesthetic worth depends on the artist's ability to govern two quite different kinds of expression. As we have seen, some artists actually need an essentially nonvisual theme. For them, conveying a social, spiritual, or other kind of message, far from competing with the demands of expressive order, stimulates it and is in turn enhanced by it. When there is such a reciprocal relationship between graphic and nonvisual expression, the results (as many of the drawings in Chapter Nine indicate) do not appear merely illustrative. It is only when a literary theme overpowers the artist and compromises his creative instincts, or when its demands are incompatible with them, that responses to both the subject and the drawing become less dynamically motivated, and more illustratively so. When picto-

*See, Nathan Goldstein, *Figure Drawing: The Structure, Anatomy, and Expressive Design of Human Form* (Englewood Cliffs, N.J.: Prentice-Hall, Inc., 1976), chaps. 1, 5–7.

Figure 11.18
AGOSTINO CARRACCI (1557–1602)
Sheet of Studies
Pen and ink, some chalk. 20.5 x 27.2 cm.
Rijksmuseum, Amsterdam

rial and literary factors clash, the result may be an illustration with some redeeming artistic worth, or a drawing weakened by the burden of nonvisual issues, but in either case there is a lessening of aesthetic depth.

To some extent, many of our responses to a subject's physical, dynamic, and psychological states are not directly visual issues. We cannot visually measure dignity, melancholy, or repose. But when such influences on perception expand to become a drawing's dominant goal by emphasizing representational issues at the expense of its abstract graphic life, the result is illustration, not art. And though some artists are stimulated by nonvisual ideas, and do their best work when spurred on by such themes, other artists, who may feel just as deeply about social, religious, or any other nonvisual interest, create works that do not address these matters through the fig-

urative aspects of their drawings. If such "messages" appear, they are felt as intangible qualities of the drawing's content.

3. the picturesque air. This problem is often sensed in works that, like illustrative ones, stress depiction at the cost of expressive order. It stems from a usually sentimental or romantic interpretation of the quaint, the strange, and the spectacular. Often such subjects do not belong to the artist's past or present environment, but are adopted because of their popularity, their exotic or unusual nature, or their literary appeal. Sometimes these subjects symbolize an earlier society. Although windmills and covered bridges still exist, it is difficult to see them objectively, because they are no longer connected to the lives most of us lead. And having been drawn and painted so many times, often for illustrative purposes, they tend to be regarded through a "filter" of earlier, more romantic interpretations. Any observed or envisioned subject may always be valid, but it is harder to respond to those we have no real familiarity with, or those which have become banal or sentimental because of overuse. The need for "squeezing" expression out of unusual situations or places subsides as we learn to evoke expressions out of the visual elements and the people, places, and things around us. It has been observed of Cézanne that "he made bowler hats out of mountains, and mountains out of bowler hats."

4. the influenced drawing. The problem here is that the influenced drawing usually lacks the conviction and daring present in the drawings it was influenced by. We do not mean drawings that show a faint residual influence of a particular artist or style. An artist who by temperament and aesthetic disposition finds he shares a point of view with that of a colleague, master, or stylistic period, is bound to reflect some superficial similarities. Sometimes, such "influences" are actually coincidence. Artists whose drawings bear some similar characteristics may not ever have seen each other's works. But even when an artist is influenced, his work is essentially original if it is not restricted by, or imitative of, the influencing works. It is hardly uncommon in the history of art for some artists, and among them some of the best, to expand upon or even to develop new concepts stimulated by the innovations and idiosyncrasies of others. After all, in being ourselves as artists, it is natural to search out "kindred spirits" among other artists, past and present, just as in our social lives we search out friends who strike us as good and wise. In both cases, influences occur. In both cases, our understanding, our abilities, and, ultimately, our freedom to be ourselves *is increased.*

But strong influences will not permit the expression of personal responses. An adopted manner is usually an imitation of a technique, rather than a concept; and whichever it is, its presence always prevents the development of genuine creative ability.

The heavily influenced drawing is often unselectively dependent on the techniques

and idiosyncracies of the admired artist. In his drawing *The Degradation of Haman before Ahasuerus and Esther* (Figure 11.19), de Gelder combines many of Rembrandt's characteristics to summon up a Rembrandtesque image. But he only succeeds in imitating a number of Rembrandt's personal graphic devices. Interestingly, such traits are sometimes regarded by the innovator as being of little importance to his purposes, or even as detrimental! As one American artist of note has observed about his imitators, "they all seem bent on exaggerating just those things I'm trying to hide in my work."

De Gelder's marks *are* strongly reminiscent of Rembrandt's handling, but they fail to convey Rembrandt's perceptual or dynamic understanding. In short, de Gelder's drawing does not convey a Rembrandt-like *content*. How could it? The lines and tones that are *necessities* for Rembrandt—the results of his negotiations between perception, feeling, and intent—all serve to amplify his *unique* and deeply felt responses. No one can summon up another's sensibility, and no sensibility can conceive and sustain the demands of another.

De Gelder's understanding of volume and design does not support the kinds of daring that are natural and necessary for Rembrandt. Note the evasive ambiguities in the forms of the figures. None of the heads or hands suggest the structural analysis, the weighty mass, the design, or the expressive power of comparable forms in a Rembrandt drawing.

Compare the bold control of the heads and hands in Rembrandt's *Three Studies of a Child and One of an Old Woman* (Figure 11.20), with those in the de Gelder drawing. Note, too, that where Rembrandt creates transitions between broad and precise kinds of handling, de Gelder's changes in handling are abrupt inconsistencies that serve no visual or expressive purpose. Where Rembrandt's washes of tone convey light and volume with certainty, de Gelder's are uncertain—sometimes rather tightly encased by line, sometimes obscuring volume, and sometimes simply inconclusive and weak. They seem somewhat unrelated to the rest of the drawing. The evenly-spaced diagonal lines that cross the center of the drawing, unlike the lines behind

Figure 11.19
AERT DE GELDER (1645–1727)
The Degradation of Haman before
Ahasuerus and Esther
Pen and ink and wash. 19 x 16.5 cm.
Courtesy of The Art Institute of Chicago

the seated child in Rembrandt's drawing, do not stay well back, but come forward and hover in space somewhere between the figure of Ahasuerus and the pillars in the background. De Gelder is uncertain about the perspective and the architectural forms on the far left, and some of those in the center background are left unclearly stated as volumes in space.

These defects suggest the limits of his perceptual, organizational, and empathic comprehension. No technique or imitation of technical mastery can camouflage such limits. The attention and energy focused on the imitating of another's point of view obstructs those abilities the artist *does* have, and further weakens the results. But the heavily influenced student or artist who begins to trust

and respect his own responses soon finds a satisfying natural freedom that imitation will never allow.

5. conflicting meanings. We sense this defect when a drawing fails to convey a consistent visual attitude, mood, or handling. It is sometimes symptomatic of a disinterest or confusion concerning a subject's structural and dynamic properties. But changes in goals and handling, after a drawing has begun, too often produce conflicting results. Such drawings reveal a weak grasp of those factors that establish unity. The freedom of response to a subject, and to its emerging equivalent state on the page does *not* extend to arbitrary changes in attitude toward the subject or to its manner of presentation within the same

325

Figure 11.20
REMBRANDT VAN RIJN (1606–1669)
Three Studies of a Child and One of an Old Woman
Pen and bistre wash with slight touches of
gray-black wash on white. 8 3/8 x 6 1/4 in.
Fogg Art Museum, Harvard University
Gift of Meta and Paul J. Sachs

drawing. For example, in a landscape drawing that is primarily tonal and concerned with aerial perspective, a sudden switch to a linear, diagrammatic exploration of the structural aspects of a house in one corner of the drawing is a glaring inconsistency (Figure 11.21).

Such conflicting goals are not uncommon in student drawings. This understandably results from experiencing the many new ideas and challenges a good program of art study provides. But conflicting interests and goals violate one of the most fundamental requirements of any art form: the organizational and expressive need to sustain a single, overall meaning. This is not to say that multiple meanings are impossible in drawing. In the example just mentioned, both tonal and diagrammatic ideas *can* be quite compatible if an interest in both is made an integral and reoccurring theme of the drawing's expressive order.

Conflicting meanings may sometimes be noted when the figurative expression is at variance with the expressive nature of the handling and design. For example, in a drawing of a figure performing some dramatic action requiring strenuous physical exertion a delicate, deliberate handling and a design that stresses horizontal and vertical directions or otherwise appears tranquil or stately will tend to weaken and contradict the figurative action.

Expression and order are the dimensions of an approach to drawing that will yield works that live. Beginners too often become preoccupied with the multiplicity of factors in drawing and disregard the general responsive direction of their work. That is, busy learning how to see, they lose sight of what it is they intend to convey. In time this seemingly unmanageable number of considerations begin

Figure 11.21

to come together, to work for the student almost automatically. Then it will be most important to recognize that perceptions and methodologies are servants that perform best when the best demands are made of them. And the demands of a sensitive analytical and empathic sensibility, perceiving and ordering in a personal way, creates original style. Style, in fact, is the key to our priorities—it reveals both temperament and intent. Therefore a search for style is not only futile, it is beginning at exactly the wrong end. *Intent* must precede a personal form for expressing itself, and brings with it the conditions that shape style. Style, then, is not arbitrary, not chosen; it is given, is inherent in our purpose.

The symptoms of basic weaknesses in responsive drawing examined here (and there are others) should provide a basis for the evaluation of our drawings that further experience will broaden. In responsive drawing the most pernicious, underlying causes of so many defects are the faulty judgments that result from an exclusive concern with imitating instead of analyzing and interpreting nature, and the employment of a sequential approach in pursuing that limiting goal. As Michelangelo's *Studies of Figures* (Figure 11.22) so well demonstrates, beginning with a search for a subject's structural and dynamic essentials provides the comprehension and control that lead to sound drawing.

What engages our participation—as well as our admiration—in a responsive drawing are the activities that suggest choices and energies contending with each other. Their resolution into a system of expressive order invites us into the drawing—not only to admire, but to participate in the negotiations that shaped them into this living system.

CHAPTER TWELVE
CONCLUSIONS

some general observations

It has been observed throughout this book that the content of a responsive drawing is the sum of its representational and abstract condition—the total impact of its depictive and dynamic meanings. A drawing's content may be shallow, interesting, or profound, according to the quality of the artist's perceptual awareness, his ability to estimate, feel, and relate; and the quality of the concepts, emotions, and intuitions that shape his responses. But the basic skills are those of analysis and empathy; we cannot interpret what we do not understand. Whatever the personal creative goals of our concepts, emotions, and intuitions, the more penetrating our perceptual inquiries the more creatively effective our drawings will be. As E. E. Cummings wrote: "always the beautiful answer who asks a more beautiful question."

And the "beautiful question" as we have seen, asks for more than proportional or structural answers; it inquires about the subject's representational *and* dynamic character, and even probes the possibilities for universal meanings that transcend the subject. The best

drawings, of whatever culture or era, suggest visual and philosophical connotations that go beyond depiction to become universal, timeless expressions.

In Sheeler's *Nude, 1920* (Figure 12.1), we sense that the drawing's content embraces an interest in form realization which goes beyond the volumetric condition of the figure's masses. There is a poetic equivocation that plays with scale and identity. The drawing *is* a closeup of a figure, its ample forms implying the fruitful properties of ancient fertility figures; but it suggests a monumental and barren landscape. It is at once realistic and abstract, substantial and illusory. The forms express both strength and pliancy, are both inviting and indifferent. Such contrasting readings attract our interest and, by their universality, will always provoke attention.

Developing the perceptual sensitivity that uncovers lasting visual and expressive qualities requires a concentration on the three main concerns of this book: first, the study of drawing as inquiry into the structure and dynamics of natural and man-made forms; second, the study of drawing's relational and expressive potentialities; and third, the study of outstanding works of art.

Hence the ongoing need for the artist—both student and professional—to draw continually, to examine the drawings of others, and to be always consciously aware that the study of nature's limitless structural and dynamic patterns is fundamental to creative growth. And we must be engaged in all of these studies at the same time. The prolific artist, unless he fertilizes each drawing with new struc-

tural, relational, and expressive demands, may only produce variants of his present range of skills and insights. Investigative drawing sheds light on nature, nature teaches us important truths about drawing, and great works of art reveal insights on both drawing and nature—they tell on each other.

The responsive artist, then, is one who never tires of examining the practices and products of drawing, or the world around him which serves as both teacher and subject. Whether like Ingres, who observed that when

Figure 12.1

CHARLES SHEELER (1883–1965)

Nude (1920)
Charcoal.
Collection of Mrs. Earle Horter

he found himself in circumstances where drawing was not possible, he would "draw with my eyes"; or the aging and ill Matisse, who would spend many hours drawing wildflowers in his garden; or Cézanne, who, when asked where he had studied art, replied, "In the Louvre," such artists experience an ongoing fascination with the behavior and patterns of the people, places, and things around them, and with the finest expressions of creative activity. Responsive artists are always inquisitive. Their perceptions—always both penetrating and innocent—search for new knowledge, new experiences. They have what has been called a "hungry eye."

Although the "long drawing"—the extended explorations of a subject's smaller forms and surface effects—is a most informing type of study, the developing artist must concentrate at least as much on those shorter drawings that test and expand his ability to see, select, summarize, and state a subject's important relationships and forces.

The brief drawing, whether its time limit is imposed by the instructor or by ourselves, sharpens our ability to analyze and express, thereby sharpening our perceptual sensitivity to the things around us. Thus the repeated practice in concentrating on structural and dynamic essentials constitutes an important part of our training in searching out other engaging subjects to draw. In this sense our perceptual sensitivity, working as a kind of visual detector, scans our environment for a significant "contact." Our creative "receiver" seeks certain kinds of stimuli. Drawing a subject that does not attract usually produces weak results.

When a contact is made, a state of excitation occurs. The artist sees potentialities for creative expression in the subject's actualities and implications, and is stimulated to draw. For some artists, almost any random collection of forms can trigger creative ideas. Others, although just as perceptually sensitive, are attracted by only a few subjects. Not surprisingly, as perceptual awareness develops, the range of subjects that attract students usually increases.

An artist's initial interests are stimulated because of a rough, general kind of perceptual analysis. Some general ideas and impulses have formed in his mind about the creative potential in a particular subject. These perceptions will have included general information about the subject's gesture, structure, arrangement in space, and the relational and emotive character of its figurative and abstract condition. These considerations overlap because they are not seen independently in the subject. For example, perceptions of a part's direction and length are simultaneously perceptions of its spatial behavior and its representational and abstract actions. And these, additionally, become factors in the drawing's design.

The order of priority of perceptual interests in the completed drawing—how much attention and development each of the above considerations gets—is, as noted in Chapter Ten, a key to the artist's content. And content is not altogether a matter of choice, but of aesthetic and temperamental necessity. One of the characteristics of great drawings is the artist's wholehearted acceptance of his own style and his own character. It is as if such drawings say for the artist, "Here I am."

Just as the brief but penetrating sketch is a useful tool in expanding our overall perceptual interests, so sometimes are the first, general perceptions themselves the main purpose of an artist's drawing. This is, of course, often so in quick preparatory sketches where the artist concentrates on a subject's figurative and abstract essentials.

The initial perceptions that stimulated Baglione's quick sketch *Group of Four Figures* (Figure 12.2), appear to be the dynamic energies of massed forms that generate the moving action of the forms toward the right side of the page. This is further conveyed by the tight enclosure of the format. Its "squeezing" pressure on the forms suggests their being forced toward the only open area within its boundaries, that is, the space on the right. The sense of forms advancing or striving to do so is also conveyed by the positions and gestures of the four heads. Starting on the left, each seems more involved with movement. The increasing tilt of the figures and the directional thrust of the lines that comprise them further add to the sense of impending movement. Note that the figure nearest to the right side is "committed" to the directed action by being in an off-balanced position. This drawing is a good example of the union of figurative and dynamic actions.

Expression also occurs here at both the figurative and abstract levels. We feel the human and plastic gestures; there is a sense of intensity and animation in both the figures and the marks.

Baglione's impulse to draw this group of observed or envisioned figures *as he did* was a response to his first perceptions of the actions just discussed. And this grasp of the subject's creative potentialities was itself made possible by his pre-set interests and instincts, as much the result of his previous drawing experiences as of his reaction to this particular subject. The scope of our ideas and impulses, the motives that make us draw, feed upon *prior* experiences as well as the perceptions we make of the subject before us. Each time we draw we nourish and expand our motives for drawing. Each time we examine a master drawing or the form and pattern of a passing cloud we add to our future creative purpose.

Among the benefits of such study is the increased awareness of the order, the relatedness of the things we see. If we do not consider the relative direction or length of an edge to other edges, we do not really *see* it; if we disregard the similarity of say, our model's folded arms and some interlaced folds in her skirt, these segments will remain more isolated from each other; and if we do not respond to the physical or visual weight of one segment in the drawing in comparison to another, the drawing's balance and unity are disrupted.

Baglione's quick sketch is profuse in the visual and expressive considerations of the responsive process, but he is responding only to those visual essentials necessary to establish the broad essentials of an expressive design.

But Snyders, in his "*Study of a Boar's Head*" (Figure 12.3), probes his subject's forms and forces more deeply. Part of the almost symmetrical design's energy comes from the smaller forms. Snyders emphasizes the rhythmic movement of forms to the left and right of an invisible border which is the vertical midline of the boar's head. Tusks, ears, and

Figure 12.2
Attributed to BAGLIONE (c. 1573–1644)
Group of Four Figures
Pen, brown ink and brown wash. 3 5/16 x 3 5/8 in.
National Gallery of Canada, Ottawa

bristles "rush" away from this unseen axis with a force that energizes the entire image. As in Baglione's drawing, directed action is a strong dynamic theme; but here, structural matters contribute to (and gain from) these forceful movements. Were the animal's head drawn on a horizontal axis, the sense of symmetry might appear obvious and dull. By tilting the head to the right and counterbalancing it with dark tones on its left side, Snyders modifies the symmetry, cancels physical with visual weight, and establishes a more compelling compositional and expressive state.

The challenge for Snyders, in carrying the realization of the forms further than Baglione does, is to find organizational and emotive employment for the smaller forms, the textures, and the values. For, the more specific and "retinal" our drawings become, the greater the danger of a randomness entering the work, of small parts and surface effects

Figure 12.3
FRANS SNYDERS (1579–1657)
Study of a Boar's Head
Pen, brown ink and brown
wash.
12.8 x 18.5 cm.
The British Museum, London

being "rendered" in an isolating and incidental way rather than adding to the drawing's overall figurative and dynamic meanings—its content.

Had Baglione developed his drawing further, it would not have evolved in a way that would deny the general responses already established. It would have developed by the inclusion of subtler and smaller relationships that could amplify the drawing's initial intent. When we begin to draw, our first perceptions—the general interpretation—figures importantly in the kind and range of responses to follow. This is another reason for confronting, at the outset of a drawing, both the subject's structural *and* dynamic essentials. The omission of either factor at the start usually diminishes its effects (and the drawing's conviction and unity) when it is added as a later consideration. Until we can begin a drawing in a comprehensive way, we cannot hope for more than narrow results.

But, advancing a drawing past the first, broad essentials *does* require some perceptions that are different from those used to

establish the first general impressions. The initial responses depend on our ability to summarize. Developing a subject's smaller specifics requires an ability to see those differences that support these summaries. Snyders is fairly specific in explaining the differences between shapes, forms, values, and textures; but the marks that explain these differences are all simultaneously engaged in various relational activities and in developing the drawing's expressive design. To perceive relationships between unlike forms and marks, and contrasts between like ones, requires an ability to differentiate between their measurable facts and their relational behavior. Obviously, good perceptual understanding is sensitive to both of these considerations.

Good perception must also be sensitive to the needs of the emerging drawing. Chapters Eight and Nine pointed out that responses to the subject, once translated to the page, stimulate new responses—those which meet the depictive, organizational, and expressive needs of the image. Sometimes, the initial stimulus comes not only from qualities perceived *within* the forms themselves, but from the artist's ideas about how these forms might be arranged on the page. Baglione's first impulse, as we have seen, is to establish a general system of visual and expressive events that takes into account the size and shape of the picture-plane. By contrast, Snyders, although he places the configuration well in the format, emphasizes the relational aspects *within* the configuration. But, to differing degrees, both artists respond to both considerations. Additionally, each artist is aware that his intended emotive theme, if it is to have impact, must participate in matters of organization and handling. Because sensitive perceptual awareness includes empathic impressions, we *can* speak of the perception of expressive as well as visual conditions. As we have seen, relational activities are always both visual and expressive.

Bonnard's sensitivity to the visual-expressive state needed to convey his meaning in *Standing Nude* (Figure 12.4) guides him to a strategy that does not rely on bold relationships. Bonnard wants to suggest the figure bathed in a gentle atmosphere. Accordingly, the figure's forms are shown as fluid and soft, their structure only lightly suggested. The gentle changes in value, the graceful, curving lines of the figure, and the foggy texture of the charcoal all promote this impressionistic air. It is even hard to tell whether this is an interior or outdoor scene. Bonnard's approach to the design is consistent with his feelings about the subject. These are not the kinds of ambiguity that come from innocence or indecision. Each is a felt, and (if we can use the term in describing a deliberate generality) "precise" response to a design where a hushed, gentle air is intended.

The easy stimulation of our creative instincts and the development of both our perceptual acuity and our level of response is best achieved by drawings that push the limits of our ability to see, relate, and react. The effort to increase our analytical and empathic understanding is a continuing necessity to the growing creative personality. The best artists have always been engrossed students all of their lives. Tiepolo's drawing *A Sheet of Sketches* (Figure 12.5) demonstrates something

of the probing kinds of study that mature artists continue to make. The drawing contains an anatomical study of a leg, several sketches of strongly illuminated heads, and several fragmentary, gestural explorations of parts of the figure. Here, there is no attempt at picture-making—he has no "product" in mind. Rather, Tiepolo is searching for additional in-

Figure 12.4
PIERRE BONNARD (1867–1947)
Standing Nude
Charcoal. 16 1/2 x 9 3/4 in.
The Metropolitan Museum of Art
Harris Brisbane Dick Fund

formation and experience with the factors of mass, light, and anatomy.

And, responses are being affected. Note the similarity *and* differences between the two centrally placed heads looking to the right. The upper, more carefully developed of the two, shows values used sparingly in the face. Here, lines carry the major responsibility for conveying volume. Below, the same forms are boldly brushed in by dark washes and there is almost no use of line. In these heads the artist seems to be testing different responsive solutions to the same forms.

Sketchbook studies such as Tiepolo's, in which no *conscious* compositional design is intended, or preparatory drawings, such as Matisse's *Seated Woman with Hat and Gown* (study for *"The White Plume"*) (Figure 12.6) which *are* conceived as designs, are, like all good drawings, attempts to expand perception and response. But, because these are both preliminary studies for other works, they show more clearly the searching, changing nature of drawings that are meant to deepen the artist's own understanding. Note the changes in the hat, shoulder, and chair in the Matisse drawing, and also the probing diagrammatic lines of the underdrawing.

Settling for challenges that fall just short of the limits of our comprehension and control helps consolidate what we know—and certainly there is a time to do that. We should, on occasion, explore the possibilities of as much as we can see and do. We must strive to be masters of as much as we understand. But artistic growth comes from an open and flexible attitude to any changes in tactics and intent suggested by our experience in drawings that question and risk, and by our educational, cultural, and social experiences.

One of the inevitable characteristics of good perceptual and conceptual growth is the increasing economy of the means that convey meanings. In responsive drawing, as in any other creative process, organizationally unengaged or repetitive elements are illogical because they are unnecessary, and weakening because they are a burden on the completed system.

In drawing, economy reveals understanding—or the lack of it. That is still an-

other reason why the traditional short poses are so important to the drawing student (and to his instructor's grasp of the student's particular strengths and weaknesses). The economy of means enforced by their brief time-span discloses the quality of a student's graphic comprehension. Of any two drawings, alike in every respect but that of the means used to state them, the simpler of the two is universally felt to be more aesthetically satisfying. It reveals a more inclusive grasp of the subject's structural, relational, and expressive character, permitting bolder, more profound summaries. As the architect Mees Van der Rohe concluded, "less is more." When an art-

Figure 12.6
HENRI MATISSE (1869–1954)
Seated Woman with Hat and Gown
Pencil. 21 1/4 x 14 3/8 in.
Fogg Art Museum, Harvard University
Grenville L. Winthrop Bequest

Figure 12.7
PAUL CÉZANNE (1839–1906)
A Corner of the Studio (sketchbook page)
Pencil. 8 1/2 x 5 in.
Fogg Art Museum, Harvard University
Marian H. Phinney Bequest

The visual-expressive meanings in Cézanne's *A Corner of the Studio* (Figure 12.7) are amplified by the artist's summaries. His severe and telling extractions from the haphazard collection of studio paraphernalia clearly communicate his discovery of two- and three-dimensional order and movement among its parts. We can more easily appreciate the pattern of these forms receding in a shallow field of space, and the taut surface tensions among the drawing's elements because of Cézanne's intense concentration on realizing these structural and organizational essentials of his subject.

A drawing's expressive meanings are also clarified by economical extractions of essentials. There is little in this collection of objects that is really engaging. It is only when we react to Cézanne's economical interpretation of their planes and shapes arranged to suggest both second- and third-dimensional activities that our emotions are engaged. Then the lines and tones and the activity they convey affect our empathic sensibilities—as they did Cézanne's. The patient, critical judgments concerning movements and edges, tones and shapes, the delicate overall balance of the elements comes from a profoundly acute perceptual comprehension—the kind that makes such evocative summary possible. Although the artist's interests are focused on a "simple" resolution of visual forces, expression, even if subconscious and muted, is part of the drawing's content.

Again, in Rembrandt's brief sketch of a young boy (Figure 12.8), extractions of essentials clarify. The patterns of abstract two- and three-dimensional forces clearly communicate the artist's judgments of what this subject's structural and dynamic essentials come down to. And, as we saw in the previous example, such a penetrating, and thus concise "essay" amplifies rather than lessens a subject's emotive nature.

But economy, like any other quality in art, when it becomes a concious goal—an effect—obstructs the sensitive perceptual and responsive behavior necessary to its natural emergence in the context of an artist's creative interests. And economy must always be judged in the context of a drawing's overall meaning. What is an economical grasp of the

ist's interpretation of a subject is as economically expressed as his aesthetic and temperamental interests permit, the magnitude of his perceptual and responsive powers is revealed. Which is why, as Henry James observed, "In art economy is always beauty."

necessary issues for one artist could be excessive elaboration for another.

In Bloom's *Landscape #14* (Figure 12.9), the subtle transforming of limbs and branches into wraith-like animals and humans, and the straining or windswept action of other branches, hand-like in their movements, conveys a bereaved, spirit-haunted mood. Bloom seems to intend the choked, intertwined

forms to be everywhere engaged in movement and change. The sense of these foreboding interactions and transfigurations as emerging from, and subsiding into, the matrix of limbs and branches benefits from the amount and complexity of these forms. But *within the context of the artist's intent*, this is an economically stated drawing. It is as directly and as simply stated as the artist's visual-expressive

Figure 12.8
REMBRANDT VAN RIJN (1609–1669)
A Boy with a Wide-Brimmed Hat
Reed pen and ink. 8.5 x 9 cm.
The British Museum, London

Figure 12.10
CAMILLE COROT (1796–1875)
A Rocky Forest Scene at Civita Castellana
Lead pencil. 31.2 x 39 cm.
The Louvre Museum

needs permit. Although a complex drawing, there are no irrelevant passages, no overworked forms or unnecessary details.

But when an artist's graphic objective is concerned with visually "simple" statements, even such intricate subjects as forest scenes can be reduced to surprisingly "plain" visual terms. Corot's *A Rocky Forest Scene at Civita Castellana* (Figure 12.10) is an impressive sum-

mary of a complicated subject. Corot's structural and organizational understanding enables him to reduce the intricate scene to an economically stated configuration of forms. Note how the artist uses value, shape-clarity, directional hatchings, and differing line weights to efficiently sort out and organize the forms in a deep field of space. And doing so creates a strong design of line, value, and

341

shape patterns that might not have survived a more naturalistic approach.

Because intent determines the degree of economy, artists, even in quick sketches, are sometimes lavish in their use of line and tone in exploring a subject's visually expressive essentials, while treating extensively developed states of modelling and illumination with a daring economy. The profusion of lines in Rose's *Two Seated Figures* (Figure 12.11) is as economical a statement as possible, given the intensity and depth of the artist's structural and dynamic search. Had Rose restricted his means *for economy's sake* to far fewer lines, it would have been as impossible to express the turbulent force he intended, as

for Picasso, in his *Three Female Nudes Dancing* (see Figure 8.34), to have employed more lines to suggest *his* intent.

Yet, in Aronson's *Rabbi* (Figure 12.12), the sensitive exploration of volumes and the play of light upon them, as well as the figure's mood of inner strength and introspection are established with a remarkable directness and spontaneity. Note especially the spare means used to convey the structure of the head and hands.

As this drawing so well illustrates, the factor of economy is sometimes extended to include the simplicity of the design concept. The artist, in reducing this configuration to a straightforward system of simple shapes, val-

Figure 12.11
GEORGE ROSE (1936–   )
Two Seated Figures (1973)
Black chalk. 20 x 28 in.
Courtesy of the artist

Figure 12.12
DAVID ARONSON (1923–   )
Rabbi (1969)
Brown pastel. 40 x 26 in.
Courtesy of the artist

ues, and masses (even the more structurally developed forms suggest their geometric basis), heightens the drawing's expressive power. For, as noted earlier, an economy of means usually strengthens emotive force.

The bold simplicity of design in Wilson's *Dialogue* (Figure 12.13) adds an important dimension of expressive meaning to the representation. The harsh confrontation of black and white values finds immediate symbolic equivalency. And, in contrasting the gentle modelling of the child's head with the more

rugged handling of the skull, the artist takes his stand.

In a surprisingly contemporary-looking drawing, *A Harvest Still-Life* (Figure 12.14), Genoels reduces his subject to a system of nervously animated lines that convey both two- and three-dimensional activities. Here, the economical use of line strengthens the sense of decorative pattern. A close examination of this drawing will disclose just how few marks are being used to express intricate representational and abstract conditions.

Figure 12.13
JOHN WILSON (1922–   )
Dialogue
Lithograph. 17 1/2 x 13 1/2 in.
Collection of the Museum of the
National Center of Afro-American Artists

Figure 12.14
ABRAHAM GENOELS (1640–1723)
A Harvest Still Life
Pen and brown ink. 6 1/8 x 8 1/2 in.
Fogg Art Museum, Harvard University
Gift of Mr. and Mrs. Charles E. Slatkin

Turner's drawing *Stonehenge at Daybreak* (Figure 12.15) shows how much can be suggested with a few bold washes of tone. Here, delineating lines are absent altogether. Turner conveys the impression of a dawn landscape in a broad, painterly handling guided by powerful perceptual skill and a determined expressive objective. Note how clearly this "simple" handling depicts grazing sheep, coach and horses, and a sense of vast space.

Rembrandt's *A Winter Landscape* (Figure 12.16) is a masterpiece of economy. The drawing's design of fast and slow directional movements, enacting the same undulations as the snow-covered surfaces, is completely fused with the character of the representa-

tional matter. In a drawing of about one hundred lines and a few washes of tone, the artist creates snow laden fields, shrubs, road, and rooftops. He even suggests the quality of the light and the feel of a silent, still, winter day. Such limitations of means should not be understood as hurdles, but as necessary confines that intensify meanings. Goethe may have had this in mind when he observed, "It is in self-limitation that the master first shows himself." Economy such as Turner's or Rembrandt's demands exquisite perceptual and conceptual apprehension and responses shaped by a lifetime of analytical and empathic interest in nature and in the relational life of marks on a flat surface.

Figure 12.15
JOSEPH TURNER (1775–1851)
Stonehenge at Daybreak
Wash drawing. 7 5/8 x 10 9/16 in.
Courtesy, Museum of Fine Arts, Boston
Gift of the Estate of Ellen T. Bullard

As noted earlier, one of the best and fastest ways to heighten our perceptual and conceptual powers is, of course, to draw as much as possible. But our drawings must not repeat old inadequacies. If drawings are not formed by a demanding level of inquiry and response, if they do not reflect an engaging dynamic life, or if they are not balanced and unified, they only strengthen the grip of old habits.

This book has been largely concerned with concepts that broaden the range of responsive options, and thus, with the breaking of older, restricting concepts. A final suggestion to deepen our understanding of drawing is appropriate here. Classes in sculpture, by enabling the student to experience more directly the structural nature of forms, and classes in two- and three-dimensional design, by helping to explore more fully the relational life of the elements and the organizational possibilities they hold, can be most beneficial. These studies can provide information and insights concerning both structure and design too often overlooked in the study of drawing. And because our attitudes toward sculpture and design are less likely to be hemmed in by our early habits of procedure or prejudice, their study helps to hasten the breakup of old notions about drawing. Old habits are insistent. Beginning a drawing by the search for the subject's gestural character is for most students an uncomfortably daring step. Many hesitate and resist. Although they may accept the logic that a cautious collection of parts cannot succeed, the familiarity of this old habit seems preferable to the anticipated ''chaos'' of a more spirited, penetrated search for essentials. Sometimes the first few attempts at gestural drawing *are* chaotic. It is natural to falter in an unfamiliar process. Here, a trust in the basic principle that governs any building process, namely, the emergence of large essentials before small specifics, may help the student over his first crucial barrier to responsive drawing. Once experienced, the many dividends of the gestural approach make a retreat to a piecemeal assembly unlikely.

We began with gesture and we conclude with it. Its importance to responsive drawing cannot be overstressed. As we develop our individual approach, even if we rely only minimally on the gestural aspects or merely keep them in mind, to accept the principle of drawing from generalities to specifics is to reverse both symbolically and actually the cautious, accumulative approach. In whatever way we adjust the search for gestural expression and the structural and dynamic issues it encompasses, to begin with the broad essentials before arriving at our own necessary particulars is the best mode of entry into the world of responsive drawing.

Figure 12.16
REMBRANDT VAN RIJN (1606–1669)
A Winter Landscape
Reed pen and bistre wash. 2 5/8 x 6 5/16 in.
Fogg Art Museum, Harvard University
Bequest of Charles A. Loeser

BIBLIOGRAPHY

The books listed below are recommended for general reading, and for further information about perspective, media, and materials. The list does not include those books already mentioned in the footnotes.

GENERAL TEXTS

Anderson, Donald M., *Elements of Design.* New York: Holt, Rinehart and Winston, Inc., 1961.

Blake, Vernon, *The Art and Craft of Drawing.* London: Oxford University Press, Inc., 1927.

Chaet, Bernard. *The Art of Drawing.* New York: Holt, Rinehart and Winston, Inc., 1970.

Collier, Graham, *Form, Space and Vision* (3rd ed.) Englewood Cliffs, N.J.: Prentice-Hall, Inc. 1972.

De Tolnay, Charles, *History and Technique of Old Master Drawings.* New York: H. Bittner & Co., 1943.

Hayes, Colin, *Grammar of Drawing for Artists and Designers.* Studio Vista, London: Van Nostrand Reinhold Company, 1969.

Hill, Edward, *The Language of Drawing.* Englewood Cliffs, N.J.: Prentice-Hall, Inc., 1966.

Mendelowitz, Daniel M., *Drawing.* New York: Holt, Rinehart and Winston, Inc., 1967.

Moskowitz, Ira (ed.), *Great Drawings of All Time* (4 vols.). New York: Shorewood Publishers, Inc., 1962.

Rawson, Philip, *Drawing.* London, New York, Toronto: Oxford University Press, 1969.

Ruskin, John, *The Elements of Drawing.* New York: Dover Publications, 1971.

Sachs, Paul J., *Modern Prints and Drawings.* New York: Alfred A. Knopf, Inc., 1954.

ON PERSPECTIVE

Ballinger, Louise, *Perspective, Space and Design.* New York: Van Nostrand Reinhold Company, 1969.

Burnett, Calvin, *Objective Drawing Techniques.* New York: Van Nostrand Reinhold Company, 1966.

Cole, Rex V., *Perspective: The Practice and Theory of Perspective as Applied to Pictures.* New York: Dover Publications, Inc., 1927.

Norling, Ernest R., *Perspective Made Easy.* New York: The Macmillan Company, 1939.

Watson, Ernest W., *How to Use Creative Perspective.* New York: Reinhold Publishing Co., 1960.

White, John, *The Birth and Rebirth of Pictorial Space.* London: Faber and Faber Ltd., 1957.

ON MEDIA AND MATERIALS

Doerner, Max, *The Materials of the Artist and Their Use in Painting,* Eugen Neuhaus, trans. New York: Harcourt Brace Jovanovich, Inc., 1934.

Dolloff, Francis W. and Roy L. Perkinson, *How to Care for Works of Art on Paper.* Boston: Museum of Fine Arts, Boston, 1971.

Kay, Reed, *The Painter's Guide to Studio Methods and Materials.* Garden City, New York: Doubleday & Company, Inc., 1972.

Mayer, Ralph W., *The Artist's Handbook of Materials and Techniques* (rev.). New York: The Viking Press, Inc., 1970.

Watrous, James, *The Craft of Old Master Drawings.* Madison, Wisc.: University of Wisconsin Press, 1957.

INDEX